MERTON AND FRIENDS

MERTON AND FRIENDS

A Joint Biography of Thomas Merton, Robert Lax, and Edward Rice

James Harford

continuum

NEW YORK • LONDON

2006
The Continuum International Publishing Group Inc
80 Maiden Lane, New York, New York 10038

The Continuum International Publishing Group Ltd
The Tower Building, 11 York Road, London SE1 7NX

**green
press**
INITIATIVE

Continuum is a member of Green Press Initiative, a nonprofit program dedicated
to supporting publishers in their efforts to reduce their use of fiber obtained from
endangered forests. For more information, go to www.greenpressinitiative.org.

Printed in the United States of America

Library of Congress Cataloging-in-Publication Data

Harford, James J.
    Merton and friends : a joint biography of Thomas Merton,
Robert Lax, and Edward Rice / James Harford.
        p. cm.
    Includes bibliographical references and index.
    ISBN-13: 978-0-8264-1869-2 (hardcover : alk. paper)
    ISBN-10: 0-8264-1869-4 (hardcover : alk. paper)
    1. Merton, Thomas, 1915-1968. 2. Trappists—United States—Biography.
3. Lax, Robert. 4. Poets, American—20th century—Biography. 5. Rice, Edward.
6. Authors, American—20th century—Biography. I. Title.
    BX4705.M542H36 2006
    271'.12502—dc22
    [B]
                        2006016047

Contents

PREFACE

Robert Lax, Thomas Merton, and Edward Rice had a clearer understanding of the issues facing Christians, especially American Catholics, than most bishops. Although not without missteps in their own lives—except for Lax who seems not to have had any—the three forged lives that were exemplary in their friendships with one another over decades, and in their prioritization of simple values, love of God and fellow man, and high standards of beauty, intellect, and tolerance for their church.

Because of their rejection of conventional norms of lifestyle and career, beginning in their undergraduate days at Columbia University in the 1930s, they might well have been the earliest "beats." But unlike most of those for whom the name was coined years later, all three were on deep spiritual searches. Their faith in God and essential loyalty to Catholicism—Rice was godfather to the other two when they converted—were with them throughout their lives, except for Rice's hiatus during one extended period. They disagreed often with the positions and practices of the church, though, and grumbled about its tolerance for mediocrity in liturgical practice, art, architecture, intellectual inquiry, and music, and its comfort with American materialism and military power.

Although very different in their ethnic origins—Lax a small-town Jew, Merton a worldly Protestant, Rice a big-city Catholic—as their friendships developed at Columbia there would be many interests that would cement their closeness—jazz musicians such as Fats Waller, writers such as James Joyce, teachers such as Mark Van Doren and—prominently—the university humor magazine, the *Jester*, and, eventually, the church—or perhaps the church as they saw it. The friendships lasted thirty years for all three, until Merton died in 1968 from an accidental electrocution, in Bangkok, at age fifty-three, then continued for the other two for thirty-some more years, until Lax died at eighty-four in 2000 and Rice at eighty-two in 2001.

Sometimes characterized as a hermit saint, Lax was a major poet, only lately gaining the recognition in America that he has long had in Europe. He lived a spare and simple life writing poetry on various Greek islands for thirty-eight years. He died in his sleep in his home town of Olean, New York, shortly after returning from the Dodecanese island of Patmos, off the coast of Turkey. Europe has long lionized this minimalist poet with a strong religious faith—translating and buying his more than one hundred books in modest quantity; interviewing him often on radio, TV, and in newspapers; making films about him; providing one-man shows of his works and venues for his readings, sometimes with jazz piano accompaniment. He has especially strong followings in Greece; in Germany,[1] where he did numerous readings; in England, where the BBC carried his poetry and interviews; in Switzerland, where in 1997 one of his poems was integrated into an oratorio with a nine-voice chorus;[2] and in France, where he lived for part of the 1950s and often visited. The United States is only lately making up for his neglect. Several books of his poetry have been published in New York in the last few years. His obituary in the *New York Times* cited his appraisal by the poet Richard Kostelanetz as "among America's greatest experimental poets, a true minimalist who can weave awesome poems from remarkably few words." At his funeral Mass at St. Bonaventure University in Olean, where major Lax and Merton archives reside, a eulogist predicted that his posthumous recognition might one day compare to that accorded Gerard Manley Hopkins and Emily Dickinson.

Rice produced some twenty books on world cultures, religion, and biography. His final work, still in manuscript when he died, was on the culture of the Indus Valley, in what is now Pakistan, three thousand years ago. In 1970 he wrote an intimate, forthright, and candid life of Merton, *The Man in the Sycamore Tree*, which evoked dismay from some of Merton's Trappist colleagues, who felt that it was rushed to publication too soon after Merton's death, was too irreverent, and made judgments on the monk's future plans that were unjustified.[3] This was not the opinion, however, of others who knew the Merton of pre-monastic days and who expressed their satisfaction that the human Merton had finally been revealed. Rice's travels to research his other books, mostly in the late 1960s, subjected him sometimes to great risk and privation. He moved solo, using the cheapest transport and eating the local diet—sometimes at the peril of his health and in at least one instance at the risk of violent death—in areas of Africa, India, and other parts of Asia unknown to most Westerners. One yield of this period was a biography of Sir Richard Francis Burton,[4] which would become a *New York Times* best-seller. Other books dealt with the hippy culture in San Francisco, with Asian-Indian and Micronesian cultures, and with Hinduism, Sufism, Islam, Buddhism, and Judaism. His black-

and-white photos from these travels, and his pictures of Merton taken at Gethsemani, are worthy of museums.

By far his principal contribution to Catholicism, though, was the creation and editing of the first high-quality lay Catholic picture and text magazine, *Jubilee: A Magazine of the Church and Her People*, to which both Merton and Lax contributed strongly in the 1950s and 1960s.

It became, in effect, their own interpretation of what being a Catholic should mean in the twentieth century. The magazine was a winner of numerous Catholic Press Association awards, and it got high praise from the national media as well. It folded, however, in 1967. Some attribute its demise to a lack of sound financing. Others fault the archdiocese of New York, which opposed the free-swinging magazine from its beginning, making it difficult to raise funds from wealthy Catholics, or to attract sufficient advertising. Still others claim that Vatican II, which took up many of the very issues *Jubilee* had articulated, made the magazine less necessary—a dubious hypothesis, since the world coverage as well as the literary and graphic features of the magazine have since had no equal in Catholic publishing. In any case it is remembered fondly and wistfully, not only by Catholic activists and intellectuals of the period but by many priests and religious and by ordinary laymen stultified by the pap appearing in diocesan journals. During its life there were thoughtful Catholic journals of opinion such as *Commonweal* and *America*, which still thrive, and in its later years the important lay newspaper, *National Catholic Reporter*, but they lacked *Jubilee's* beautiful art, layout, typography, poetry, and marvelous picture essays featuring Catholics, Protestants, Quakers, Jews, Hindus, Buddhists, and others little known to most Catholics.

Merton, the Trappist monk whose conversion to Catholicism is told in his best-selling autobiography, *The Seven Storey Mountain* (1948), was by far the best known of the three. He wrote prodigiously throughout his life on a stupefying range of subject matter—spirituality, history, politics, war, contemplation, biography, monasticism, prayer, art, mysticism, Zen Buddhism, liturgy, and social justice. His books, essays, letters, poems, and political tracts attracted millions of readers. A monk for twenty-seven years in the Order of Cistercians of the Strict Observance—the Trappists—he renewed the zeal of many adherents to the church of Rome whose belief in a merciful God had been numbed by the humdrum sermons of many parish priests. His writings were consumed avidly by members of other Christian denominations, to whom he helped build bridges. They also pricked the psyches of many a nonbeliever, and they opened windows to the four other major religions whose creeds were not well known to most Christians—Hinduism, Buddhism, Islam, and Judaism. More than three decades after his death there is an International Thomas Merton Society with branches all over the United States and in many parts of the world, a Merton Center, Merton symposia, Merton curricula for high schools, Merton Web sites, Merton films, Merton archives in at least five universities, Merton annuals and seasonals, many Merton biographies, Merton Ph.D. theses, and even regular excursions to his birthplace in France and his hangouts in New York.

Through the years, although their get-togethers became infrequent, the three men sent each other hundreds of letters—rollicking, ruthlessly candid, eclectic in subject matter—and using language so full of inside-argot that scholars may never understand their full import. While Merton's letters to a wide circle of intellectuals, poets, literary greats, and religious and political figures are amazing in their depth and range of subject, they do not match for candor his correspondence with his two oldest and closest friends—and theirs with him. With the publication of the complete Lax–Merton letters, and the availability in university archives of the correspondence among all three, a trove of material exists—covering a period of over thirty years for Lax, Merton, and Rice, and over a sixty-year-plus period for Lax and Rice.

The writings and drawings of Lax, Merton, and Rice in the Columbia *Jester*—all three were gifted caricaturists—differed very little in range of subject from what could be read in other Ivy League magazines of that genre—satirical poems, flip essays on politics and world developments, insightful but sometimes savage reviews of plays, musicals, and jazz records. But the *Jester* in their years was superbly creative, serving a discriminating academic community that appreciated the fact that the content went beyond humor to deal with issues confronting the students. All three friends served as editor-in-chief of *Jester* at one time or another during the period from 1937 to 1940 period, wrote articles, contributed clever cartoons, and each got strong encomiums from their Columbia peers. Each would go on to justify those praises while living lives that disdained trappings, social distinction, and material possessions.

It is unlikely, however, that they themselves would have envisioned the directions that their lives would take.

* * * * * * * * * * *

Acknowledgments

It is too bad that I did not begin this book until 1997. Millie and I had known Bob Lax since 1952 and Ed Rice since 1953, and so we had missed more than forty years during which we could have recorded conversations and anecdotes. Also, with introductions from these two, we could have interviewed Merton at Gethsemani, private as he was, before he died in 1968.

In 1997 I had just finished a book on the dominant figure in the Soviet space program, Sergei Pavlovich Korolev. Published by John Wiley, that book was well received, and I considered other possible books related to my field—thirty-seven years in aerospace. But Millie said: How about a book on Lax, Rice, and their long-time friend Thomas Merton, and focus on their impact on American Catholicism, which is, after all, in troubled times?

I agreed, and I set out on the task, starting with my own memories as well as Millie's and those of our four now-grown children, all of whom had known Lax and Rice intimately. Probably more than half of the book is based on interviews or recollections—with Lax whom we first got to know during 1952–53 when we lived in Paris, in New York when he worked for *Jubilee* magazine in the 1950s and early '60s, then on his Greek islands over the next thirty years during which we also met about once a year in various European cities; with Rice in New York at *Jubilee*, which he started and then ran from 1953 to 1967, at his homes in Manhattan and Sagaponack, Long Island, or in Princeton during his visits to our home. Although we never met Merton, all of us talked about him often; we read most of what he wrote, and we wrote down memories of him not only from Lax and Rice but from some of his closest friends at the Abbey of Gethsemani.

Many people helped me with their personal memories of Lax: first and foremost, his niece Marcia Marcus Kelly; her husband, Jack; and her sister, Connie Brothers. Adding anecdotes were Marcia's brother Dickie and her cousin Soni Holman. Paul Spaeth, director of the Friedsam Library at St. Bonaventure University in Olean, New York, showed me how to delve into the Lax and Merton archives and answered many phone queries.

Emil Antonucci, at great personal sacrifice, sustained Bob Lax in his writings for many years as his publisher with Journeyman Books, made brilliant illustrations for his poetry, shot films with him, met him at the dock when he came to New York, visited him in Greece, and accompanied him to numerous venues, especially the summers at Art Park near Buffalo in the 1970s.

In later years, the late Bernhard Moosbrugger took over the publishing of the Lax books and had much to remember when we interviewed him in Zurich and on Patmos, as did Gladys Weigner, his partner at Pendo. In the poet's later years I was helped a lot by John Beer and Sarah McCann, his research assistants on Patmos.

I spent hours and hours reading the letters of all three protagonists to each other in their archives at Columbia, St. Bonaventure, Georgetown, and Louisville. Rice's son, Chris, and his wife, Liza, were enormously cooperative in allowing me to pore over boxes and boxes of Ed's papers, letters, and photos in their Princeton home. Numerous times I accessed more of the same in the Georgetown University archive, managed by Nick Scheetz. Ted Rice very kindly allowed me to pay the permission fee for the use of two copyrighted prints of his father's photos of Merton. Ed's sister, Carol McCormack, was forthcoming with memories of Ed's parents. Mary Cummings, who helped to tend Ed during his last years, generously shared her own writings about him. Dolly Jagdeo, who was a rock of support to Ed during his sicknesses, was free with her recollections.

I much appreciated the stories I was told about Rice, Lax, and Merton by Jim Knight, a survivor from the Columbia crowd, who was on the *Jester* magazine staff, lived it up with them in Olean in the summers of 1939 and 1940, stayed in touch over the years, and probably knew the three men the most intimately of anyone. His own "The Merton I Knew" can be read in full at www.therealmerton.com.

Many Merton memories came from the anecdotes and the letters of Lax and Rice, but immensely important was the help I got in person, as well as by phone, from Merton's colleagues at Gethsemani, especially Brother Patrick Hart, who had been Merton's secretary in his last years, and Father John Eudes Bamberger, who was one of his counselors, both of the Order of Cistercians of the Strict Observance (O.C.S.O., or Trappists). Monsignor William Shannon, who has written prolifically about Merton, gave me a long interview at Nazareth College in Rochester. Patrick O'Connell's *Merton Seasonal* was a steady source of material about the monk, as was the Merton Center at Bellarmine College during the domain of Jonathan Montaldo and, in recent times, Paul Pearson. O'Connell made numerous corrections in the advance proofs, for which I am sincerely grateful. I learned much about Merton as well from the *Merton Annual* and from the biennial meetings of the International Thomas Merton Society and the New York meetings of the ITMS group at Corpus Christi in New York, run by Anne McCormick. Clarification of Merton's Buddhist experience in his last days in Asia came from Harold Talbott, who accompanied him on some of his travels during that period.

I read avidly, of course, the writings of all three in *Jubilee*, where I served on the editorial advisory board from 1954 to 1967. For other *Jubilee* memories, I am obligated to former staffers Oona Sullivan, Ned O'Gorman, Wilfrid Sheed, photographers Charles Harbutt, Frank Monaco, and the late Jacques Lowe, as well as Lowe's former wife, Jillen Ahearn, a faithful worker in the *Jubilee* vineyard. Their daughter, Victoria Allen, Lax's godchild, had precious memories as well. Mary Anne Rivera's remarkable three-hundred-page Ph.D. thesis at Duquesne University on *Jubilee*, written only a few years ago, was a rich reminder of the highlight articles that the magazine published in its lifetime. I thank longtime *Jubilee* subscriber Rose Bernal for back issues of the magazine that I did not have.

My own family figured large in this project, starting with Millie, of course. Not only did she have the idea for the book; she participated often in interviews with Lax in many places, with Rice in Sagaponack, and with Merton's friends in Kentucky. Our daughters, Susan and Jennifer, each made big contributions, Susan with editing and text corrections, Jennifer with her own interviews with Lax on Patmos and Rice in Sagaponack. Son Jimmy helped build Sag Henge, Ed Rice's astronomical oddity in his Sagaponack backyard and took long walks with Lax in the little town of Rondo, Spain. Chris spent some weeks receiving gentle counseling from Lax on Patmos.

Others who gave me valuable material were Yuri Zonov, Judy Emery, Moschos Lavagardos, Steve Georgiou, Paul Cristiani, better known as the acrobat Mogador, Trappistine Sister Sheryl Chen, and Benedictine Sister Sheila Long.

Kate Skrebutenas, reference expert at the Princeton Theological Seminary library was invaluable in finding Merton writings, as was Mary Lou Hartman of the Princeton Public Library, who also enabled me to acquire somewhat rare books by interlibrary loan. Another important resource at PPL was Bob Keith, who taught me how to use my laptop to paginate the whole book.

Finally, a deep thanks to Frank Oveis, who approved the book for Continuum International and provided astute and important editing through its final phases.

Thank you all.

Permissions

Books and articles quoted or cited in the text under the usual fair use allowances are acknowledged in the footnotes.

Excerpts and photos from the works of Thomas Merton, Robert Lax, and Edward Rice are with the permission of the following institutions: Ave Maria Press: *A Merton Concelebration*, 1981. Columbia University Press: *Columbia Poetry 1938, Columbia Poetry 1939; Jester* magazine. Farrar Straus & Giroux: *The Courage for Truth: The Letters of Thomas Merton to Writers*, by Thomas Merton, edited by Christine M. Bochen, copyright © 1993 by the Merton Legacy Trust; *The Hidden Ground of Love: The Letters of Thomas Merton on Religious Experience and Social Concerns*, by Thomas Merton, edited by William H. Shannon, copyright © 1985 by the Merton Legacy Trust; *The Road to Joy: Letters to New and Old Friends*, by Thomas Merton, selected and edited by Robert E. Daggy; *Mystics and Zen Masters*, by Thomas Merton, copyright © 1989 by the Merton Legacy Trust. Grove Press: *Love Had a Compass: Robert Lax Journals and Poetry*, edited by James Uebbing, 1996; Hanging Loose: *One Island*, by Robert Lax, 1976. Harcourt Brace Jovanovich: *Love and Living*, 1979; *The Seven Storey Mountain*, 1948; *The Sign of Jonas*, 1953. HarperCollins: *A Search for Solitude*, 1996; *The Coming Catholic Church*, 2003; *The Intimate Merton*, 1999; *Learning to Love*, 1997; *The Other Side of the Mountain*, 1998. Journeyman Press: *The Circus of the Sun*, 1959; *R. L. New Poems*, 1962; *Fables*, 1970. Robert Lax Estate c/o Marcia Kelly. Lax materials in the Lax Columbia University Archive and Merton and Lax materials in the Friedsam Memorial Library, St. Bonaventure University. Louisiana State University Press: *The Selected Letters of Mark Van Doren*, edited by George Hendrick, copyright © 1987 by Dorothy Van Doren. Merton Annual: *Robert Lax Poems*, vol. 1, 1988, pp. 35-54. Merton Legacy Trust: Above mentions plus the Merton archive in Columbia University Rare Books and Manuscripts, Butler Library. New Directions: *Lax Kalymnos Journals, 33 Poems; Merton 30 Poems, Figures for an Apocalypse, The Geography of Lograire, Thoughts on the East, Zen and the Birds of Appetite, Cables to the Ace, The Asian Journal*. The *New Yorker*: Lax poems: "Greeting to Spring," May 4, 1940; "A Radio Masque for My Girl Coming Down from Northampton," June 15, 1940; "Poem of Gratuitous Invective Against New Jersey," July 6, 1940; "The Man with the Big General Notions," October 10, 1942; "Breeze on a Lexington Avenue Local," November 29, 1945. W. W. Norton: *Thomas Merton and James Laughlin Selected Letters*, edited by David Cooper, 1997. Georgetown University Edward Rice Archive in the Lauinger Library. Edward Rice photos, copyright © Edward Rice III, Santa Fe, NM. University Press of Kentucky: *When Prophecy Still Had a Voice: The Letters of Thomas Merton and Robert Lax*, edited by Arthur W. Biddle, 2001, copyright © Robert Lax Estate c/o Marcia Kelly and Merton Legacy Trust. Voyages: Robert Lax poems and text, edited by William Claire, 1968.

1

SEEDS OF UNORTHODOXY

Eccentric Paths from Olean, Europe, and Brooklyn to Morningside Heights

So now is the time to tell a thing that I could not realize then, but which has become very clear to me: that God brought me and a half a dozen others together at Columbia, and made us friends, in such a way that our friendship would work powerfully to rescue us from the confusion and the misery in which we had come to find ourselves. . . . —Thomas Merton[1]

Two of those "half a dozen," Robert Lax and Edward Rice, would remain among Thomas Merton's closest friends and correspondents through his lifetime, and continue to be friends with each other for another thirty-some years after the monk's death. At Columbia the three were often in daily, and nightly, communion about "the confusion and misery in which we had come to find ourselves." The United States, in the 1930s, was largely inattentive to Hitler, Mussolini, Franco, Stalin's purges, the Japanese rape of China; the huge unemployment that was reducing many families to misery; the degradation of what had been fertile western farm land; and the exploitation by large U.S. companies of Latin American labor.

While it was Merton who seems to have felt the prevailing injustices most keenly, all three could properly be grouped with, as Murray Kempton wrote years later, "a number of Americans of significant character and talent [from the thirties], who believed that our society was not merely doomed but undeserving of survival. . . ."[2] All three, as well, had their social and cultural values influenced by teachers who were among the best minds at any university. "I have undercut all hope of claiming that Columbia made me a success," wrote Merton. "On the contrary, I believe I can thank Columbia, among other things, for having helped me learn the value of unsuccess. . . ."[3] The teachers exerting that influence were the likes of Joseph Wood Krutch, Jacques Barzun, Lionel Trilling, and Mark Van Doren. "Such people," he wrote, "taught me to imitate not Rockefeller but Thoreau. . . . I ended up being turned on like a pinball machine by Blake, Thomas Aquinas, Augustine, Eckhart, Coomaraswamy, Traherne, Hopkins, Maritain, and the sacraments of the Catholic Church. After which I came to the monastery in which (and this is public knowledge) I have continued to be the same kind of maverick and have, in fact, ended as a hermit who is also fully identified with the peace movement, with Zen, with a group of Latin American hippie poets, etc., etc."[4]

The maverick-hermit description also fits both Lax, who would write poetry in tiny houses on various Greek islands for thirty years, and Rice, who would give American Catholics a much richer understanding of their religion with *Jubilee* magazine in the 1950s and '60s, aided strongly by both Merton and Lax, then wander the world and end up writing in a potato farmer's shack in his last thirty-five years.

The beginnings of the three friends, each born at the outset of World War I, were very different, ethnically, religiously, educationally, and geographically. Lax, a Jew, came into the world in Olean, New York, on November 30, 1915, the third child, after two daughters, of haberdasher Sigmund Lax and Rebecca "Betty" Hotchner. Sigmund had moved his business from New York to the little town in the far western part of the state when his city customers dwindled. "Sigmund Lax Progressive Clothier" read his sign on the shop at 180 North Union Street. Betty had not been happy about the move, but eventually became active in what culture there was and showed an ecumenical instinct, which might have influenced her son in later life, by singing in both the Methodist and Presbyterian choirs while attending the synagogue she had helped found.

Merton had been born ten months earlier, on January 31, 1915, in Prades, France, near the Spanish border. His father, Owen, a New Zealander, and his mother, Ruth Jenkins, an American, were both painters who had met in Paris. Father was a nonconscientious Protestant. Mother sometimes attended Quaker meetings. Young Tom's rearing, recollected in great detail in his autobiography, *The Seven Storey Mountain* (1948), was chaotic, as his parents moved about in the early years of his childhood. He was only an infant when they came to the United States to live near her parents on Long Island.

Rice, the only born Catholic, and the youngest of the three, was delivered "on a kitchen table" in his parents' home in Brooklyn on October 23, 1918. His father, also Edward Rice, was a banker. His mother, Elizabeth "Elsie" Becker, had been one of five children orphaned when her father, August Becker, who ran a saloon in Park Slope, died.

The early education of the three was also disparate. Lax went to public schools in Olean, got excellent grades, and lived the normal life of a small town American boy. His father, mother, and his older sisters, Gladys and Sylvia, all doted on him. Gladys, known as "Gladio," who was eleven years older than her brother, remembered that "he was always smart, and, even as a little boy, could repeat jokes verbatim."[5]

As a child, Bob was interested in theater, even building stage sets in his home. He was also a dedicated reader and spent much time at the local library. Bob's grandparents were Reformed Austro-Hungarian Jews. The men and women sat together in synagogue, unlike in an Orthodox Jewish community. The family moved back to New York for a time in the late '20s because Betty was unhappy with the sterility of Olean life, but they soon had to go back to Olean because Sigmund could not make a living in New York. Making the best of it, Betty helped found a Conservative synagogue in Olean where the Jewish population, although small, probably only a few dozen families, was very close-knit. Betty was the oldest daughter in her family and Gladys says that she was very ambitious for her own family. She was determined to help develop the culture of Olean and dug into community affairs. She got the YMCA built, and also a town swimming pool where she herself taught swimming. "She had come from an important family in Europe, with servants," Gladys said, "and it's no question that our intellectual bent came from her. She took evening courses in Olean. . . . She lived almost her entire married life in Olean, but she didn't enjoy it—it was like living on a desert island. She had perfect reason to dislike it. She spent the whole summer season, is my impression, going to Chautauqua. Maybe she went every year. . . . She would take proper clothes, dress for dinner. . . . Kids were taken care of. . . . She took it for granted that we would all go to college." Gladio and her sister Sally [Sylvia] both went to the University of Michigan. As for Bob, Betty "recognized his special talents and tried to get him as good an education as possible."[6]

Merton had a much more exotic upbringing. In his first years he was taught at home—and evidently well taught—by his mother, becoming an avid book reader with a keen ear for language. It seems, however, that he was displaced in her affections by his younger brother, John Paul, who was born when Tom was three. Three years later she died, just after the family had returned to the United States. What followed for Tom was a succession of schools whose locations were dictated by his father's peregrinations. First it was "the rickety grey annex of the Public School"[7] in Douglaston, Long Island, near his maternal grandparents; then Bermuda, where he was a student at "the local school for white children where I was constantly punished for my complete inability to grasp the principles of multiplication and division."[8] When his father left Bermuda for New York to sell paintings, he became a truant for some months. Then it was back to Douglaston, where he went to school while living with his grandparents, and while his father journeyed to the south of France and to Africa to paint.

Rice had Quaker schooling, because his mother, although a regular attendee at Sunday Mass, felt that the parish schools in the neighborhood were too narrow in their views. She sent young Ed to the Friends School on Schermerhorn Street in Brooklyn, where he was first exposed to the Quaker emphasis on simplicity in life style, art, and furniture, an influence that would remain with him through his life. He had been born with an eye condition called congenital columboma, what he called "cat's eye," an eye with a fixed focus. He did not have trouble reading as a child, although he did in later life.

As with Merton, Rice, too, felt a lack of maternal love, although he states that lack more strongly than might be warranted. "A lot of what I did later in my life was in reaction to an awful childhood," he said in an interview.[9] When pressed for examples of maltreatment, he merely pouted that "[s]he threw away my Brownie camera." His mother, one of five children who became orphans when their parents died, married Edward Rice, the senior, who had grown up in Greenwich Village. He got a job on Wall Street working for the August Belmont Company, "holding up the numbers for stock sales." Over the years he advanced in position, providing a comfortable life for his family, even during the economic slump of the '30s. Ed junior was the eldest of three children. Brother Donald was born in 1920, and sister Carol in 1929. Carol questions her brother's memory of their parents. "I don't know where his negative statements come from," she said. "I remember our mother as a warm, active, person who kept a nice house. My father was strict, but he was good to us, had a good job, and took us to the Adirondacks in summer. In 1929, when Ed was eleven, his father took him and brother Don on a 'grand tour' of Europe."[10]

The Rice family had lived in a large house in Bay Ridge, an upscale section of Brooklyn. Ed's high school was Poly Prep, a well-regarded nonsectarian school in Brooklyn, where the academic demands were very high, and where he won a prize as the best-informed student in his class. Latin, Greek, and modern languages were part of the regular curriculum, and stiff assignments were handed out in English composition, grammar, and literature. His Poly transcript shows a B- in English and mostly Cs in his other courses, but the high reputation of the school must have been a factor in his admission to Columbia. Every Monday and Wednesday there was an Anglican prayer service at Poly, but "I was dragged to Mass by my mother and went to confession every week," Rice recalls.

While their childhood formation was very different, Lax, Merton, and Rice each showed early on a common characteristic—fierce creativity.

Lax, at age eleven, had his first poem published, in the *Olean Times Herald*. It was 1927, just after Charles Lindbergh had made his historic solo flight from New York to Paris. Seventy years later he would recite it from memory for friends:[11]

> It happened on a fair May night
> When Lindbergh made his nonstop flight
> From New York to Paris he was to roam
> Over land of trees and sea of foam
> With nothing to eat but sandwiches five
> How could he ever get there alive?
> Straight to LeBourget Field he flew
> And everyone cheered for the Red, White and Blue
> In my moral this truth you'll find
> Keep faith and bravery first in your mind

Young Bob took clarinet lessons from a German music teacher when he was in eighth grade, and he formed with several friends Lax's Oleanders, a group strongly influenced, he says, by Fred Waring's Pennsylvanians. That was the end of the musical fling, though, after about three or four sessions of a couple of hours each, playing songs such as "Sleepytime Gal."

Like Rice, Lax got a trip to Europe as a youngster, maybe at age thirteen, in the company of his sister Gladys. But neither had lifestyles that were comparable to Merton's in terms of sophistication. When Merton returned to France with his father in 1925, at age ten, he felt that he was back in "the fountains of the intellectual and spiritual life of the world to which I belonged."[12] He had already learned French and was enrolled as a boarder at the lycée in dull, gray, Protestant Montauban. French lycées, he would write in his journal, "are probably close to monasteries as they are now . . . courtyards surrounded by actual arched galleries. You went everywhere marching two by two in line."[13] It was not a happy time. He was harassed by schoolmates—"fierce, catlike little faces, dark and morose," and he was kicked and pushed around. He lived in a dormitory where he "knew for the first time in my life the pangs of desolation and emptiness and abandonment." But the deep and lasting influence of French culture throughout his life is reflected in his remark about this period that "it was France that grew the finest flowers of delicacy and grace and intelligence and wit and understanding and proportion and taste."[14] The two stayed in Montauban, on the Languedoc border, for only a short time. "What a dead town!" he recalled, and he remembers that his father "told me to pray, to ask God to help us, to help him paint, to help him have a successful exhibition, to find us a place to live."[15] On to the attractive medieval village of St. Antonin, fifteen miles away, traveled the pair, and Owen began to build a house. Here, Merton's religious consciousness, and even an inkling of his meditative future, emerged in the village, which was dominated by a central church with a high spire. "Oh, what a thing it is, to live in a place that is so constructed that you are forced, in spite of yourself, to be at least a virtual contemplative!"[16]

It would seem that a major influence on his eventual Catholicism was brought to bear on him by the Privat family in the Auvergne town of Murat. His father boarded with the Privats in 1926, presumably to paint the Auvergne countryside, and Tom was a periodic visitor on school vacations. Serious Catholics, "They inspired real reverence, and I think, in a way, they were certainly saints . . . by leading ordinary lives in a completely supernatural manner. . . ." In any case, they left a strong mark on the eleven year old. "I owe many graces to their prayers, and perhaps ultimately my conversion and even my religious vocation."[17]

Owen, after stints in the Mediterranean towns of Marseilles and Cette, went off to London for an exhibition of his work, and on his return dropped the bombshell that he would abandon the house-building and go back to England, and Tom would go with him.

Enter another set of life-forming adults—Owen's Aunt Maud and Uncle Ben—living in the town of Ealing, in the western part of London. Maud was "so like an angel," but had a disciplined character, warning young Tom: "Boy, don't become a dilettante" (presumably, like his father). School would be at Ripley Court, presenting another uncomfortable entry into new classes, new classmates, and teachers. Now thirteen, he knew no Latin, felt "more or less as if I were an orphan or some kind of stray . . . ," and "had the humiliation of once again descending to the lowest place and sitting with the smallest boys . . . and beginning at the beginning." But Ripley Court turned out to be a happy place, the students much more pleasant than those at the lycee. And finally Tom was going to church—albeit "dressed up in the ludicrous clothes that the English conceive to be appropriate to the young . . . and found many occasions of praying and lifting up my mind to God."[18]

In 1929, at age fourteen, Tom went to a public school—Oakham, a "decent little school in the Midlands"—where today a chapter of the

International Thomas Merton Society thrives. Grandfather Jenkins, a modestly well off executive for the New York publishing company Grosset & Dunlap, paid the fees. Tom's learning challenges were formidable—trigonometry, Greek, Shakespeare, nineteenth-century European history, but the religious exposure was absurd. The chaplain, a former rower at Cambridge, said that "One might go through this chapter of St. Paul and simply substitute the word 'gentleman' for 'charity,' as in 'A gentleman is patient, is kind; a gentleman envieth not. . . .'"[19] The headmaster, F. C. Doherty, however, was wise enough to see that Tom could finesse getting a certificate in mathematics, in which he was weak, and go for a higher certificate in French, Latin, and the classics, which would better prepare him for a try at Cambridge University. It was at this time that Tom Bennett, his godfather, reentered the picture. "He was to be the person I most respected and admired and . . . had the greatest influence on me at this time in my life."[20] Living in the Bennett flat in London, the precocious fifteen-year-old read many books. He mentions among the authors, Evelyn Waugh, with whom he would correspond as a monk. He spent hours listening to American jazz records—Armstrong, Ellington, King Oliver, and others—a passion that he would share with Lax, Rice, and other Columbia friends. Bennett and his French wife, Iris, took him to Paris to see the paintings of Chagall, Braque, and Picasso. They also exposed him to the writings of Gide, Hemingway, Waugh, D. H. Lawrence—and James Joyce, who would be a major influence on Lax, Rice, and him during summers spent together in Olean in 1939 and 1940 as well as later in their correspondence.

In the summer of 1930, grandfather Pop Jenkins "made over" to Tom "the portion of my inheritance and threw open the door for me to run away and be prodigal."[21] Then on January 18, 1931, he became even freer to be prodigal when, alas, Owen Merton died of a brain tumor, leaving Tom without either father or mother when he was not yet sixteen.

In 1933, at eighteen, he went to Italy, then came back to America, spending the summer as a barker at the Chicago World's Fair. He entered Cambridge in the fall to study French and Italian in preparation for the British diplomatic service, at Dr. Bennett's insistence.

Bob Lax's teenage years in Olean seem straight out of Andy Hardy. He lived in a neighborhood of big Victorian houses, some with porches all around. He ice skated at Bradner's Stadium, where in summer a class-D baseball team played its games. There were three movie houses to go to—two of them now gone, and the third, the Palace, which once had vaudeville, would be razed for an Eckert's drug store. Antique movie posters, which hang these days in the Greek-Lebanese restaurant on Main Street, portray films that Bob could have seen—*Moby Dick*, *My Little Chickadee*, with W. C. Fields, *Animal Crackers*, with the Marx Brothers, and Lilian Roth. Films of the Marx Brothers would be favorites of Lax, Merton, and Rice at Columbia. Unlike Merton's reading fare of Waugh and Hemingway, Lax got from the local library *Jerry Todd* and *Poppy Ott*. Early on he demonstrated an ineptitude for mechanical things that would stay with him for life. When he was about sixteen he went with Benji Marcus, Gladys's husband, to the motor vehicle bureau to be tested for a driver's license. Coming back after a poorly executed test drive, the inspector shook his head and said, "This is your brother-in-law's car. I don't like your brother-in-law so I'm going to pass you."[22] Lax, in this writer's fifty-year memory, was never seen driving a car.

The Lax family was moderately religious, observing the high holidays at the B'nai Israel Conservative synagogue. Both Betty and Sigmund are buried in the small Jewish cemetery in town. Lax's niece, Marcia Marcus Kelly, daughter of Gladys, estimates that there were probably about one hundred Jewish families in Olean when Bob was growing up. Now, she thinks, there may be only forty, and the synagogue has no rabbi. But there was no anti-Semitism in Olean then, and there isn't today, she says.

After his Lindbergh poem Lax didn't think about poetry again until high school. Still unhappy with provincial Olean, Betty lobbied a reluctant Sigmund to once more try New York. The family moved to Elmhurst, Long Island, and Bob went to Newtown High School, where he had as a classmate Ad Reinhardt, who would be a famous abstract expressionist painter. Reinhardt became a close lifetime friend of Lax, as well as of Merton and Rice, starting in their years at Columbia.

Lax's rhymes in the *Newtown Lantern* ran to the outrageous, such as in "Hymn to My Innards":

How beautiful my gastric juices
Turning to their sundry uses
Soup and steak and beans and pie,
Beer and Scotch and Gin and Rye[23]

Young Bob was offered a fellowship to study poetry at Columbia under Joseph Auslander. His poem from that period, "The Siren," is unlikely to have impressed Auslander:

Her liquid eyes are Garbo-like
Her lacquered lips are weepy

She doesn't look exotic though—
Just a little sleepy[24]

Lax didn't accept the fellowship, in any case, because, "I didn't like the idea of taking a course on studying poetry. I had liked my high school courses, and later Mark van Doren's course, but that was more on literature than poetry."[25]

Rice had been badgered by his parents about what he should study as he began his freshman year at Columbia. His mother wanted him to forget about studying art, which was his passion, and become a doctor so as to take over an uncle's practice. He was also interested in the Russian language, but his father said, "No son of mine is going to take a Communist language."[26] The pressure to study medicine was released tragically, during his freshman year when his mother died of peritonitis from a ruptured appendix. But Ed began to get poor grades at Columbia. "I went to art class rather than chemistry or whatever," he said in a 1986 interview. "I remember my father getting out a fancy belt he bought in Brooks Brothers and he just beat hell out of me."[27]

None of the three were in the same class at Columbia. Lax and Merton were both Class of '38, but Merton, with Cambridge credits, would graduate in February while Lax would be a regular June graduate. Rice was in the Class of '40 but would actually leave before the term ended, without graduating, having neglected his premed courses. He had played on the lightweight football team and was a drummer and clarinetist in the marching band.

Merton rowed for one season with the lightweight crew, ran cross country, played a lot of solo jazz piano, and was active in a fraternity. Lax wrote lyrics for the Varsity Show and was for one year editor of the *Columbia Review*, but his ancillary activities were focused mostly on what became the most intensive involvement for all three: *Jester* magazine.

In 1937 Lax had been editor-in-chief, while Merton was art editor. On his staff was Reinhardt, who had been *Jester* editor himself in 1934-1935 and who was, in Merton's words, "certainly the best artist that had ever drawn for *Jester*, perhaps for any other college magazine. . . . Everything he put out was original, and it was also funny . . . for the first time in years *Jester* . . . was not just an anthology of the same stale and obscene jokes that have been circulating through the sluggish system of American college magazines for two generations."[28]

Reinhardt had written a serious self-appraisal of his 1934-1935 *Jester* editorship for the 1935 *Columbian*. Describing his own thought process in the third person, he wrote that "He did not pretend to the life and laugh of the party of his predecessors . . ." and asked himself if he "[s]hould . . . cater to a crowd which loves belly-laughs and dislikes Slate and Robinson and Freedgood [other classmates on *Jester*] and Lax, who demand a corresponding acuteness to be appreciated." His decision was to do both, devoting the first five issues to "an attempt at popularity" and "the latter ones . . . more an attempt at moment and merit." He cited a Lax satire on Dorothy Parker, subtitled "Mourning does not become Lady Poets," as "the best piece of verse published" during the year and reprinted it in the yearbook:

> The nation knows how you must feel;
> We're sure your heart will never heal.
> But we don't need your sad confession;
> The nation's got enough depression.
> **Desist! Please stop! Please weep no more!**
> **Your sour pen becomes a bore!**
>
> The vengeance which you seek sad maid
> Was no doubt by another paid.
> The guy you've taught us to abhor
> Was probably killed in the Civil War.
>
> Perhaps you can locate the house;
> In the relics at a museum;
> But if your charm is like your bawl
> I'm sure there was no man at all.
> **To hags who sing of shattered hope**
> **Let my gift be sufficient rope.**[29]

The style of Ivy League college days in the 1930s is reflected by an announcement in *Jester* of the Junior Promenade to be held in the Grand Ballroom of the Ritz Carlton Hotel (razed in the 1950s). Tickets: $5. Ads were for Prince Albert pipe tobacco; Jacob Ruppert beer; Camels (in four color, with a caption that quoted a secretary as saying, "Camels put more fun into eating and smoking too"); Brooks Brothers blue gabardine trousers for $8. Barry Ulanov, later a well-known jazz critic and a professor at Barnard, reviewed the new Victor, Brunswick, and Decca recordings of Tommy Dorsey, Chick Webb, Benny Goodman, Fats Waller, and Teddy Wilson.[30]

Poetry tended to the ultra light-hearted. In a 1936-37 issue Lax had this poem, with no apologies to Ogden Nash:

The ant's a stupid little thing,
He works his tail off in the spring.
The grasshopper, whose sloth is native,
 Is winter warm and procreative.
I'll keep my thoughts on the mantis within me,
 Because I'm afraid they'll start praying agin me.

Rice was accepted as a staff member when, as a freshman in 1936, he brought some of his high school cartoons to the *Jester* office on the fourth floor of John Jay Hall, and was accepted by a group that included Merton, Lax, and Ralph Toledano, "a Trotskyite at the time," Rice recalled, "and . . . later [as Ralph de Toledano] . . . a columnist for the liberal *P.M.* magazine and still later an arch-conservative.[31]

But it wasn't just humor that marked *Jester*'s content in those years. Serious issues were dealt with, although usually sarcastically. The 1936 Roosevelt-Landon presidential campaign had been the butt of a satire by Merton. He invented a candidate named Evander Crotch, "the only archconservative candidate in this campaign . . . all the other candidates are directly or indirectly supplied with Moscow gold." He writes that William Randolph Hearst and "his boss, Alf Landon," had stolen the Crotch platform. He quotes Crotch: "the drought would be far less serious if it would only rain a little," and "I am told that a few of the unemployed are losing weight, and becoming thin and peaked. . . . I can only conclude that the unemployed are not eating their spinach."[32]

Columbian, the university yearbook, reported that the 1937-38 *Jester*

> regained to a large extent the goodwill of the Campus. Due to its large circulation, it was truly able to represent and reflect student opinion for the first time in many years. In this function [it] stepped out of the role of "college comic" and tried to create for itself a new personality which would combine both the elements of a humor magazine and a clearing house for ideas pertinent to university life.
>
> It was, therefore, not strange when the Christmas Issue appeared with an eight-page antiwar section consisting of the famous Goya etchings (from Desastres de la Guerra), a serious poem by Ralph de Toledano, reproduction of Spanish and German propaganda posters, and Chinese-war sketches by Tom Merton.

That issue had a striking cover, captioned "Peace on Earth," depicting Mussolini, Hitler, and Franco riding camels à la the Three Wise Men and gazing at the star of Bethlehem while cradling bombs.[33]

Merton and Lax, both talented caricaturists, drew many of the cartoons. Typical of Merton's were luscious nudes and leering males. Caption on one: "But she has no Raison d'etre," and on another, "Now toin
around, and tell me more about Brahms." Lax did marvelous faces with
a few bold strokes—one series especially good to illustrate Merton's
short essay "The Question of the Beard."

Columbian went on to write that "In the process of extracting copy
from the student body, the editors of *Jester* had the good fortune to discover Ed Rice, a writer-artist of exceptional merit who will in all probability move into the editorial chair and from there to greater things.
To him, more than to any other individual contributor, goes the credit
for making this a successful *Jester* year. Then there was Robert Lax, ex-
editor of the comic and present editor of *Review* . . . [and others who]
devoted their efforts and their wits towards filling up the year's pages,
as did Tom Merton. . . ."[34]

Lax spoofed an anonymous poet—illustrated by a Merton nude—in
June 1939:

> Summer is icumen in
> (Lhude whistle traffique coppe)
> Sparrewe peepeth, poodle leapeth
> Aardvark sleepeth in the zoo;
> Summer is icumen in
> Murie sing cuccu.
> Busse upon the Dryve ironne
> Sauntre saylors in the sunne,
> Traffique maketh toote and screeche,
> Longen folk for Brighton Beache,
> Summer bringeth awful dinne,
> Shut-up, dmne cuccu!

Both Merton and Rice became campus activists, while Lax abstained
with the characteristic unwillingness to become involved in activism that
would stay with him in later life. "In those days," said Rice, "the war in
Spain was a big topic. We also got involved in supporting labor strikes,
like the miners in Harlan, Kentucky, and we picketed Macy's over their
labor policies."[35] Rice remembers dealing with these issues over lunch
or dinner with Merton almost every day during those years.

Both Lax and Merton give extraordinary credit to Mark Van Doren
for his influence on their appetite for learning. Rice, unfortunately,
never took a course from Van Doren. Merton wrote, "It would not be
exactly true to say that he [Van Doren] was a kind of nucleus around

whom the concretion of friends formed itself: that would not be accurate. Not all of us took his courses, and those who did, did not do so all at the same time. And yet nevertheless our common respect for Mark's sanity and wisdom did much to make us aware of how much we ourselves had in common."[36]

A Shakespeare course taught by Van Doren turned out to be the occasion for Merton meeting Lax for the first time. His description in *SSM* of the event, of Van Doren's class, and of Lax is classic:

Taller than them all, and more serious, with a long face, like a horse, and a great mane of black hair on top of it, Bob Lax meditated on some incomprehensible woe. . . .

[In the course we were] considering all the most important realities, not indeed in terms of something alien to Shakespeare and poetry, but precisely in his own terms, with occasional intuitions of another order. . . . Mark's balanced and sensitive and clear way of seeing things, at once simple and yet capable of subtlety, being fundamentally scholastic, though not necessarily and explicitly Christian, presented these things in ways that made them live within us. . . . This class was one of the few things that could persuade me to get on the train and go to Columbia at all.

It was this year, too, that I began to discover who Bob Lax was, and that in him was a combination of Mark's clarity and my confusion and misery—and a lot more besides that was his own.

To name Robert Lax in another way, he was a kind of combination of Hamlet and Elias. A potential prophet, but without rage. A king, but a Jew too. A mind full of tremendous and subtle intuitions, and every day he found less and less to say about them, and resigned himself to being inarticulate. In his hesitations, though without embarrassment or nervousness at all, he would often curl his long legs all around a chair, in seven different ways, while he was trying to find a word with which to begin. He talked best sitting on the floor.

And the secret of his constant solidity I think has always been a kind of natural, instinctive spirituality, a kind of inborn direction to the living God. Lax has always been afraid he was in a blind alley, and half aware that, after all, it might not be a blind alley, but God, infinity.

He had a mind naturally disposed, from the very cradle, to a kind of affinity for Job and St. John of the Cross. And I now know that he was born so much of a contemplative that he will probably never be able to find out how much.

. . . In those days one of the things we had most in common, although perhaps we did not talk about it so much, was the abyss that walked around in front of our feet everywhere we went, and kept making us dizzy and afraid of trains and high buildings. For some reason, Lax developed an implicit trust in all my notions about what was good and bad for mental and physical health, perhaps because I was always very definite in my likes and dislikes.[37]

"We did a lot of heavy drinking in those days," recalled Rice, "I was one of the heaviest boozers but Merton drank, too, Lax not so much. We would buy quarts of beer on Friday night, or go to bars like the Gold Rail, Flynn's . . . sometimes we drank Scotch and Bourbon. We might down a half pint each in the movies."[38]

Academics, though, were serious stuff for all three men. As a freshman Lax took geology, French, an English course in verse writing, and a music course in pianoforte, sitting in with Ad Reinhardt. He and Ad also took Meyer Schapiro's history of art, Irwin Edman's esthetics, and Randall's history of philosophy. With Ad he remembers going to a Bartok concert by the Budapest String Quartet and to lectures by André Malraux and Gertrude Stein. As a sophomore, his French course was in literary masterpieces; he took on the Renaissance in a comparative literature course; he began Italian, philosophy, zoology; and he dug into a classical civilization course called "Rome and the World of Today." Junior year brought a colloquium on important books, English literature from 1590 to 1797, the Shakespeare course under Van Doren where he met Merton, more Italian, and medieval Latin. He continued as a senior with the colloquium on important books, English literature from 1798 to the present, and medieval Latin, and piled on French literature, two history courses—one on nineteenth-century European thought and one on the social and political development of the United States since the Civil War—advanced English composition, and a course on modern drama and playwriting. The colloquium on books was taught by Jacques Barzun, the distinguished literary figure, then in his thirties, who would publish a masterful cultural history of the West when he was in his nineties.[39] The latter wasn't yet finished when Lax said this to me one day in Patmos, "It doesn't worry him that he may not be able to finish it but he keeps at it. . . . I'm trying to get the *Love Had a Compass* book to him."[40]

Merton had entered Columbia in February 1935 with advanced standing, getting substantial French, history, and Italian credits for his work at Cambridge. Starting as a second-term freshman, he jumped right into history of the French novel, the philosophy of art, a course in Western civilization, and the same course in English literature from 1590 to 1797 that Lax took. In summer school he began Spanish, and one does not wonder why his French became so elegant when noting that he took a course called "L'Esthetique de la langue française du XVIe siècle à nos jours."

Merton's language capabilities were truly amazing. Lax recalls watching him one day say goodbye to an international busload of young musicians, "all in their own languages, and he'd even switch from one dialect to another. If Merton was talking to a British lord he'd speak like a British lord, if he was talking to a Swami he sounded like one. . . ."[41] His facility in French, Spanish, Italian, German, and Latin was remarkable.

But his intellectual curiosity extended to science as well. He went for botany as a sophomore and continued the geology that he had started as a freshman. Both subjects he would get to use often in the fields of the Trappist monastery in Gethsemani, Kentucky. Also in his sophomore year he took on two additional sophisticated French courses—French critics of the nineteenth century and French literature of the Renaissance. He continued Spanish, added German, and—one wonders why—a course in American constitutional law. Junior year in 1936-37 brought two more French courses, one on literature to the end of the fifteenth century, and one on the French novel from 1885 to 1936. He kept going with botany, geology, and Spanish, and added the Shakespeare course by Van Doren. His final half year, up to February 1938, was absorbed with more English literature, a course in the aesthetics of English poetry, and his first ventures into economics and astronomy. His A.B. degree was conferred on February 23, 1938, but he did not participate in the graduation ceremony until that June.

Rice, still influenced by his mother's admonition that he prepare for a career as a doctor, in his freshman and sophomore years took some pre-med courses in which he did not fare well—among them physics and chemistry. His language choices were French as a freshman and German as a sophomore. Pursuing his determination to become an artist, he took a studio class in drawing, then, as a junior, a studio class in painting, two history of art courses—one on ancient, medieval, and Renaissance art and one on the development of modern art, and no less than four English subjects—eighteenth-century Restoration drama, biography, advanced composition, and literature after the death of Shakespeare. As did Lax and Merton, he took geology, and he kept up the painting studio as a senior, along with two more art courses—one on Oriental art and one on commercial art. He added Italian, medieval

Latin, psychology, and history of U.S. social, economic, and political policy. The course in Oriental art, he would later say, influenced some of the graphics he used for *Jubilee* magazine. Although a tepid Catholic, Rice kept up his attendance at Mass and maintained an interest in the different kinds of Catholic worship. "The Eastern liturgy particularly appealed to me and a group of friends, and we, including Merton, would go all over New York to attend different ethnic services."[42]

Rice would leave school, having encountered academic difficulty, before he would have graduated in June 1940. His transcript shows he owed $6 in infirmary fees.

Knowing how much time the three students put into *Jester* work, and how intensively they caroused, it's hard to understand how they managed their academics.

Lax's poetry got high praise from some of his distinguished teachers. Irwin Edman, himself a noted poet, wrote a longhand note praising one of Lax's poems. "Your 'Antony and Cleopatra' was very fine, especially the latter part, really a major poem in theme and in execution. Real music and imagination."[43]

Asked about the poem many years later, Lax wrote, "I composed it on the spot, during a final exam Van Doren gave us in his Shakespeare course. All he had said during his lectures about Antony and Cleopatra was inspiring, both to me and to Merton. So on the final exam, I found I was writing those lines. It was the only question out of eighteen or so that I answered. So Mark couldn't give me an A on the examination. He gave me an A- instead. And that's old Mark for you. When Merton read it, he liked it, and I think that's when he asked me to give him my thoughts on how to write poetry. And we were off to the races."[44] Alas, the poem could not be found in any of the Lax archives.

Merton describes a characteristic of Van Doren that seems to have been especially meaningful to him and to Lax since it heightened their motivation to write poems: "And for him poetry was, indeed, a virtue of the practical intellect, and not simply a vague spilling of the emotions, wasting the soul and perfecting none of our essential powers."[45]

Poems by Lax and Merton won the university's Mariana Griswold Van Rensselaer prize, Lax in 1938 as a senior, Merton in 1939 as a graduate student. One marvels at the bountiful output of poetry by Columbia students in those years, although perhaps it's not so surprising when one considers their teachers; besides Van Doren and Edman there were William Rose Benet, Lionel Trilling, Joseph Auslander, Leonora Speyer, and others. Lax's prize-winning poem was a prophetic piece, foreboding New York's difficulties in modern times, titled "Last Days of a City":

How do the men about to die
In rural places prophesy
The fate incumbent? What dark flight
Of dreams forewarns them in the night?
By what deep wonder are they shown
The gaudy raiment of the bone
Unbuttoning? The ribs laid bare,
The silly empty-socket stare
Of eyeless dead Neanderthals?
What whispered note, what flute-voice calls
That these men feel before their time
Disintegration into lime?
In pastoral song a city dies,
Its face averted country-wise.
With gilded smile and perfumed breath
It makes a pattern of its death.
With dying ear attentive yet
To tightened string and flageolet
It skims in barge of silver sound
The tides of voices underground.
A city's very laughter damns
Itself in its own epigrams,
And all the warning death would bring
Is dissipate in murmuring.[46]

The following year Merton, as a graduate student, had six entries in the annual poetry volume. His prize winner, titled "Fable for a War," reflects his disgust with the Axis powers:

The old Roman sow
Bears a new litter now
To fatten for a while
On the same imperial swill.
The cannibal will dig
And root out Spanish bones beside the pig.

Germany has reared
A rare ugly bird
To screech a sour song
In the German tongue:
Tell me if there be
A sparrowhawk for such birds as he?

The parrots lift their beaks
And fill the air with shrieks.
Ambassador is sent
From the parrots' parliament:
"Oh see how fine I fly
And nibble crackers got in Germany."

Europe is a feast
For every bloody beast:
Jackals will grow fat
On the bones after that.
But in the end of all
None but the crows can sing the funeral.[47]

An important, it would seem even life-shaping, development for both Lax and Merton occurred in 1937. Lax had read Aldous Huxley's just-published *Ends and Means* and persuaded Merton to read it too. The appeal of the book to the two idealists might have stemmed from lines like these on the very first page:

There are some who believe—and it is a very popular belief at the present time—that the royal road to a better world is the road of economic reform. For some, the short cut to Utopia is military conquest and the hegemony of one particular nation; for others, it is armed revolution and the dictatorship of a particular class. . . . There are others, however, who approach the problem from the opposite end, and believe that desirable social changes can be brought about most effectively by changing the individuals who compose society. Of the people who think this way, some pin their faith to education, some to psycho-analysis, some to applied behaviorism. There are others, on the contrary, who believe that no desirable "change of heart" can be brought about without supernatural aid. There must be, they say, a return to religion. (Unhappily, they cannot agree on the religion to which the return should be made.)[48]

Three pages later are Huxley words that could well have been an early influence on the eventual choice, for both Lax and Merton, of the ascetic, contemplative life:

It is difficult to find a single word that will adequately describe the ideal man of the free philosophers and the founders of religions.

. . . The ideal man is the non-attached man. Non-attached to his bodily sensations and lusts. Non-attached to his craving for power and possessions. . . . Non-attached to his anger and hatred; non-attached to his exclusive loves. Non-attached to wealth, fame, social position. Non-attached even to science, art, speculation, philanthropy.[49]

Huxley hit home with the future Merton when he pointed out that the ideal of nonattachment has been "systematically preached" for over three thousand years—"in Hinduism. It is at the very heart of the teachings of Buddha" and for the Chinese in Lao Tzu, by the Greeks with the Stoics, and then through the Gospel of Jesus which he says is a "gospel of non-attachment" to worldly things, and of attachment, instead, to God.[50]

Huxley probably struck another responsive chord with Merton when he contrasted some of the characteristics of the rites of "the masses" of both Christians and Buddhists with their contemplative centers:

Christianity, Hinduism and Buddhism have in common certain vulgar aids to devotion for the masses, such as, in some of their places of worship, gaudy colours, the same tripe-like decorations, the same gesticulating statues; the nose inhales the same intoxicating smells; the ear and, along with it, the understanding, are lulled by the drone of the same incomprehensible incantations, roused by the same loud, impressive music.

He terms those features "fetters holding back the soul from enlightenment and remarks that they are conspicuously absent from the chapel of a Cistercian monastery and the meditation hall of a community of Zen Buddhism."[51] In just a few years hence, Merton would be a monk in one of those Cistercian monasteries.

A man who adhered to the gospel of what Huxley termed "nonattachment"—who had virtually no worldly possessions, in fact—would soon arrive on the Columbia scene in most unusual circumstances, and he would have strong effect on Lax, Merton, Rice, and their classmates. His name: Mahanambrata Bramachari. A holy man from Calcutta, Bramachari, then age thirty-five, moved in with Lax and his roommate Seymour Freedgood in 1938, having arrived from Chicago five years earlier. A Hindu monk, he had been designated to represent his Vaishnava Order at a World Fellowship of Faiths, to be held coincident with the Chicago World's Fair of 1933. With little money he had made his way from India, depending on the grace of God and the generosity of strangers, by ship from Bombay to Venice—sleeping on deck each night—then by train to Genoa, Paris, Le Havre, then by ship to New York and finally by bus to Chicago. Throughout the trip he wore only a homespun skirt and turban and subsisted on handout vegetables and bread. For two years in Chicago he stayed in the home of one of the conference officials, then got a scholarship that permitted him to earn a Ph.D. from the University of Chicago in 1937. Throughout the four years he lectured before clubs, high schools, and universities, giving an astounding 364 lectures in 63 cities while studying during the latter two years for his doctorate. Lax described how he came to Columbia:

> my room mate [Seymour Freedgood]'s girl knew him in chicago and told him that if he came to new york he could stay with us.
>
> he went all around the country that way, people who liked him sent him to see their other friends. he wasn't any trouble at all, took up very little room, was often so quiet you went out of your way to ask him questions, and being a hindu he was not very costly to feed. that is how i came to know him. he came to stay with us in new york in spring of 1938, when i was studying for my last college exams. he wore a yellow turban, a white toga and a cape the color of pea soup. the girls in chicago had given him a pair of blue sneakers.
>
> the first day he came we sat around the room asking him questions. where had he been, he had been to chicago, springfield, denver, yellowstone national park. ok that was enough. how did he like america. he liked it as well as any place else. was he lonesome. he also told us about the sanskrit alphabet.
>
> that night my roommate went home and bramachari slept in the room adjoining mine. early the next morning. . . .
> goodmorning he said
> good morning
> i have been reading the poems of william blake
> . . . and stood silently as though waiting for a thought.[52]

Bramachari's influence on the Columbia friends was profound. Merton would write years later that "Dr. Bramachari came into my life precisely at the moment when I stood at a crossroads, and my encounter with him helped me to decide upon the road I myself must take. . . . Indeed, one of the main things I learned from Dr. Bramachari was a lesson he taught not so much by his words as by his life: the lesson that one can and must entrust himself to a higher and unseen Wisdom, and that if one can relax his frantic hold on the illusory securities of everyday material existence and abandon himself peacefully to a supreme Will he will himself find freedom and peace in that Will."[53] It was Bramachari, ironically, who led Merton to read some of the Christian classics, like the *Confessions* of St. Augustine. He also helped Merton to realize how important it was that Western man get to know the East. "Ever since that summer day in 1938 [when they first met in New York] I have realized how true it is not only that East and West may meet, but that they *must* meet, not in the chance collision of alien cultures in which one seeks to impose upon the other the patterns of power and technology, but in a profoundly human exchange in which each culture finds itself in the other."

Lax, too, was deeply influenced by the holy man, and kept in touch with him for years. In 1993 he wrote Bramachari from Patmos that "you opened a door to life for all of us. We knew it then, and none of us has ever forgotten the blessings that came to us through you. . . . I am 77 years old now and happy to be living on this little Greek island . . . with you and Merton (and our other friends) for company. Both you and he often come to me in dreams . . . sometimes in the same dream too, one metamorphosing into the other."[54]

The Columbia friends, it must be said, had been conditioned for the arrival of the Hindu holy man by their own readings in 1937 and 1938, including Huxley's paean to Hinduism, described earlier. But then the quest for spiritual enlightenment headed toward serious Christianity. Merton would soon discover Thomas Aquinas through scholar Etienne Gilson, and then the philosopher Jacques Maritain, and often shared his thoughts about these thinkers with Lax. Also influential was Mark Van Doren, whose own temperament was "profoundly scholastic in the sense that his clear mind looked directly for the quiddities of things, and sought being and substance under the covering of accident and appearances."[55]

After getting his undergraduate degree in February, Merton stayed on at Columbia as a graduate student, working on his M.A. in English. His thesis was entitled "Nature and Art in William Blake." He went to his first Sunday Mass at Corpus Christi, and soon had consultations with the pastor, Columbia's Catholic chaplain, Father George Ford, about becoming a Catholic.

Lax got an apartment near Columbia, and his mother joined him near the end of his senior year to help him put together his senior thesis. "There was always someone taking care of Bob's mechanics," his cousin Soni Holman remembered.[56] He got his B.A. in June, was voted best writer in the class, and elected to the class hall of fame. While Merton's new-found zeal for Catholicism was on the rise, during the subsequent summer, well into his work on his master's degree, he was clearly not immune to more worldly attachments, and he retained a college undergrad's lingo in his letters. He wrote Lax from Douglaston about the tiring trip he had from Olean where he had just spent a week with Lax, whose family had once again given up on New York and returned to the little western New York town:

> The girl [Pat Hickman] met me in New York and we came home where it was very cool and we refreshed ourselves some. I could hardly walk to bed when I got home for the great aching of the limbs, back and groin, for that the refreshment was of a merely spiritual nature.[57]

In another letter to Lax he reported that he expected *The Nation* to print his "Blake review" and that he was writing movie reviews. Girls were still on his mind. "This last week I had many carnivals with my Chicago girl [Pat Hickman], all kind of festivals I did. . . ."[58]

He later complained that Lax had not written. "Sir, are you bogged up in your cabin . . . is there no mail service, is it eating and drinking and feasting all day, is it watching the birds fly about and no thought of friends?"[59] Lax responded with, "I was laying an egg. Lots of things: torpor, stupor, mama coming home, slate and freedgood coming and not coming, letter to n. flagg (who did write) [Flagg was Lax's girlfriend] and graduation people, opening cottage, tying my shoes. . . ."[60] Lax's brother-in-law Benji Marcus, who owned the cottage outside of Olean that would become the abode of Lax, Merton, Rice, and other Columbia brethren in the summers of 1939 and 1940, wanted Lax, Merton, and Bob Gibney to start a magazine, "but he doesn't know how much backing and I don't know what sort of a magazine or whether it would[n]'t be better to get a job with something already started, but he keeps saying it but I think he keeps thinking of Life and Time or anyway a thing that would make lots of money. . . ."[61]

Merton, in these months, was intensively into his Blake thesis. "Me," he wrote Lax from his apartment across from Columbia's Butler Library, "I have worked like a dog, ten twelve hours a day, sweating over dirty old books. . . . I have studied William Blake, I have measured him with a ruler, I have sneaked at him with pencils and T squares, I have spied on him from a distance with a small spyglass, I have held him up to mirrors, and will shortly endeavor to prove that the prophetic books were all written with lemon juice and must be held in front of a slow fire to read."[62] In spite of his sweat over the Blake thesis, it has been judged harshly over the years. Merton's biographer, Michael Mott, wrote Bob Lax in 1982 that it was "[h]alf baked and actually badly written."[63] At the time, Merton was experiencing strong spiritual stirrings: "I think to go and read pieces of Aquinas, and I think to read about Zen Buddhism."[64]

Only days later, however, Merton's vestigial carnality emerged. He admonished Lax, "Listen, for Christ's sake, why don't you go to Boston to N. Flagg and maybe I'd go up to Boston and stay with some people and then we'd all get drunk? Except the fool girl I would be staying with has got a fallen womb or some beetles in her cunt, and so she doesn't drink or laugh much."[65]

But not long after he took a step in a direction that would radically change his life. On November 16, 1938 he was baptized and received his first communion at Corpus Christi Church on 121st Street, with Rice as godfather. Lax, Sy Freedgood, and Bob Gerdy (another *Jester* stalwart), all Jews, were witnesses. Lax would tell an interviewer many years later what he thought had drawn Merton to Catholicism. It no doubt applied to his own eventual conversion as well:

> I think the feeling of God's concern for the world, God's mercy toward sinners, actually made a strong appeal. I think it never occurred to him that that was at the center of Christianity. But it seems to me, he certainly supernaturally moved toward all this because he'd be sitting in his room reading, and suddenly he hears a voice inside him saying "Go to Mass," and soon after that he hears a voice saying "Go and become a Catholic."[66]

Merton's own account of the conversion, written three years after his baptism, reveals how certain books influenced him:

> until I read his [Aldous Huxley's] *Ends and Means* just about four years ago, I hadn't known a thing about mysticism, not even the word. The part he played in my conversion, by that book, was quite great. Just how great a part a book can play in conversion is questionable: several books figured in mine. Gilson's *Spirit of Medieval Philosophy* was the first and from it more than any other book I learned a healthy respect for Catholicism. Then *Ends and Means* from which I learned to respect mysticism. Maritain's *Art and Scholasticism* was another—and Blake's poems. . . . Joyce's *Portrait of the Artist* got me fascinated in Catholic sermons(!) What horrified him began to appeal to me. . . . Finally, G. F. Lahey's life of G. M. Hopkins: I was reading about Hopkins' conversion when I dropped the book and rushed out of the house and went to see Fr. Ford."[67]

* * * * * * * * * * * * *

2

SPIRITUAL HIPPIES

Writing, Carousing, Praying in Olean; Taking Over Jester; Lax Published in the New Yorker

> It was probably one of the original hippie colonies. . . . We wrote, drank, read, went to the movies, played jazz—Armstrong, the Chicago crowd, the Austin High School gang. We had a windup phonograph for 78's with bamboo needles. We sometimes fell down dead drunk, playing Royal Garden Blues, Beiderbecke, Whiteman, Frank Teschmaker. We would read Joyce—Finnegan's Wake. Several installments had appeared. Ulysses had been banned. Merton was also reading religious works—St. John of the Cross, St. Teresa of Avila, the Bible.—*Ed Rice*[1]

Such goings-on characterized most of the summers of both 1939 and 1940 at the Olean cottage owned by Bob Lax's brother-in-law, Benji Marcus, husband of his sister Gladys. It was a tranquil place, on a lovely wooded hill on the outskirts of town, but the interior of the house was always in a state of chaos. It was occupied mostly by Lax, Merton, and Rice, but there were various others, including, at different times, Seymour Freedgood, Bob Gerdy, Bob Gibney, Jim Knight, John Slate, and girlfriends Nancy Flagg, Jinny Burton, Peggy Wells, and Lilly Reilly.

Early in 1939 Merton had received his master's degree in English. He then left his 114th Street apartment behind Columbia's Butler Library and moved to Perry Street in Greenwich Village, having decided to go for his Ph.D. Lax was tutoring the children of the manager of the Hotel Taft. One of the children, Stephen Lewis, wrote a book that included memories of Lax from 1939 and visits to the Taft by Merton and Bramachari. The ten-year-old, and his younger brother Peter, listened, he wrote, with "Tom on the floor . . . to Bob on books, spiritual rebirth . . . and descriptions of Olean . . . so vivid we walked the streets . . . both tried to explain eternity to us." It must have been heady stuff for the two boys. "What happens after eternity? they asked. 'More,' said Tom. 'What after more?' 'A hundred times more than everything since time began,' said Bob, adding, 'And that's just the first minute.' Peter looked as if he were going to cry; Merton looked a little upset himself."[2] Lax and Merton talked on the phone in those days almost daily. But they wrote to each other as well. A letter from Lax to Merton in April, which might never have been mailed, reveals how spiritual their communications could be when they weren't being hippies. "What's good is to love yourself and your neighbor as yourself and love both and all in the love of God. For if you love one wholly you love all wholly and if you love any partly you love all only partly, and a man who can beat down the heathen in himself can beat down the heathen in Tahiti as well. Now no more balanced sentences."[3]

It's interesting that it was Lax, the Jew, still not baptized a Catholic, whose counsel to Merton was most meaningful at the time. As he wrote in *SSM,* Merton felt that "although I had gone before him to the fountains of grace [presumably referring to his own baptism], Lax was much wiser than I, and had clearer vision, and was, in fact, corresponding much more truly to the grace of God than I, and he had seen what was the only important thing. I think he has told what he had to say to many people besides myself: but certainly his was one of the voices through which the insistent Spirit of God was determined to teach me the way I had to travel."[4]

At some time during this period Dan Walsh, who had been a student of Etienne Gilson at the University of Toronto and who taught a popular course on Thomas Aquinas at Columbia, took Merton to meet Jacques Maritain, a noted Thomist, at a session of a Catholic book club. Thomism, long neglected, was having a revival, and the subject fascinated Merton. Walsh would turn out to have a major influence on Merton's religious directions, and so would the writings of Maritain, who would visit Merton when he became a monk. In turnabout, Merton would influence Walsh, years later, to become a priest, although not a Trappist.[5]

But Merton still had strong secular inclinations. He wrote Lax a while later from shipboard on the way to a vacation in Bermuda, mainly about girls, "larfing," and champagne. He wasn't quite ready for the cloth.[6]

Then, however, a talk with Lax seems to have changed his whole focus. It occurred one evening in spring when he and Lax were walking along Sixth Avenue in the Village. Merton recounted the incident in *SSM,* and it has been cited often. The dialogue went roughly like this. Lax asked bluntly:

"What do you want to be anyway?"

"I don't know; I guess what I want is to be a good Catholic."

"What do you mean, you want to be a good Catholic? What you should say is that you want to be a saint."

"How do you expect me to become a saint?"

"By wanting to."

"I can't be a saint."

"All that is necessary to be a saint is to want to be one. Don't you believe that God will make you what He created you to be, if you will consent to let Him do it? All you have to do is desire it."[7]

The next day he told Mark Van Doren that "Lax is going around saying that all a man needs to be a saint is to want to be one." Van Doren responded, "Of course." Merton went out and bought the first volume of the works of St. John of the Cross and began underlining some of the sentences, which, "although they amazed and dazzled me with their import, were all too simple for me to understand . . . too naked, too stripped of all duplicity and compromise for my complexity, perverted by many appetites."[8]

It was not long afterward, in June 1939, that Lax, Merton, and Rice began their first summer at the Marcus's cottage. The house, just outside of Olean, had three bedrooms. Lax's family and Rice's father provided the three men with basic income, but not much. "My father was glad to have me out of the way, and we didn't spend a lot," Rice remembered. Sometimes the day began at dawn. Merton typed in the living room, Lax in the garage, Rice outdoors except in cold weather when all three were in the living room. They had no newspapers or radio, but sometimes they went to the movies downtown. "We had a contest to see who could write a novel the fastest. I wrote one in about 10 days called *The Blue Horse*—never published," Rice told me. "Lax wrote *Spangled Palace* which Gerdy and I turned into a musical we had in mind for Vera Zorina.[9] Merton wrote versions of a novel [presumably *Labyrinth*, which was also titled *Straits of Dover* and *The Night before the Battle*]."[10]

There was reading material aplenty, most of it courtesy of Father Irenaeus of the St. Bonaventure library, who "with reckless trust abandoned all the shelves to us."[11]

Jim Knight wrote an autobiographical novel focused on his hometown of Atlanta. He remembers that they were all arrested for exploding firecrackers on July 4 near St. Bonaventure, and that he and Merton were thrown out of a bar in Erie, Pennsylvania, to which they had hitchhiked, after Merton played raucous drums. Lax recalls that Merton would play on hand drums at the Olean house, "and it was like he was communicating with Bramachari in India. He also played piano as a percussion instrument."[12] "Merton intimidated me in those days," Knight says. "I was a yokel from the South . . . he was much more sophisticated, with his French background . . . he would talk about Huxley, Graham Greene." Today Knight feels that "people are making a plastic saint out of him . . . he had an impish, devilish grin and was certainly no saint in those days." As rambunctious as were their ramblings, Knight says the group never got involved with drugs.[13] That, however, is at variance with what Nancy Flagg, then Lax's girlfriend, recalled in a magazine piece written years later, namely, that they smoked a lot of pot.[14] Neat and clean they were not. Rice recalled:

> The Marcus house was always a mess, dishes in the sink sometimes for days. There was a cleaning woman sometimes [sent to the cottage by Lax's sister Gladys once a week], but we cooked our own meals. We'd buy the food at the A&P, eat Graham crackers, hamburgers, drink Jim Beam bourbon, sit in the balcony at the movies and drink. There were some frightful Lax–Merton arguments about subjects like St John of the Cross. Merton threw a book on the ground in the middle of one of them. A lot of the things they were arguing I didn't know anything about, like Blake and Donne, but I was interested. I was only 19, they were in their early 20s but three years makes a big difference at that age. Lax was always throwing out his back doing things like tieing his shoelaces. Then he got a terrible infection from Shredded Wheat. A piece went into his palm and it was infected for two weeks.
>
> I had a girl friend in Rockville Center that I went home to see. Merton and Lax were kind of anti-feminine in those days. Merton was sexually active but he could be derogatory about women. Lax had a so-called romance with Nancy Flagg but he never put his arm around her.[15]

Knight says that Gibney had Peggy Wells sleeping with him and Sy Freedgood had a girl.[16] Lax's nephew, Dick Marcus, a youngster at the time, remembers that

> they all had beards and Rice's father paid him once to shave . . . they used to set up card tables to type. Merton and Rice were usually barefoot. At night they would sometimes sit out front and watch the lightning strikes in the valley. Freedgood, who had been an Eagle scout, led us on walks in the woods. One of my friends and I put a packing crate from a refrigerator up in the tree and built a ladder

to it while Rice and Gibney watched us. Then they took over and expanded it to a big platform high in the trees that maybe 50 people could stand on. They'd sometimes go up there and write. I went up and got scared, it was so high. Rice and Gibney were both good swimmers. Gibney could hold his breath for two minutes underwater while he swam half way across the lake.[17]

In a letter to Lax dated July 14, during a brief return by train to New York with Rice, Merton wrote, "I . . . get ready to send my novel to Farrar." He went to the post office with the manuscript [*Labyrinth*, presumably] and, indulging as he sometimes did in hyperbole: "The guy tell me eighty dollars, (it weighs five and ½ pounds) . . . and [I] felt better about sending it express for 25 cents."[18]

Shortly after, Merton wrote to Lax of much drinking of Barbados Rum Collins back in the city, going to the World's Fair, and he observed that "New York seems to be so full of nice dames and W[ilma] Reardon certainly looked to me the most beautiful thing in the world but I guess it's all right for a visit and no place to live, New York . . . I hope very much to get back to Olean and finish the novel."[19] He might have meant revising the novel since the earlier letter told of having already mailed it off to "Farrar" [at that time Farrar and Rinehart].

Staying in Olean Lax got a job as a radio announcer on the local station. A lengthy and newsy Merton letter in late August complains about the city's heat and reports that he and Rice bought some Balinese records and that "Rice gave me a shock with the beard off. . . ." A visit to the Museum of Modern Art drew praise for "some picasso called seated woman oh boy . . . cezannes . . . one Juan Gris, and even one chirico and I was happied by the Miros okay, and one Stuart Davis." His reading ran to Dante and a French author named Valerie Larbaud,[20] who was "some good guy, too" and he got "mild amusement" from the Broadway production of Anita Loos's *Gentlemen Prefer Blondes* and from a spy movie, *Clouds over Europe*, which he saw with Gibney.[21]

Lax, still a worshipping Jew at the time, wrote in September that "Once more it rushes to the Jewish vespers [presumably Yom Kippur]." His reading was becoming more and more Christian, though, as he told Merton, "S. J. of the C. [St. John of the Cross] I have finished this afternoon. . . ."[22]

Merton responded with apprehension about the oncoming war [Poland had been invaded by Germany on September 1]. "I can't say I got one clear idea in my head, not one unless it is to make some tentatives to grab a runout powder to some nice safe place such as a tiger's den, although I still say if you don't want to go to W[ar] you don't have to, . . ." and then, "As to St John of the Cross, sure keep it as long as I don't send a worried letter askin for it fast, because if I do it means I am building a raft on which to paddle to Chile and this will be one of three books I want to take and hold over my chest to stop enemy bullets as I go through the Panama Canal. I don't see why every American boy should not build himself such a raft."[23]

He visited Jinny Burton, a Barnard girl, in Virginia over Labor Day, after first going to Mass at St. Francis of Assisi, next to Penn Station. Although there were wild parties, it was not a completely pleasant stay since he suffered an impacted wisdom tooth while there and needed five stitches in his jaw when he got it extracted back in New York. His reading in those days: "Here on my shelves, Pascal, Saint Augustine, Thomas à Kempis, Loyola, The Bible, Saint John of the Cross (no—Lax has that)."[24]

Merton wasn't the only one of the three friends who was thinking about the priesthood. So was Rice, although it's doubtful he was as serious as Merton seems to think he was. In his journal Merton wrote:

I don't know why I should have been a little surprised when Ed Rice said he had sometimes thought of being a priest. . . . Rice's difficulties are the same as mine. . . .

First: he thinks of the Jesuits. That's what I started out with, too. I suppose in my case it was because of working on Hopkins.

Second: he is afraid he will no longer be able to "write the way he wants to." That is, freely, using any kind of language that presents itself.

Third: he is not particularly anxious to get married, any more than I am. And so it goes. I wish Rice would come and be a priest, too, and I know it is God's will he should because every vocation is of God.[25]

It seems surprising that Rice would consider becoming a priest at that time since his Catholic convictions were not at all deep. "I went to Mass every Sunday," he recalled, "to a French church on Morningside Drive because my parents told me to go." However, he said "I never remember talking about my Catholicism . . . a lot of Catholics on campus in those days were Fascists." What discussions Rice, Merton, Lax, and friends did have were often in hangouts like The Chemist, a sandwich drugstore, Flynn's bar at 109th and Broadway, Gil Godfrey's and Pete's tavern. "We smoked Camels—'Lucky Strike Green Has Gone to War' and we often spent evenings listening to Dixieland at Nick's in the Village. Merton came in one night drunk and told us he was going to become a priest."[26]

Even in those days, Merton was very interested in Buddhism. "Ted deBary, whose wife was Catholic and who became a convert himself, was head of the Asian department at Columbia and he and Merton would have great discussions about Buddhism," remembered Rice.[27] But deBary, who has had a distinguished career as a scholar of Asian languages and culture and is still teaching at Columbia at this writing, does not recall Merton's interest in Buddhism as serious.[28]

In October Merton got a grant-in-aid for courses toward his Ph.D., and his journal reports having told Dan Walsh over a beer that he had been accepted into the Franciscan novitiate for entry in August 1940.

"I made up my mind," he wrote Lax, "about the monastery and now the monastery only has to make up its mind about me." The Franciscan monks that he encountered at St. Francis of Assisi entranced him: "all day long there are crowds of people there, for confessions and sermons and benedictions and all kinds of prayers to God: and there is not anything else in New York, not any place, not any office or any bright guy's typewriter or any gay dame's room full of congas or any museum full of El Grecos or any Library, even full of Dante that is as good as that one church where the monks are busy hearing confessions and praying and preaching."[29]

When Columbia's fall 1939 term started, Rice, now a senior, became editor-in-chief of *Jester*—a job that both Lax and Merton had had before him—and he continued to have both friends on the staff, although neither was enrolled at Columbia. Rice had been awarded a Silver King's Crown award and was elected secretary of the class of 1940, the only fraternity man [Psi Epsilon] elected a class officer, and he had lunch or dinner almost every day during this period with Merton.

Reinhardt continued to provide his friends with drawings for *Jester* even after his graduation. He would also, a few years later, while forging an outstanding name in art—his paintings today hang in the world's best museums—somehow make the time to contribute to *Jubilee*, and to Lax's poetry pamphlet, *Pax*. He would correspond regularly with all three friends through his lifetime, which ended, unfortunately, in 1967 when he was only fifty-four.

But in these years he was still an unknown, struggling to get recognition as a WPA artist. After a visit in early 1940 with Reinhardt, Merton wrote of him in his journal that "I think Ad Reinhardt is possibly the best artist in America . . . his abstract art is pure and religious," a somewhat ironic appraisal in the light of the painter's Communist convictions. But Merton regarded Reinhardt's painting as "completely chaste, and full of love of form and very good indeed." Going farther, quite stretching things, he said, "He'd make a good priest: a better priest than Gibney or Freedgood or Lax . . . because he wants to really do something like a priest."[30]

Merton's reflections on Reinhardt's politics led him to a tough-talking diatribe in the same journal entry on capitalism, a system he would castigate through his lifetime. In words that could well be valid in contemporary times he came down hard on

> . . . economic determinism—a sort of Calvinist predestination operating through forces let loose by the wickedness of a few selfish and crafty men.
>
> For the world to avoid damnation, the masses must come to life, realize that they are all powerful, that their reason is mighty and perfect, and take over from the self-destroyed capitalists.[31]

He was not easy on his new-found Catholicism either, blasting its cultural inadequacies in his journal only weeks later: ". . . it is one of the singular disgraces attached to Catholics as a social group," he wrote, "that they, who once nourished with their Faith and their Love of God the finest culture the world ever saw, are now content with the worst art, worst writing, the worst music, the worst everything that has ever made anybody throw up."[32]

While working on his master's degree, Merton was an instructor in English composition three nights a week in the extension program at Columbia. His journal entries during this period are full of analyses of his own intense efforts to love God. Once again he enlisted Lax's counsel.

> When I said that it was hard, if you were attached to drink and women and pleasures and ambitions, to love God and even to pray to him, Lax said nothing should be hard. That is of course true; what he meant is, just as I did, that you should be so full of the love of God as to be no longer attached to these pleasures, so that it would no longer be *hard* to abandon them. . . . [But] we are all weak and selfish and proud, and all bear the burden of Adam's sin; but Lax does not hold with any doctrine of original sin. And he would have the love of God be easy, and so would Christ and so would the worst sinner, the unhappiest of all: and so it is easy, that is plain . . . when you have put down your sins and desires, then it is easy.[33]

Merton turned out to be a very good teacher, and he became quite fond of conducting his classes. He wrote Lax that

> I got a chance to work full time as an instructor to Barnard College for girls only I don't think that will make me quit the [Franciscan] monastery because there is right now only violence or some sudden adverse judgement on the part of the monks could keep me out, and I guess if I wasn't to get into the monastery I would not be a cheerful fellow at all. Also I wish I knew when it was going to

begin, because I am sick of novels, and although I am not sick of teaching, but like it better every time. Only I want to be a monk first and then teach and write next.

But still I am going to see the english dept guy about it . . . and I will make no attempt not to be hired, just in case there are delays about the monastery or trouble. And if I wasn't going into the monastery I would certainly like very much to teach in Barnard because I think it would be mild and suave and pleasant to instruct maybe one fine dame like Burton or Reilley or Eaton in a whole class of Camilles, even.

Teaching is candy, Wotta happy clars. They write essays about the funny sheet and the movies and now precisely I got them writing a big dirty argument whether money stinks and defiles the hands like pitch or not, and whether everybody ought to love everybody.[34]

While his teaching was going well, Merton's own writing was frustrating him during these months. He had suffered rejection after rejection from book and magazine publishers. "How many envelopes I fed to the green mailbox at the corner of Perry Street . . . and everything I put in there came back—except for the book reviews."[35] Here too he got blunt advice from Lax, who criticized him for aiming too wholeheartedly at success, wanting to see his name in print. "His [Lax's] whole attitude about writing was purified of such stupidity, and was steeped in holiness, in charity, in disinterestedness. Characteristically he conceived the function of those who knew how to write, and who had something to say, in terms of the salvation of society."[36]

But the harsh comments of reviewers hurt Merton deeply. A reader at Macmillan, he wrote Lax, "said the characters were copied from Hemingway and the writing was copied from Joyce, and I myself sounded like a smart fellow only the reader wisht I didn't argue so much about religion in the book."[37]

A couple of months earlier Merton had written something in his journal that might have signaled what would become the inclination to write *The Seven Storey Mountain*: "I think everybody in the world wants the people to read his autobiography, or his letters or his diaries or his state papers or even his account books. . . . Lax spent the summer writing an autobiography after he had spent the spring writing a journal. The best novel of the age—*Ulysses*—is autobiography."[38]

But Merton lectured himself, quoting St. Theresa of Avila in *The Interior Castle* as saying, "we must not dwell on self-knowledge alone, but pass on from it at once and go seeking God's love above everything. . . . I was so preoccupied with self-knowledge that I didn't know anything about anybody else's feelings."

Rice and Merton spent a weekend in Washington in December, in a "very bad" hotel. Merton called the Corcoran and Freer gallery exhibits "ridiculous," was impressed by the Dominicans singing Vespers at their seminary, but was condescending about the Catholic University environs. "When you have seen the solidity of things in Europe—when you have seen Rome, it is odd to see something so raw, so unbegun. But maybe it is already a big thing and the best thing in the country, and please God it may someday be very great and wise and solid and rich and a source of wisdom and riches and light for all this part of the world." He continued in a gloomily prophetic tone, "Because this hemisphere needs it, and will need it more, because after the war, or as the war goes on, this country is going to be more and more lost as the civilization of Europe (on which America, being still a province, depends) destroys itself."

Perhaps Merton can blame Lax, at least partially, for getting him started at writing letters to literary luminaries that he admired. "I wanted to write Joyce last spring and I got sore at Lax for writing to Dorothy Baker[39] this summer but now I want to write to Saroyan."[40]

Merton took a vacation in the spring of 1940 to Miami and Cuba (apparently with funds from his grandfather). He wrote copious notes in his journal and lengthy letters to both Rice and Lax. To Lax he wrote from Camaguey that he was "knocked clean out on my feet about 28 times" by a singer named Angelillo, and went on rhapsodically, "I don't think there has ever in the history of the world been anything except church music equal to flamenco songs." He did not fail to check out the Cuban church. He went to some monasteries, made friends with "one wonderful priest in the Carmelite monastery" in Havana, "which was all full of statues of St. John of the Cross and St. Theresa."[41] He included in the letter "the first real poem I had ever written," inspired by La Caridad, the virgin who is Queen of Cuba, in the Basilica of Our Lady of Cobre in Santiago. He titled it "Song for Our Lady of Cobre."

> The white girls stir their heads like trees,
> The black girls go reflected like flamingoes in the street.
>
> The white girls sing as shrill as water,
> The black girls speak as loud as clay.
> The white girls open their arms like clouds,
> The black girls close their eyes like wings;
> Angels bow down like bells,
> Angels look up like toys,
>
> Because the heavenly stars stand in a ring,
> And all the pieces of the mosaic, Earth, get up, fly like
>   birds.[42]

Lax wrote back that he thought the poem so good he was sending it to the *New Yorker*. There is no record of what the magazine might have done with it.

Lax, Merton, and Rice each kept journals through their lifetimes, Merton and Lax quite faithfully, Rice spasmodically. While Merton put down his journal's significance—"If there is no important change in our lives as we go on there is no point in keeping journals"[43]—he ignored his own advice, and his journal writing eventually became pure habit. In any case, he made voluminous entries up to his death. Lax's entries are not as detailed or as introspective as Merton's but include some of his most refreshing poetry starts. Rice's often seem to have been written during periods of depression. He was having academic difficulty when he made this entry just before failing to get his degree in 1940:

I always feel that I have to apologize every time I write some journal: it seems like a dumb diary when ever I begin it again; do Merton or Lax feel the same way?

. . . A week ago Wednesday I wrote instead of studying for my italian test which was the next day and I got a C, twenty two mistakes one of the lowest marks in a class that never receives any F's. Thursday night I was drunk, I forget how. Friday afternoon, when Knight [Jim] and I went downtown to see Gerdy [Bob] and to get my glasses we had hangovers; we came back, bought a fifth of Milshire, drank all afternoon, shocking I suppose Merton, Rosenstein and de Bary who came around in the afternoon, then went to the movies to see Of Human Bondage where I almost passed out, and had to keep walking back and forth to the can trying to keep from falling over. That night we went to the Lion's Den, after drinking a lot of beer, where I was very drunk still. . . . [44]

The next pages recount Rice's hangovers—including one that persisted during his walk back from Sunday Mass—and more drinking escapades with Gerdy, Knight, and a few others, some fistfights with other Columbia students, and some interludes writing "some very good stuff" for *Jester,* "full of imagination."[45]

Rice, who would in later years establish himself as a gifted writer, was uncertain of his writing capability at the time:

Today I got everything I have written together that I could find and separated it into three piles, first what I either have to get out of the house or burn (these are mostly mine and merton's pictures from last summer), what I can leave around (term papers), and what I want to take to Olean next week with me.

So far today no novel writing; just shitting around college, and sitting in the gold rail with flynn and doc emrich while the class day ceremonies went on.[46]

Missing the class-day ceremonies was a consequence of Rice's failure to get a degree. That must have depressed him, and in the same journal entry he groused, albeit with somewhat peculiar logic, about how "Harry" was mucking up *Jester*, the magazine that he felt was his baby after having worked on it for three years:

> The more I look at Harry's Jester the worse I feel, because here he had ruined the pretty make-up I have perfected, misused the ideas I told him, and abused the privileges of the press in an entirely different way from how I abused them.[47]

In June the trek was made once again to the Olean cottage, this time including—besides Lax, Merton, and Rice—Bob Gibney, Bob Gerdy, Jim Knight, Sy and Helen Freedgood, Peggy Wells, Nancy Flagg, Norma Prince, and maybe others. Rice recalled that "[w]e talked a lot about dreams. Lax talked about dreams involving his mother. I was at war with my own mother [he must have meant 'had been at war' since she had died during his freshman year at Columbia]."[48] Merton's mother had died very early in his life. Years later Lax told an interviewer that the Olean cabin was a compelling sanctuary, a place where the friends could work, and "because we felt we could do something that was going in the opposite direction from the whole commercial world. We'd already had brushes with that world, and we didn't like it."[49]

A major setback to Merton occurred in June when he was told that the Franciscans had rejected his application to enter their order. Apparently, his own revelation of his indiscretion in Cambridge scotched his chance, although the friar who gave him the news had apparently had other misgivings about Merton's suitability for the order. It was a dark time, but in retrospect the rejection would lead him eventually to a much more fulfilling life than he might have had as a Franciscan.

But his time with Rice, Lax, and the others at the cottage was not as carefree as it had been the prior summer. All three worked on their novels, typing together on the kitchen table amid messes of dishes. Merton, remembered Rice, was babbling in his sleep and keeping everyone awake with his raucous laughter. He sometimes went into the woods to say the rosary or read Aquinas's *Summa* or Augustine's *Confessions*. There were expeditions in Rice's junk-heap car to small hotels with bars, or to St. Bonaventure for books. Merton later destroyed his journal covering the period, but the range of subjects mentioned in the June to August entries from Rice's journal illustrate how broad were their introspections—writing blocks, jazz, the French surrender, the

Willkie–Roosevelt election, going to Mass with Merton, yoga exercise with Lax, more on the filthy kitchen, and speculation on U.S. entry into the upcoming war, including an outrageous statement by Rice that it might be best if the Germans were to invade and conquer America.

Certainly the most successful writer of the Olean friends during 1940 was the twenty-five-year-old Lax, who had no less than four poems published in the *New Yorker* in seven months, an achievement that may well still be without precedent at the magazine. His "Greeting to Spring," with references to "darkened Paris" and "parties at strife," was published May 4, 1940, just weeks before the Nazis marched down the Champs Elysées. An excerpt:

> At an outside table, where the sun's bright glare is,
> We will speak of darkened Paris . . .
>
> Over the plans of the parties at strife,
> Over the planes in the waiting north,
> Over the average man and his wife,
> *Lo, the sun walks forth!* [50]

The very next month the editors gave him what might have been unprecedented space for a long poem—it ran in two columns across a full page. The title was "A Radio Masque for My Girl Coming Down from Northampton," which looked forward to Nancy Flagg's visit from Smith College. Two stanzas:

> Other days are gray,
> Today will be bright;
> Other days are dull,
> Today will be pretty;
> Other days are Monday, Tuesday,
> Wednesday, Friday, Saturday, and Sunday,
> But today, today will be Thursday.
>
> Other days are wet,
> Today will be dry;
> Other days are cold,
> Today will be warm;
> Other days say, "Wake up, stupid,"
> Today will say, "Good morning, Arthur."
> Other days are Monday, Tuesday,
> Wednesday, Friday, Saturday, and Sunday,
> But today my girl comes, today will be Thursday. [51]

He told Merton about Flagg's impending visit in one of his Joycean takeoffs:

Oh Maistyer Meetin,
How lung have I help beneeps the hegelstroms of imargination the ungunned feuerbachs of deliht? My girl dancy flutes is in tune from north chaplin and tomorrow I will see her wile the clock bings in the novcent horissimus of the sun's dumb golden eagis. what breaknecks will be eke in wop flourecent palaz, beaneggs wat fakely glowering water wool we nod wizder conuming the uncoprehestive exactimentos most lightly give my the clown of dimones at sniffs gobbage.[52]

Merton was even more into Joycean language. In his journal he tells of having written three pages of it in a letter to Lax:

And I liked writing it, too. That's the way I want to write. And it can't be sold. Just because it can't be sold doesn't mean it can't be read. I could mimeograph it and send it around. I have a clean stencil, right here in my room. And I don't mean send it around to just anybody: only to people I know. Jinny, Lilly, Lax, Gibney, Rice, Knight, Van Doren, Dan Walsh, even (those mad) professors in the Graduate School of English at Columbia. That's what I want to do. Write like poor Joyce. I pray he comes to heaven.[53]

Only three weeks after "Radio Masque" was published Lax got space in the magazine for a deft satire on New York's neighboring state across the river, called "Poem of Gratuitous Invective Against New Jersey." One stanza:

Graysuited Hudson like an endless freight
Rolls past the Drive, its motion separates
Manhattan gneiss from traprock Palisades
And us from Jersey. Here, moored and motionless,
The fuelling barge awaits a signal.
There minutemen stamp for the hour of action.
Here the machine awaits the word of man.
There the machineman motivates himself.

Roll on, Hudson, keep us still from Jersey.[54]

At the end of the summer of 1940, Merton wrote Lax from Urbanna, Virginia, where he had been again visiting Jinny Burton, in a state of depression. He didn't know what to do. Having been told that the Franciscans didn't want him, he was afraid that he might get drafted. "No monastery. Maybe look for a job," he wrote.[55]

He wondered about becoming a member of the Franciscan Third Order, but didn't follow through, went to an oppressively hot New York, and saw his brother, John Paul, who had not been accepted as a Naval Reserve officer, then went back to Olean, where he got a job as a $45-a-week English instructor beginning in the fall. He taught three classes in English literature and started a new novel, *The Man in the Sycamore Tree*, a title that Ed Rice would resurrect in his biography of Merton (1970).

It was on October 17, 1940 that he began writing a new journal longhand in a spiral notebook. Mott writes that he did not begin to type his journals until *The Cuban Journal*, published as *The Secular Journal* and continued as what became *Conjectures of a Guilty Bystander*. It was in this period, says Mott, that he "gave in to a sexual passion and committed adultery with an unnamed woman."[56]

With the war in Europe now going full blast, he was given a chance to broadcast a peace plea on the local radio station, WHLD, where Lax had worked earlier. He told Lax about the experience:

Deleriously happy to hear you have been deployed as poetastical consul to the Nose Talker's weekly [*New Yorker*]. . . . This morning with my dapple coats and pied hats and flowered gloves, towed by a copula dolphins by sneed to the Ray-de-do Smation, where I confused myself by prizing open the raves of the zither with a bench, in odder to shove diaments, sapwires and other forms of candyglass in between the interstates of the wind to be freely distreputed about all over the nations soundboxes, for all, indiscriminate, to catch by their big folding ears. In fine, over Question WHDL I mouthed a short speaks, untuttled: "Ploctions of the Privad made Published, or my Driary dictated to Plebs, or a Leapf trun the Me-mores of Herr Senor and rad over the ear."[57]

The congratulations about being hired by the *New Yorker*, it develops, were premature since Lax wouldn't land the job until early 1941.

* * * * * * * * * * * * *

3

The War, the Monk, the Manhattanites

Merton to Gethsemani; Lax to the New Yorker; Rice a Godfather Again

It is curious to reflect, after more than sixty years have passed, on the contrast between the impact that the onset of World War II had on most Catholics of draft age and on Lax and Merton. Most of us who were eligible in those days marched lock-step into the ranks of the military, and our patriotism soared as we enlisted. Rice was ready to join, but not Lax and Merton, whose detestation of war was palpable. In early 1941 all three friends were faced with being drafted. Although none were, the possibility hovered over them through the year. Eventually, both Lax and Merton would be classified as conscientious objectors. Rice, with bad eyes that would plague him all his life, would be classified 4F, although he would have been willing to fight. "I expected to be drafted," he said, "and was going to volunteer to join the Marine paratroopers. I was a crazy mixed up kid. Everyone in those days expected to be drafted and killed. I was not drafted because I was classified as legally blind. I had a mal-formed iris, what they called a 'cat's eye.' Kids made fun of me. I couldn't focus one eye. When I took pictures I focused with the left eye."[1]

Neither Lax nor Merton had disqualifying physical ailments—although both were borderline hypochondriacs through their lifetimes—but it was their pacifist convictions that held sway. In March, Merton wrote Lax that

> I put in my 10 cents worth of conscientious objection, that is all the ten cents' worth I could squeeze out of being a Catholic: namely that I would refuse combatant service but not non-combatant service like medical corps, etc. I give as much argument as was in me to give why I don't want to be killing people, and as

far as I'm concerned that is all I worry about: if get in the medical corps I make no more complaints, nor seem to swear as much as I do now. . . . [2]

Merton looked back on that period in *SSM,* writing that "If I had objected to war before, it was more on the basis of emotion than anything else," but now "God was asking me, by the light and grace He had given me, to signify where I stood in relation to the actions of governments and armies and states in this world overcome with the throes of its own blind wickedness." Strong stuff. His decision was to make "an application to be considered as a non-combatant objector: that is, one who would willingly enter the army, and serve in the medical corps, or as a stretcher bearer, or a hospital orderly or any other thing like that, so long as I did not have to drop bombs on open cities, or shoot at other men."[3]

Lax, before getting conscientious objector status,[4] had to undergo the same humbling experience that befell many another young American in those months. He addressed Merton with one of the myriad names that the two would coin for each other over the years, and used a racial epithet that was, unfortunately, common for the times:

Oh, Myrtle. . . . Among the draft they did force me naked in a room with a thousand jigs in a similar condition and direct me harshly to piss in a Dixie cup which I could not. They did fumst me and pummel me and direct me to an impractical truck. They did transfix me with needles, startle me with bright lights, pound my kneecaps, and sound with unsharpened pencils my ears.[5]

Lax's horror of war and killing was certainly equal to Merton's. In fact, he had a respect for life that included all beings—even insects. A visitor to his home in Patmos recalls that she was not allowed to dispose of a spider on the window sill but told to put a glass jar over the insect, slip a card underneath, and release it outside.

When asked for his rationale in becoming a conscientious objector, he showed a text he had actually written out in 1941:

My objection is to taking human life. My desire is to help preserve lives that are endangered. . . . My belief is that a single God, good and loving, rules the universe. I believe that His authority extends to every event, large and small. I believe that in this scheme man is particularly blessed with a conscience to advise and a will to choose between good and evil action. The religious writings in

harmony with this belief and which seem to me of great importance are The Ten Commandments, the 23rd Psalm and the Lord's
Prayer. These express for me the goodness of the Lord and the
proper faith and right behavior of man.[6]

His Columbia archive has a poem, undated, but someone has written
on it that it was composed "just after Pearl Harbor":

> I believe that all the people should stop their fight
> I believe that one should blow
> A whistle or sing
> Or play on the lute or say very quietly into a microphone
>   that whatever they think they are doing it is wrong.
> The same world as we knew when we loved the people is
>   still here.

Lax's main preoccupation, once he was relieved of the obligation to
serve in the military, was his own writing, which was giving him frustra-
tions, as revealed in an entry from his journal in early 1941:

> I would like to be known as the author of fables but i don't seem
> to like writing them. I don't seem to like writing anything except
> the stuff that flows without any feeling in the head, of thought.
> Still when I have written a fable i like rereading it, I get a (kick)
> out of it. . . . [7]

It turns out that it was one of his fables that got him his job at the
New Yorker. In February 1940, E. B. White, one of the stars of the
magazine's staff, wrote Lax from his home in Brooklin, Maine:

> I didn't like the looks of your book [which Lax must have sent
> him] (I get an awful lot of junk sent me by terrible people) so I let
> it get bogged down under a lot of stuff; but today I pulled it out as
> a last desperate stand against doing any work myself, and I got a
> lot of pleasure out of it. So did my wife [Katharine White, also on
> the *New Yorker* staff], which is more to the point as she is never
> mistaken about anything, whereas I can sometimes be taken. In
> short, why don't you let us submit this to the New Yorker and see
> if they don't want it? . . . I am willing to share it with the western
> world if you have any desire for publication and I have never seen
> a graduate of Columbia, 24, who didn't, nor do I want to, par-
> ticularly.

The "book" was a fable, "The Man with the Big General Notions." The first two and the last stanzas:

THERE was a man who said, "Why eat cake when all you want is bread? Why eat frosting when all you want is cake? Why eat cake and frosting when all you want is bread and candy?"
The man was accounted very wise, and he thought it was a true account.
When he went to build a house he said, "Why get brick when all you want is HARDNESS?"

> So he got a big rough stone
> And on top of the stone he put a bone
> And on top of the bone he put a box
> And on top of the box he put a bar
> And on top of the bar he put a beam
> And the pile stood five feet high
> And tottered And then it fell to the ground.

And the man said, "Why should I buy a bed when all that I want is SLEEP?"

> So he went to sleep
> And the dog went mad
> And bit the cat
> And the cat ate the fish
> And the fish ate the snail
> And the tree caught fire
> And the molasses ran
> And the snow melted
> And the hat fell down
> And the cover fell in the forest pool
> And so did the shell
> And so did the gum
> And so did the tape
> So did the bar
> So did the beam
> So did the box
> So did the bone
> So did the glue
> So did the stone.
> Some man.
> Some house.[8]

The fable was published eventually, in the October 18, 1942 issue of the *New Yorker*, but before it came out White arranged for Lax to be interviewed for a job at the magazine. However, it would take some time for the bureaucracy to operate. In the meantime Lax wrote Merton that

one sits in ones room and waits for 11:30 when he will call for the 300th time the pharoah of cecil b de mille's ten commandments, mr lobrano . . . aw whats the matter, no job?

and this man will say, almost a job, mr apes, almost an excellent job in our fine fairy pavillion at 15¢ a week, but i must ask a certain mr ulano who is in sun valley now and will not be back until he has visited mexico, armonk, and miami.[9]

Earlier that day he had been even more morose in his own journal:

Before 11:30 I answered a letter of mertons which come that very morning. When I was a line from finishing it, I called lobranol. he said I'd have to come down tomorrow (today) and see mr shuman about a job which it looks as though it will be open. "it is what we call a bread and butter job." having to see one more guy, about a job that was still indefinite and could be described as bread and butter. i finished mertons letter, looked at my quickly saddening face in the mirror, turned out the light and lay on the bed, feeling sorry, not for myself, see, because i knew somewhere right below the surface that it was all going to be all right, that nothing they could do to me would do me any real harm, but that such a brave plucky little fellow, apparently so alone in the city, should be so carelessly treated.[10]

When he was hired he was given the title of Assistant Poetry Editor and assigned to "winnow through the submissions, answer letters to the editor and, if anyone came to the office who wanted to shoot the editor, they sent me out."[11] It became a dreary existence, but he got to observe some the magazine's legendary characters, like James Thurber and Janet Flanner.

the job maybe it ain't stupid but right now i spend all the time being dazed and worried. the being dazed is still the stupor i had in olean which hasn't let up for a second. . . . . I don't know what I'm scared of, maybe the boscool coffee people. it's not as though everybody was a prince: lobrano i like fine, more each time i talk to him . . . i met thurber who is tall, like 6/4, and almost blind not being able to find the knob on a door . . . most spectacular of the assbeaten refugees is janet flanner the paris letter dame 75 years old, yesterday she was talking about some poor philadelphia girl she knew, and kept saying "this . . . this kid" like she was translating from gamine. . . .[12]

He was assigned an office next to another legend, the humorist S. J. Perelman, much to the latter's annoyance. Perelman had just returned from an unhappy stint in Hollywood.

He told me that even the trees out there would die if they weren't propped up. They would leave him things he should write parodies about and he didn't feel like writing them and he was sort of down . . . and what was worse about it was that I was in the next office typing away . . . this young guy writing away. But here I was going through mental anguish myself . . . can I push this one more day? I was writing my journal and these long sort of suicide notes page after page—once I typed out "I hate it here"—and this was the time I was going through things like what sort of church I should belong to and everything else and how do I feel about being in New York.[13]

Lax sent Merton still another letter of rhapsodic disillusionment with his job:

. . . my subconscious life, long considered the wellspring of poetry and my chief entertainment in months of despair has become, dear tomols, almost as tedious as my waking day, aye more, for in the day i have such diversions as the chocolates moulted, riding the alabastors, or crouching 43 street against the likes; now in the nights i lie still in bed to the accompaniment of the most realistic dreams . . . altogether i was glad to hear the merry clap clap of mrs gibney outside the door, the yell of the bluejay. . . .
. . . mr white come to the office this week and we play a lot of dodgem in the dumb halls, twice in the past two seconds he has gone past the door him about to say hi, me to replay ow; i'm sure we'd have a swell time if we was to sit down and talk, him being so worried and myself the same, but the natural bashfulness of us both as well as a certain Hottentot decorum he observes will keep that from happening one is sure.[14]

Still somewhat in a funk he wrote Merton again, but this time with a bit of brightness shining through:

worry a little, get happy a little, get unhappy a little. such full days.

maybe i'd do more if i didn't keep asking myself what i was. tonight i sang the ballad of perse o reilly from finnegans wake, a good ballad.

tonight i walked in times square, the lights and buildings seeming visible with a new clarity and exciting to see like a new place in the 5 o'clock brightly glowing, darkening blue sky with bright stars in it. tonight the stars are bright too, and this morning like i said, the sun was bright, the sky and air clear.[15]

But the cheeriness did not last. Here is what he had to write about the state of his personal health:

hangover: feel like rusty wire stretched tight.
headache: rusty wire stretched tight between the ears.
   who is skinny: I am
   whose hair feels unhealthy: mine
   whose muscles of the upper leg are tight and tired: mine
who is against doing anything that seems an effort: I
who nevertheless does plenty such things, often the most foolish? I.
who looks like a busted balalaika: me
   who nevertheless is happy with this small dark, adequate, having electric light, heat and not much noise, room: I am.
   who heard yesterday lying on his bed talk in the court that might have been in a court in venice, marseilles, cairo, all the cities of the world: me.
   who say colored children climbing the steps of mount morris park like the shadowless angels climbing the steps of heaven:
   Who seen the city, who seen the pigeons appear and disappear?:
   Who seen one day at Mt Morris park a colored boy climb inside the grating and leaning way over very carefully, looking out at the playground below, hit the bell: bong, with a stick, and then very stealthily, as from a coconut tree, climb down again, stand on the flag stones, look around and leave the place: me i seen him.[16]

His essential downbeat feeling about the job was in contrast to his father Sigmund's pride that he was working there. Merton, then at St. Bonaventure, recalled meeting him in the lobby of Olean House hotel in Olean, "beaming like a golden statue" over the news of his son's position. Maybe, Merton speculated, "if in the future all the editors were to listen to him, the New Yorker would get good again."[17]

But Lax would have had to be transformed if he were to make an important contribution to the New Yorker. He was very much in a funk, and his bosses could not have been very happy with him. Jottings from his journal:

right this minut i don't want to teach school or work in a factory or go to friendship house or join a monastery, or do anything but swim and i have an infection on my leg.

flies hang all around, on the leg on the table on the paper, at night its mosquitoes, there is no sleep . . . i am hungry, there is a green fly bouncing around my leg there is a black fly sitting on the typewriter, i have a headache, my shorts are tight, the bird swings up and sits on a tree, there is nothing he can do there but hop from branch to branch, what i need is wings and an obligation to fly. the butterfly bargains among the tired grass.

i am sleepy, i am hungry, i guess i want to get into trouble.

look, if i'm going to lose my job in two weeks because i don't write good letters and haven't contributed much comment and don't show any interest in advancement, i think you make a mistake. you hired me because you liked my stuff. you think i can write and i think i can do something. even if i can't write comments maybe i can write poems, and while i don't need your assurance that i won't starve it would make me happy to have it. if you would say the job is for 6 months or even 4 months ok. But if I'm just here until the business manager gets mad at me, I'd rather be selling tickets at a translux [a movie house].[18]

Lax, in these days, became very serious about Judaism.

I really tried for a while to be an Orthodox Jew, which no one in the family was. In high school I had read the Old Testament but my mother, who was a Reformed Jew, tried to tell me not to read it—just love God and neighbor. Leviticus did scare me but I felt that at some point this middle way business wasn't right. If you're going to be Jewish, really be Jewish. That was great news for me but it was hard on my family. "Do we have to feed him kosher food when he comes home?" my sister Gladys said. . . . It probably was wrenching for the New Yorker to have somebody growing a rabbi's beard in those days. The Old Testament says you should have one, and you shouldn't use a razor. I went to a Conservative rabbi to ask about the beard and about where I could live and eat kosher and he said, 'it doesn't say you can't use an electric razor, just a clipper" and he sent me to a landlady and the first thing she offered me was Spam.[19]

Continuing on his spiritual search was Merton, who revealed to Ed Rice a craving for asceticism, an unhappiness with his writing, and a disposition to blame some Catholics for wars because they are "nothing but wiseguys and gyps and crooks." He mentioned also that Rice might want to teach art at the college:

Holloy Rous.

. . . this summer i think maybe to give a course in the divine dante, and they all think that is a good idea here, so i read the divine dante all day and all night. Also some finnegans wake. also maybe the best english poet living, if he is still living, is a welsh guy called dylan thomas, some poet. no fake like this auden, eliot, etc etc, but a real true poet, plenty good. him i read a lot too. . . .

. . . i gave up movies in disgust, and either i will sit on my hands and wait for summer and the circus or else give up everything merely for a penance, but i wont go to the movies for a long time anyway because it will be lent in two seconds, time to shut up shop. Not that they shut up shop around here, by any means, but stuff themselves with bigger and better vegetarian delicacies or else sling dispensations around like snowflakes, but I got an idea the church is too easy in this country and everywhere else and it is because, not the Church, but Catholics everyplace are nothing but wiseguys and gyps and crooks that there are so many wars, consequently we should all do penance, four guys for everybody. Except it turns out that there are a hundred million of them doing penance already too that we don't know anything about. i also think of making a retreat in Holy Week at the Trappist monastery in Kentucky.

what I did is become a Franciscan Tertiary. this is a very good thing to have become, for a guy who cant be a priest. it has a sort of a rule: that a guy should pray and do penance and no longer be dirty or mad or a wiseguy, but love peace and be poor and all day and all night love God. This rule was made by St Francis and Dante was a tertiary and a whole lot of Saints were too. It is not a club like the children of Mary, it is a religious order.

In the five days following my reception as a Tertiary i writ five poems and the meaning of this is obvious; even though all five were not very good, three are certainly all right for me, good as anything i ever wrote before, anyway. . . .

i think all the publishers hate my novels very much, the second worse than the first, but i don't care because i still think the second is better than the first, and anyway it is very nice here and sunny and i sit in my room and write and write all day and all night, very busy, never talk to anybody much and when i dont write, read the divine Dante or teach a class for ten minutes or say prayers. First in importance is saying prayers, second in importance is writing poems and books, third in importance is reading the divine Dante, fourth in importance is talking to people, fifth in importance is the publication of novels or poems and nowhere at all in this scheme comes movies or visits to Olean or even cokes, thats how nice it is here. maybe you cld be art teacher.[20]

On February 19, Merton had become a member of the Franciscan Third Order and began to wear a scapular under his shirt. Rice, though born a Catholic, always disclaimed any responsibility for his friend's conversion to Catholicism. He must have raised his eyebrows, though, over Merton's new passion for the church about which he, himself, was only lukewarm. Religion did not, in any case, have a high priority in his life. His professional ambitions were jumping around circa 1941.

Merton wrote in his journal that "I hope Rice sells the new children's book about night clubs he just wrote."[21] There's no record of what happened to that project.

Rice's first salaried job after Columbia had been as a $15-a-week "mat boy" for a midtown advertising agency. He left after a few months to work for Dell Publishing, becoming managing editor of *Film Fun*. He wrote captions for photos and organized "one-shot" issues like a biography of General MacArthur for newsstand sales. The pay was $25 a week, not bad for the times, and the work gave him good training in production and layout.

He later went to work for the Children's Aid Society, writing fundraising letters, then became editor of *Time In*, a radio magazine. In 1944 he would get real editorial jobs, first at *Look* magazine's foreign edition, then, in the same year, at *Collier's*, where he did a book called *Movie Lot to Beachhead*, for which he got no by-line. He freelanced a *History of War*, with pictures, for Dell, for $100, then went to work for *Parade* magazine. On the side he was also writing—and painting—seriously. Lax wrote Merton that Rice "has almost finished a novel and did about 12 oil paintings, two of which I seen and these are good."[22]

Merton visited Lax at the *New Yorker* in March, and found poetic inspiration in one of the offices, only weeks after he had had a poem rejected by that magazine.

sitting quiet in the room full of desks, where Lax works with Mrs Sayre and some fuzzy-headed dame who keeps calling up and

asking what's on at the movies—in that room around noon time
I started a good poem—good enough. Mark Van Doren read it in
the subway, and liked it.[23]   .

In the same month Merton was given a 4E status in the draft. "i will
not appeal," he wrote, "there is only one more remote class: 4F, lunatics
. . . i think my chaff bor must have been confused and perplexed by the
close-print pages of argument i gave them why I didn't want to kill the
leaping Italian, the mathematical hun."[24]

A few weeks later, he made the retreat to the Abbey of Gethsemani
referred to above in his letter to Rice and it was mind-blowing:

> This is the center of America. I had wondered what was holding
> this country together, what has been keeping the universe from
> cracking in pieces and falling apart. It is this monastery if only this
> one. (There must be two or three others.)[25]

But, the draft was still hovering. "My draft board is full of lies, it
turned out. I am really 1B, after all, and not a convict, off to hoe the
trees."[26] His zealous Catholicism did not mean that he was uncritical
of his fellow worshippers, as in his counsel to "Joe," possibly Joe Rush,
a Catholic Worker friend:

> Everybody wants to be happy: most people are miserable as
> hell. . . . Do not let yourself be confused by the Catholics who act
> as if Christ promised them money, Buicks, success, jewelry, if they
> went to Church on Sundays and said the right kind of things at
> the Rotary club and read Social Justice. I tremble to think of what
> those guys have got in store for them, if only for the scandal they
> cause.[27]

Lax does not recall just how long he lasted at the *New Yorker* but it
was probably not much more than a year—at least until Labor Day 1941.
But even fifty years later he had vivid memories, of "Harold Ross going
up and down the halls . . . Thurber and Joel Sayre barking to each other
out the windows on a summer day, and William Shawn, although a tough
manager, being so shy that he had to be the last one out of the elevator . . .
but I had to be the last one out, too, it's a wonder we ever emerged . . .
'after you, after you,' neither of us could do anything about it."[28]

One major yield of the period, however, was the beginning of what
would become perhaps Lax's greatest and certainly his best-known

work, *The Circus of the Sun*. It was not published until 1959, but it was a *New Yorker* assignment in 1941 that led to its creation.

> I was shambling down some downtown street. I had left the New Yorker by then and I ran into Leonard Robinson, who was still there. He said he was on his way uptown to Riverside Drive where there was a circus family that they wanted him to interview for Talk of the Town and did I want to come along. I said yes. So we got to this apartment—the door was opened by this midget lady, she curtsied and let us in and introduced us to the members of the family . . . the father came out and shook hands with me and it was like meeting a long lost uncle. Then the kids came out—Mogador, then about 17, younger brother Pete, about 15, and sister Hortense. Mogador was the family spokesman. I guess I had never seen people like that in my life—it meant that much to me. Everyone who knew me said I didn't talk about anything else. Robinson wrote a nice article but they took umbrage at something—maybe an adjective describing Hortense.[29]

After leaving the *New Yorker* Lax worked for a while with the homeless in Harlem at Friendship House. It was run by Catherine de Hueck, who actually was a Russian baroness. The de Hueck part of her name came from a Belgian nobleman she had married. Merton had seriously considered working with her, as an alternative to joining a monastery, when she came to St. Bonaventure to lecture, and he spent some time at the House in the summer of 1941. He persuaded Lax to join the dozen or so people on the staff. Not known for adeptness at any kind of manual work, Lax

> mostly sat around, was in charge of the library, talked and talked to visitors and all kinds of poor black people, as well as one famous black poet. One day I was asked to mop the floor. I must have looked hopeless, maybe not even knowing which end of the mop to use, when a stranger came along and took the mop from me and did the job. . . . [30]

The baroness recalled the incident. Lax had been sent across the street with the mop to the House's storefront. After two hours she went over to find out what was going on. There was Lax standing in water, the dry mop in his hand, scribbling a poem about mops and floors. During this period Lax lived in a room about ten blocks away from Friendship House in a downtrodden neighborhood. It must have been at 207 West 144 St. from which he wrote a letter in 1941 to his sister Gladys. It says something about his lack of security there when he tells her that

> 35 W 135 St [where apparently Rice and some other Columbia friends were living] is best for mail. . . . The room is fine—large—with two windows and a good bed—hot and cold water which is unusual up here. The woman I stay with gives me breakfast—fruit, hot cereal, toast and coffee—I have the other two meals with that gang at 135th street. I'm still working in the library, handing out clothes and taking things to the post office. We've been having parties and fancy dinners every day for a week. The kids we work with are very good, gentle and smart . . . one of the staff workers told them I was a great dancer so I get along fine with them.

Not all of his memories of the place are as rosy. He recalled that "The walk home could be something to think about. Once a drunk came out of a bar, looked at me and said, 'Why you . . .' and went to hit me, but he didn't. Another time I had to bound to the door of my house to get away from a very aggressive guy."[31]

Lax was still trying hard to be a good Jew.

> We got little food, whatever came along. But if it was Spam I couldn't eat it. And they worked on Saturdays so I would spend those days at the Jewish Theological Seminary. I was really running around on both sides of the question. I tried to become Orthodox but the more I read of the Old Testament the more I felt I was seeing the New Testament prophesied in it—through prophets like Isaiah.[32]

He was probably at Friendship House for less than a year, keeping in touch with Rice at *Parade* magazine, and by correspondence with Merton at St. Bonaventure. Collaborating with his friend Alex Eliot, who had been a colleague at *Time*, he made a film, "photographed over the transome of Friendship House and onto the street. I think we still have got the film."[33]

In September Merton wrote Lax, Rice, and other buddies from Columbia days a tightly typed letter proclaiming his own boredom and his concern about the impending war. His young brother John Paul, who had visited him in Olean in May, was a bomber pilot with the Royal Canadian Air Force. Excerpts:

Chr Messieurs Chums:

Bonabon hola! Humble bonjours! Bonabon soir, we grumble, in the jours of the midi and the soirs of the apres-midi. . . . Time crumbles apace! Autumn cedes to the reaches of September and settles grossly into the incipient laps of October! . . . The ceilings shake with the ferocious laughter of the monks. The vacuum cleaners of the ten thousand sleeping students roar in the halls alleys and passageways and drown the timid radios of afternoon. . . .

. . . Only a few minutes ago I ran with a shout to the immense files of correspondence concerning my three unsold novels and read them until I fell over in a sorry daze, I must say. I have absolutely no mottoes one way or the other to express either lively indifference or affectionate scorn for the publishing business which I cannot comprehend as it is too vast, too universal, too titanic, too rich, too glorious, too subtle, too fine and too astounding for my sheepish thought.

. . . when will he tell us the *news*? When will he end our suspends, and scatter with shouts the newsier, chattier fragments of importantest Olean gossips? Whom lives Raoul? Which stints in the frilled curtains of the Olean house with fashionable what? . . .

. . . Well, that is enough of that, all the rest I know about is war stocks, preferred preferentials, and the news from my brother who will probably be a captain in the Canadian Air Forts within a week. . . .[34]

He was still considering Harlem at the time. In fact, he told the baroness in October that he would join her in January. But his spiritual calling was coming on strong. At lunch in New York, on the day after Thanksgiving, Mark Van Doren asked him, "What about your idea of being a priest?" He replied, "I think God's Providence arranged things so that you would tell me that today," and as he parted with his Columbia mentor he said, "If I ever entered any monastery, it would be to become a Trappist." He and Lax, two days later, made a retreat at the Convent of the Holy Child on Riverside Drive. Father Paul Hanley Furfey of Catholic University conducted it, and it affected both men deeply. Lax, in fact, had to leave the chapel to get air because "he began to get the feeling that the place was going to fall down on top of him."[35]

Merton went back to Olean where he got another notice from the draft board, ". . . now I am to appear for re-examination," he wrote in his journal. "They have changed the rule about teeth. If I pass this time, it means I might be in the army by January—in 1-A." But his opposition to serving in the war was resolute, "I have no interest in human wars. Wherever I am, I am a citizen of the Kingdom of God and fight only as a soldier of Christ—killing nobody."[36]

He sought counsel on his decision to join the monastery from a Franciscan priest at St. Bonaventure, Father Philotheus (Werner Boehner), who was for years later an important influence on both him and Lax. Philotheus told him there was no reason why he couldn't go into a monastery and be a priest, but asked, "Are you sure you want to be a *Trappist?*" His response, "I want to give God everything," satisfied the friar.[37]

He sent his clothes to the baroness, left those books he would not take to Gethsemani for the St. Bonaventure library, threw "three finished novels and one half-finished novel . . . in the incinerator," and sent to Van Doren all of his poems, his copy of *Journal of My Escape from the Nazis*, another journal, and an anthology of religious verse. "Everything else I had written I put in a binder and sent to Lax and Rice who were living on 114th Street, New York."[38]

On December 6, 1941, the day before the Japanese attack on Pearl Harbor, he wrote Lax, "Finally has come the time to go to the Trappists and try to get in. I cannot explain this except to say it in a lot of different ways: time to get out of the subway and go away to the clean woods; or time to get out of the party full of smoke and pray in a clean bedroom, like before sleeping and resting the way it is sweet. It is time to stop arguing with the seven guys who argue inside my own head, and be completely quiet in front of the face of Peace. . . ."[39]

That peace would be experienced, with intermittent spells of emotional crises, for the next twenty-seven years. Merton entered the Abbey of Gethsemani on December 10 and on his first evening wrote out a poem that he had composed "by way of a farewell to Bob Lax and Mark Van Doren."[40]

Not everyone thought that Merton's entry into the Trappists was a good thing. Gladys "Gladio" Marcus, Lax's sister, recalled in an interview years later, "I was upset when Tom joined the monastery. I felt that from my point of view he was really losing himself, a desperation move. However, I was wrong, not knowing anything about Catholicism. It wasn't desperation. He wanted to serve humanity by serving God . . . he has had a real influence on thousands, millions. It's awesome to think that someone of his stature was just . . . here."[41]

Lax must have envied Merton's decisiveness in making his commitment to the monastery. Although Mark Van Doren had written Merton that Lax seemed "happier at Friendship House than I have ever seen him," Lax did not stay there long. He soon took the next turn in what was becoming a very uncertain career path.

I had a habit—if someone comes along in a car and says he's going somewhere, I hop in. Bob Mack, Benji's nephew, came along and said he was going to North Carolina. I hopped in. The head of the English department was nuts about *New Yorker* and when he heard I had worked there he hired me. I taught freshman English but did my best to turn it into creative writing. I also took courses in the English department and the Philosophy department. I stayed for one academic year and then some more, got a fellowship in the Philosophy department and worked for about a year towards a PhD. The students liked me. Those people who didn't were the ones who didn't think I should be bringing jazz records—like Billie Holiday—to writing class. Why did I introduce jazz? If you are going to write poetry you better have some rhythm. The students were good—I would get them to write their dreams . . . mythical or psychological dreams . . . wonderful stuff.

Some of the administrators didn't like me giving everyone A's. I got a letter saying the marks were seriously out of line. Either correct, conform to the graphs or don't come back. I didn't come back. Well I had thought they all deserved A's because all of them were doing their very best! What more do you want of a person? One girl I really . . . even with that philosophy I couldn't give her an A. I gave her you know some sort of passing grade, and she was just reduced to tears of joy. She never . . . she had a dream in which I had been fired and she woke up crying.

While I was at North Carolina I wrote some parodies, like *Autumn in the Marathon* for the *Carolina* Magazine, about a Greek restaurant named *Marathon*.[42]

Lax's fellowship at Chapel Hill could have been renewed each year for seven years but he had had enough of academia, and he would leave before getting his Ph.D., which would have been on St. Thomas Aquinas. His study of the great medieval philosopher-theologian deeply affected him, however, and very likely influenced his eventual decision to become a Catholic.

Merton wrote Lax a very long letter on November 21, 1942, almost a year after his entry into monasticism. The first surviving letter to his old friend from Gethsemani, it is a classic of spiritual contentedness.

It is very good and sweet to be always occupied with God only, and sit simply in his presence and shut up, and be healed by the mere fact that God likes to be in your soul, because you like Him to be there. And in doing this you also love your neighbor as much as you could by any action of your own: because God cannot be in your soul without that having an effect on other people, and not necessarily people who have ever heard of you.

. . . a lot of my brothers are really saints, and it makes you happy simply to see them walking around full of God.[43]

That's a letter to the same friend who, only a few years earlier, had participated with Merton in the girl chasing, hard drinking, and general dissipation of the Columbia and Olean days. The same letter invited Lax to come to Gethsemani, offering to pay his way, and gave news of his brother, soon to be lost in the war:

The Abbot says, if you want to you may come here for two weeks & sit & do as you like & pray & think, and as for the money getting here and back, if you write & tell me you are coming, right away I will send you money, enough for coming & going.

. . . My brother [John Paul] was here, & baptized, very happy, in July. Now he is in England, with the Canadian Air Force, & writes good letters.[44]

It says something about how profoundly Lax was struck by the letter that he addressed Merton, in his response, as "F Louis," the only time he would ever use that appellation. "Yr letter I showed to Gibney, Gil, Roger, Leila, Lennie," he wrote. "This week to Rice, Gladio, Mark Van Doren. All said what a beautiful—" The sentence was not completed.[45]

About a year later, on December 18, 1943, Lax appeared at St. Ignatius of Loyola Church on Park Avenue in New York. Rice—who was to be his godfather and who had also been Merton's godfather—said to him, "Take off your hat, Lax, you're not in the schul." Father O'Pray, the Jesuit who would baptize him, wondered if he knew enough about Catholicism to take the sacrament. "I told him what I had been reading in North Carolina. . . . St. Thomas, St. Augustine, St. John of the Cross, and he said, "You don't have to study the catechism, you're ready to go. Bag him boys."[46]

Soni Holman, Lax's New York cousin, said that Bob's decision to become a Catholic was respected immediately by his Jewish family, although she points out that the baptism occurred shortly after the death of his beloved mother. "I once asked him, though, why he had become a Catholic and he said, 'Because I believe the Messiah has come.'"[47] When the friars at St. Bonaventure, to whom Lax's father, Sigmund, sold suits, asked him, "What do you think of Bob becoming a Catholic, he said, 'If my boy Bob did it it must be all right.'"[48]

Asked if it was "wrenching" for him, as a Jew, to become a Catholic, he answered a questioner, with a chuckle, "Well, I took my time about wrenching. Going through all that and becoming a Catholic had a long history for me, but I wouldn't have missed it for anything . . . at the time my picture of Merton in the monastery, although it was erroneous—him in a little hut just being a monk all by himself—was always in front of my eyes when I was in North Carolina. That did mean a lot to me and did direct a lot of my activities, and I'm sure that it directed my studies, too, the idea that I would study Saint Thomas Aquinas or do lots of things or come into the Church."[49]

On Christmas eve in 1943, Lax made a visit to his monk friend, experiencing the kind of travail that seemed often to befall him when he traveled. He wrote Ed Rice an eight-page handwritten letter recounting the experience. He first took a train from Indianapolis—it's not clear how he got there from New York—to Louisville, where he stood, with Laxian patience, in a long information line while his connecting train to Bardstown, Kentucky, pulled out.

So then I had to stand at the outskirts of Louisville in an attempt to thumb to Bardstown, about 39 miles away. it is 9 o'clock Christmas Eve, very cold, many cars go past without stopping. Finally one stops. . . . I get in the car [with] a 16-year old stable-attendant and a middle-aged horseback rider, both very drunk. . . . They offer me a drink of something abominable; I tell them no & then the car begins to weave over the roads, very loopy driving, going off on both sides, shining a ten-thousand watt spot light into the eyes of all comers, & coming closer to a head-on crash than I've ever been in my life. This for 40 miles. The driver, a sentimental fellow but quick-tempered, is named Harry. The stable-boy is named Blondie. Blondie keeps dropping off to sleep. Harry keeps waking him up & asking for another drink out of the Three Feathers bottle; he also keeps lighting cigarettes, dropping them in his lap, standing up whilst he drives and looking for them on the seat. [Next sentence illegible but it must have explained how he managed to get out of the car.]

Then through the kindness of a parish priest & a devout drugstore proprietor in Bardstown I get a ride with one Freddie Pigg who is driving to the monk house for midnight Mass. He has to drop his girl off at her house first & they talk to each other about somebody who doesn't fit in at Bardstown at all, goes against all native customs, is certain to run into trouble. When the girl gets out F. Pigg explains that the obnoxious character comes from New

York & that that explains a lot. Later by an obscure method he finds out that I come from New York, he says it isn't coming from N.Y. that makes the guy an outcast, its that he's a Jew. So then I explain meekly that some of my best friends and all of my relatives are Jews; so he says, "Oh well this one's an Orthodox Jew." After that we don't say anything till we get to the monk-house.

. . . Inside the monastery, once you get past the anti-necking pamphlets in the Gate House; all was beauty.

First I thought I seen Merton standing near the altar, head shaved & looking healthy. Then I wasn't sure it was him [illegible] . . . the monks came forward to receive communion looking devout, then I was sure I saw Merton, looking most devout of any. Head bowed, eyes down, he goes right past but doesn't see me. Next day at a pontifical mass he has a lot to do, holding the Abbot's crosier, which looks like a shepherds crook, kissing it, handing it to the Abbot, kissing the Abbot's ring, retreating, picking it up again later, taking various positions around the altar, at one point sitting on some steps looking out at the people. There are only three of us in the audience part & this time I believe he did see me.

All this ritual action he does like Merton, or maybe like Chic Boyer, very devout but with some extra polish and precision like when he does the Conga.

That afternoon a monk takes me to see the Abbot, wise, saintly, dignified 70 year old who looks sort of like your father, only with [illegible] smile & a continuous chuckle about something. Merton says he is always telling him to eat plenty because lots of saints are eaters; but they watch the Abbot who hardly eats a thing. I saw where he sleeps, on some kind of straw mattress [illegible].

While I am talking, a bell rings, the Abbot pushes a button to unlock the door & Merton comes in, full of jokes. The Abbot tells him I'm a Catholic & he is very glad about this. . . .

That afternoon the Abbot tells him he can come up to my room & we talk from 2 to 5. He's writing [about] Cistercian Saints, reading St Augustine, St Thomas?, St Bernard's sermons, the moralia of Gregory the Great. The Lives of the Saints is very simple & full of interesting stories. One about Ida de (Lelay?) [illegible].

He asks after all the fellows & says you shld come there when you can.

Heres some details

Choir monks: Merton is one: wake at 2 sing till 4, work till 6, sing again, Mass, then breakfast 2 oz bread & coffee made out of barley & rye. High Mass till 9:30; work maybe physical maybe study till 11, lunch—in summer an after lunch rest period—in winter none—after lunch work till 4—physical like wood-chopping, some study, 4 o'clock Vespers 5 supper—more bread, fruit coffee. Big meal comes at noon, soup maybe & vegetables, good brown bread, cheese. Read after supper, Salve Regina, very fine service—then bed at 7. Choir: white habits, no beards, clipped heads. Lay brothers: brown habits, beards, clipped heads. Work between 3 & 6 P.M. on most of the days.

Second time I saw Merton he told me: Once he went up to the organ there, started to play a hymn & it turned into St. Louis Blues.

A guy came there who didn't understand the place. During his first week they were out in the fields, hoeing weeds & he says to them in sign language, "What are we, slaves?" & starts making Volga boatman gestures. Leaves a week later.

Merton heard another one saying to the novice master: "Ah, let me have just one cigarette." This same guy later went around talking to everybody & finally left.

Merton said he got to laughing very hard one day at a joke he remembered. The joke was "Who was that lady I seen you with."

He says a millionaire wanted to endow another abbey in San Francisco. Wrote the Abbot about it. Only catch was he wanted to have it inside the gates at Luna Park & charge admission.

Brother Barnabas, the baseball player, is a very nice guy. Nobody around the place [illegible sentence] . . . lay brothers all big guys. One in the kitchen was allowed to talk. Told me he was going to be a baseball player in Detroit. They all look very happy & healthy.

Choir seems to be divided between very pious types & happy ones like Merton. Mostly, I guess, he looked healthy.

Lots of young guys & also more old men than there are in the whole town of Olean.

On the wall it says, "Friend, if you want to enter here, leave your body outside, there is only room for your soul."

Merton says it's the Abbot's responsibility to look out for their health & the monk's to forget all about it.

They all got cold shots when winter set in.

They have a hospital section. Also a public address system, so spiritual reading at the refectory can be heard by the patients.

They are reading "A Companion to the Summa" by Walter Farrell. Another sign says [illegible].[50]

The news of Lax's baptism had come to Merton in dramatic fashion, during the third of the great Christmas Masses. He had turned from the altar after the kiss of peace exchange, "And suddenly I find myself looking straight into the face of Bob Lax." Merton's joy at his dear friend's conversion was in contrast to the reaction, some time later, of Bob Gibney who, Lax told Merton, said, "You were a Jew and now you're a Catholic. Why don't you black your face? Then you will be all the three things the Southerners hate most."[51]

Lax went back to New York with some of Merton's poems, half from his time in the novitiate—including "For My Brother Reported Missing in Action, 1943"—and half from the St. Bonaventure days. He gave the poems to Mark Van Doren, who sent them to James Laughlin at New Directions. "I think him a fine poet," Van Doren wrote Laughlin. "Strangely, considering the strictness of the Trappist vows, he has continued to write poems in the monastery. . . . It doesn't seem to me to be keeping the vow of silence, but us heathen benefit whatever it is."[52] They would become Merton's first published work.[53]

❊❊❊❊❊❊❊❊❊❊❊❊❊❊

4

LITERARY TRIUMPHS

Merton Writes Seven Storey Mountain; Lax, *after*
Stints with Time *and* Hollywood, *Writes* Circus
Classic; Rice Leaves Pathé *to Start* Jubilee

There could hardly have been more contrast between the experiences and moods of Merton and those of his two close friends than what prevailed in the mid-1940s. Merton had been on a high for more than two years—since entering Gethsemani—when, on March 19, 1944, the feast of St. Joseph, he took his simple vows, advancing one more step toward becoming a full-fledged member of the O.C.S.O. (Order of Cistercians of the Strict Observance).

Lax, though, was coming off an unhappy year at the *New Yorker* and unsettled periods in Harlem and North Carolina, while Rice was stumbling as he tried to make his way into the commercial world of magazine publishing.

Neither Lax nor Rice had achieved anything like financial stability. Lax was mostly broke—partially sustained by his haberdasher father— so it was fortuitous that Merton had filed a legal document on February 14, 1944, giving his old friend the yearly dividends from the Grosset and Dunlap stock he had inherited from his grandfather, modest as they were.[1]

Rice's financial lot was equally precarious. He, too, needed doles from his father, a successful Wall Street broker.

Also in 1944 James Laughlin of New Directions, encouraged by Mark Van Doren, published Merton's first book, *30 Poems*, in his Poets of the Year series. It is somewhat surprising that Laughlin accepted the poems since, as David Cooper, who edited the Merton-Laughlin letters, recalled, Laughlin admitted that "Merton's early religious poems, except for their color and vigor of imagery, do not particularly interest me. There is something facile about them."[2] Nonetheless Laughlin would go on to publish many Merton books, and would become a close personal friend. Here is the fourth and last stanza of one of the poems in that first volume, manifesting the monk's continued anger at the war and his high level of spirituality. It is titled "An Argument: Of the Passion of Christ."[3]

> The cry that rent the temple veil
> And split the earth as deep as hell
> And echoed through the universe,
> Sounds, in bombardments, down to us.
> There is no ear that has not heard
> The deathless cry of murdered God:
> No eye that has not looked upon
> The lance of the crucifixion:
> And yet that cry beats at the ears
> Of old, deaf-mute interpreters,
> Whose querulous and feeble cries
> Drown stronger voices, and whose eyes
> Will let no light of lances in:
> They still will clamor for a sign!

Laughlin had questions for Van Doren about the kind of contract that should be offered, and to whom it should be sent. Van Doren responded that he would ask Lax for advice—should the contract go to him [Van Doren] "as representative or agent" with royalties going to the monastery, or "directly to Merton or the abbot"? "I have asked Lax to fire an answer back, and you may hear next week."[4] Recognizing Lax's business naiveté, it's a wonder that Van Doren expected such crisp action. In any case, the contract went, eventually, to the monastery, as did the contracts for all other Merton books in his lifetime.

At Christmas time Lax made another visit to Gethsemani and told Merton he should be writing more poems. Merton, however, had not thought it was "God's will," and his confessor agreed, but then the abbot told him, on the feast of the Conversion of Saint Paul, January 25, 1945—"I want you to go on writing poems."[5] That Easter he sent some new ones to Lax for passing on to Van Doren. "I have very little time to write them & none to work on them a lot & make corrections—or type out better copies."[6]

Lax was having good success with his own poetry. The *New Yorker* had published two more of his poems in 1944 and then this one in 1945, "Breeze on a Lexington Avenue Local,"[7] revealing a nice eye for city scenes:

> The flower merchant drops his pack
> And leans against the sliding door;

Wind, beautiful but blind,
Stirs petals on the iron floor.

In Lax's archive at Columbia, there is a penciled postcard dated 1944 from Robert Lowell which seems to refer to some kind of collaborative activity, "I hope before the year is out we will be able to accomplish what we planned." Whatever was "planned" never came about, evidently.[8] He brooded about his writing in a very downbeat entry in his journal:

Your whole trouble, Charlie, and we may as well talk about your whole trouble as anybody elses, because you won't be able to fix anybody elses until you are able to fix your own which you know better than anybody elses, your whole trouble is not being able to stick to anything long enough to get good at it. . . .

Writing, i figure, is what you ought to stick to, it's the one thing you've got a pretty good start on and sometimes have done o.k. with. drawring is maybe ok to kid with.

One thing about writing is ideas of silence. . . .

Second is a feeling that if you aren't writing a letter or a book on charity you aren't doing what you ought to do.

Third is a feeling that because M V D [Mark Van Doren] and Slate said once are you still writing the journal you ought to be still writing the journal. . . .

Fourth is the idea that unless you are writing noel cowid plays, movies, new yorker articles, note comment or cole porter songs, you are wasting your time.

fifth is the idea that unless you are travelling from county to county with a guitar singing spirituals and preachin the gospel you are wasting your time.

sixth is the idea that you are never wasting your time, but yes you are.

seventh is the idea that unless you are doing whatever some body asks you to, you are doing something silly on your own hook.

eighth is the idea that unless you are eating or sleeping you are wasting your time, unless you are exercising.

ninth is the idea that when you are eating or sleeping you are wasting your time, unless you are getting an idea for a novel (you don't know what it is because you've never read one).

tenth is the idea that anybody who isn't either dead and in heaven or horizontal and on a psychoanalyst's day-bed is wasting his time.

eleven is the idea that waking or sleeping, alive or dead you are just the nicest little fellow you ever met. [9]

In the summer of 1945 Rice met Margery Hawkinson, a very pretty Mount Holyoke graduate who lived near his Brooklyn home, and who worked in the censorship section of ABC television. He would court her for two years, then get married, and move into an apartment in Greenwich Village at 58 Bank Street. "Margery wanted to get married," he reminisced. "I would have drifted along. Marriage is a difficult thing. The church doesn't instruct you. A twenty-year-old priest instructed us. What did he know? I wanted a lot of kids. Margery only wanted two. She wanted a country club life."[10]

Rice got a job at RKO Pathé News and continued his creative writing, but without much success. "Over the years," he later remembered, "I've written five unpublished novels, and I did a musical comedy with Bob Gerdy for Vera Zorina. I wrote a scenario for a Universal Pictures film that was never made, and I was offered a job in Hollywood but I didn't accept it."[11]

Lax, in October 1945, was hired by an unlikely employer: *Time* magazine.

It was not a good match. His explanation:

Rice may have told me they needed someone up there and gave me the name of Jim Crider, who was doing the hiring. They had some vacancies, one in the religion department, one in the film department. I said religion sounds good to me. But then they asked me what religion I was. I said Catholic. They said they can't have anyone who is committed to just one religion do these stories, so it was the film department. I guess James Agee had just left as critic. The editor, Tom Matthews, said to me, "Do you like films? Because the last editor we had didn't like them." I said I didn't mind them, something like that. . . . I certainly didn't tell him I ate them up. So I got the job.

They send you to the movie with a senior editor and a researcher, and you go to what they call screenings. You sit through the show and the senior editor is making up his own mind about what he sees and the researcher writes down in the dark what she thought you laughed at or anything like that so you'll have the line ready to quote for your review. Then you write your review and it goes to the senior editor. They call it group journalism. On one review I remember writing that it was an average melodrama. The senior editor added, "just head and shoulders above the average." So I realized what group journalism was like, what a satisfaction it was going to be. I don't remember what film it was. But I'll tell you it was average.[12]

Lax recalled three of the films he reviewed—*Spellbound, Lost Weekend,* and a Noel Coward war propaganda film called *In Which We Serve.*

I was told by my eye doctor that it was ruining my eyes. . . . I was seeing four movies a day . . . and it was bad for me, not just for my eyes. Nancy Flagg read my reviews and was sickened by some of them. But if you look them up remember the senior editor might have made a few changes.[13]

The *Time* stint lasted only five months, until February 1946. Alexander Eliot, a distinguished art editor and critic, was on the *Time* staff in those years, became Lax's life-long friend, and would put him up at his home in Greece when Lax first went there in 1962. He says that "Bob was fired because the editors couldn't figure out from his reviews whether he liked the films or not. 'Is that bad?' I said. 'I would have thought that getting beyond mere "like" and "dislike" was the first essential step in criticism. Perhaps you were disturbed by his subtlety of mind. I empathize with that.' Ironically, some years later a book of reviews by James Agee was published but some of the reviews were actually by Lax—there were no bylines in those days."[14]

The departure from the *Time* organization had not been abrupt. "Nobody quits Time, that's a slap in their face," Lax said. "They found a way that I should work for Life, but I only stayed there about a week. By that time there was an opening at Parade." This would be Lax's fourth magazine job within five years. At *Parade* he was told that "We personalize our stories. When we do a story about bucks, it's from the buck's point of view. Groan. I knew what we were in for. We had a department something like, 'Truth is Stranger Than Fiction.'" It was run by his old Columbia friend Robert Gibney. "We were just making up the contributions . . . week after week. Some man had an alarm clock that he kept in the pouch of a kangaroo. When it went off the kangaroo would come over and tap him on the shoulder to let him know that morning had come. That kind of thing."[15]

Next up for Lax was Hollywood, where he worked for two years in the script department at Sam Goldwyn studios. How did he get there? This is from Lax's Hollywood journal:

Mike Beam [a friend from North Carolina days] and I drove out in an open 1941 Plymouth convertible, starting right after Labor Day [1946]. Mike had been offered a job out here last spring. I had never officially been offered one, but Arthur Ripley Jr. had written his father [Arthur Ripley Sr., a director] a letter about me. . . . There was nothing I wanted to do in New York. I wanted to drive across the country. I had just come back from 2 pleasant trips, to Bermuda & Grenada, & I had developed a liking for traveling. . . . Before I started out I asked Arthur Reef of *Parade* magazine to make me official West Coast representative of the magazine. . . . There was also a strong possibility that I would be earning my living by writing weekly stories for Parade.[16]

Eliot recalls that Lax sent him a message when he got settled. "Am writing swamp-cries for Maria Montez!" Actually he had gone to work for Ripley collaborating on a screen play for a film called *Siren of Atlantis,* starring Montez, Dennis O'Keefe, and the French actor, Jean Pierre Aumont. It was an adaptation of a novel by Pierre Benoit that had already been made into a successful film in Germany. The producer, Seymour Nebenzal—"Seymour . . . crazy" said Ripley—had come to Hollywood to remake the film. The thirty-one-year-old Lax got $125 a week for the research and then a somewhat higher salary as a screen writer. He stayed on the picture from early 1947, when the story conferences began, until June 1948, when the cutting was almost finished, living in a place called Castle Argyle. "Where else would ya live in Hollywood?" he guffawed as he recalled the period during an interview in 1997.[17]

Hollywood made him feel unholy, as he explained to Merton. "I'm still in need of a lot of spiritual guidance," he wrote. "I can't believe that a good life can be this idle. I wonder what the great unrecognized sin has been?"[18]

Realizing that his friend needed succor, Merton wrote back promptly. He had made his solemn vows on March 19, 1947, and said, "I go around singing inside about it all day." He then offered unrealistic career counsel: "About Hollywood I myself would think I want to get away from it. . . . If you stay there why don't you write a movie about Charles de Foucauld since you are all full of research on the Sahara. He was a Trappist then he was a beggar at the door of a convent in Jerusalem then he was a hermit in the Sahara & finally the Tuaregs killed him."[19] Lax must have sucked in his breath after reading that although in retrospect it was prescient advice since Lax would, fifteen years later, hole up by himself on various remote Greek islands, living practically as a hermit for almost four decades.

The same Merton letter revealed that "Harcourt Brace is publishing the autobiography [*The Seven Storey Mountain*] & all the fellows are in it." More advice: "At present I would not say to you to be a Trappist, unless you get some strong & special urge. But I do think you ought to pray to God and ask for a vocation to the priesthood. Anyway, pray to him and ask him for a definite vocation, that is important & I would do that."

Although going for the priesthood was not in the cards for Lax, neither was Hollywood. *Atlantis* got a devastatingly negative review from, ironically, Lax's former employer, *Time* magazine. This was the plot: Aumont and O'Keefe are foreign legionnaires who stumble on the sunken city of Atlantis while on a mission in the African desert. Montez is Queen Antinea, who romances both guys. A review can be called up even now on the Internet's *All Movie Guide*. Here is a sentence: "Of the many deliriously awful Maria Montez vehicles of the 1940s, Siren of Atlantis may well be the worst, though it's not without its campy pleasures."[20]

There were no new film opportunities to entice him. He wrote Merton that a plan for making a movie out of Thomas Wolfe's *Look Homeward Angel*, which could have been interesting, was dropped and others were ludicrous, like "one called Johnny Macbeth is about a gangster who got to be head of a mob by killing Big Duncan, at his wife's (Lily Macbeth's) instigation. The ghost Banky shows up at the dinner party."[21]

"Well, by then I had had enough. Another car door opened—it was Andy Soybell's, a young composer friend who was headed back to New York. . . . 'Not alone you don't go,' I said, and I hopped in."[22]

It was high time to get back to serious writing. Early in 1946 he had had still another poem published in the *New Yorker*. For those Lax readers who may be familiar only with his cryptic abstract poetry of more recent years, here it is, "Truth Compared to the Light of Day," replete with rhymes:

> Sun hath one pivot, night and day,
> Toward which we haste, then turn away.
>
> So Truth, at our sweet system's center,
> Sees us approach and then resent her.
>
> Sun lights his system like a part.
> (The universe is mostly dark).[23]

Merton's writing was about to hit new heights, but not without encountering temporary disappointment. After, in 1946, New Directions had published the second volume of his poems—*A Man in the Divided Sea*—he was told that his autobiography, *The Seven Storey Mountain,* had been rejected by the Trappist censors, "not on theological grounds, but as unripe for publication. . . . I am held to be incapable of writing an autobiography 'with his present literary equipment' and I am advised to take a correspondence course in English grammar." Cynicism about his routine in the monastery began to emerge. "The Cistercian life is energetic. . . . We go out to work like a college football team taking the field. . . . Trappists believe . . . Anything that makes you suffer is God's will. . . . We seem to think that God will not be satisfied with a monastery that does not behave in every way like a munitions factory under wartime conditions of production. . . . We think we have done great things because we are worn out."[24]

The thirty-two-year-old Trappist, soon to become famous, was in the dumps, and had even thought of discontinuing his journal writing. "I continue writing this journal under obedience to Dom Gildas, in spite of my personal disinclination to go on with it," he wrote in March 1947.[25] Imagine the loss if he had stopped. But he wouldn't, and he would still be making insightful entries more than twenty years later—as in his last weeks before his tragic death, when he had a bad cold, sore throat, could breathe only with difficulty in the coal-polluted air of Darjeeling and Dharamsala, and yet write paragraph after paragraph of complex thoughts on subjects such as Buddhism.

But there were sterile days, even in these early years. The completion of his solemn vows failed to stir him. "So yesterday I made my solemn vows. I do not feel like writing about it. This does not mean that I am not happy about profession. But I am happy in a way that does not want to talk."[26]

In the next month he was still trying to boost himself up: "the monotony of the life," he wrote, "sometimes makes us so dejected that we cannot seem to do anything about it. What we need above all are words that will make us love one another and advice that will strengthen us to overcome evil with good."[27]

The evil of the times seemed to be consuming him. The title poem of *Figures for an Apocalypse,*[28] published in 1947 but probably written at the end of World War II—after the dropping of the nuclear bombs on Japan—was sixteen pages of relentless foreboding and warning of what was happening to his adopted country. The whole volume seems more a versified tract than poetry. Segment III is headed "(Advice to my Friends Robert Lax and Edward Rice, to get away while they still can)":

Time, time to go to the terminal
And make the escaping train
With eyes as bright as palaces
And thoughts like nightingales.
It is the hour to fly without passports
From Juda to the mountains,
And hide while cities turn to butter
For fear of the secret bomb.
We'll arm for our own invisible battle
In the wells of the pathless wood
Wounding our limbs with prayers and Lent,
Shooting the traitor memory
And throwing away our guns—
And learning to fight like Gideon's men,
Hiding our lights in jugs.[29]

He expressed his deep disappointment with what he considered the prevailing evil of his adopted land in "A Letter to America":

America, when you were born, and when the plains
Spelled out their miles of praises in the sun
What glory and what history
The rivers seemed to prepare.

Then came an ominous third stanza:

How long are we to wake
With eyes that turn to wells of blood
Seeing the hell that gets you from us
With his treacherous embrace![30]

Mark Van Doren praised the book, and in particular its concluding essay in which Merton wrestled with the conflict between his contemplative desires and his writing. "Nothing has touched me more deeply," he wrote to Merton, "than the problem you pose on page 110, and somehow solve on page 111."[31] The "problem" as stated by Merton in the essay "Poetry and the Contemplative Life" is "what if one's religious superiors make it a matter of formal obedience to pursue one's art, for some special purpose like the good of souls?" His solution, or rationalization, is that "we can console ourselves with Saint Thomas Aquinas that it is more meritorious to share the fruits of contemplation with others than it is merely to enjoy them ourselves."[32]

But Van Doren's comments on *Figures* were not all positive. "Your new poems," he wrote, "are very rich—sometimes too rich, I think, for the thin blood outside those walls. I mean, the phrasing runs too often in parallels, and admits too many epithets; result, a tincture of monotony." Then, as if to soften the harshness, "If that is heathen criticism, let it pass. Substantially, the poems are powerful. The "Duns Scotus" is the best. . . . I suppose Bob [Lax] has copies." [33] "Scotus" was, in fact, one of the few upbeat poems in the volume. It cited "the music of Our Lady's army!"

> For Scotus is her theologian,
> Nor has there ever been a braver chivalry than his
>   precision.
> His thoughts are skies of cloudless peace
> Bright as the vesture of her grand aurora
> Filled with the rising Christ.[34]

Laughlin, too, had his criticisms of Merton's poetry, and even passed on the criticism of others, notably, in 1948, T. S. Eliot, who was spending some of the war years in Princeton. Eliot, he said, "is most interested in your work, but thinks it is very uneven, and he wishes you would strive more toward form."[35] Then he asked if Merton could have Van Doren or Lax send him some more poems to show Eliot. Merton responded that he'd get Lax to make some suggestions.

Lax, Merton, and Rice, in these years, would each have experiences with the rites of the Eastern Church that would stay with them throughout life. Lax's did not come about until he moved to Greece, but both Merton and Rice had exposures in the late 1940s that affected them profoundly. Merton described the visit of some Eastern clergy to Gethsemani in 1948:

> . . . the place was full of priests of the Byzantine-Slavonic rite who . . . ended up singing two Masses a day and Benediction and the last night they were here they were still singing. . . .
> The Eastern rite—we got a good look at it this time—is in many ways impressive. I like seeing priest, deacon and subdeacon all praying together at the altar with their hands up in the air like the *orantes* in the catacombs. . . . Their Mass gives you a greater sense of the reality of the Mystical Body.[36]

Rice, about six months after Merton had made that entry, recorded this in his own journal:

Ever since I first discovered the Byzantine rite, my head has been
filled with the memory of the music and the churches and the
people. I want to tell everyone about them, bring everyone to the
services. But what can you do in this world? Nobody really seems
to care. (I've brought Gerdy, Lax, Freedgood, the BW [his wife
Margery], and Flynn, but outside of Lax, none of them seems to
care enough to go back, although they all express the hope for
phonograph records.) I can hardly wait for Sunday to come, and
after it I have this terrific music, these wonderful thoughts of what
the Liturgy has said and what it means to me, unable to communicate them to anyone.[37]

He would, in fact, communicate those thoughts through many articles, beautifully photographed, on Eastern rite churches and communities in *Jubilee* magazine over its fifteen-year existence from 1953 to
1967, some of them written by Merton and Lax.

Although Merton's problems with censorship of his manuscript for
The Seven Storey Mountain were not entirely solved, the book finally
emerged in 1948 from Harcourt Brace Jovanovich, the publishing
house of one of his Columbia friends, Robert Giroux. Rice, in his post-
mortem biography of Merton (1972), claimed that the manuscript was
"bowdlerized" by the censors, and that an original copy does not even
exist today. Rice was probably mistaken. In his journal Merton indicates that besides Giroux's copy he gave one to Sister Thérèse Lentfoehr, which is at Columbia, and there is another in the Merton archive
at Boston College. But it's not clear how much the abbey censors had
stricken from the copy that went to Giroux, who then cut out a large
amount of material he might have thought too pietistic, very likely
improving the readability.

Merton himself does not mention any manuscript manipulation
in his journals, and when Lax wrote him a congratulatory letter he
acknowledged it with enthusiasm:

Thanks for the beautiful letter. One of the best things I liked
about *The Seven Storey Mtn.* was the index which they fixed up
at Harcourt Brace and which came to me as a surprise. It made
me wish I had mentioned a whole lot more people in the book.
It reads like a big party on the night before judgement day, with
everybody invited by Providence to be in this book also invited to
go to heaven in a big yacht provided by prayers of the ones who
were the biggest saints like Francis, Saint and Blake, William and
Michel-de-Cuxa, Saint. . . . I get this wonderful exalted feeling

that we are all going to ride into heaven together and that Christ
will get glory in the work of His love that united us all together in
ways that we will never understand until then. . . .

Right now very busy trying to fix up a fancy picture book about
the Abbey for our centenary. Some very classy photographers from
Lousibille were out here twice and they were very good. One of
them is a kid 19 just out of the marines but he works like Rice
works, with the same kind of seriousness. . . .[38]

By this time, Merton had accepted the kindness of Sister Thérèse
Lentfoehr, herself a poet and a teacher at various universities. She
would transcribe his longhand notes—not always easy to read—serve
as his sounding board and adviser on poetry and devoted factotum for
the next thirty years, although they met only once, at a Gethsemani
picnic in 1967. The Merton-Lentfoehr file in the Columbia archive is
very substantial. In early 1949 he wrote her that he now had a different
place, much more agreeable, to write in the monastery.

The new Father cellarer, at the beginning of the year, took over
the room where I was working. That left practically nowhere for
me except the rare book vault. And now here I am behind a double
iron door in this silent monastery, and surrounded by twelfth century manuscripts of St Bernard. It is simply wonderful. It is a mir-
acle that I do any work at all. The constant temptation is to sit still
and taste the beautiful silence. I have permission to come in here
in the "interval" after the night office on certain feasts—around
four thirty a.m.—and study old liturgical ms, missals, antiphoners
etc. What a meditation![39]

Lentfoehr took her responsibilities as Merton's helper with such seriousness that she began to examine the Merton materials in the Columbia University library. He wrote her that he hoped she wouldn't have
her "sensibilities" damaged by what she found—presumably the nude
cartoons he had drawn for the *Jester* in the late 1930s.

Thank you also for the card from New York. One thing distresses
me: it is the thought that you may have been led to ferret around
in the Columbia library until you unearthed some skeletons in the
closets of Columbia of fifteen years or so ago. If you did, then I
have no need to assure you that those skeletons are certainly skeletons and there is nothing in those closets to edify a religious. I
am only thinking of your sensibilities. For my own part, I ought at

least to be able to accept the humiliation of my past as some kind of penance. After all I ought to do something to make amends.

On the other hand you will be glad to hear that the priesthood is very close now and that they have arranged the ordination for Ascension Day, May 26th.[40]

The ordination took place on that day, in 1949, as scheduled. It was the same year that saw the publication of *Seeds of Contemplation*, meditations, "The Tears of the Blind Lions," poems, and *The Waters of Siloe*, a history of the Cistercians.

A big Columbia representation came down from New York for the ordination ceremony. Lax, though, probably journeyed from Connecticut College for Women, where he had taught English for the prior academic year of 1948-49. His cousin, Bob Mack, who was head of the English department, had arranged for Lax to replace a professor who was sick. Merton's account of the ordination:

I could not begin to write about the ordination, about saying Mass, about the *Agape* that lasted three days, with all those who came down to attend. Perhaps some day it will come out retrospectively, in fragments. . . .

. . . I am left with the feeling not only that I have been transformed but that a new world has somehow been brought into being through the labor and happiness of these three most exhausting days, full of sublimity and of things that none of us will understand for a year or two to come.

. . . So I gave communion to Nanny [Frieda Hauck, who had helped to raise Merton back in Long Island] and to Dan Walsh and Bob Lax and Ed Rice and Bob Giroux, who wore his U.S. Navy jacket, and to Tom Flanagan who came with Ed, and Rod Mudge who came with Dan and to McCauliffe who wrote here about poetry. But I couldn't give communion to Jay Laughlin or to Seymour [Freedgood].

. . . Now I know that I had the whole Church in America praying for me and I am scared and consoled by so much mercy and by the sense that I myself have contributed practically nothing to the whole business and that I have been worked on and worked in, carried upward on the tide of a huge love that has been released in people, somehow, in connection with a book printed over my name: and on this tide millions of us, a whole continent perhaps, is riding into heaven.[41]

Seeking some of the religious fervor he caught from Merton at Gethsemani was his friend Rice, who composed a wistful note around this time—perhaps to his friend Bob Gerdy:

oh: this is what is happening: i am going up to Graymore [*sic*] monastery for a few days to save my soul. if I don't come back by friday, call my poor old daddy and tell him where I am. if I am not back in a week from today, send him the enclosed letter but don't soak off the stamp before you do.

. . . I am sorry for being so melodramatic about this trip, but it is the ham in me coming out for the last time.

Give the rest of the fellows my compliments and tell them they ought to repent themselves.

Get it right, Y'rs[42]

Merton asked Lentfoehr to stop by Rice's apartment at 54 Bank St., New York, and pick up "some snapshots he took down here, and some other old ones perhaps."[43] These photos show most of the ordination visitors mentioned above but do not show Lax, Merton, and Rice in the same frame—and, alas, no such picture was ever taken in their lifetime, evidently. Rice's photo of a blissful Merton after his ordination, in straw hat and traditional Trappist robes, and many others he took on visits to the abbey in later years, are heirlooms.

In the summer of 1949 Lax got to do something he had been aching for. He got a $400 advance from a publisher—maybe Duell Sloane & Pierce—to do a kind of reporter-at-large article on traveling with the Cristiani Brothers circus through parts of western Canada. Some fifty years later he recalled the experience:

I was to fly out and meet them in a big border city in Saskatchewan and travel with them to Saskatoon. Mogador met me at the plane and it was as though we'd just seen each other yesterday. I'd ride in the cab of Mogador's truck and take notes all the time as we talked. It seems we'd drive all night, then sleep just a little before it was time to raise the tent in the morning. More likely, performers slept late and circus grips did the tent-raising, still, performers had to be on hand to install trapezes, tight-wires and nets.

I lived and ate with the performers—the food was great. The first draft of my book was all full of breakfast menus. . . .

Played just one role with them, not at every performance, but they allowed me to play the clown for maybe about 10 days.

Another clown would say, "What's your name?" I'd say whatever. He'd say, "My name is milk. Shake." Another: I was carrying a bag and fishing into it and bringing out a flashlight. I fished and fished and finally came out with a flashlight and I was amazed by it and that got a laugh.

They were all farmers in that part of Saskatchewan. One day a whole farmer family with a baby was watching me do this panto-mime with the flashlight . . . the baby was sober as a judge. I was in a tramp suit. It was only a slight adjustment to what I was wearing all the time. I pulled out the flashlight and the baby smiled and they all sat back and relaxed. I started to walk away and the baby was following me. It was quite a triumph.

I was out of advance money by the time we got to Saskatoon. Mogador lent me fifty dollars so I could fly back to New York, and I mailed it back to him from the Virgin Islands where I'd gone to visit Nancy [Flagg] and [Bob] Gibney.[44]

He never wrote the article, and is not sure if he ever returned the $400 advance, but the material he gathered became grist for the *Circus of the Sun,* which would be published ten years later, in 1959.

Forty years after, the late Paul Cristiani (Mogador, the acrobat, in *Circus)* remembered with great warmth his friendship with Lax. "You gotta like him, you don't teach anybody to have a funny walk and make good faces."[45] For his part, Lax remembers the Cristianis for, as he told Mark Van Doren, their "unearthly sweetness and grace [having] taken him in as a poet and philosopher without portfolio." Van Doren eventu-ally met Mogador at lunch in New York with Lax. "Mogador was hand-some and lithe, but scarcely more articulate than his friend, so that I did most of the talking. But I learned that he had studied dancing under Balanchine to perfect his balance." Not long afterward Van Doren went to a Cristiani Brothers performance, traveling to Massachusetts from his home in Connecticut. "Mogador bounded out to greet us; assigned us the best seats in the tent; and during the show perpetually bowed and waved to us, so that we felt very important." Van Doren wrote about the show to Lax, whose reply was one word: "Gee!"[46]

Not long after returning from Canada, Lax accepted an invita-tion, and an airplane ticket, to the Virgin Islands from his former girl friend, Nancy Flagg, then married to his old Columbia buddy Bob Gibney. Ad Reinhardt, not having yet made his mark as an abstract painter, and recently divorced, went with him. Lax had visited Flagg and Gibney in Bermuda on their honeymoon. Why were they in the Virgin Islands?

Well, they were tired of New York certainly. Gibney, at least, perhaps Nancy, too, maybe they both had come into some money from the deaths of their parents. I had just come from traveling with the circus and was trying to write the circus book. I spent most of each day on the book, although I did go for a swim each day. The form of *Circus* changed a lot. Since I had thought it was going to be a reporter-at-large piece it included every menu or every meal I ate while I traveled with them. It was all magical with me. Ooh, corn flakes! As it went along it got to be more and more a poem.

I got sick at some point, some stomach disorder, maybe from eating too many avocados. . . . I had eye trouble . . . had it back in New York, too. I went to the hospital in St. Thomas. I remember an Anglican chaplain coming by my bed and saying things like, "Anything good happening?"[47]

During that hospital sojourn he wrote a lot of *Circus*, including a very funny poem that describes the lion tamer, "Colonel Angus," who interrupted a chat to go into the cage with chair and whip, then left the lion "furious . . . with his paws against the door" while he "Scurried from the cage" and calmly ended the interrupted sentence with, "I think it was Pasadena."[48]

What did he do for money in those days? "Same as always, just waited for some. We had to go to St. Thomas for mass . . . and Reinhardt would come with me." He, a Communist? "Yes, and he went to Gethsemani once with me. He was an open person, not a committed Communist like his first wife was. He came from a Lutheran family . . . Lutheran, German, the works." Were there any people there you could talk to about God? "Sure, both Gibney and Nancy." It was there Lax heard about the Holy Year, the Marian Year [1950]. "At the church I heard a voice inside me that said, 'You'll be there.' I have a lot of voices inside me, but I took that one seriously."[49] He did go to Rome later, after writing *Circus*.

Lax's affection for Flagg is transparent in this journal entry, written on the day of his arrival with Reinhardt, having been met by Gibney at the airport in St. Thomas:

> Nancy dressed in fair colors,
>   walking like princess,
>   came to the end of the pier
>   wept
>   so beautiful.

Swim. No suits. Masks and fins. Gibney pursuing fish, could catch them bare handed. . . .

Drink, before dinner. Martinis. Conversation. Dinner: goat curry, mango chutney.

Nancy roasts & grinds own coffee, makes bread, grows vegetables, makes mango chutney, guava jelly, all ice creams, johnnycake, works out own dishes of native fare, makes dresses, keeps house immaculate, writes stories, stays beautiful.

Have 6 cats: George & the Princess, Eddie, Hazel, Lucille. Ok, 5 cats. . . .

Gibney makes beds, tables, chairs, repairs motors & tools for natives, catches lobsters, turtles, spears fish, sets home made fish pots for the cats. Two days ago speared three lobsters. Yesterday a big flopping sting ray. Lobsters for us, sting ray wings for cats. . . .

Gib being outspoken conservative, Reinhardt retiring liberal. All day Reinhardt makes abstract watercolors for New York art show. Virgin Islands colors & grace of line beginning to make appearance in pix. Gib against abstract art, "Bastardize extraordinary talents, shouldn't waste them on this."

They play jazz records. The eye business keeps me from going up hill where I do my writing. . . .[50]

Gibney, although a hard drinker, was very athletic. He could swim great distances under water, and he would tightrope walk on a cable, with a balancing rod—not all that hard—but he did it while carrying his kids.

His judgments of Lax's writing and Reinhardt's painting were harsh. Flagg would write that Gibney "deplored the direction that Lax had taken: he felt that Lax's supple, shimmering wits were wasted on his false-simple 'concrete' poems." He also wrote, in his journal presumably, that "Merton's book left me with the feeling that he'll deserve martyrdom so essential to canonization." He "ranted against Reinhardt and the whole new 'Culture Industry': Genet, blah, Poor Reinhardt's one-upmanship in purple-on-purple. Welded auto parts. Pop. Rauschenberg. Warhol. Bridget Riley. SHIT! . . ." He wrote Reinhardt himself that "I tend toward the thoroughly unreal and naïve wish that everything that has happened to the world since 1750 be repealed." Flagg writes that Gibney's only hero was Samuel Johnson, and he "clouted Reinhardt with proofs that Andrew Wyeth was the one contemporary painter worth considering."[51] Lax and Reinhardt remained oblivious of their friend's harsh criticism.

Lax's eye trouble was from exposure to the Caribbean sun. He put a patch over one eye, which was sensitive even to moonlight. One night they all drove to the house of one of Nancy's friends and drank a lot. Everyone was hung over the next day, and Gibney felt bad about not writing.

Some thirteen years later Flagg, a talented writer who had worked for *Parade* in New York, recalled the daily doings of the quartet in a magazine piece.

It evokes the mood of the Olean days and is titled "The Beats in the Jungle," and leads off with this quote from a Wilfrid Sheed article called "The Beat Movement Concluded," which had appeared in the *New York Times Book Review* of February 13, 1972: "Much of the Beat life style existed among a small group at Columbia University as early as 1939." Flagg's article makes it clear that the beat lifestyle was still very much alive in 1949 in the Virgin Islands:

Five cats were the only company we kept. So we were delighted when the poet Robert Lax, Gibney's great friend and Columbia roommate, promised to come and spend the summer with us. No doubt Thomas Merton would have come along too, if he hadn't been living austerely enough already, in a Trappist monastery. (Merton's much-edited autobiography, "The Seven Storey Mountain," had been published the autumn before, to the scorn and merriment of his friends. "We got a free copy of Merton's book," Gibney wrote to Lax. "I can't put him any closer to grace in a cowl than I could to sin in a straw hat.")[52]

Flagg's description of her two guests on their arrival at her abode: "Even after the rigors of the trip down from New York, both Lax and Ad looked just as usual—Ad plump and shrewd and self-contained and benign, like a Buddha or a baby; Lax as skinny and shaky and ungainly as a foal, and just as clearly destined for grace."[53]

She wrote that she had first met Lax when she was fourteen. That would have been in 1936 when Lax was a sophomore at Columbia and she was perhaps a precocious freshman at Smith. She is proud that "The first full-page poem ever published in the *New Yorker* was written by Lax for me ['A Radio Masque for My Girl Coming Down from Northampton,' see chapter 2]. When was that? 1940. So I was eighteen by then, and taking poems as a matter of course. All my vanity was still intact; I hadn't yet met Gibney."

Ed Rice felt that Flagg really loved Lax, and he probably returned her love but seriousness about women was not part of his makeup. His publisher Emil Antonucci once asked Lax why he never married. After a pause he said, "I'm a unicellular organism." Flagg transferred her affection to Gibney since she could get no response from Lax, thought Rice. It was not an easy marriage, though. In the article she recounts Gibney's depression, as well as Lax's. She says that Gibney's

blocks were so many and so massive that they became his castle. Lax too seemed to be, indeed boasted of being, an aesthetic basket case. He couldn't repeat his early successes with The New Yorker. That summer on the cay, he was supposed to be writing for Duell Sloan a straight journalistic book about some circus acrobats of his acquaintance. He couldn't write it. ("The Circus of the Sun," a dizzying sequence of high-wire poems, wasn't published until 1960 [sic, 1959], and then not by Duell Sloan.) But the sort of thing he was doing, and was ashamed of doing—those small slopes and ropes and ladders of words, on all those flyaway scraps of paper—swung him up to his present rarefied reputation.[54]

Maybe "rarefied" but largely unrecognized, except in some circles in Europe, one would say, although there are some Americans who feel his poems will one day become classics. Flagg recalls, in the article, an afternoon with Lax that reveals his own self-doubt about the quality of his work:

One afternoon, with the sun like an axe to our skulls, Lax and I plodded up to the top of the cay to admire the peacock-blue view, a full circle of stupefying beauty and boredom. Lax seemed depressed. Perhaps I was trying to cheer him up, perhaps to cheer myself about Gibney's chronic depression. Anyway, I said, "It's not fair. There should be a good acceptable name for the sort of talent you and Gibney have. Not for formal writing. Discipline, organization, all that stuff. But for the wonderful talk and jokes and journals and letters to friends."

Lax wasn't cheered. "There is a name for that sort of talent. That's what they call posthumous talent."[55]

Flagg and Gibney took note of a characteristic of Lax that stayed with him all his life—his klutziness. Flagg cited in her article this Gibney remark in a letter he wrote from Boston during one of his escapes from the islands: "I stay constantly irritated (not seriously, but you know) when he can't seem to open a can or light the lamp or a fire, or get into a boat without being lowered in a sling. . . ." Lax's talent was elsewhere and, even in the environment of ennui that seemed to hover over the Flagg-Gibney complex, he showed it with some substantive writing on Circus.

He returned to Olean and concentrated on making his notes into a long poem, "and I had Father Philotheus [a long-time friend, on the faculty at St. Bonaventure, who was also Merton's spiritual adviser for some period of time] keeping me at it. 'You be here by 8 in the morning and you start writing.'"[56]

He looked back on his sojourn with Flagg and Gibney in a note to Merton:

i'm home again in the attic; stayed at the island till October 15. it is a fine island, but house too small for three people [Reinhardt must have left earlier] not singing trios, me and gibney good duets, old songs and some new; nancy, solo, with defiantly lonely arias from the rustic cavalier. . . .

i wrote about the acrobats and am still writing in gladio's attic. many words, much paper, but nothing like a finished book.

Want to make a movie ballet of Juggler of Notre Dame. Mogador Cristiani turning the right kind of somersaults. i wish we could make it in the Church, for the Church. . . .

i wrote a lot of psalm-tones on the island. i think they all need working on; but i will send them to you when i can retype them.[57]

Even then, it seems, Merton was on the lookout for sanctuaries more isolated than Gethsemani, as he queried Lax in a letter of several densely typed pages that included his own doings and musings, as well as reflections on the teaching of theology to the novices, and a revelation of his eclectic musical tastes. Excerpts:

Thanks for the letter and the list of poems and the news of Gib and Nancy. Is Virgin Islands any good for a monastery?

I am not writing, too busy teaching mystical theology and a big orientation course for novices to get into the liturgy. I have suddenly woken up to the fact that somebody needs to be teaching theology the way St. Augustine did and not the [way] textbooks used in seminaries do. . . .

Anyway, pray that the classes may work out. It will certainly do no harm to stop writing now for a while and all this will build up easy into a better book than I ever thought of before. If God wants it that way.

Naomi Burton [Merton's agent] wants to come down here and persuade me to lie low for a while and she does not believe that this is exactly what I am doing. I have manufactured a private boardwalk out behind the old horsebarn which is half destroyed and there I walk up and down and make up songs that I will never be able to write down, partly King Oliver and partly Stravinsky or somebody and partly gregorian chant. It is about the only way I can pray but it is mildly pacifying and doesn't disturb the cloud where God is. I say it is the only way I pray—no—there is a big opera starts inside me when I get in choir but it is strictly opera and for me Il Trovatore isn't prayer and I shrug it off, when I remember. . . .

Then he reminded Lax of his passion for the Bible, and revealed an interest in mysticism:

Gee, read the Bible.
    I have been nuts to go so many years in the monastery without reading Scripture all day and studying about the prophets. Claudel writes awful good about Scripture and there are many in France many priests beginning to wake up and find out all about it too. . . .
    There is a priest living as a hermit in India, knows all about indian mysticism and thinks that maybe India will someday be the hope of the Church. People keep writing from India we should start a monastery there, but Fr. Abbot say no. also a bishop from switzerland wrote, wants american trappists. French-swiss-german-dutch trappists no pep, he says. wants american trappists. . . .
    Me hide in Kentucky jungle behind horsebarn rain-snow-hail sing king oliver all night. Good bye. God Bless you, Gladio Benjie Dick Mary Davis all people at Bonas everybody in Olean. Holy and Happy Christmas. In Corde Jesu.[58]

It was not going to be a happy Christmas for Rice, whose journal showed him plunged in gloom:

Fraud
Despair
Gloom and misery everywhere
    It's always three o'clock in the morning . . . in the dark night of the soul. Who knows how lonely a man can be? Who can express his own dark night, even to himself? How can we communicate to each other except through Jesus Christ? Who is to cement society together except Jesus Christ? It seems there are two dark nights: the one before the light is given you, and second after. I am still in the first, and how terrible can the second night be![59]

The mood was still with him on New Year's Eve when he, nonetheless, set some goals that seem very modest: "Another year gone. The two most depress[ing] times of each year—Oct 23 [his birthday] & today. My projects for next year—painting & completion of Great Expectations, which I am picking up for the sixth or seventh time." His comments on art in this same entry are prophetic because they would show up in the remarkable art that would characterize *Jubilee* magazine, soon to be born. "It seems to me that the best art of the present is spot art—simple drawings, often symbolic. Good because it is used as an aid to other things just as medieval and byzantine wall drawings and decorations were used as an aid to worship. Spot drawings are a quick guide to content of a story or article."[60]

A few months later he would lose his job at RKO Pathé, but it would give him time to begin to develop the *Jubilee* concept. While *Jubilee* was germinating in the 1950s, *The Seven Storey Mountain* was becoming a galloping best-seller. It was sending droves of young men and women into monasteries and convents, as well as faltering Catholics back to Mass. The book has sold several million copies over the years, has been translated into numerous languages; and its fiftieth anniversary paperback edition, printed in 1998, is still selling briskly. Even in England, a country not especially congenial to Catholicism, particularly American Catholicism, it was received warmly. The English title was *Elected Silence*, and Evelyn Waugh wrote Merton that it

has had a very respectful reception here—not particularly understanding in most cases, but it has been chosen by the magazines and papers as an important book. One ass, V. S. Pritchett was rather offensive about it in the New Statesman and I am having fun with him in the correspondence columns.

Apart from its primary, religious value the book is doing good service, I think, in showing England a side of America they seldom meet.

They think of America as a kind of Coney Island and it is a great thing for them to learn of Gethsemani.[61]

Rice would comment on the book's success in his biography of Merton, written in 1972: "Tens of thousands of people saw themselves in Merton, felt his anguish over the black and the poor, war, the deadening effects of industrialization in its vast uprooting of humanity. If he had never written another word (and he hoped not to), it would have been a landmark of the twentieth century. But it was, he sensed, not an end but a beginning."[62]

One of the many people profoundly touched by *SSM* was a young medical student in Cincinnati named John Eudes Bamberger, later a Trappist priest and psychological counselor at Gethsemani to Merton himself. In those days Bamberger had no intention of becoming a monk. "I was living a life of prayer when I was [later] in the Navy, and continued to do so as an intern, but the calling to be a monk, somewhat influenced by *The Seven Storey Mountain*, became strong."[63]

Another was Ernesto Cardenal, the Nicaraguan poet, who later vexed Pope John Paul II with his activities on behalf of the Sandinistas. Cardenal, who also became a Trappist at Gethsemani and a novice under Merton, recalled that he was twenty-three when he read *SSM* as a student at Columbia, just after it came out, and then read "all his books, and also translated his poems into Spanish."[64]

The book had another big impact: it prepared the climate for *Jubilee*, which became a magazine of unprecedented artistic and literary quality among Catholic publications. Although Merton and Lax each figured in its birth, and each wrote for it and recruited writers over the years, the brunt of the work—the conceptualization, the fundraising, editing, art direction, article solicitation, and business management—was done by Ed Rice. The name, probably thought up by Merton, came from *Jubilate Deo* (Praise God), and carried the subtitle *A Magazine of the Church and Her People*.

Rice's initiative in launching the magazine came at an opportune time in his life. His friends were concerned about him, just let go from RKO Pathé in a downsizing dictated by the new owner, Howard Hughes. Lax wrote Merton that the firing was "to all an obvious good, but for right now worrisome."[65] Rice's own journal entry from 1950 reflects his doldrums.

Reading my 1939-40 journal. My whole empty life is epitomized in those childish, self conscious scribblings. There's an account of a week which turns my hair—nothing but drunkenness and foolish posturings.

Reading some old letters by Merton, about 1940-41, when he was at St B's. He had all the ideas, but I never paid any attention to him. There's one letter in particular, from 1942 when he was at G [Gethsemani] which sums up the whole business of religion. I read it then, but it made no impression. I guess I wasn't ready to be saved then. Perhaps that is why I escaped the war, escaped being killed in my drunken stupors, escaped serious illnesses, because I wasn't ready for salvation. Now I have an idea of it—but what will happen?

Looking through that old journal is a shattering experience, all right.[66]

Work on the magazine concept brought him out of it. He wrote Sister Thérèse Lentfoehr, probably in early 1950, that "Bob Lax and I are trying to start a Catholic picture magazine—about 3/4 pictures and 1/4 text. I hope you will be among our first contributors."[67] He outlined the magazine's plan in some detail to Merton:

Lax just passed on a letter from you. I was going to write you about the magazine, but I see that Sister Therese has already done so. She has offered us some material of yours. We certainly would like to use it—we need it in fact—and we hope that you will let us use some of it, although we are going to be very careful about the way we handle it.

The magazine is a strange business. All of a sudden I can see that chaos of my years on Film Fun, Look and the other stupid places falling into a pattern, because that was the only way I could get the experience to edit the magazine. God has been leading me along the edge of a precipice. I did a lot of worrying because none of these things made sense, until now.

We asked some rich Catholics for money. They all said the magazine wouldn't sell, that Catholics are dopes and don't read. Now a backer has appeared out of nowhere. He is a Jew and is one of the smartest and holiest men I have ever met, and is full of confidence about the magazine. He thinks it is a terrific idea, says that what he wants to know first when he goes into a project is, is it good, and then he'll worry about making it pay.

He says whatever we run is fine. He is taking us to the Cardinal for his blessing. It will take a month or two to work out the business deals, but the whole project looks good.

What I'd like to run in the magazine is stories about Friendship House, Negro Catholics, St Therese (using the pictures of her before they were retouched), French worker priests, Peguy, Stravinsky (wrote a good mass). Matisse (now painting a church), Russian Orthodox mystics, Catholic Eastern rites, a Franciscan Oil Research Laboratory, the Desert Fathers, St John of the Cross, stigmata, Abraham, the Apocalypse, Visions, etc. There is good picture material for all of them. We won't worry about intellectual levels. We'll run a story about St Benedict Joseph Labre—would you like to write it? I have a good Picasso picture, of a poor beggar, to illustrate it.

We want to show the Catholics (and the rest of the world) what a terrific thing the Church was and is and will be, and how it has a place for everybody, that the Orthodox and the Protestants should come back fast. We'll leave the stories about laying cornerstones of rectories to the Brooklyn Tablet.

. . . I hope you will write. Margery and I have been praying for you.[68]

Merton kept close track of Rice's effort and asked Lentfoehr to help out. "I thought often of you stopping by Ed's place, and I hope you did not get into any mischief in the Village. I wonder how his magazine is coming along. . . . I didn't tell Ed anything about you but I shall certainly ask him if you are wearing yourself out!!"[69] He appended a longhand note in pencil suggesting that she do something for the magazine herself. Merton reassured the nun that her appearance at Rice's apartment was not improper. "Your account of your visit to Ed fascinated and charmed me. I rarely get any news from him, and it was good to see into his apartment. . . . Don't worry, I didn't bat an eyelash at your knocking on the window—except in surprise at the thought that you would think I would be surprised."[70] An interesting entry from 1950 in Rice's journal portends how his critical ear for high quality liturgical music and his astute eye for good church art would be manifest in issue after issue of *Jubilee*. It also shows his continued interest in the Eastern church.

Mass at Church of the Holy Trinity, Magyar Greek rite . . . poor singing. last week & two weeks before St Mary's Melkite and Our Lady of Lebanon Maronite in Bklyn . . . liturgy sung pretty well . . . art terrible. Ikons are bad, and they all have Barclay Street statues. In each of these I have the desire to rush up & destroy the art, start all over again.[71]

Merton continually boosted Lax's poetry to James Laughlin, his New Directions publisher, writing in January that "Bob Lax wrote a swell poem about Our Lady which ought to go in any anthology under the sun but especially the one you are planning."[72] Laughlin passed on it, however, and then, later in the same year, Merton wrote again, this time about the circus book that "maybe you ought to see."[73] Laughlin would eventually publish a segment from the circus book in one of his annuals, but he never felt that he could afford to use the extensive white space that accompanied most of Lax's poetry in later years. Lax sent Merton, in April, an early specimen of his lean stanzas—perhaps one of the first examples of Lax poetry written in geometric shapes that he would mail to many friends over the decades. This one was a simple circle made up of the words "Power Wisdom Love Power Wisdom Love At Play In Every Act Of Every Being."[74]

A short while later, Lax reported how he was proceeding with the *Circus* book. "I come to Bonas [St. Bonaventure] each day and write in the art room. I've got quite a few words now on the acrobat book, but still haven't tried to put sections or even paragraphs together. . . . I also suspect that when it is all written down I will look it over and see that it could all have been said in a simple sentence and that the year of jabbering was only for myself."[75]

Lax wrote Sister Thérèse that "[m]ost of my friends, I think, have disowned me for my self-imposed silence. . . . I have wanted to send some of the poems I wrote last year in the Virgin Islands. The book, of course, has been taking up most of my time and thought, maybe more than it should; I'm hopeful that it will be in some sort of readable shape by the end of the summer. . . . Your deeply perceptive (and very complimentary!) criticism of those few circus poems makes me believe you would be its best critic."[76]

Merton's own writing was on a roll, but, having signed a new long-term contract for four books with Harcourt Brace Jovanovich, he worried about the impact that the commitment might make on his solitude. "That probably means the final renouncement forever of any dream of a hermitage . . . meanwhile my work is my hermitage because it is *writing* that helps me most of all to be a solitary and contemplative here at Gethsemani."[77]

By September of 1950 Lax reported to Merton triumphantly, if with some restraint, that "the circus book is either finished or not. when i get back to Olean (maybe the middle of next week, i'll have it typed and read it and see.) there is a lot of it, but i don't know if it goes together." In the same letter he told of more traipsing about. He had gone to Combermere, Ontario "chez the baroness de hueck in the believe me far north. . . . I may go to Rome for this proximate cause: a Quaker girl I knew last year . . . [Theodora "Teddy" Colt Flynn, of the Colt weapons family, a student of his at Connecticut College] is marry a Frenchman name of Jean François [Bergery] . . . she says now she wants me to come and meet him and I guess convince her more about the Church. (Meet them in Paris; from there go Barefoot to Rome.) She sends me tickets to do this with. So maybe yes."[78]

He did go, stayed at first in the Bergery apartment on the Right Bank and was godfather to their child, as he had been godfather to Bergery herself. He spent a lot of time, however, at L'Eau Vive, a retreat house in

Soisy-sur-Seine, a village outside of Paris that had once been the grand home of Madame Pompidou. It was now rather shabby but still carried an air of gentility and was surrounded by beautiful meadows and trees. There were stations of the cross through the woods and broad unmowed fields that burst with seasonal wildflowers, such as buttercups. Such Catholic intellectuals as Jacques Maritain would spend days there praying and meditating. A serene Franciscan priest counseled guests on sunny days while seated in the shade of a huge chestnut tree. Lax did some serious writing there and Millie and I visited him on several weekends in 1952-53, enduring the cold of the high-ceilinged bedrooms, warmed only by a wood fire, but stimulated by the holiness of the other guests. There were dignified, plainly dressed French ladies, spinsters, and nuns, right out of Mauriac novels. A Canadian diplomat who had served as a judge in the Nuremberg trials would prostrate himself in front of the altar throughout Mass. Jean Vanier, later to found L'Arche, an organization that even today serves men in Europe and Canada who have developmental disabilities, was one of the regulars. We had never seen such holiness. There were also polyglot students from all over—Greece, New York, South Dakota, Paris—and some bizarre drop-ins, like Allen Ginsberg, who recorded in his journal that he had been "sent to work under Bob Lax" and arrived "with trunk." No explanation of what the "work" was, or who sent him to Lax.[79]

Merton, at around this time, had a stay in the hospital where he was diagnosed with colitis—"they found no ulcers." He was put on a diet in the abbey infirmary and allowed to eat meat. He wrote Lentfoehr that the baroness in Combermere had wanted Lax to be another Benedict Labre, but that "is too heroic. Bob is already a Labre in the ways of the spirit. . . . At the same time he does not have the comfort of feeling that he can subsist without aspirins, dry socks, and a shower-bath every day." He asked if the nun had received from Lax a copy of "Journal of My Escape . . . ," which he, himself, had not seen "in ten years."[80] Sister Thérèse was often Merton's confidant on matters spiritual. He told her how impressed he had been with the devotion that the sisters in the Louisville hospital showed to the rosary, benediction, and the litanies and noted in his journal that "something of Catholicism was lacking in Gethsemani on this account. . . . I would never do without the rosary."[81]

A subsequent letter went to Lentfoehr on the eve of the pronunciation of the dogma of the Assumption during the Marian Year. "I shall have a special prayer for you on tomorrow's big day. This is Our Lady's age in the Church and the definition proves it. . . . What divinely instituted Church would hesitate to declare this dogma on the grounds that a few stuffy English deans would take offence! There is only One Church and she knows what she is doing." That breath-taking remark reflects a faith in the hierarchy that would turn to cynicism in the years to come.[82]

In 1951 Lax headed for Marseilles. The city had been formative for him, connecting him with the fishermen he would become very fond of in later years in Greece. It also confronted him with the writings of St. John of the Apocalypse. James Uebbing writes, in fact, that one of the reasons that Lax would go to Patmos years later was "because there had been a picture of Saint John on the wall of his room in Marseilles. He lived in that room (in a cheap hotel) for months, and in the evening the very last rays of the sun would highlight this portrayal of the Apostle, busily writing in the cave of the Apocalypse. A simple response to a simple moment. Simple matters have shaped Lax's life—a simplicity that is real enough to be disarming at first sight."[83] Uebbing cited the poem "Port City" as a striking manifestation of it.

An excerpt:

> i had
> been coming
> toward that
> city
> since
> the beginning
> of time
>
> i had
> been coming
> toward
> that city
> and singing
> that city's
> song[84]

Merton reported to Sister Lentfoehr that he had heard from Lax in Marseille at just about the time he himself had been made "Master of the Students." He was beginning to send parts of his journal to Harcourt Brace for printing, and he thanked the nun for typing it out. "For the first time my publisher has received from me a legible manuscript. Maybe you ought to get part of the royalties. I heard from Bob [Lax] in Marseille and sent him the poem about St. Agnes (from the journal) which he thinks he will print somehow privately with one of his own and one of Mark Van Doren's." The poems appeared in Lax's poetry flyer, *Pax,* which would debut in 1955 and be distributed to a few hundred friends and colleagues. "I told him to go to La Salette and hope we will all feel the effects of his prayers to Our Lady for us."[85]

A few weeks later he told Lentfoehr of a poem that Lax had sent him, "a beautiful long poem written for Our Lady in Marseilles. . . . Surely that one deserves a place in I SING OF A MAIDEN if you ever revise it!"[86] Soon, however, Lax was headed not for La Salette but in a quite different direction, although he had a spiritual advisor who urged him otherwise. It says a lot about Lax's malleability in those days that he could be influenced by strong, and especially by holy, personalities. "Pere François de Sainte Marie," he told me many years later,

> was from Lisieux, I think. . . . I came to him once with about fifteen things I wanted to do . . . work with poor in Marseilles; live in a cave outside of Marseilles as a hermit; work at L'Eau Vive; a number of other things. They all sounded pretty good. He was sitting there and he just drew a circle and he said, "This is the year, you spend this many months here, this many months doing that, and it was so wise and calm." Days or weeks after I got a letter from Rice saying, "Come home immediately we need you here." And so, there went all those projects.[87]

What Rice needed him for was the launching of what would become *Jubilee* magazine. Rice had continued to work on the concept from 1950 to 1953. At first he had been thinking of putting out a thirty-two-page biweekly that he could offer for fifteen cents a copy. He was optimistic that he could attract national advertising. He had a plan to get ten investors to put up $10,000 each to cover the startup costs, but he couldn't pin down the ten investors.[88] A few months later he came up with a different strategy, suggested by Sister Thérèse. He would get 50,000 subscribers to pay $5 each for a share of stock that would include a year's subscription, giving him $250,000 to pay for "almost two years of publishing" with a goal of reaching 100,000 subscribers "by the end of the first year." That plan proved wildly overoptimistic and was substantially revised before the magazine actually came out in 1953.[89]

Merton's involvement with *Jubilee* was not as immediate as Lax's. He had turned down an offer from James Laughlin to be on the masthead of a publication called *Perspectives,* stating that "it seems better that I should not be. The reason is that Father Abbot has got me refusing all such offers—rightly—otherwise I would be on all sorts of magazines etc etc. . . . I had to say no to Ed Rice too, for his picture magazine."[90]

Fortunately, the abbot did not veto Merton's participation in *Jubilee* as an author and as a personal advisor to Rice. He would write dozens of articles for the magazine over the years and be responsible for persuading many notables to submit pieces.

In May of 1953, the same month that would see the first issue of *Jubilee* come out, Lax had another poem in the *New Yorker*—a harbinger of what would emerge six years later as a complete book of poems under the name *Circus of the Sun*. The small poem was titled simply.

Circus

The silver morning shifts her birds
From tree to tree.
Young green fires burn along
    the branch.
The river moves but each wave holds
    a place—
Pattern of knives above the
    juggling tide.

Now in the south the circus of the sun
Lays out its route, lifts the white tent,
Parades the pachyderm,
And pins the green chameleon
    to the cloth.
Coffee mists rise above the gabbling
    cook tent.
Aerialists web above the tumblers' ring.

Behold! In flaming silk, the acrobat,
The wire-walking sun.[91]

* * * * * * * * * * * * * * * * * *

5

JUBILEE'S HEYDAY

Rice the Mastermind; Lax the Rover; Merton a
Major Contributor; Circus Comes Out

Catholics who remember what a powerful impact *Jubilee* magazine
had on those itching for change in the pre-Vatican II 1950s—lay
and religious alike—are tempted to believe that it was no less than
a twentieth-century intervention by the Holy Spirit. "The church was
dominated by sixteenth- and seventeenth-century Spanish pessimism
in those days," recalls Ed Rice. "I thought this is not God. God is
love. Priests were telling us that God punishes those he loves most, that
women were handmaidens of the Lord. That was wrong. God is your
friend. We tried to reflect that in the magazine."

Tens of thousands of Catholics and many non-Catholics—circulation, including newstand and back-of-the-church sales, was 72,000
at its peak—found that *Jubilee* did just that, providing much-needed
nutrition during a time of meager diet on diocesan pap. *Commonweal*
and *America* and precious little else were available for those trying to
get beyond the church's dogmatism to learn what being Catholic really
ought to mean in the twentieth century. But unlike those worthy publications, largely opinion journals, *Jubilee* had wonderful pictures, taken
by top-notch photographers, marvelous art layouts, beautifully written
stories about Catholics and non-Catholics living extraordinary lives in
ordinary situations. It gave readers objective insight on the spiritual
quests of other Christian sects—Methodists, Lutherans, Quakers,
Shakers, Presbyterians, Congregationalists—and offered well-documented pieces on the other four great religions, Judaism, Buddhism,
Islam, and Hinduism. It exposed many parochial school-educated
Catholics to thinkers they had never heard of—Jacques Maritain, Karl
Barth, Etienne Gilson, Leon Bloy, François Mauriac, Hans Küng, Karl
Rahner, Martin Buber. Many priests and nuns began to look to *Jubilee*
as a literary oasis in their diocesan deserts.

Jubilee was dramatically innovative graphically, and it covered for the first time for American Catholics a lot of not very well known Catholic, Protestant, Jewish, Buddhist, and Hindu thinkers; introduced a number of European and Asian intellectuals, the Montessori movement, Mother Teresa, John Kennedy, Eugene McCarthy. The magazine's impact on laymen was sometimes life changing. James Forest, later one of the founders of the Catholic Peace Fellowship, said, in a 1999 speech, "Among religious magazines, there has been nothing like it before or since. . . . If I should find a chest of gold coins buried in our backyard, I'd love to start it up again. It was one of the publications I read faithfully from the time I entered the Catholic Church—I was 18 when I crossed that border—until it folded."[1]

Some of *Jubilee*'s articles led to movements that have stuck to this day. A good example was the revival of the Montessori method for teaching children. It was sparked by a *Jubilee* story in the September 1953 issue[2] on the late Nancy Rambusch, who began the first new Montessori school in the United States in decades, in Greenwich, Connecticut. This one had a big impact on my own family. My wife, Millie, on reading it, decided that she—a mother of three small children— would take the training to become a certified Montessori teacher. We just upped and moved to Greenwich for a year, renting our home in Princeton, New Jersey, so Millie could be in the first new class of Montessori-qualified teachers. I changed my New York City commute from Princeton to Greenwich, and the two oldest children—Susan, six, and Jimmy, five, enrolled in the Whitby Montessori School, which had been founded by Rambusch and her supporters. Mario Montessori, son of the legendary Maria, founder of the movement in Italy in 1922, personally gave Millie her certificate after nine months training. Returning to Princeton, she and two other women started the Stuart Country Day School of the Sacred Heart, with Millie teaching Montessori to the preschool classes. Stuart today, one of Princeton's architectural gems, has almost five hundred pupils, and has spawned a separate boys school.

Jubilee's cover subhead, *A Magazine of the Church and Her People*, was an apt characterization of its simultaneous loyalty to the church and independence from it. One of its flyers said that "JUBILEE's editors are Catholic laymen, but the magazine encompasses the thoughts, words and actions of all men of good will." It goes on to characterize the magazine with a credo that seems even more badly needed these days than it was fifty years ago, although one winces when noting the exclusively masculine language common in those days.

Jubilee takes an uncompromising position against gee-gaws, claptrap and clutter. Jubilee's normal tone is friendly, fair and helpful. Jubilee doesn't pick needless battles, but since its prime interest is Man and his role in the world, Jubilee is never quiet about the injustices perpetrated in the name of mankind, team play, or "getting the job done." Jubilee reports, examines, interprets (and cajoles) man in relation to his work and play: in politics and international affairs, in the home, office and factory, in his religious and intellectual life. Jubilee pays special attention to the problems that mark our times: the clashes between cultures, the breaking-down of barriers, the demons of the 20th century upon traditional values.

Such promotional rhetoric was backed up strongly by articles that had been covered in prior months:

"Christianity and voodoo." "The patience of God." "War, peace and the A-bomb." "Liturgical music on LP. . . ." "When Al Smith ran for president." "Japan's new literature." "Detroit's Lebanese. . . ." "An American in the USSR." "Notes on art by Thomas Merton." "A national scandal: The plight of Mexican migrants in the U.S." "Taena: A utopian community in practice." "Scholarships for Negroes." "A basic paper-bound library for $35." "Ordination in Dachau." "Am I my brother's keeper?—An Asian speaks to the West." "The Church and the worker." "The sense of silence." "Spain's America." "Psychosis, neurosis and religion." "German war novels." "The Corbusier chapel." "The Ukrainians." "The Church and the Negro." "Dostoyevsky: Dramatist of the Soul." "Jacques Maritain at 74."

The magazine's existence, though, caused pain to some church leaders, notably the archdiocese of New York in the tenure of Francis Cardinal Spellman, one of whose spokesman told Rice that "If the Church needed a picture magazine it would have one."[3]

Rice was a fine writer, an excellent artist, and a gifted photographer himself, but he was also a superb editor and production expert, and spent a large part of his brutal schedule getting other writers, artists, and photographers to work for a pittance; supervising a small staff and an army of volunteers; doing layouts and preparing promotional programs singlehandedly; and fighting with printers and bill collectors. While his frugality and innovative genius enabled him to publish the magazine on a shoestring, he was perpetually in debt.

He accumulated a small pot initially—about $35,000—by selling $100 stock packages to 351 people. Then he sold, for $5, subscriptions that included a $1 share of stock in the enterprise, called AMDG Publishing Company (for *Ad maiorem Dei gloriam,* for the greater glory of God—some of us parochial schoolers were taught by the nuns to write the initials AMDG on our homework). He was following a precept that was inspired by papal encyclicals (Leo XIII's *Rerum Novarum* and Pius XI's *Quadragesimo Anno*). Rice was let down by wealthy Catholics, who never responded to his importunings. I became a member of the magazine's advisory board early on, and personally experienced rebuffs to numerous pleas for investment from some who seemed to be logical prospects. My request for an audience with the Joseph P. Kennedy Foundation never even got an answer in spite of relentless follow-ups. I would ask wealthy Catholics to consider a $25,000 gift, then back down to $250 serial notes, then be happy if I sold a one-year subscription. I was very pleased when one fellow bought twenty. Other affluent Catholics were equally unhelpful. Clare Booth Luce told Rice that instead of pushing *Jubilee* he should join the *Life* staff and make it a better magazine.

Rice recalls that there were some colorful characters on the staff in the early days, and some bad episodes came with the good.

I had to fire a business manager for what today would be called "sexual harassment" of a secretary—who later committed suicide. By and large the staff was hard working—people like Peggy Mannix, Marie Moore, Edith Jones, put in long and arduous days. Robert Reynolds, from Chicago, was hired as managing editor and took on a big load. Ann Cannon ran the book store and was a receptionist. We hired some photographers as young kids who later made national reputations—Charles Harbutt, Jacques Lowe. Lowe had been a refugee, his mother a Jew in France. Later he made a big reputation taking Kennedy family pictures.[4]

But it was Rice who did most of the day-to-day work. "I was editor, managing editor, art editor, and production editor," he recalls. Lax, titled roving editor in recognition of his peripatetic travels, sometimes got Rice angry for not making more consistent contributions, but he submitted both articles and poems, helped attract other writers, and was a charismatic presence for the staff and the Wednesday night cadre of envelope-stuffer volunteers when he was in New York. Lax had not even been aboard in New York when *Jubilee* got started in 1953, although he had been advising Rice about the magazine's concept for several years earlier. Rice had asked him to be managing editor and had sent Lax a prospectus in about 1950. The answer, in letters from

Olean, was that the concept was "tremendous" and suggested a slew of possible magazine titles, his favorite being *Magnificat*.

But Lax's own role would not be so substantive as managing editor. He was off to Paris where he would write poetry, some of it for *Jubilee*, but mostly he worked for a short-lived literary journal named *New Story*, edited by the American Robert Burford. Weekends he would often go on retreat to L'Eau Vive and would get spiritual infusion from one of several Franciscan priests who counseled guests under the giant chestnut trees. Although he would not return to New York until the mid-1950s, he sometimes stimulated articles for *Jubilee* by European Catholic luminaries such as Jacques Maritain.

The first issue of *Jubilee* came out in May 1953 with a beautiful cover story on a not-very-extraordinary subject—Communion dresses. It was illustrated with lovely Jacques Lowe photos. The fare inside was more diverse and hard-hitting. "The Church and the Cold War," by the veteran *Commonweal* writer John Cogley, showed pictures of Ukrainian priests, hooded to avoid reprisals on their relatives, testifying about the terrible acts being committed against the Eastern Catholic Church. Another piece, also with fine photos, showed the work of New York waterfront priest John M. Corridan, later the inspiration for *On the Waterfront*, the movie starring Marlon Brando. There was an insert of eight pages of beautiful woodcuts on thick, lilac-colored paper by the German artist Walter Mellman; the first of many engrossing interviews over the years with brilliant Catholics, this one with John Gilliland Brunini, executive editor of the *Catholic Poetry Society*; a picture story on the beautiful family of a French refinery worker in Normandy; a Bob Lax piece on the Cristiani circus; a profile of Venerable Bede, the eighth-century English Benedictine scholar, by Sister Thérèse Lentfoehr; and a picture story on Manhattanville College of the Sacred Heart. To Catholics supposed to be guided by the Legion of Decency movie pronouncements on what was and what was not see-able, Frank Getlein's intelligent movie reviews were startling, including one on the fine film *Man on a Tightrope*, having to do with Communism in Czechoslovakia, that "contains no preaching on the American way."

The reaction to the issue from readers, particularly the clergy, was ecstatic. A Benedictine monk from St. Meinrad's in Indiana wrote, "Keep up this pace and you'll rejuvenate the whole Catholic press. May your circulation go up in leaps and bounds." A Maryknoll priest said, "Jubilee takes its place in the front ranks of all Catholic magazines." But long-suffering laymen were enthusiastic too. A Pennsylvania reader said, "Every literate or illiterate Catholic should eventually be a subscriber."

Merton finally got permission from the abbot to write a piece for *Jubilee*. It was about St. Bernard of Clairvaux, and it appeared in the magazine's fourth issue, in August 1953. He sent the article to Rice via Sister Thérèse, remarking cautiously that Rice should "check it out with the New York diocesan censors "just in case."[5] That article[6] tipped his hand on the kind of message he thought twentieth-century Catholics ought to be getting by characterizing the twelfth-century Cistercian in words that might well have applied to himself. Bernard, he wrote, "was a great contemplative. And because he was a contemplative he never ceased fearing to be a mere man of action."

At the time, he did not even know if *Jubilee* had made its debut, writing that "the copy that may or may not have been sent me got into the ashcan instead [he eventually got it]."[7] He actually missed Rice's deadline for the article, but it got in anyway. He told Lentfoehr that "I cannot meet deadlines, I fear. . . . It seems that monks do not belong in magazines." Nonetheless, Merton would write many articles for the magazine over the fifteen years of its life, and he would continue to encourage Rice. "Tell him from me," he wrote Lentfoehr, "to keep his chin up & that we are praying for his magazine to succeed, if God wills it."[8] Subsequent Merton pieces over the years included many that nudged Catholics toward action.

Others pushed for more aggressive attitudes by the church in the direction of unity with other religions, a subject on which Merton was passionate. His biographer, Michael Mott, quotes a strong entry from one of his restricted journals dated April 28, 1957. It seems almost arrogant in the implication that what he did personally was crucial to the cause of Christian unity:

If I can unite in myself, *in my own spiritual life*, the thought of the East and the West, of the Greek and Latin Fathers, I will create in myself a reunion of the divided Church and from that unity in myself can come the exterior and visible unity of the Church. For if we want to bring together East and West we cannot do it by imposing one upon the other. We must contain both in ourselves, and transcend both in Christ.[9]

Through Merton's intercession there were contributions from many noted writers whose views of their faith were eclectic—Brother Antoni-nus (William Everson), Daniel Berrigan, Henri de Lubac, Ernesto Carde-nal, Jean Danielou, Dorothy Day, Dom Aelred Graham, John Howard Griffin, Jacques Maritain. Also a contributor was the aforementioned Sister Thérèse Lentfoehr, a member of the *Jubilee* advisory board who would have a prodigious correspondence with Merton over many years. Revelatory, to Catholics at least, were articles on Buddhism from such authorities as Thich Nhat Hanh and John Wu, both Merton correspondents. Merton's letters to Lax, Rice, and Sister Thérèse over *Jubilee*'s lifetime reflect his deep involvement in the magazine and the issues on his mind.

One of the early subscribers was Emil Wcela, later a Long Island bishop, who had been a seminarian when *Jubilee* made its debut.

At Immaculate Conception Seminary in Huntington we were interested in liturgical reform and the role of the laity and Jubilee was dealing with those subjects. Jubilee was stylish, a real step forward in Catholic publishing, it caught the spirit of the times. Nobody knew what was happening in the Church in those days . . . we were interested in reports on the religious life, and so Merton's articles were devoured. . . . Jubilee broadened our perspective . . . up to that time we were essentially exposed to one book—a theological manual.[10]

The morale of the staff soared. However, there were personnel problems. Besides the sexual harassment case cited earlier, two young staffers died of cancer, one woman jumped to her death from a window, and Rice had to deal regularly with the emotional problems of his severely overworked people. He had his own family problems, as well, as his Episcopalian wife, Margery, although initially supportive of the venture, began to resent the magazine's drain on Rice's time and finances.

By and large the staff was very competent, very hard working, and some were promoted from volunteer to clerical to editorial work. Oona Sullivan, later a Ford Foundation executive, followed that route and eventually became managing editor. She remembers that Rice offered to upgrade her from volunteer to secretary in a letter (1956) while she was on vacation in Italy:

the hours are long and the work is hard and all the rewards are in heaven. Besides secretarial work, you'll also have to do some research and writing and possibly some routine promotional jobs. We can pay $60.

Rice couldn't resist asking his unhired staffer for "foreign reports" if she knew of any.[11] He was enterprising in coming up with ways to get articles, even from foreign countries, without paying for travel. Bernhard Moosbrugger, later head of Pendo Verlag, Zurich, which would publish many of Lax's poetry books, went on assignment to South America with his partner, Gladys Weigner, with tickets given *Jubilee* in 1956 in payment for ads in the magazine from an Argentine airline. He stopped in Brazil, where Weigner wrote a cover story, with lovely photos by Moosbrugger himself, about the famed cleric who championed the poor, Dom Helder Camara.[12]

Jacques Lowe recalls having been assigned by Ed Rice to go to Europe in the mid-'50s, traveling steerage, to make photos for several *Jubilee* stories. Lax was to be the writer.

So I landed in Paris and went to Lax's office in the old building where *L'Humanité* [the Communist newspaper] was. It was a tiny office occupied by *New Story* magazine, which was edited by Lax's friend, Bob Burford. Burford was behind his beat-up desk, Lax sitting on top another desk. I told Lax which stories we were supposed to do: Catholic youth, Sisters of Mercy, a few others. He said, "Relax, relax, these are boring stories. We'll go see the gypsies, and the circus in the south of France."

"What do those stories have to do with *Jubilee*? I asked."

"Everything has to do with *Jubilee*," he said. "Don't tell Rice, we'll just do the stories."

There was a big transportation strike in Paris so we hitchhiked all the way to Ste Marie de la Mer, the gypsies' gathering place. "Let's go see the King of the Gypies," Lax said, and we walked up to his trailer and Bob identified himself as an American journalist and said, "We'd like to go around the camp first, and in the meantime Jacques would like to leave his camera bag here (I suppose he didn't want the gypsies upset right away by the sight of a camera)." I nearly pissed in my pants. I had a single old Nikon with two lenses, the only camera I owned, but we left it with the King and, of course, it was safer there than it would have been in a bank vault. And we got a wonderful story.[13]

In spite of his resourcefulness and frugality, however, Rice was always under the gun for money. In 1958 he sent this memo to members of his editorial advisory board:

I'm sure all of you will remember many days during this time when it looked as if we would never publish another issue.

Each year is somewhat better than the previous one, but when we are still unable to make ends meet this is like saying that we are less poor than ever before. The 1957 fiscal year was the best we've ever had, on an overall basis. It started strongly, but immediately after Easter we experienced a disastrous slump which almost finished us [income was off $11,000 from the $40,000 of 1956]. We were fortunate in sparking a revival with the July issue, which sold some 72,000 copies [our basic sale was then about 44,000 copies monthly]. The August issue sold 55,000 copies, the December issue, 60,000. These sales and a fair amount of advertising, plus the rental of our expired subscribers list, gave us the strongest two quarters of our history. . . .

We have been severely handicapped by a shortage of personnel. Bob Lax has been seriously ill since August with arthritis and is just beginning to feel better. Bob Reynolds [who had shared a heroic burden with Rice] left in September to work with *American Heritage*; he has not been replaced, partly because we have not been able to find the right editor, partly because of the tight budget. We could use more secretarial help. . . . [14]

The advisory board was in no position to provide much financial advice. Members, besides myself, included several liberal-minded priests and nuns such as Mother Eleanor O'Byrne, then president of Manhattanville College of the Sacred Heart, Reverend John Osterreicher, author of books on Jewish-Catholic dialogue, and Sister Thérèse Lentfoehr. They were more likely to be able to either write for the magazine or suggest authors than to provide advice or initiative in getting money or advertisers. Advertisers, alas, never did come through in great numbers. Reasonably loyal were Catholic book publishers—Sheed & Ward, P. J. Kenedy, Universe Books, Pantheon Books, Newman Press, Doubleday Image books. Other ads came, sometimes, from the Irish Tourist Bureau, Gethsemani Trappist cheese, and a distributor of yellow and green Chartreuse liqueurs. But there weren't enough.

Jubilee became a spawning ground for young writers who would go on to brilliant careers, such as Richard Gilman, Ned O'Gorman, and Wilfrid Sheed. "Our artists and writers were a bit crazy. They could not have worked on a staid magazine," says Rice. "Actually *Jubilee* was a kind of extension of *Jester*—an unstructured creation. I tried a structure, with departments, but it didn't work."[15]

Crucial to the magazine's rising reputation was the month in, month out work of Rice's two old and dear friends from *Jester* days—Lax and Merton. Merton wrote dozens of articles for *Jubilee* over the years, was responsible for attracting many authors, and Rice gives him much credit for the magazine's initial impact. "A lot of Catholics," he says, "were struck emotionally by Merton's book [*The Seven Storey Mountain*] and his ordination. I think Merton started a whole new movement and that he is still the most significant religious figure in the world today. He told the Church to bug off. He was thinking and writing about what was important."[16] It now seems clear that Rice's risk in starting *Jubilee* had been greatly reduced by the meteoric success of *SSM*, which had been published only about five years before *Jubilee* appeared in 1953.

Pals from the old Columbia *Jester*'s crowd pitched in in the early years as well, including Ad Reinhardt, then gaining reputation as a painter, who made marvelous black-and-white sketches to illustrate some of the articles.

Volunteers were abundant and willing. It was the era of Addressograph plates, and many an hour was spent by earnest, mostly young, single and idealistic Catholics, carrying trays of them, entering subscriptions, changing addresses. Romance came along sometimes, as when one staffer, Jillen Ahearn, married photographer Jacques Lowe. Alas, the marriage didn't stick, although the union produced a daughter, Victoria, whose godfather is Lax. Lax, Ahearn-Lowe remembers, "took care of our hearts and souls. He was my spiritual teacher . . . he'd meet with me in the cafeteria up the street and we'd sit there for hours." As for her job on *Jubilee*, she says, "I was a slave—worked for $28-30 a week in an airless, windowless back room doing address changes, writing letters to subscribers." But she was happy to be around Lax, Rice—"he had vision, humor, intelligence"—and such other writers as Wilfrid Sheed and Richard Gilman. Of Gilman, later a drama critic for the *New York Times* and a professor at the Yale Drama School, she said, "I was his first fan—he would write long, brilliant historical articles and then nervously read them to me." She says that the *Jubilee* staff had a "passionate camaraderie . . . we totally believed in our mission."[17]

Gilman has written of his *Jubilee* days in a memoir. A Jew who became a Catholic, he remembered that the church, before his conversion, "seemed to me pinched, blind and joyless; it gave off an atmosphere of sullen ignorance, of meanness precisely in the realm of the spirit."[18] *Jubilee*, by contrast, "purveyed humanism within a Catholic framework"[19] with a staff imbued with what Gilman called "a spirit of democratic ardor."[20] When he came to Rice looking for a job in 1954 he was asked to sell subscriptions. He was spectacularly unsuccessful. Getting potential customers—mostly parish priests—to buy "was like trying to talk to eskimos." Eventually he became an editor, and he recalls working ten- to twelve-hour days at $60 a week, and becoming, he says, responsible for about half the writing in each issue, sometimes using pseudonyms such as "Boris Yampolsky" (to give authority to articles on Russian Orthodoxy). He also reviewed books and remembers getting a thank you for one review, and a subscription renewal, from Flannery O'Connor, who became his friend until her death. Lax was an important presence to Gilman, a "secular monk," he calls him, but with a "Jewish, almost Talmudic, flavor to his wit." He remembers receiving a postcard from Lax that said, "Where There's an Oy, There's a Vey."[21]

Gilman remembers Rice as "[a]n aloof, unemotional man . . . I remember telling him once that if a boss couldn't pay his workers much money then he ought to give them love, but the truth was he did neither." The fact is, however, that the staff had much admiration for their skilled and devoted editor, and Gilman concedes that morale was always "amazingly high."[22]

But severe financial problems hovered constantly. To boost income the imaginative staff came up with resourceful, sometimes offbeat, ideas. An article on Chancery handwriting produced a bonanza of orders for the Osmiroid pens it called for. There were Our Lady of Monserrat statuettes, paper umbrellas, and a Book Club. Prices were cheap, too cheap one would think, in retrospect. For $10 one could get a book per month for six months by such authors as François Mauriac, Ronald Knox, Anne Fremantle, and Merton. A ten-months introductory subscription was offered for $3. Merton's morality play, *The Tower of Babel*, was available for 25¢, and no charge for shipping and handling! Even taking into account the fifty-year-plus passage of time the prices seem ridiculously low.

Content of the magazine, looking back on some of the issues, was of remarkably consistent high quality. Beautifully photographed stories on off-the-curve Catholics like the stigmatic Padre Pio were balanced by pieces on exemplary diocesan figures. A twelve-page article on the diocese of Worcester, Massachusetts, showed Bishop John J. Wright, then in his forties, saying a funeral Mass, investing new priests, broadcasting the rosary on radio, saying a Mass for shut-ins, and administering to a family of French-Canadian parishioners. Wright's message to those Catholics who might not have been without bigotry: "The Church has no nationality. Its language is prayer." And another to those who might have harbored anti-intellectualism: "Perhaps Father John Tracy Ellis is accurate in his suggestion that such conformity may be part of the pattern by which our people have in all things sought to demonstrate how thoroughly 'American' they are . . . contempt for the intellectual life is . . . utterly out of harmony with authentic Catholic tradition."[23]

A great deal of attention was paid to other than Roman Catholic Christians. James Forest, who had been with the Catholic Worker and is now head of the Orthodox Peace Fellowship, based in Holland, remarked in a 1999 speech about the generous space *Jubilee* gave to the Orthodox community:

> In the hundred or so issues I looked through, there was hardly one that didn't have something in it about eastern Christianity. It might be a photo portrait of life in St. Catherine's monastery on the Sinai or a text about the Desert Fathers or something as small as an ad promoting the sale, by Jubilee, of icon reproductions or recordings of Byzantine chant. A question I cannot answer is what inspired Jubilee's passionate engagement in what must have seemed to many readers a somewhat esoteric form of Christianity. Was Jubilee helping fuel Merton's interest in the Orthodox Church, or was it mirroring his interest?
>
> In any event, Merton was deeply moved by photos of Orthodox monastic life that would appear in Jubilee. I recall Merton showing me a photo in Jubilee of an Athonite monk, a man who looked older than Abraham. He was standing behind a long battered table in the refectory while in the background was a huge fresco of the Last Judgement. The monk's head was bowed slightly. His eyes seemed to contain the cosmos. "Look at him," Merton said. "This guy has been kissed by God!"[24]

Merton was a constant promoter of the magazine, sometimes exaggerating Rice's privations as publisher in his exhortations to get his friends and correspondents to subscribe. He wrote to one friend, an English schoolteacher, John Harris, who was responsible for putting Merton in touch with Boris Pasternak, about "a magazine you ought to know about, Jubilee . . . edited by my godfather, Ed Rice, who lives in a slum with his wonderful wife and kids, in order to put everything he has in producing *one* decent magazine in this country (Commonweal is fair, and so is Cross Currents)."[25] The Rice home was hardly a slum, but, in fact, it had been rough on Rice's family getting the magazine started. His account of the early years:

> When we got married Margery resigned from the job she had at ABC. Ted was born in 1951 and Chris in 1954. We were living at 58 Bank Street, then 150 Waverly Place. At first Margery was behind the project. Then the work load I was carrying and the time I was spending got to her. I was editor, managing editor, art editor, production editor. I put in 12 hour days routinely. I was still

working at Warner Pathe for $105 a week. I would go to Jubilee at 7:30 A.M. after feeding the kids. I would also have fed them at 1 A.M. I got to Warner Pathe, would work on a U.S. or Canadian news reel, maybe do Spanish and Portuguese newsreels for Latin America, then go off to Jubilee. Margery told me I should get a job on Wall Street and make some money.[26]

Wilfrid Sheed, who was on the *Jubilee* staff from 1959 to 1961, recalls it as

a hot place to be in those years . . . there were all these characters dropping in—Kerouac might come in with a jug of Muscat and some poetry he had written on the subway . . . it was a place where Catholics had a chance to meet each other. There were vibrant theologians, like Yves Congar . . . and we had good parties . . . the volunteers were a part of the place. . . . I remember volunteers like Joe Califano's wife [secretary of labor under Lyndon Johnson]. . . .[27]

Sheed recalls

we strove to outslob each other in dress—if neckties were worn, it was around the waist—and my own particular makeshift office consisted of a drawing board in the middle of a clearing, from which I could hear every conversation in the joint. Rice had practically a real office in which we tended to eat sandwiches, and Robert Lax had another next to the fire escape, so that he could duck onto it and crouch when he didn't feel like visitors.[28]

"We were all drawn to Lax," he said, "although he wrote little for the magazine . . . as an editor he would reduce the text as much as he could. You didn't want Lax to get near your papers. He'd unsort them. One day he totally messed mine up. He was so mild that, if you went to the local Lebanese restaurant with him he'd always order what you ordered . . . there was something monastic about him."

Ed Rice, said Sheed, hardly talked. "'Nice piece' is all you might get from him. He wasted a lot of time trying to get money, without success, out of rich Catholics." Rice's notable unsuccess in this work was one of the reasons why the staff was paid meagerly. "I got about $50 a week," Sheed recalls, "but I only went to work a couple of days a week. I would sit at a desk, be given a clipboard and told to 'straighten this out,' 'look at this press release.' Sheed understates his contributions. His movie reviews were extremely literate, and pungent, although his father, Frank Sheed, founder of the Sheed & Ward publishing company with his wife, Maisie Ward, once said that "Wilfrid reviews movies the way a pigeon reviews monuments." Sheed eventually quit to go to Spain. "Then I went to work at *Commonweal* and my pay was doubled."[29]

Another major contributor to *Jubilee* was Peter White, who came from the family of the famous architect Stanford White. He lived in Box Hill, the once-luxurious manor house built by Stanford in a wealthy enclave in St. James, Long Island. A graduate of the class of 1938 at Harvard, where he studied history and music, his father—a nonchurchgoing Episcopalian—was a senior partner in McKim White (Stanford White's firm). Peter went to Germany to school in 1932-33.

> I could read French and German so one of my early assignments for *Jubilee* was to review the play *The Deputy*, written by the German author Rolf Hochhuth.
>
> I realized that some five and a half hours had been cut from the original German version for its New York presentation. . . . The play raised a lot of questions. It dealt with a story that the pope (Pius XII, Eugenio Pacelli) had gotten word from some Catholic German officers that the Jews were being rounded up in Holland. He told the Dutch bishops about this. The Germans intercepted the pope's coded message and were angry. . . . I was interviewed about the play on TV and got a lot of flack from the clergy for not defending the pope. . . . [30]

White was one of the *Jubilee* staff members assigned by Rice to develop questionnaires about topical subjects, selected for their timeliness and, perforce, sensitivity. "We did one asking the clergy about their satisfaction with the Church and got some explosive answers. The Chancery let it be known that they did not like the magazine."[31]

Most issues of the magazine included well-written pieces on the liturgy, the saints, and other Catholic staples. But *Jubilee* made a mark with articles on outstanding Catholics largely unknown to most readers—the artist Sister Corita, the British economist Barbara Ward, the spiritual writers Yves Congar, Karl Barth, Henri Nouwen, and a young Albanian nun named Mother Teresa of Calcutta, who made *Jubilee* her first stop when she came to the United States.

Rice was constantly innovating and experimenting with production techniques.

We tried a lot of ideas—like children's pullouts, one I remember was for a "Daniel in the Lions' Den" piece that worked quite well. . . . We developed techniques for using black and four-color as cheap as black and one-color, any way to be creative and still save money because we were always behind in our printing bills and sometimes got threats from the printer.

Merton sent in a fantastic list of ideas. We did stories on the Orthodox churches, Hinduism, Buddhism. Some priests would write to us and say we shouldn't be publishing this heretical stuff. I didn't care and Merton didn't. There were, however, some articles that I wish I had not done—like one on women as handmaidens to the Lord. We did an eight-page article on birth control and got a letter from a priest saying this was not a topic for discussion. But we got heart-rending letters from readers. We also did a piece on "Why They Leave the Church" and another on "Divorced Catholics." Those caused complaints from Cardinal Spellman via Monsignor Kellenberg, who later became a bishop.[32]

Rice sometimes gave assignments to people who simply showed up on his doorstep, as long as he didn't have to pay them. Charles Harbutt, later a noted photographer, recalled that in 1955, when he was twenty and about to be a senior in journalism at Marquette University, he went to see Rice with an idea for an article on the last boatload of displaced persons coming to the United States under the Catholic Refugee Services program. "Ed said go ahead. . . . I met the boat in New York, with no instructions from Ed—he never gave any, it was wonderful—and I photographed and wrote what became an eight- to ten-page article, my first published story."[33]

Harbutt was hired at $25 a week when he got out of Marquette, and, since *Jubilee* had no darkroom, he used one above Ad Reinhardt's painting studio on Broadway and Waverly. He stayed on the *Jubilee* staff until 1959 doing both photography and writing. Stories ranged from one on the Swiss monks who brewed Grande Chartreuse to one on a parish priest's efforts to get better working conditions for migratory farm workers in South Jersey.

"Both Rice and Lax were good text editors," he remembers. "If you worked with Lax you didn't need Strunk and White. My eight pages of pictures and his forty words caught the whole story." Harbutt made the pictures for another Lax story on the Cristiani circus, and later did the cover picture for Lax's *Circus of the Sun*. "We all felt that Lax was a saint, a kind of mysterious, clown saint."[34]

The fact is that Lax didn't stay around *Jubilee* very long after its beginnings. His title as roving editor was on the mark because he seemed always to be banging around Europe, and he was constantly working on his *Circus* poem. A letter sent back to *Jubilee* and some other friends in June 1954 from Corps d'Isère in the French Alps—where he had been staying at the monastery of Notre Dame de la Salette—asks for names from *Jubilee*'s Addressograph files so he could send circular letters to "one or three hundred . . . friends and *pax* subscribers [his own slim poetry magazine, which appeared irregularly for a few years starting in 1955]. . . ." He wrote: "i get here yesterday with a big wicker basket and a trunk, three suitcases and a typewriter, this is more business than i have ever ridden around with."

One of Lax's visitors at la Salette was Mark Van Doren, who remembered that

I shall not forget the delight in his long face as it looked out from a window where he was waiting . . . as he walked with us up and down the paths of the orchard and garden. He did not know the name of any plant or tree, but he knew how beautiful each one of them was, and he still knew—but without speech—how unspeakably fair the whole of creation looks when nothing is permitted to stand in its way.[35]

Merton got a card from Lax at la Salette that simply said, "Hoy!" "I don't need more than that to know he is happy," he commented in a note to Sister Thérèse.[36] Lax himself wrote Sister Thérèse that it is the "most peaceful place in the world & one of the most wonderful. Very close here to you and Tom and Ed. The air—the rocks—the water—the character of all things here is stern, and gentle—rare. Yet recognizable. Had a happy time too at Lisieux—thanks for sending me on that errand."[37]

Lax's friends would hear several times from the Corps d'Isère mountain top, a site so beautiful that even today one thinks of going there. The communications were, typically, postcards of four or five words decorated with a tiny yellow sun. But on one occasion, very much an exception, he included a piece of prose, not often used once he began his abbreviated style of poetry.

thinking again about grass, trees and mountains, the little lakes, the flowers, i was thinking about the thing to do with nature, when you're out among nature is to listen to it, and watch it, and look deep into its eyes in a sense, as though you were listening to and watching a friend, not just hearing the words or even just watching the gestures but trying to guess, or get a sense, or share the spirit underneath it, trying to listen (if this isn't too fancy) to the silence under the sound and trying to get an idea (not starting with any pre-conceived formulation) of what kind of a silence it is. how's nature feeling today, this minute, what does she seem to be saying, what is she trying to say with all her trees grass flowers and mountains she cannot. there is a kind of opening up of the floodgates (of consciousness) of the soul, which lets all nature, all the summer-green, sky-blue phenomena rush in, and all the black nothing beneath it, and all the silence under it, and all the twisting spirit that motivates it, and will not let it rest, but pushes it forward, and all the joyous calm beneath it, that speaks the final word. you see and hear. . . .

. . . so that when you speak (if you have listened as you should) you speak not only for yourself but for all of nature (leaves and streams) and also for her Lord. . . .

. . . And so our life becomes not only an imitation (and a sharing in the life of) Christ who comes to us in the darkness of mystical adoration, but also of his multitudinous reflections (innumerable facets in harmonious continuity) of His power, wisdom, and love, which we have seen and heard—absorbed into ourselves and rendered back—of His magnificent and inexhaustible creation.

The letter that included this prose also contained verses that already show the minimalist style that would become his hallmark, "written in bewildering circumstances somewhere near Villeneuve-St. Georges":

I
climb
a ladder
of swords
&
juggle
torches

all up

and
down
the other side:

step
off

the
bottom
rung,

swing
the torches
till
they
smoulder,

lay
them
on the
ground
&
bow.

Also in this letter is a record of who was on the staff or a member of the close-in *Jubilee* family—some forty-three people he wanted to "say hello to."[38]

In 1954 Lax published what would be his last poem in the *New Yorker*, enriching that issue's humor and giving debut in the magazine to his new terse style. It was titled "Solomon's High Dive." He later said, and he could have been kidding, that he had gotten wise to the magazine's practice of paying $6 a line for its poetry, and therefore the three words, 26 letters plus exclamation point, strung together at the end of this poem—precipitevolissimevolmente!—earned him $163 [editor's note: Sol Solomon is a carnival high diver]:

Wisdom plunges with a full gainer
layout into the lake of fire;
Sol Solomon
scrambles with the speed of a spider,
the ape's agility, and nautical grace
to the top of the ladder;
on hangman's platform,
with lifted arms,
his hands rain benediction on the crowd.
The music stops,
lake blazes,
and Sol plunges;

wisdom, with full turn, plummets
into the fiery pool.

P
r
e
c
i
p
i
t
e
v
o
l
i
s
s
i
m
e
v
o
l
m
e
n
t
e
!

The phoenix rising splashes flame.
Sol Solomon, sun of wisdom,
climbs from the tank, bows to
beholders, and flicks back
into the dark.[39]

Lax returned to New York in the mid-1950s and lived, primitively, in an apartment paid for by *Jubilee*, more a flophouse than an apartment. Tom Cornell recalled that when he was in college in Connecticut in 1956, Lax invited him to live in the place, in characteristic Laxian hospitality. The two had met through a mutual friend, Joe Rush of the

Catholic Worker, at an Irish bar near Penn Station. As Cornell recalled the experience in an article in CW years later, the apartment, on Avenue A and 11th Street, was

[u]p three flights, apt dark, bulb burned out, Bob felt around and found a bed. "You can sleep here." Next A.M.: four others in apt (3 rooms, condemned for human habitation after WW I but reopened to meet housing crunch after WW II, not painted "since the fall of the Czar") . . . bought a pack of bulbs and put them in and moved in Sept after buying a bucket of paint and a brush. Jubilee paid the rent on this apt and a twin next door as "hospitality suites" for visiting writers. One WC for 4 apts on landing. Bathtub in each kitchen. No heat or hot water. $20 a month rent. Other Jubilee apt guests had key to use their stove and fridge. Cold!
. . . Rarely speaking, Bob Lax was a presence. Living with this mainly silent man, I learned how important simple presence can be. He was there. That glum, bitter cold winter of '56-'57 subdued us all. There was not much of Bob's playful nature on show. I huddled in the only stuffed chair we had, with my overcoat on, reading, while Bob stalked. He needed space to walk back and forth to compose his lines. Finally, he and Joe found a heated apartment on Ludlow Street that had a corridor he could walk. But by then, the cold had seeped into Bob's bones, always to burden his health.[40]

Lax's cousin Soni Holman remembered how quiet the poet could be. "He had a wonderful capacity for listening," she recalled,

but he could also be quiet for long periods. I remember going with him to John Slate's house. Bob had just come back from France and we took him to a Ravi Shankar concert and belly dance. Slate said, "Hi" and the two sat there, with hardly any words exchanged. . . . They had a kind of symbolic language—chuckle, words, pause. He talked the same way with Reinhardt.[41]

Alfred Isacsson, a Carmelite priest now attached to Transfiguration Church, Tarrytown, N.Y., recalled how spiritual a person Lax was.

This bearded man in a long overcoat used to come to our first Mass [at Our Lady of the Scapular, 28th St & First Ave], 6:45 A.M., which I invariably celebrated. I felt so sorry for him because he seemed so cold in the New York winter and he was so friendly. . . . one day our provincial, Donald O'Callaghan, saw me talk to this man and told me to invite him down to our dining room for a cup of coffee. For an outsider to come into our dining room in 1959 was unheard of but the bearded and overcoated man made the grade. He became a regular. It was only then that I learned his name was Bob Lax. Being a St Bonaventure alumnus, I knew well of Thomas Merton and Bob Lax.[42]

Lax wrote a poem about Elias the Prophet, founder of the Carmelites, for *The Scapular*, the magazine that Isacsson edited. Isacsson said the poem, for which he paid Lax "a few dollars," is as much a self-portrait of Lax as it is about Elias:

Nobody knows what makes a man a prophet. He usually doesn't want to be one anyway. God builds a fire in him; then he begins to do the things a prophet does, and to be what a prophet is.

He works at every moment with the Holy Spirit; he learns to choose. He watches and listens: not to every sight and every sound; but to the sight that is a sign, the sound that is a whisper of the Lord.[43]

The *Jubilee* staff—except for Rice, Lax, and later Ned O'Gorman—never got to meet the monastery-bound Merton, although it is fair to say that most staff members read his books avidly, and Rice would pass around his periodic Merton letters. In his roundup preface to the August 1953 issue, Rice wrote that ever since *SSM* had been published, five years earlier, there were rumors about Merton's status, that he

had left the Trappist monastery . . . become a Carthusian , a Jesuit, a Franciscan, that he had taken a wife and gone to Hollywood to live on his new found wealth and direct the story of his life. Other reports claimed that he had flown to Rome to advise the Pope, he had broken away from the Trappists to start a new order. He was seen on the beach at Cannes and in the gambling casinos of Monte Carlo. He was reported dying of rare and mysterious ailments; remote cousins of friends of the rumor bearer, lying in the adjoining hospital bed, had indeed witnessed Merton's last moments.[44]

In fact, Merton was, as Rice put it, "safe and sound in Gethsemani, living the austere and humble life of a Trappist monk," and he was at an apex of his productivity.

Since *Jubilee* travel money was virtually nonexistent, staff often depended on the generosity of the subjects of the articles, sometimes sleeping in church rectories, as Harbutt recalls. "Days were long—10 to 9 usually—and raises infrequent. . . . I was upped to $75 a week when I got married."

Although sensitive issues were covered—like contraception—the magazine eschewed politics. But articles about political personalities who were living exemplary lives were good fare. The thirty-seven-year-old Democratic congressman from Minnesota, Eugene McCarthy, later a candidate for president, got a six-page picture story in August 1953 because he "Brings Christian Principles to Politics" [and is] . . . "strongly influenced by the Benedictine approach."[45] Reynolds and Gilman wanted *Jubilee* to endorse Adlai Stevenson in his 1956 run, says Harbutt, but Rice and Lax felt it would be a mistake.

Especially memorable to Harbutt is a 1959 story about Fidel Castro. "There was a kind of Lincoln Brigade of artists, including me, who got on a plane to Havana on January 2, 1959. Batista had left Cuba on December 31, 1958. I wrote a 'Report from Cuba' for *Jubilee*'s March 1959 issue, after that trip." Using the pseudonym "Manuel Garcia" [Rice, as mentioned by Gilman, was not above using pen names to make it look as if he had more people on his staff], Harbutt reported, among other things, that "a dynamic organization of Catholic intellectuals . . . were members of one or another of the revolutionary factions and a few have managed to gain responsible jobs in the new government." But Harbutt's views, like many others at the time, proved to be overly roseate. He concluded that "in the long run, Castro's reform can do little but good for Cuba."

Harbutt's involvement with activist Catholics was at a peak during the days of *Jubilee*. He had been a conscientious objector and had worked with Ammon Hennessy of the *Catholic Worker* who, according to the diocese of New York, "had an erroneous conscience." Harbutt became involved with the Association of Catholic Trade Unionists, siding with the cemetery strikers against his own diocese. His fervor for Catholicism was eventually quenched when he and his wife were threatened with excommunication by their Brooklyn diocese for having Mass in their home. He started to feel "screw it about official Catholicism. It seemed at pains to assert that whatever I believed wasn't kosher." These days Harbutt is a nonbeliever.[46]

Harbutt was not the only one naïve about Castro. Here is what Merton wrote in the same year to Sister Thérèse:

I am enthusiastic about Fidel Castro in Cuba: a terrfic [*sic*] person, who against all odds (both the U.S. and the Reds were lined up with Batista against him!) has liberated Cuba for the sake of an ideal and not for political gain. He is a good Catholic, and the Archbishop of Santiago once intervened and saved his life when he was likely to have been killed.[47]

Another of *Jubilee*'s passions was for high-quality religious art, a subject in which not only Rice, but Merton and Lax as well, had extremely strong views. Merton laid his on the line in a November 1956 article. He came down hard on much Christian art, and did not spare the monasteries. "Religious art is practically dead," he wrote. "The total insensitiveness to the sacred, and to the life and character which enable an art to measure up to the holiness of God's house and of divine worship, is a disturbing symptom of the ills of our time. . . . This insensivity . . . is the fault of materialistic society . . . the only thing monastic orders as such have done for art in our times has been the revival of the Gregorian chant [by the Benedictines] at Solesmes."[48] He later wrote to Sister Thérèse that he didn't realize that his article would come out "looking so belligerent."

During these heyday years roving editor Bob Lax turned out some wonderful articles from Europe. While not showing up at the same pace that Rice hoped for, they were artistic and poetic gems. Not as accomplished a photographer as Rice, or the *Jubilee* professionals like Harbutt, Lowe, and Frank Monaco, Lax nevertheless had a perceptive lens. His May 1956 article on *Piccolo Casa*, Turin's Little House of Divine Providence, was beautifully written and the pictures were marvelous. The *Casa* was actually a hospital city of 9,000 people, mostly rejects from other hospitals.

Jubilee was well in the vanguard of publications dealing straightforwardly with racial subjects. An article in 1955 revealing some of the problems that Negro Catholics had with their church produced a barrage of favorable letters.

Jubilee pumped exuberantly for practices it felt that Catholics were neglecting, like reading the Bible. Merton might have had an influence on Rice's decision to deal with that subject, having complained to Lentfoehr that Christians knew very little about the Old Testament. In agreement was the English Catholic Alexander Jones, who wrote a piece that said, "It is ominous and disturbing . . . that the word 'Bible' has a Protestant ring in Catholic ears. . . ." He then came out strongly for Catholic families to purchase the remarkable new *Jerusalem Bible*, a one-volume distillation from forty-three books compiled by the Ecole Biblique.[49]

Merton eventually published in the magazine what he described as "about the eighth version" of his *Tower of Babel* play, which Rice sold to readers for 25¢ a copy. Merton sent Sister Thérèse, in 1955, the full manuscript of the play and in the enclosure letter told her of his continual difficulty with the censors. "I finally caught on to why your Christmas present did not reach me: it was the book about the Carthusians. . . . Anything eremetical is considered bad for cenobites, and it is kept outside the iron curtain. . . ."[50] The next year he reported to his nun friend that

In the last year Father Abbot has requested that I gradually cut off all writing activities. . . .

. . . with me writing is less a talent than an addiction. Father Abbot hopes I can be cured of it now, and so do I. . . . I have been at the typewriter since the second year of my novitiate, and it has not all been worth while or healthy for me, even though Our Lord has seen fit to bring good out of it for many souls. I am glad to have the respite from writing, with the few special ones with whom I was still in contact, like you, and one or two Benedictines in France, and Dom Leclercq, and Ed and Bob and Ad Reinhardt and a few like that. . . .[51]

In his twenty-seven years at Gethsemani, Merton, although in constant correspondence with Lax and Rice, was visited by them infrequently, although perhaps more frequently than by any others. Merton recalled a visit from Lax in 1956 in a letter to Sister Thérèse,

Bob Lax was down. It was the first time I had seen him in seven years and he was in good form. It was a happy visit, and I was glad to see him again, though he no longer has a great mane of hair. Jubilee, it turns out, is going to print some of the Sacred Art notes [referred to above], and I am pleased. I know you will be too. And too I have been writing a few poems—since the Tower of Babel is coming out with other poems at the beginning of '57 if we all live that long. I am sending one of the poems. Lax has another [of] which I have not copies, and I am hoping to get a copy from him. . . .[52]

Lax's letters were always a morale builder for the sometimes down-in-the-dumps Merton. An especially exultant letter arrived in 1958 from the then forty-three-year-old poet who was still striving for recognition. His long-germinating book, *Circus of the Sun*, was about to be printed, with the help of the brilliant artist-publisher Emil Antonucci, who had done much work for *Jubilee*. Antonucci was only a couple of years out of art school and was striving to make it in the professional world as an artist and graphics designer. At the time Lax was living in Jackson Heights, Queens, "with 1-2 Oblate Benedictines, the one a lab assistant (ex-Carthusian), the other a pious steamfitter (the same). . . ." He added this:

> News item, item of news, news flash here, as follows, viz: Emil Antonucci, artist & big friends with Jubilee—it was him who designed the tree bk of poems on original Jap magnolia—hath gained & been awarded a googie withers felongeschaft [Guggenheim fellowship], with, as one of his special projects, the project of designing & publishing the long abandoned circus book (this last sentence was punctuated with a jab of penicillin from the nurse . . .) Now the problem (and one which you will not be slow to prehend) is that there is not circus book. In one wild moment I thought I wld send you the pages (40 or 75) I hold in my hand, & beg you to make a rapid selection among them. "This lives," you will say, and "this, this lives but little."
>
> At other times I think of drinking strychnine or clubbing myself on the head with a power jac [sic].[53]

The Circus of the Sun came out in 1959, published by Antonucci's newly created publishing house, Journeyman Press, illustrated by his own line drawings. It was a beautiful fifty-six-page book with a cover photo by Harbutt of the dark silhouette of an elephant against the illuminated interior of a circus tent.[54]

My wife, Millie, and I are privileged to have copy number 39, signed by both Lax and Antonucci. The book has wonderful poems, one of the most treasured of the Harford family. "Penelope and Mogador" is about the acrobat Mogador's comeuppance while showing off on horseback for Penelope, the aerialist. Our daughter, Jennifer, twelve at the time, got an A at Stuart Country Day School of the Sacred Heart for her essay on the poem.

The book's first long poem, *The Morning Stars,* printed in italics, is especially powerful:

> *Have you seen my circus?*
> *Have you known such a thing?*
> *Did you get up in the early morning and see the wagons pull*
>   *into town?*
> *Did you see them occupy the field?*
> *Were there when it was set up?*

Did you see the cook-house set up in dark by lantern-light?
Did you see them build the fire and sit around it
*   smoking and talking quietly?*
As the first rays of dawn came, did you see
Them roll in blankets and go to sleep?
A little sleep until time came to
Unroll the canvas, raise the tent,
Draw and carry water for the men and animals;
Were you there when the animals came forth?
The great lumbering elephants to drag the poles
And unroll the canvas?
Were you there when the morning moved over the grasses?
Were you there when the sun looked through dark bars of
*   clouds*
At the men who slept by the cook-house fire?
Did you see the cold morning wind nip at their blankets?
Did you see the morning star twinkle in the firmament?
Have you heard the voices of the men's low muttering,
Have you heard their laughter around the cook-house fire?
When the morning stars threw down their spears,
*   and watered heaven . . .*
Have you looked at spheres of dew on spears of grass?
Have you watched the light of a star through a world of
*   dew?*
Have you seen the morning move over the grasses?
And to each leaf the morning is present.
Were you there when we stretched out the line,
When we rolled out the sky,
When we set up the firmament?
Were you there when the morning stars
Sang together
And all the sons of God shouted for joy?

Merton was captivated by the book and arranged for copies to be
sent to numerous friends, including Czeslaw Milosz, to whom he wrote,
"I wish you could see one good book, though, that is unknown, by my
friend Robert Lax—*The Circus of the Sun*. I'll ask him to send you a
review copy for *Kultura*. It is an expensive limited edition, beautifully
done. Lax you would like."[55] Merton took numerous opportunities to
praise the book, calling it

a tremendous poem, an Isaias-like prophecy unique in simplicity
and purity of love that is not afraid to express itself. The circus as

symbol and sacrament, cosmos and church—the mystery of the primitive world, of paradise, in which men have wonderful happy skills, which they exercise freely, as at play. But also a sacrament of the *eschaton*, our heavenly Jerusalem. The importance of human love in the circus—for doing things well. It is one of the few poems that has anything whatever to say. And I want to write an article about it. [He never did, alas.][56]

He urged James Laughlin to publish "a volume of [Lax's] Circus stuff" at New Directions, but it never happened. Asked why it did not, Laughlin said that he wanted to publish some of Lax's poems, but "there was so much white space around them he didn't feel that he could spare the pages required." When the book finally came out a delighted Lax wrote Merton that "Charlie Van Doren read the circus poem (some of it) on the televisions early in the morning & it is very good. Mark is cry, Dorothy cry & everyone is happy."[57] It must have been the NBC *Today* program, on which Charles Van Doren, Mark's son, was a regular for some time, before he became involved in the quiz scandals. Merton sent a copy of *Circus* to his friend Ernesto Cardenal, calling it "truly magnificent, a whole cosmic meditation." Cardenal translated it into Spanish and arranged to have it printed in Mexico.

Lax told the poet William Packard in an interview that "I don't think I could have written the Circus book without travelling with the circus, knowing the family well, and travelling with other circuses subsequently. I like being immersed in that life, and still feel immersed in it in some way. It was a happy world to live in, a good world for me."[58]

In the same year that *Circus* was published, 1959, Merton sent to Sister Thérèse, for transcription and transmission to Rice, an article for *Jubilee* about Boris Pasternak, who had been forced by the Soviet government to reject the Nobel Prize the previous year after having first accepted it. The layout of the Merton article was a stellar example of Rice's creativity. A black-and-white photo of Pasternak's head, the top clipped off just above the brow, ran across a two-page spread. Merton's copy was on an insert of sixteen quarter pages of sepia newsprint—that's right, *quarter* pages. The first quarter page repeated only the piercing eyes, knit brow and noble nose of the poet, and the last only his ear. Page two contained just a quote from a Pasternak poem:

My sister is Life, and today in a downpour
Of spring rain she burst upon the head of all:
But people with watch chains were haughtily peevish
And politely explained, like snakes in the corn.

Very powerful image. In the article, titled in red script "Boris Pasternak and the people with watch chains," Merton made the point that "the hero of Doctor Zhivago is not only the obscure doctor . . . not only Pasternak himself, not only Russia, but mankind—everybody. In the West. . . . Perhaps we can taste a little vicarious revolutionary joy without doing anything to change our own lives. To justify our own condition of servility and spiritual prostitution we think it sufficient to admire another's integrity."[59] Rough stuff on the readers.

Jubilee won seven first prizes from the Catholic Press Association in its first three years, and was given recognition by the national press as well. *Time, Newsweek,* and the *New York Times* all ran very favorable stories. *Today,* a Catholic media journal, said it was "unexcelled in the general Catholic-magazine field for the verve and originality of its presentation" and reported that one special issue sold 115,000 copies.

The outlook was very bright as the end of the 1950s approached.

****

6

Vatican II: Before and After

Jubilee *Interprets the Council*

Aching issues faced all Catholics at the start of the 1960s, but *Jubilee* seemed up to dealing with them, with Rice and Merton in the vanguard while Lax stayed his usual noncombative self.

What would happen at Vatican II, which was about to begin? What should be the actions in the aftermath?

How were Catholics to handle the moral implications of the Cold War, which was raising the specter of nuclear annihilation?

What about the behavior of the church hierarchy with respect to such matters as abortion, birth control, race relations, celibacy, the status of women, lay participation, government policy toward the poor, the Third World, environmental degradation, ecumenism?

How could the church's liturgy, music, art, architecture inspire, rather than so often depress, its worshippers?

The overworked and underfunded *Jubilee* staff was fortified, in considering these questions, by the realization that the magazine was having a profound impact on American Catholicism as manifested by this kind of reader response: "To read your magazine is to feel truly catholic. Your presentation of the vital Church from all parts of the world makes one love the God who inspires the greatness in hearts to accomplish the things portrayed in your pages," wrote a Colorado reader.[1]

But the magazine's appeal was to the aesthetic as well as to the inspirational. Almost forty years later Lax, on his Greek island, told me what he thought was the magazine's significance.

Jubilee was lively, creative and beautiful, and that's something that a lot of, particularly religious magazines, never thought of being—I really think that's why it made such an impact. Rice wouldn't let an issue go out unless it was beautiful—and so it got good reviews, won prizes, not because its point of view was so liberal or progressive. I think it's because people felt, "It's a magazine for the greater glory of God." That was what impressed me about

Rice so much right from the beginning—in *Jester* and everything else. He might not be able to give you a lecture on why this figure here, that photo there, he just knew—like having absolute pitch.[2]

Rice's enterprise in getting exclusive material, especially when he could get it free, was remarkable. Whenever he got wind of upcoming travel by a friend he would pounce. When he learned that I was going to Warsaw in 1964 for a space congress he asked me to seek out and interview Stanislaw Stomma, the only practicing Catholic in the Polish Parliament. I did the interview and wrote a short, straightforward piece, but with the skillful editing of his managing editor, Oona Sullivan, and a simple layout using my black-and-white photo of Stomma, it looked both beautiful and authoritative in the magazine, testifying to the stubborn faith of the beleaguered Poles.[3]

A few years earlier Ed got me to write an article on the theological implications of the search for extraterrestrial intelligence in the universe. Once again, Sullivan's editing and Rice's imaginative color layout heightened the credibility of the piece. It's fascinating to read it decades later, recognizing that an actual search was for a time funded by NASA and continues these days under the auspices of SETI (Search for Extraterrestrial Intelligence Institute) in California.[4]

There is no question that the regular intercession of Merton with prospective authors was a major factor in *Jubilee*'s success. In 1960, for instance, he wrote the Polish poet Czeslaw Milosz, later a winner of the Nobel Prize, that "I will also send you some copies of the magazine Jubilee, which is very good in its way, and run by good friends of mine. It would be wonderful if you did something for them, though they don't pay very much."[5] In this case, alas, nothing was forthcoming, but his influence on others was continual.

Merton also lost few opportunities to boost Lax's poetry, hoping that his friend would eventually get the recognition he deserved, as in this note to Father Kilian McDonnell, the editor of the magazine *Sponsa Regis*: "I hope you haven't lost courage in regard to Lax's poetry—it is really good, simple stuff and worth a try; I think it is deeply spiritual, in all its transparent simplicity. Too simple at first sight. I hope you will use it."[6]

Sullivan, one of the hardest workers on the magazine, was also one of the least eccentric. "The magazine was staffed mostly by extremely bizarre Catholics who loved the Church. Everybody had his or her own spiritual crisis," remembers Ned O'Gorman, who concedes that the description applied to him as well as to others.[7]

Now a noted poet who has been running schools for three- and four-year-olds in Harlem for more than thirty years, O'Gorman worked for *Jubilee* from 1961 until 1965, first as a volunteer, then literary editor, then senior editor. "It was a fabulous magazine," he says. "I finally got paid, $35 for an essay that I worked all day on."[8] His assignments ran a huge gamut, including interviews, essays, and reviews of books, plays, and movies. He interviewed the graphic artist Sister Corita, in her habit ("I have a picture of her, Mark Rothko, and me"), Karl Rahner in Greenwich Village, Flannery O'Connor in Georgia, Ralph McGill in Atlanta during the civil rights marches. He marched himself, joining 200,000 others, mostly blacks but many courageous whites—including priests, enthusiastic girls from Manhattanville, and Cardinal Cushing—in Washington in August 1963, producing a *Jubilee* piece that reminded Catholics that "The world had made a demand on it, on the Church, that could not be answered by referring to a communique from the chancery, dogma, prudence, politics or Rome."[9]

O'Gorman was at his most ebullient with his reviews of movies, books, and plays. Of Zero Mostel, in *A Funny Thing Happened on the Way to the Forum*, he wrote, "[he] has made from the clay and syrups of his wit and genius a figure of comic energies and staggering art that cracks open the mystery of laughter."[10] Of Tennessee Williams's *The Night of the Iguana*, on the other hand, he said, "This is an ugly play and I think here of Ad Reinhardt's statement: 'Artists are responsible for ugliness.'"[11]

O'Gorman was one of the few people who was on long and intimate terms with all three protagonists in this book. He visited Merton at Gethsemani, and his poetry talents were praised by the monk. "I hung out often with Reinhardt and Lax," he says, and he recalls a "magic time" when he visited Lax in Athens in the winter of 1965 while on his second Guggenheim fellowship: "we had dinner on the roof of the Grande Bretagne, walked on a snow-covered Acropolis at night. The light Moon brought out every detail. We walked and talked for two days." Rice, he considered "a genius. I worshipped him. He would sit in his office with a scissors and out would come this beautiful magazine." He remembers "magnificent dinners" at the Rice apartment, prepared by Ed's wife, Margery. And there were luncheons at the homes of wealthy New York Catholics like the 92 St. apartment of Mrs. Robert Hoguet, "where as many as 20 guests might include the likes of Oliver LaFarge, Martin D'Arcy, Father George Ford, Princess Bonacampani. There were Irish maids. It was a *Jubilee* assignment to go to the Hoguets."[12]

Merton had a natural inclination to stir things up, whether with the abbey, church officialdom, or the whole of society. He got the idea in 1960 to enlist James Laughlin and Bob Lax in organizing some rump sessions at Gethsemani, involving maybe "ten or twelve groups a year, small ones: writers, beats, protestants, buddhists, intellectuals, who knows, even politicians. . . . Why not you, Lax, Kerouac, and a few other assorted people picked by the two of you, make an expedition down here and we could solve the problems of the world for two or three days, perhaps on the edge of some quiet lake. . . ."[13] Nothing materialized, however, and it's doubtful that the abbot would have given his permission anyway.

In April and May of 1960 Rice went to South America to seek support for a Spanish-language edition of *Jubilee* that he had been encouraged to believe could be successful. He wrote bullish letters to Margery about the prospects for support from stops in Buenos Aires, São Paulo, Rio de Janeiro. In hindsight one wonders if the quest had any more realistic chance of success than did his forays in the United States. Was he escaping the scene of a shaky enterprise, or maybe getting away from a marriage that was coming apart? In any case, he found no Latin American sponsors.

Merton expressed his concern about Rice's perambulations in a letter to Lax:

What befalls Ed Rice? Feast in the leather conches of Brasilia, or fasts in the footsore wastes of Matto Grasso? . . . What were the conversations and reactions of Ed with all the famous peoples who were not there? . . . Any of my highpowered introductions work or did they cause him to be pursued with Latinamericdan writs, bulls, injunctions, projections, and fistfights? Tell me every detail. . . . What says Ed to the Patagonians? The German minority? The Italian majority? Do the japs in Brazil sit by the Tocantins with their Zen? [14]

He wrote Sister Thérèse that she should "not be surprised that Ed has not written. He has been wandering around South America. I have not heard from him either, though I sent a couple of long articles to Jubilee weeks ago. Lax is holding fort there [NYC], and therefore he does not write. They are always in some kind of quandary."[15]

A reason for Lax's "quandary" was probably his uncertainty about his own plans. He had revealed months earlier, for the first time, the notion that he might end up in Greece, where, in fact, he would, and spend some thirty years there.

my plans, my plans . . . i wld go and visit my friends alexander eliot
and his wife and two children (for one day) in greece and and then,
and then, on to mt athos for perhaps three weeks, three months.
(do you know any of the kids there?). rice thinks he knows someone who is archmandrake of constantiniple and runs a notions
store on 7th street. how glad i would be to go to such a mt. not
right this minute, but perhaps toward august, september, october.
emil antonucci says he will lend me carfare for the voyage, and rice
will send me currants and sheep cheese . . . cesar Vallejo [Peruvian
poet] the poems are in galley for el paho [Pax, Lax's poetry flyer]
. . . here then is a rough first galley of pax, but it will be narrow
(narrow as sin) with a black border all around . . . Yrs, Bishop
Hurley[16]

That making money was not the end-all of *Jubilee* is clear from the
fact that some of the articles were severely critical of some church-
related organizations that might have run ads. Wilfrid Sheed's critique
of Catholic funeral parlors is an example.[17] That piece, and one on
the religious goods industries, "earned me the richest hate mail from
these usually sanctimonious groups that I ever hope to see," wrote
Sheed in a memoir.[18] With Charles Harbutt's photos of the saccharine
and cheesy merchandise, the latter piece, titled "The Barclay Street
Image,"[19] mostly just quoted what the enterprising salesmen said, such
as, "What we have displayed reflects what the people want," and "The
two or three percent who go for modern statues are Catholic in name
only. Traditional statues are what religious statues are supposed to be."
"After all, a church should be gaudy, beautiful and rich." The second
article, published a few months later in 1960, impaled the funeral parlor
industry. "Equipped with little more than their basic black coats, their
caskets, embalming fluids and euphemisms, the morticians of America
have given death a facelifting such as it hasn't had since ancient Egypt."
No wonder that nowadays there is a growing trend among Catholics
toward cremation, with the remains placed in a simple pine urn such as
those made by the Trappists in Iowa.   ˙
     But the article hit the fan with the morticians, as Lax wrote Merton:
"ho, ho, ho, me, depression, yuletide dementia, very acute . . . Catholics, and esp cath funeral directors whom we attacked last week, are
after us with shovels. . . ."[20]
     The month-in-month-out excellence of *Jubilee* in the 1960s was such
that concentration on just one month—January 1960—reminds one
of how exceptional a publication it was. Highlight articles include the
following:

- An eight-page picture story on St. Louis Priory, a prep school that followed the concepts of the English Benedictines, placing a high premium on scholarship, and a "rigorous form of Christian education." The school's attractive, contemporary buildings were designed by the architectural firm that built the St. Louis air terminal.[21] The piece followed earlier ones on other precedent-setting Catholic schools, such as St. David's in New York's upper East Side, and Whitby School in Greenwich, Connecticut, the first Montessori school to be started in the Montessori renaissance.

- An essay on Blaise Pascal (1623–1662), the French scientist-polemicist-religious thinker. Peter White, in his article on this author of the *Pensées*, called Pascal "probably the most brilliant man of his time." Besides his amazing work in the sciences—"In attempting to solve a friend's gambling problem he worked out the mathematics of probability from which we derive the actuarial science used in the insurance business as well as in pari-mutuel betting"—he did original work in hydraulics, vacuum phenomena, calculating machines ("the first workable one ever made"). He eventually became a serious student of theology and scripture, becoming a flaming Jansenist before dying at the age of thirty-nine.[22]

- A report on a priest who served some ten thousand mostly Indians in a gigantic region of the Northwest Territories of Canada called Dog Rib, "saying Mass atop sleeping bags . . . a hundred miles from nowhere, dragging logs across the lake for an Indian privy . . . bearing a face full of mosquito welts; carrying his canoe over a five-mile portage, hoping to catch some sleep in a smokey, crowded shack with ten other people . . . walking fifty miles in the slush, coughing blood from freezing lungs as he runs behind his team of dogs . . . [he] remains above all a warm person, jovial . . . sympathetic, cultured."[23]

- A striking example of Rice's dramatic use of white space: two sentences, in very large black type across two-pages, containing a quote from a Leon Bloy letter to Jacques and Raïsa Maritain—"WHATEVER MAY BE THE CIRCUMSTANCES, ALWAYS PLACE THE *INVISIBLE* BEFORE THE VISIBLE, THE *SUPERNATURAL* BEFORE THE NATURAL. BY APPLYING THIS RULE TO ALL YOUR ACTS, WE KNOW THAT YOU WILL BE INVESTED WITH STRENGTH AND FILLED WITH PROFOUND JOY." Rice put the words, "*INVISIBLE*" and "*SUPERNATURAL*" in pink!

- A sixteen-page section responding to Pope John XXIII's call for an ecumenical council to discuss Christian unity, including a report on

Protestants and Catholics in Germany;[24] a study of Nicolai Berdyaev (1874-1948), a Russian intellectual who greatly influenced Christian thought ("He was one of the first to understand that the catastrophe of Russia's revolution was a catastrophe of the intelligentsia. He saw how modern industrial civilization threatened to dehumanize man")[25]; a full-page excerpt by Moses Maimonides, using the same pink that colored the Bloy quote, from an A.D. 1172 letter that admonishes the Jews of Yemen to "Keep ever in mind the event on Mount Sinai, "the pivot on which our faith turns"; a six-page photo "scoop" on religion in the Soviet Union, by an American photographer whose very presence with a camera in one of the few Orthodox churches still open at the time in Moscow demonstrated unusual courage.[26]

Jubilee was one of the first American publications to give attention to Pierre Teilhard de Chardin, the controversial French Jesuit paleontologist who had been silenced by the Vatican. Rice sent Merton a copy of Teilhard de Chardin's *The Divine Milieu,* and Merton wrote Sister Thérèse that he "liked it very much," but he nevertheless showed a sensitivity to the criticism of de Chardin that was already being expressed by church authorities. He told the nun that he

did a review article praising it. Of course I wanted to make clear that this was just a review of *this book* and not a general approbation of all T de C.'s work (and in any case I have not yet read the Phenomenon of Man). The censors of the Order were true to form. They went into a panic, and the General took it up. Gave the article to some professor in Rome. The latter said there was really nothing wrong with the article but Rome wanted Catholic magazines to keep silence about Teilhard de Chardin right now, and that it would be much better if I did not say anything.[27]

Jubilee, of course, was not about to be silenced by Rome on Teilhard, having already in December 1959 published a long review by Wilfrid Sheed of *The Phenomenon of Man* that concluded, "His book arrives at a fortunate moment. There is hopeful talk these days about a Catholic intellectual revival. Our reaction to *The Phenomenon of Man* (already a widely recognized masterpiece) will indicate whether we are serious about this. It will also indicate whether we have mastered our squeamishness about evolution."

Merton, however, *was* squeamish—not about evolution but about the attitude of his superiors. Rice was persistent in wanting him to write something about Teilhard, but Merton felt it necessary to turn him down, with colorful cynicism:

Well, I now have the final supreme decision about the Teilhard de Chardin article. It is that this must not make the appearance. It must not put forth the snout. It must remain in the hole or warren. It must go the way of all other well meaning attempts to say T de C is all right. The Jesuits have not bless T de C. Nobody has bless T. de C. Rather they have muttered at him, nay, mumbled. It has been handed down by the Magisterium, says a prof in Rome, Lord only knows who, but he made the decision, it has been handed down he says that the Catholic reviews should make the profound silence at least with regard to this article. We are in profound silence, and I for my own part in most profound silence being more profoundly silent than anybody else on this rather noisy planet.[28]

Mark Van Doren often served as chronicler of Lax's doings in his letters to Merton.

Lax has just left with his beard after three good days during which he agreed with everything I said, and as usual I said plenty. . . . We love having him here. . . . His favorite topics are always you and Rice. I must know Rice better—only once have I seen him, at Jubilee. He is a legend merely, but believe me, a rich one. Bob's beard, if you must know, is quite French and quite distinguished—not long and square, but pointed like a 16th century poet's, or a savant's of any time. Only two white streaks in it suggest that 25 years have passed since I first saw him.[29]

Jubilee kept up its momentum with the start of 1961, printing a piece titled "Chinese Classic Thought"[30] by Merton that seems even more prescient today than it was then. He had written Lax months earlier that the piece was on its way, "if Jubilees want twenty pages Chinese Classic, here you are man. . . . Of this wrote to Rice and he is waiting to ponder on the question. You help him. . . ."[31] Reading the opening paragraph, one marvels that it was written forty-four years ago!

We of the West still hold instinctively to the prejudice that our world and our civilization are the "whole world" and that we have a mission to lead all others to the particular cultural goals we have set for ourselves. But the world is bigger than we think, and its directions are not always those that we ourselves have envisaged. Besides, "our" civilization is falling apart. The destiny of the whole human family has, it is true, been practically in our hands for several hundred years. Times are changing. Asia and Africa are beginning to claim their active share, for better or for worse, in directing the fortunes of mankind. At such a time it is vitally necessary to understand the traditional thought of the greatest and most powerful of the Asiatic nations: China, India and Japan.

Merton goes on to say that "contact with Eastern thought can renew our appreciation of our own Christian heritage," recommends that colleges teach the Asian classics, reviews Confucianism, Taoism, and, briefly, Buddhism (the latter a "late arrival" that "does not belong to the classic period of Chinese philosophy") and ends with the apocalyptic admonition that "If the world is to survive and if civilization is to endure or rather perhaps recover from its present eclipse, we must hope for a new world-culture that embraces all civilized philosophies."

On a nearer-term front, Merton, who had become incensed over the increasing attention to possible nuclear warfare, wrote a piece called "Original Child Bomb" that took up the entire issue of Lax's poetry broadside, *Pax*. It was laid out with a compelling design by Antonucci. He sent a copy to James Laughlin and added, "There is to be more of it. That is the best I can do about this non-violence bit."[32] "As you say," he wrote Laughlin, "it is a terrible and central issue. This country is getting sicker all the time."[33] He had been asked for the piece by the beat poet Lawrence Ferlinghetti, "but since Lax has been promised it and has it and is going ahead first, then that seems to settle the matter."[34] It was naïve of Merton to think that a piece on the bomb in Lax's tiny publication, which went to a few hundred mostly friends, would have much of an impact; but his passion was great, and his respect for Lax's Don Quixote-like *Pax*, was great. "I think the latest Paxo is without a moment's hesitation the most superlative and supreme. I think it contains the best poems I like O'Gorman, and these I think are bursting in all directions with fantasy. You should get some prize."[35]

Some months later Merton told Laughlin that he wanted to do a "hardhitting book" on nuclear warfare. "Ed Rice," he told Laughlin,

sent me one [book] . . . God and the H Bomb with Tillich and Sheen [Paul Tillich and Bishop Fulton J. Sheen] and all the big wheels in it, religious like. . . . But I think with our stuff we are much more solid and tight and hit a great deal harder. . . . In a word, I think as soon as we get this stuff together and look at it in a bunch we will be ready to roll. And I will get busy on the preface when I see it all together. Will have to get the preface in the works way ahead of time because of the censors.[36]

The book eventually appeared as *Breakthrough to Peace,* edited by Merton (New York: New Directions, 1962).

Jubilee, as it neared the end of its first decade of publication, was ever nudging its readers to upgrade their aesthetics as well as their faith and their sense of activism. One wishes heartily that the architects of today's bingo hall churches in the United States had been disciplined to read the thoughtful article on church architecture and liturgy by Father H. A. Reinhold in February 1962. Inspiration might have come from his description of some of the beautiful churches in Europe, such as the basilica of Santa Sabina in Rome (the first Catholic church in which Merton had felt motivated to pray), which Reinhold hailed for its

. . . great simplicity. A plain brick and tile building with large ala-baster windows; an atrium with wood carved doors; a spacious nave; an enclosed space for schola singers; low *cancelli* surround-ing the sanctuary with its clergy benches and the simple altars facing the congregation: unpretentious—wonderfully propor-tioned—ascetical and spare. There is no doubt that in this church the liturgy can be performed with maximum participation . . . the worshipper is drawn to the structure's *raison d'être.* The liturgy in itself, with its vestments, lights, readings and processions *is* the essential adornment of this great church.[37]

Ahead of its time, Oona Sullivan wrote a remarkable fourteen-page report on narcotics addicts, illustrated with stark photos by Harbutt and Lax, calling attention to the work of one of the few priests deal-ing with the problem, Father Daniel Egan, a Greymoor friar. The piece is harsh on the relatively little work being done by the church. "It is embarrassing to discover how many addicts are former altar boys and how many are the sons of ministers . . . the church above all cannot stand by . . . addiction to heroin is a symptom of a deep-rooted spiri-tual sickness, and a diabolical answer to the spiritual quest of the man without faith in God."[38]

Consistent features were portraits of individual Catholics of note, including foreigners not likely to be known by Americans. Frank Monaco, based in London, made sensitive black-and-white photos and profiled a group of English converts in 1962—Countess Albemarle (Diana Cic-ely), a leader of charitable causes; Margaret Majendie, a prison social worker; Pamela Frankau, the novelist; John Walter, a director of *The Times*; David Pelham James, a Tory member of Parliament and explorer; Meriol Trevor, who did a study of Cardinal Newman; and Basil Christopher Butler, the Benedictine abbot of Downside.[39] In the following year Monaco wrote and photographed an absorbing eight-page article on Catholics at Oxford University. It is striking how much the undergraduates in his pictures, with their insouciant, almost arrogant stances, resemble those in Evelyn Waugh's *Brideshead Revisited*.[40]

An article that O'Gorman wrote about his trip to Rome to cover the opening of Vatican II in 1962 evokes much nostalgia, forty-plus years later, about what occurred there, and how frustrated has been the effort to implement some of what had seemed to be so promising. No other prose written about the council was quite like O'Gorman's. "The rains, 2500 bishops, watched by Telstar, and the Holy Spirit, descended upon Rome on the eleventh of October 1962. The mystery of Christ's Church in all her lusty brilliance and primitive lineage came, in pageantry and ritual, to announce the will of the Father."

Unmentioned by O'Gorman, although he could probably have guessed the fact, was that there were only twenty-two women auditors and about three thousand men in total at the council. "A woman's voice was never heard during the Council deliberations," recalled a Catholic woman activist years later.[41]

O'Gorman's admiration for the pontiff brimmed at the start of the opening ceremony, "Pope John, with jeweled glove and satin slipper, is such a complete, simple man, never at odds with ceremony. He draws even august ceremonies like this away from mere Renaissance jangle and intrigue. In his masterly way he made St. Peter's the possible abode of great actions, high deeds and torrents of grace."

As with many others he had exultant optimism about what he hoped would occur during the council. "Castle San Angelo and the towers of Santa Maria Maggiore were aflame with burning pots of oil as if to announce that the spirit of a new Pentecost would descend upon Rome, that on the morrow the fathers would rise up, and in spite of electronic machines, the court, the vanities and intrigues of men, the root of Jesse would spring forth in a rich and radiant Spring."[42]

Cautiously optimistic about the council's prospects was Merton, who had counseled Rice just weeks before the opening, "Don't worry about the Councils. Holy Ghost did not die yet. He can fool all the viships and worships." But then he added, "I admit I think the council is going to end up with a lot of well meaning ordinary joes in the rank and file (you and me) sitting with thumbscrews firmly attached from now until finish. And all the worships running around unregenerate and with bigger cadillacs and longer cigars, and no more peace than a hill of fire ants."[43]

Alas, that pessimism proved to be warranted when what emerged over the years after the council was much dousing of fresh ideas, as well as a virtual shutdown of talk about such crying issues as birth control, celibacy, papal infallibility, the role of women and laymen in general in the church. Even the liturgical and church music reforms did not accomplish what had been hoped.

Just before the council had convened, in its October 1962 issue, *Jubilee* had printed an article by Sullivan, "Behind the Council," that reported on the "secrecy-shrouded preparations" and then analyzed a remarkable document—an audit of the Roman Catholic Church performed by the American Institute of Management (AIM).

The secrecy, wrote Sullivan, "traditional in ecclesiastical and diplomatic circles in the past is less comprehensible today, especially to representatives of the press." Parenthetically she pointed out that Monsignor John E. Kelly had resigned his post as information head of the National Catholic Welfare Conference, "allegedly because the poor information service being given by the Vatican press office will make it impossible for [his bureau] to keep the general public in the United States adequately informed on council proceedings." Not a good start, raising a "rash of speculation," wrote Sullivan, "ranging in tone from outright cynicism to almost naïve optimism. . . ."[44]

It's ironic that earlier AIM audits, in 1956 and 1960, had given the church extremely high marks for efficiency. The audit itself was an extremely useful document for council followers. It summarized succinctly the twenty church councils held in history, and gave encyclopedic information on the preparatory commissions and secretariats for Vatican II, providing names of their presidents, the numbers of members, the consultants and staffs. Some foreboding of the largely conservative aftermath of the council is revealed by the fact that only nine of the 440 people serving on preparatory bodies were laymen, and more than 300 had some connection with the curia.

In December 1962, Peter White, *Jubilee* staffer and father of eleven, summarized a trenchant survey performed by a French quarterly on Catholic family life. His comments offer an ironic backdrop to the council's failure to deal with the issue of birth control. Many of the survey's one thousand respondents, he wrote, "seemed profoundly perturbed by problems of birth control, noting that certain kinds of psychic imbalance, or nervous depressions are frequently the result of pregnancies following one another too rapidly, or of continence heroically practiced . . . what struck those who studied this material, perhaps most of all, was the state of moral and psychological anguish in which some of these couples have been living for years."[45]

The magazine stayed hopeful through the council's deliberations. In March 1963, a Church of England observer, Canon Bernard C. Pawley, personal representative of the archbishop of Canterbury, wrote that "some Catholic doctrines may be freshly interpreted at the council: papal infallibility, for example, may be restated in a way more acceptable to non-Catholics."[46] No way, it turned out.

Major figures in the council's discussions emerged in the magazine's pages, most of them little known heretofore to *Jubilee* readers. There were articles by the thirty-five-year-old Hans Küng, who had just completed a tour of the United States, and by the Right Reverend Nicholas E. Persich, C.M., the personal theologian of Cardinal Ritter of St. Louis. It is sad to realize how emphatically Father Küng was later silenced since those days when he was described, as *Jubilee* put it, as "[a]mong the 'new wave' of European theologians happily influencing the Fathers of the Second Vatican Council" with his "candid yet irenic critique of the Church." The critique was contained in Küng's new book titled *The Council, Reform and Reunion* (published by Sheed & Ward), whose reception, "here as in Europe, can only be called jubilant."[47] Thankfully, Küng's stature is restored, and he is today perhaps the best-selling Catholic theologian in the world.

Father Persich, in a nine-page article titled "Inside the Council," seems to have been one of the many whose views proved overoptimistic. He was on the mark in recognizing that "[w]e have nearly lost sight of the fact that the principle of subsidiarity has a practical application in ecclesiastical, as well as civil, government; we have forgotten that personal responsibility and private initiative are necessary to the life of the Church." But his expectation that "this thinking was shared by bishops from every part of the world when they arrived at the Council . . ." did not convert into movement that would go beyond the papacy of John XXIII.[48]

Since photographers were not allowed into the council chambers the Persich article was illustrated with beautiful pencil drawings made in and around St. Peter's by Franklin McMahon, providing *Jubilee* readers with a graphic insight on both the proceedings and the trappings.

A quite full, and very human, account of Vatican II by Francis X. Murphy, a Redemptorist priest who wrote under the pseudonym Xavier Rynne, was published in 1999.[49] The book is fascinating reading today; the six hundred pages cover the proceedings and intrigues of the four sessions held over a three-year period from October 11, 1962 to December 8, 1965. In *Jubilee* Rynne prepared readers for what became a barrier to church reform at the council, namely the curia, with an excerpt from one of the pieces he had written for the *New Yorker*.[50] It began with a recollection that in the nineteenth century, "Two forces took possession of the Roman Curia—a fear-inspired ruthlessness in dealing with every semblance of non-conformity in theological thought, and a determination to explain the traditional doctrine of the Church only within a rigid framework." That intransigeance persisted into the twentieth century and "saddled the Church with a backward and frequently ominous outlook on the modern world." It proved telling in subsequent Vatican II decrees on numerous subjects, including doctrine, scripture, and, wrote Rynne, "the moral aspects of psychological research and psychiatric practice."

Merton was not heard from on the subject of the council in *Jubilee's* pages, possibly for fear that he might get into hot water with his superiors. He kept up his contributions to the magazine, however, into the '60s, calling attention to prophets with a long view of history who were being ignored. In March 1963, he commented eloquently, and alarmingly, on the writings of one such prophet—the German Jesuit, Alfred Delp, who wrote journals while awaiting execution in 1945 for being a member of an underground anti-Nazi organization. Merton's introduction to the journals is very hard on Christianity as it enters what he describes as a "new era [in which] the social structures into which Christianity had fitted so comfortably and naturally, have all but collapsed. The secularist thought patterns which began to assert themselves in the Renaissance, and which assumed control at the French Revolution, have now so deeply affected and corrupted modern man that even where he preserves certain traditional beliefs, they tend to be emptied of their sacred inner reality, and to mask instead the common pseudo-spirituality of the outright nihilism of mass-man."[51]

Delp himself was in despair, writing that "Spiritually we seem to be in an enormous vacuum. . . . Scarcely anyone can see, or even guess at, the connection between the corpse-strewn battlefields, the heaps of rubble we live in and the collapse of the spiritual cosmos of our moral and religious convictions as revealed by our behavior."

There is nothing upbeat in the Jesuit's memoir, even when considering the potential role of the church. "Both as individual Christians, and as the corporate community, the Church, we have in recent times failed in our dealings with our fellow man, failed in our assessment of situations and spiritual realities. . . . We have every reason to be shocked and ashamed. Of course the Church still has skillful apologists, clever and compelling preachers, wise leaders; but the simple confidence that senses the right course and proceeds to act on it almost unconsciously is just not there."[52] Rough stuff, from a doomed priest of the church which so sadly let down its people when dealing with the Nazis.

Merton's *Jubilee* writings in this period ranged from the sermon-like, such as "The General Dance," to the angry, such as "Religion and the Bomb." In the former he lectured that "[t]he more we persist in misunderstanding the phenomena of life, the more we analyze them out into strange finalities and complex purposes of our own, the more we involve ourselves in sadness, absurdity, and despair. But it does not matter much, because no despair of ours can alter the reality of things, or stain the joy of the cosmic dance which is always there."[53]

In the "Bomb" article he became furious, warning that "there are many possibilities of accident, miscalculation and plain confusion which might lead to a first strike in the name of Democracy, Liberty and—Christianity!" and "if we become apologists for the uninhibited use of naked power, we are thinking like Communists, we are behaving like Nazis, and we are . . . destroying our own Christian heritage."[54]

The magazine continually did its part in ecumenical outreach, as in a long article—sixteen pages by Sullivan titled "Joyous Mystics,"[55] with striking photos by Burt Shavitz—on the Lubavitchers, an "intensely joyful and intellectual" branch of Hasidic Judaism based in Crown Heights, Brooklyn. A reader whose name could be Jewish called it "absolutely astounding" and said it "will surely help to bring about the fraternal love that should exist between Catholics and Jews."[56] A few months later, a commentary on the scripture of Islam, "The Koran,"[57] appeared, authored by the late Princeton University scholar James Kritzeck (he died years later of AIDS). "It is unjust," Kritzeck wrote, "to regard the Koran as no more than a manual for Islamic conquests; and that is practically the only image that Christendom has ever had of it." He recounted a touching experience where he felt that he "witnessed ecstasy, as St. John of the Cross defines it, only once in my life . . ." watching a young boy in a mosque in Istanbul reciting the Koran "enrapt, barely in this world . . . reciting for God alone."

The "Letters" column in *Jubilee* was month-in-month-out one of the most interesting features, attracting as it did, communications that were often as informative as the articles, and which regularly included transmissions from non-Catholics. For a time in 1963, for example, the column was a veritable forum of almost scholarly discussion of Gregorian chant. Four years earlier, in the November 1959 issue, Dom Ludovic Baron, O.S.B., had called the chant, "the voice of Christ in His Mystical Body," and explained that "If you think of plain-chant as any other music, you will completely miss the point, because you have not entered into the spirit of the liturgical drama and its characters."[58]

It would be well for those church leaders of today who don't seem to realize how many Catholics are turned off by the humdrum, often saccharine, hymns that characterize most Masses, to read Dom Ludovic's article, and also the letters from readers on the subject from three different *Jubilee* issues in 1963. Ethel Thurston of the Pontifical Institute of Medieval Studies in Toronto started it off by stumping for a revival of Gregorian chant: "The readers of Jubilee who have been brought up in European towns or in some fortunate parishes in this country will realize to what an extent Gregorian Chant illuminates the words of the Mass, banishes depression and tedium, encourages spiritual thoughts. It fits the Mass better than any other music. . . . Good music and the hierarchy seem to have drifted further apart than they have in past ages, and the latter appear to be captivated by good souls who manufacture the most tiresome of cliches, the killers of mystery, the ungifted." However, she made an emphatic point in the same letter—a response to the piece on the use of the vernacular recommended by respondents to the Vatican II questionnaire (see above)—that "If the vernacular is to be employed for the Mass and Office, it must be *firmly* understood that the Gregorian Chant cannot be transferred to any of the new languages. This is because the chant, unlike some music, is extremely subtly and intimately allied to the weight and sound of the words to which it was originally written . . . [it] cannot be set to another language without awkwardness which will amount practically to caricature."[59]

That letter triggered two firm objections two months later. One came from an Episcopalian named George A. John Porthan of Nashota, Wisconsin, who said that the Episcopalians "have been singing Gregorian chant, with English texts, for some time now. It *can* be done; it *is* done; and it *is* done without damage to text or music."[60] The other was from another Episcopalian, a missionary priest named Beverley D. Tucker writing from Sapporo, Japan, who wrote that not only can chant be sung successfully in English, but also in Japanese and other languages. "I know something of the beauty of Latin for plainsong," he wrote, "having once sung in a Roman Catholic choir, but English has its own beauty and for most of us it speaks to the heart as Latin never will."[61]

Ms. Thurston responded, somewhat condescendingly it must be said. "The Anglicans have made wonderful contributions to church music with their performances of Bach, Schütz, Händel, Fauré, their construction of Baroque organs, their excellent boy choirs and choir schools. Gregorian in English is not one of their distinguished achievements."[62]

Merton himself probably urged Rice to tout Gregorian chant, having gone on record on the subject himself in *SSM:*

Gregorian chant that should, by rights, be monotonous, because it has absolutely none of the tricks and resources of modern music, is full of a variety infinitely rich because it is subtle and spiritual and deep, and lies rooted far beyond the shallow level of virtuosity and "technique," even in the abysses of the spirit, and of the human soul. Those Easter "alleluias," without leaving the narrow range prescribed by the eight Gregorian modes, have discovered color and warmth and meaning and gladness that no other music possesses. Like everything else Cistercian—like the monks themselves—these antiphons, by submitting to the rigor of a Rule that would seem to destroy individuality, have actually acquired a character that is unique, unparalleled.[63]

Rice led a continuing crusade for high-quality church music based on his own taste, a taste nurtured in the jazz cellars of New York and months of listening to his own and Merton's and Lax's classical and jazz records during the Columbia years and the Olean summers of 1939 and 1940. He would buy good church music records and sell them through ads for the "Ikon Guild" on the inside back cover of the magazine. One ad listed tapes of chant by the Trappists of Citeaux, the Benedictine monks of En Calcat, the choir of Santa Susanna in Rome, a Mass for the Dead by Spanish Benedictines, and one that covered the whole church year—fourteen 45-rpm records at $2 each.[64] Another ad describes twenty-one records or tapes—at the unthinkable-for-today prices of $4 to $7.50—of Slavonic, Byzantine, Melkite, Romanian, Coptic, Eastern Monastic, Russian and Greek Orthodox music as well as Catholic folk music. One of the latter, the *Missa Luba* album from the Belgian Congo, was bought by the Harford family for $3. My children, teenagers at the time, were entranced, especially by its bongo-beat version of the Credo.[65]

There was deep mourning throughout the world, and especially the Catholic world, and perhaps more especially the *Jubilee* readership, when John XXIII died at eighty-one on June 3, 1963, only two months after he had released the encyclical *Pacem in Terris* while tirelessly preparing for the second session of the council. Xavier Rynne termed the pope's convocation of Vatican II, as well as the encyclicals *Pacem in Terris* and *Mater et Magistra*—which updated Leo XIII's *Rerum Novarum* on social teaching—as his "three most considerable claims on history's attention. . . ."[66]

The German sociologist and historian Dr. Edgar Alexander, then living in New York, wrote in *Jubilee* that *Pacem in Terris* "stands as the final testament of a Pope who had endeared himself to the world for his simple goodness and his fatherly concern for all men, Christian and non-Christian. . . . Even some Catholics were astonished at the openness to the world shown by the Holy Father in his declaration that freedom and peace are conscience-binding norms in politics and social affairs and also in religion."[67] The impact of the encyclical, the first one addressed not only to Catholics but to "all men of good will" still reverberates. It was a remarkable document, covering, as Dr. Alexander enumerates, "the freedom of the human person, the governmental and social orders in which men live together, the political and social rights and duties of the citizen, political cooperation among nations on a legally ensured basis of international order, peace and nuclear disarmament [and] the possibilities of a dialog between Christians and those who hold different views, including Marxists and Communists."

A noted Jew, Joseph Lichten of the Anti-Defamation League of B'Nai B'rith, wrote in *Jubilee* the following month, "The death of few men in living memory aroused such universal sorrow as that of Pope John XXIII, whose philosophy was perhaps summed up in this greeting to a Jewish delegation in October 1960: 'I am Joseph, your brother.'" Lichten felt that the pope's "extrordinary charity has led some of the Catholic Church's severest critics to see it in a more favorable light."[68]

Back to the subject of birth control went *Jubilee* in several 1963 issues. First came a review by Wilfrid Sheed of Dr. John Rock's book on "the pill."[69] Sheed called it, "one man's explosion of impatience over the Church's official birth-control position and, for better or worse, I believe it echoes the feelings of many."[70] Later that year Rosemary Radford Ruether, who is even today one of the most articulate writers in the United States on women's issues, made the point that in the church "there has been little willingness to give a hearing to new ideas or dissenting opinions" on the matter of birth control. "It is assumed," she wrote, "that all forms of contraception except rhythm are immoral. . . . Yet it is precisely this 'moral argument' that is so unconvincing to non-Catholics, many of whom believe that the family is weakened rather than strengthened by the Catholic position."[71] These two articles may well have helped to cause the magazine to disappear from the back of numerous parish churches. A priest responded in a letter to the editor that "If Mrs Ruether wants a scientific treatise on the irrevocability of the Church's teaching [on birth control] she can read 'Questions on Marriage,' the latest book by Fathers Ford and Kelly, America's leading theologians."[72]

Merton was in the magazine again in September 1963 with a long review of a novel by a young black man, William Melvin Kelley. He called the book[73] a "parable which spells out some of the deep spiritual implications of the Negro battle for full civic rights, and for a completely human status, in the world today."[74] Merton jabbed the Catholic conscience with the remark that Kelley's book, and those of "Negro writers like James Baldwin, Jonathan Williams and many others . . . must be read with deep attention. They spell out a message . . . not to be found anywhere else at the present moment, and on the acceptance of which the survival of American freedom may depend."

Much angrier on the subject was O'Gorman, who wrote in March 1964 his impressions of a trip through parts of the South. "Jackson, Mississippi is hell," he wrote, ". . . [and] bears an evil we must all suffer, we must all expiate, we must all mourn."[75]

Reinforcing the magazine's concern with having Catholics understand the religious convictions of other sects, Merton wrote a fascinating piece a few months later on the Shakers, whom he called "American celibates and craftsmen who 'danced' in the glory of God."[76] A disappearing sect, since they generate no new families, they had values that impressed Merton deeply. They were "meticulous workers, with a passion for order, cleanliness, simplicity, practicality and economy of means . . . [a] perfect fusion of temporal and eternal values, of spirit and matter . . . living according to a kind of inspired eschatology in which ambition, personal gain and even quick material results were not considered important." Right down the alley for Lax, Merton, and Rice.

It was in this period that Merton and Lax had an extremely interesting exchange of letters on the relationship between Catholics and Greek Orthodox. Lax wrote, on May 1, 1964:

here it is good Friday among the orthodox . . . the following questions are in my mind: how do we know we're right and they're wrong? . . . (why do we think we shouldn't give up our special claims and just become one church among the orthodox?).[77]

Merton's response, only a week later, is so startling that it is surprising that it hasn't been quoted more in Catholic circles, especially after the call for ecumenism was heralded in *Pacem in Terris*:

Between us and them is no difference of faith, is no difference. Is not a whistle of a significant difference. . . .
. . . Difference between us and them is politics, chum. Is a historical question of politics which neither you nor I nor that monk you spoke about got any time to bother with. Let the politicians figure it out. Let the Vatican figure it out. . . .[78]

Although money problems plagued Ed Rice, he had needed more space for his staff in the early 1960s, and so he moved the magazine from the one-story office at 377 Park Ave. South to more commodious quarters on three floors at 168 E. 91st St. Ads were still not coming in as had been hoped. Some book publishers stayed loyal—such as Harper & Row, advertising Dorothy Day's new *Loaves and Fishes*; Sheed & Ward, with *Prayers* by Michel Quoist and *The Council in Action* by Hans Küng; and Doubleday's Image Books, which advertised nine books, including those by Romano Guardini, Henri Daniel-Rops, and Dan Herr. The back cover plugged fifteen-month *Jubilee* subscriptions plus a book thrown in for $6—*World Crisis and the Catholic*, featuring Konrad Adenauer, Mayor Giorgia la Pira, Karl Stern, and Christopher Dawson.[79] In other issues there were ads for Catholic tours—one by Irish International Airlines, one by Lufthansa—and even an ad for Chartreuse liqueur. There were all too few of these, however.

Jubilee did not cover the assassination of John F. Kennedy at all in the months after the traumatic event in November 1963, probably because of the voluminous coverage in the world media, and perhaps lacking the heart to deal with such a painful subject after having written extensively about JFK in his electioneering days and his early years in office. In 1960, just after the election, Robert Hoyt had analyzed the phenomenon well, concluding that "[t]here is history to be made, grave perils to be met, the nation needing leadership; a man with gifts should be at work, and he need not describe the work in the standard vocabulary of the lay apostolate to make it a worthy expression of his humanity and his Catholicism."[80] After Kennedy's death there were no solemn reflections, only two ads to commemorate him—one of them for a large picture book costing only $3.95, *America the Beautiful*, which used text from Kennedy speeches and which Cardinal Cushing called "the finest memorial of this wonderful man and dearest friend, that I have seen."[81]

By 1964 Lax had been two years in Greece and was writing poems intensively. Van Doren had recorded in an earlier note to Merton that "He [Lax] talk Merton all the time. Him Greek now, him gone for good, except he'll be back, with no difference visible."[82] Lax had entrusted to Van Doren the task of reading his poems and even editing them, but Van Doren was reluctant, and Merton got the job. Van Doren commiserated with him:

Lax's poems will be a job to edit. I tried it once, with no luck for Lax, who said he liked my selection, but I wasn't sure he did, nor could I be sure myself that I had done it right. The job in your case will be complicated by the existence of what I call his raindrop poems, among which I simply couldn't choose. I have told him I wasn't strong for these, and maybe I hurt his feelings. They produce a queer result for me: instead of brevity, loquacity. . . . Now I admit that some of them have seemed better than others; but for the life of me I couldn't say why, and I don't intend to grope for reasons. Lax is a fine poet, naturally, and I rejoice that you are undertaking this work; but it will be work. Good luck—and actually, if you ever have specific poems that you want to trade views about, by all means let me see them. There are few books I'd rather see than Poems by Lax, even if (looking back) I don't sound that way. I do, I do. . . . [83]

Lax evidently changed his mind about the idea of having Merton edit his poems since there is no further mention of that subject in either of their journals.

Nostalgia wells up when reading a beautiful picture story that took up eight pages in *Jubilee* in April 1964. Was there ever anything more serene than Dominican nuns, in the now-disappeared classic white habits, going about their work among the grindingly poor? In this case it was Sister Violeta and her fellow religious—she the only doctor in 26,000 square miles of jungle in the fetid bays of central Brazil where garbage is dumped and diseases breed wildly.[84]

The same issue had Wilfrid Sheed writing incisively and bitingly about "the most controversial play of our age," *The Deputy,* by Rolf Hochhuth. Sheed acknowledged that "many Catholics would generally like to share in the guilt of the Jewish massacres" by the Nazis, but "this lop-sided emphasis on the papacy has led us to the point where Pius XII must stand scapegoat for the whole of Christendom. . . ."

The articulate, and sometimes angry, Anne Fremantle deplored Vatican II's "casting aside" of Latin, in May. ". . . no more dropping into Mass in Abyssinia, Bolivia, Calcutta, through Yucatan and Zanzibar and finding always the same Mass with the same responses going back for more than a thousand years . . . it will be a long time before there are missals in Tamil and Telegu, in Aztec and Tolmec, in Romansch and Ladin."[85]

The *Jubilee* crusade for reconsideration of church thinking about birth control continued, with "Marriage, Love, Children II," which included sixteen pages of letters documenting the opinions of particular Catholics, like the woman with nine children who had had five miscarriages, a bad case of varicose veins, for whom "rhythm didn't work" and "abstinence was impossible."[86]

In June 1964, Merton made his first trip back to the old scene of his gamboling with Rice and Lax in New York, although he saw neither old friend. It was a clandestine trip that he had been given permission to make to the city coincident with the visit there of the ninety-four-year-old Zen master, Daisetz Teitaro Suzuki. He dropped into his old room in Butler Hall at Columbia, had long talks with Suzuki, said Mass several times by himself at Corpus Christi "at Our Lady's altar before that lovely Italian medieval triptych—no word for it," and took note nostalgically of New York's noises, "Drums, bongos, the chanting of songs, dogs barking, traffic, buses like jet planes. Above all the morning light, then the afternoon light. . . ."[87]

Later in the year he wrote for *Jubilee* a tribute to Flannery O'Connor, who had recently died. She had been

> disconcerting to some Catholics . . . because she did not make a point of including an obvious "Catholic message" in her work . . . her stories and novels . . . do not hand you a message on a silver platter. . . . Now Flannery is dead, and I will write her name with honor, with love for the great slashing innocence of that dry-eyed irony that could keep looking the South in the face without bleeding or sobbing. Her South was deeper than mine, crazier than Kentucky, but wild with no other madness than the crafty paranoia that is all over the place, including the North![88]

The magazine began to shrink in size in the latter part of 1964. It was now sometimes forty-eight pages, not always fifty-six. An article by Charles Curran, which O'Gorman solicited, sped up the downturn in revenues as parish priests ordered the magazine removed from their churches in protest against the theologian's liberal views on birth control.[89] Rereading those views, carefully worded in five-and-a-half pages of dense type, it is difficult to understand today how they could have been so controversial. "Although artificial contraception is considered objectively wrong," he wrote, "there are times when, even objectively thinking, it is the lesser of two moral evils. Theologians admit that a confessor can counsel the lesser of two evils in a given situation." In the same article he argued—on the subject of another mode of contraception, namely, the "pill," that "[t]heologians, like scientists, must experiment constantly. Theological discussion and dialog will test the validity of the arguments for and against antiovulant pills."

Ed Rice got *Jubilee* into the travel business in the fall of 1964, laying on a twenty-two-day tour of the Holy Land and Italy on El Al Airlines, and it would be followed by other trips sponsored by Lufthansa, by Air France, and by Irish International Airlines. One of the participants in the Holy Land trip wrote that it was "the greatest travel bargain in my experience," with "informative explanations at every site of religious or historical significance."[90]

Merton once more agitated for social change at the start of 1965 with a *Jubilee* six-pager in which he cited the similarity of the position of Gandhi to that of John XXIII.[91] "Gandhi's principles," he wrote,

> are . . . extremely pertinent today, more pertinent than even when they were conceived and worked out in practice in the ashrams, villages and highways of India . . . especially for those who are interested in implementing the principles expressed by another great religious mind, Pope John XXIII, in *Pacem in Terris*. Indeed this Encyclical has the breadth and depth, the universality and tolerance of Gandhi's own peace-minded outlook. But neither can it be built on vague liberal slogans and pious programs gestated in the smoke of confabulation. There can be no peace on earth without the kind of inner change that brings man back to his right mind.

A subject besides marital sex that has gotten even more contentious in the last forty years was described in *Jubilee*'s February 1965 issue by the eminent German Jesuit theologian Karl Rahner. Titled "The Pope and the Bishops," the five-page article is followed by three pages of deeply sensitive black-and-white photos of Rahner in New York made by Rice.[92] The article, excerpted from the book *Inquiries,* reminded readers that the bishops are "the direct representatives of Christ himself and not simply of the Pope," even though, he premised at the outset, "the pope, as an individual, has full, direct, ordinary and general episcopal primacy of jurisdiction over the whole Church and each of her parts and members—including the bishops—[and so] then the monarchical constitution of the Church is axiomatic for Catholics." But, he pointed out, "a monarchical constitution is usually understood to mean a hereditary monarchy and not an elective one, whereas the pope is at least *de facto* elected." The text bears study today in the light of the continued controversy over the power of bishops vis-à-vis the laity, as well as vis-à-vis the Vatican.

Rice, in February 1965, fired Ned O'Gorman after what had been months of clashes in personality. "I'm arrogant, I have a bad temper, I explode when I don't get my own way," O'Gorman recalled, in an interview in 1996 at the school for Harlem little ones he now runs. A tantrum involving the destruction of furniture might well have been the climactic trigger, but Rice claimed that O'Gorman had not been straight up in some instances, such as having allowed himself to be misrepresented as *the* editor, not *an* editor, of the magazine. This O'Gorman denies. It must be said that Rice himself had been having wild swings of mood, probably fueled by financial and marital problems. His relations with his wife, Margery, were stormy, and he had begun what, over the next several years, became affairs with three different Indian women. O'Gorman recalls that the first, a beautiful tan-skinned Brahmin, who had been one of the *Jubilee* volunteers, "would sit langorously on a rug in the middle of the office wearing a lovely sari, Ed would sit down next to her and Margery might come into the office and start screaming."[93]

Even with the loss of O'Gorman, *Jubilee* stayed at a high level in 1965. The "Report from . . ." section, which often led off the magazine, continued to have marvelous perspective and documentation. Typical was a "Report from Canada" in February coauthored by a Paulist, Paul Doucet, and a layman, Denis O'Brien.[94] The authors called for Catholics' "deliverance from 'Quebec's Jansenist shudders'" and delivered a blistering attack on the Canadian church's outmoded approach to Catholic education. Interestingly, though, they commented that "French Canadians have become so conditioned to aggiornamento that the reform movement in the Church, especially with the liturgy, is far more advanced in French than in English Canada."

Merton suggested to Laughlin, in 1965, that the letters he and Lax had exchanged over the years might be published in the *New Directions Annual*, but Laughlin did not think so and Merton respected his friend's judgment. "So just keep one [packet, presumably] for the file and send another down here. I will let it be part of a collection and that will be that." About sixty-five of the letters—funny, irreverent, full of inside stuff, covering the period from 1962 to 1967, interspersed with several poems by both writers—would be published in 1978 as a slim book, *A Catch of Anti-Letters*.[95] But there were hundreds of letters that did not make the volume, many of them revealing of Merton's mood swings, such as this one to Lax from April 1965 when he was spending time at the hermitage but had not yet been given permission to live there: "Yes, it is true I sleep in the woods, I eat in the woods, I come down to the monastir only to say an occasional fie upon the commandant and to subvert the troops. Or to write five or six novels. In my house I resist war. I resist everything. This why the hermit life is called the piece de resistance."[96]

In the summer of 1965 Lax, then three years in Greece, and by then living on Kalymnos, wrote Merton a sympathetic letter about his recent stay in the hospital with a slipped disc, "is it slipped back in place? 50 years is not very old for an author. you must stand on your head as much as possible and take care of yourself."[97] A few weeks earlier Lax had come up to Athens, with a small subsidy from me, to take pictures for my aerospace journal at the International Astronautical Congress.

While sitting at the edge of the Hilton Hotel pool he tried to teach me to stand on my head, and then to strike the yoga lotus position, but I failed in both. His picture taking sometimes failed, too, as he was insufficiently aggressive in trying to photograph the first-ever meeting between Soviet cosmonauts and American astronauts, which was important enough to make *Life* magazine, as well as the appearance of Queen Frederika and her son, King Constantine, at the sessions. The paparazzi simply pushed him out of the way. Subsequently, over the years, he took some good pictures for my reports at congresses in Belgrade, Constance, Stockholm, Lausanne, Madrid, Graz, Brighton, Prague, and Paris, although he still had the problem of being elbowed aside by more aggressive photographers at the ceremonial events and I would have to buy these pictures from the offical congress photographer for my report.

Van Doren wrote Merton in October that he had received a birthday greeting [his seventy-first] from Lax and "a long thin poem about how the sea moves like a dancer. It does so move in the poem; but I appreciate your problem, in case you haven't solved it yet."[98] The "problem" probably had to do with Merton not knowing how to deal with the poem, which was probably "Sea & Sky." It took up over one hundred pages with largely the single words "sea" and "sky"—the rest white space—in a Swiss journal.[99]

Rice, hard up for personal income and not drawing much out of *Jubilee*, made several photo essays at the end of 1965 for the religious series called *Directions 66*, which aired on ABC-TV on Sundays. One was on the Worker Priests, another on the Benedictine monasteries at Mount Saviour, Regina Laudis, Weston Priory, and Christ in the Desert, and a third on the final session of the Vatican Council.

In January 1966, Merton wrote Laughlin about the possible exhibition and sale of some of his drawings. "I think the nuns up at Manhattanville College . . . would probably be happy to have an exhibition" and suggested that Laughlin and Naomi Burton "take a few of them in custody so to speak and hang them up somewhere. The rest could go to Bellarmine. Or better still we might sell a few of them. Ed Rice is coming down. I can talk to him about it."[100] Rice arrived a few days later and they had "a good talk," but there is no indication that an exhibition of drawings was discussed.[101] In any case, an exhibition was eventually organized with the help of Sister Thérèse and, according to Brother Patrick Hart, who became Merton's assistant, it traveled to various universities, including St. Louis, Marquette, and Loyola of New Orleans before some twenty drawings that remained unsold ended up at the Merton archive at Georgetown. During Rice's visit the two drove out "to Edelin's Hollow and saw the sunny silence and stillness of the place. . . . Rice took pictures. We came back and had supper in the hermitage."[102] Merton wrote Lax that "Ed Rouse was here. . . . We opened up the sardines dutifully but it did not come back any of the old days, we are all too serious now for the old days, there is so much of the new days, so vast, so heaped up, so oppressive, so lamentable, there remains no time for the old."[103] Rice told Merton of troubles he was having with Margery but evidently did not mention his interest in the Indian beauty he was romping with at the *Jubilee* office.

Merton offered his friend counsel on his marital problems a few weeks later, advising him about "being careful to make the break with Margery in the least dramatic and painful way, and meanwhile it will be rough."[104] A second letter, shortly afterward, responded to Rice's general miseries and took off on the church as possibly a source of the problems.

First big thing is not to get so damned attached to the angst that all you are able to do is tread the mill and keep it going round and round. . . . There is every serious reason why the life of the Catholic Kirk should induce all forms of neurosis and anxiety and everything else right up the line. The way the Christian faith is lived is so schizophrenic that it is a wonder one can be at the same time a Christian and sane. I mean to say a Christian according to the pattern and the approved forms. You think I got fun here? Man, you think more. You think I got no angst? Man, think again. I got angst up to the eyes.[105]

The financial problems of *Jubilee* had reached still another level of crisis, and so Merton chimed in on that subject as well.

One thing is the whole question of Jubilee: you have been counting on it to make sense out of "Christendom" and it has been doing a good job, better than you realize. But not the job you want it to do for you. It will get you nothing but debts. It will not get you any sense of spiritual meaning. It will not make you happy. But it is still a good thing. Only you better get someone to help out with the twenty thousand [the debt at that time, soon to grow larger] . . . can't you get someone like Sheed and Ward to own it and lose money on it? Meanwhile getting yourself out from under the business bushel and just editing it like fun?[106]

That advice was not needed by Rice since he had already begun to offer the magazine to various publishers.

****

7

ROMANCES, DEATHS

The Nurse; Loss of Columbia Pals, Then Jubilee

A s Rice's marriage to Margery came apart—she would eventually get a divorce by Mexican decree in Ciudad Juarez on May 2,
1969—he began to travel in the Near East, leaving the management
of the magazine largely to Oona Sullivan. He sent back vivid picture
stories from his stops—an American family in Jordan, Catholic pilgrims in Jerusalem, the Chaldeans and other spiritual leaders in Iraq.
Before leaving New York he had completed an article on Merton for the
March 1966 *Jubilee*—including a sensitive cover portrait of the monk,
and six pages of wonderful shots taken at the hermitage and around
the monastery grounds during his January visit to Gethsemani. The
piece commemorated Merton's twenty-fifth anniversary of entry into
the Trappist community. He "still follows the contemplative life in all
its purity and strictness," said the copy, a comment that seems ironic in
retrospect since it was just prior to the five-month period, from April to
September 1966, when Merton had his affair with the nurse, identified
in his journals as "M" [and then in 1998 by a *Washington Post* journalist as "Margie Smith," who, said the article, eventually went back
to Ohio and married a doctor and raised sons, and "has never once
spoken publicly of Merton"].[1] It is no wonder that Merton wrote in his
journal that he was embarrassed when M was examining the picture
story in his presence.[2]

It was just before his travels began that Rice wrote a television script
for a program that featured Merton, but the TV people butchered the
project, leading an embarrassed Rice to write from Iran that "I was so
disgusted with the tampering that . . . I should have demanded that the
program be cancelled, because it was a violation of our friendship and
also just added more nonsense to the T.M. legend."[3] Merton so disliked
the program that he wrote Jay Laughlin that "they messed up Ed's
original ideas and made the whole thing a bit silly if you ask me. Hence
I am all for avoiding that kind of jazz in the future. Let's stay scrupu-
lously away from the popular especially Catholic press."[4]

The same letter to Laughlin enclosed a copy of a journal that Lax had been keeping on Kalymnos, and which he had sent to Mark Van Doren, who—not knowing quite what to do with it—sent it on to Merton with these comments: "I hope it can be published—with as few editorial tidyings as possible. Typos, yes; but the hesitations, the vaguenesses (not really that), the gentlenesses, the Laxnesses—keep those, tell Doubleday. You might be tempted to write a preface, and include a few mad letters."[5] Van Doren, in transmitting the journal, characterized well the life style of the poet, then fifty-one-years old and in his fourth year in Greece:

He walks about the island, talks to the sponge fishermen, looks out at the sea (he never tires of that, as it never tires of being there), goes to hear singing and watch dancing, gets concerned about the fishermen who may not return from their perilous voyage to the waters off Africa where they dive for sponges and sometimes die in the act, sleeps, thinks, writes poems, and tells himself he will probably be there forever, as perhaps he will be. He also mentions pretty often a very handsome girl (he has sent me pictures of her) who lives with her mother and weaves rugs on a loom. I have no idea what his Greek is like but clearly he communicates with this girl (no name yet), and he even claims he has told her about me, though I doubt that he tells her I tease him about how I think he will end up by marrying her. He says if he does marry her it will be only so I can come there and kiss her. Well. Do you want it? I didn't mention another incessant activity: photographing. He has shot every person on the island, I imagine, over and over, as well as the little white house where he lives. Kalymnos (Calymnus to the Romans) has never been so visible before; images of it go fluttering over the Aegean like so many butterflies, never perhaps to rest again.[6]

Whatever happened to the girl who weaves rugs is not known. He never mentioned her to the Harfords, certainly, but Van Doren must have told Lax's Columbia classmate, the poet John Berryman, about her since he later wrote Berryman that "I'm not sure I should have spoken about the rug girl, but then I did, didn't I? Use your judgment about speaking of her yourself. He's shyer than ever, you know."[7]

Merton's own comment to Lax on the Kalymnos journal was:

It is the great book of each evening it was come from Mark Doorstops with encomiums too far short of the truth. It is the Everest of Journals. It is the Kachenjunga of Poems. It makes me want to

throw over everything especially the back operatio and come to
Kalumpups. You got plenty social life in Kalopsis. Now it is gypsies
the social life, now dinner in the ships, now ouzos in the café now
the spinning lady for which I have deepest respect the spinning lady
has beaten all the hossus and just sits quiet and spins with the Buddha mind. . . . Here's what I do. I hide your treasure in garbage and
I put in the hands of New Direction. . . . It will be an eyeopener for
the dustraps in the parlor of New Distinctions.[8]

When Merton sent the journal to Laughlin at New Directions he
included the comment, "I know it looks a little mad at first, but if you
are patient with it you will see it is really a fine book, and can easily
be edited into the kind of shape that will not terrify the reader. It has
wonderful stuff in it. . . . I hope you can use it."[9] Laughlin did, but not
until nine years later when he placed an excerpt from the journal in his
New Directions Annual.[10] A portion of one entry shows Lax's fascination with the interactions between the islanders:

all over the island [Kalymnos], and wherever two or three greeks
are gathered, conversation proceeds and the subject at hand is seldom the actual theme of what's being discussed. each participant,
and all who hear, listen to the undercurrent, drawing the serious
conclusions, if any, from that, getting to know each other better
and better from the surface of the bavardage.[11]

Here is another excerpt, written in vertical columns: in mostly single
syllables:

what
do
you
do

(they
ask
me)

i
write
what
i
see
(i
say)

like
a
recording
angel

(some
re-
cord)
(some
angel)[12]

Merton kept plugging for Lax's poetry in letters to prominent people, such as Henry Miller, to whom he offered an analysis of the reason for his friend's lack of acceptance, "I regret that I never got to Greece, and envy Lax who is batting around in the islands there now. I can understand that his poems did not click: I suppose you have to know what is in all the blank spaces."[13]

Rice made another visit to Merton in 1968, two years after the M romance had ended, but evidently the affair was never discussed, and Rice would make no mention of M in his Merton biography, *The Man in the Sycamore Tree*, which was published four years later, in 1972.

How much Merton might have told Lax about his romance with the twenty-five-year-old nurse—she was born a few months before he entered the monastery; at fifty-one he was twice her age—is conjectural. When I asked Lax straight out in 1997 in Patmos whether Merton had ever mentioned M in their correspondence or meetings, he said uncomfortably, and for him evasively, "I think he did." I did not press for more information. Whatever mention of M Merton might have made to him would likely have been in conversation during Lax's final visit to Gethsemani in June of 1968—since the subject did not appear in their frequent correspondence. Lax and Merton exchanged nine letters during the M period, April to September 1966—five by Merton and four by Lax—and none mentioned her, which seems strange since Merton had always been candid with his best friend. The letters of that period are, in fact, typical of the free-form, lingo-loaded missives the two wrote to each other over the thirty years of their friendship. "Here is in the hospitalio," Merton wrote Lax on April 7, 1966, a few days after he had met the nurse while recuperating from disk surgery. "Big strong girls rush in to give me the bath though I lie to them that I have already had the bath." He wrote in the same letter that "Rice wishes to travel so he will never have to come back. . . . I would have traveled there & stayed traveling up and down. . . ."[14] That seems to forebode Merton's own future travels and Rice's oncoming penchant for visiting exotic places.

Evidently Merton eventually revealed the M romance to Sister Thérèse, who wrote a longhand note, in red ink, on the back of an envelope—now in the Columbia archives with the other voluminous Merton-Lentfoehr correspondence—that said, "Three letters of this year—were destroyed [double underline]—I thought it best, for in them Merton had confided in me a personal problem (the nurse, etc.) which I felt (should something happen to me, would not be 'safe' in hands of others—though it is known (I believe) by a discreet group in Louisville)."[15] Whatever the letters said they would not likely have matched the ardor, and candor, that Merton displayed in his own journals, such as this entry recounting an Ascension Day picnic at the peak of the affair:

We ate herring and ham (not very much eating) and drank our wine and read poems and talked of ourselves and mostly made love and love and love for five hours. Though we had over and over reassured ourselves and agreed that our love would have to continue always chaste and this sacrifice was essential, yet in the end we were getting rather sexy. Yet, really, instead of being all wrong, it seemed eminently right. We now love with our whole bodies anyway, and I have the complete feel of her being (except her sex) as completely me.[16]

The nature of the injury that had put Merton into the hospital where he met the nurse was described to Sister Thérèse in some detail, at a time, June 7, 1966, when the romance, unmentioned in the letter, was hot and heavy: "In fact it is an old injury and the disc had deteriorated. Not slipped. Had to be entirely removed and replaced with a bone graft from the hip. . . ." His amours, however, did not diminish his writing productivity. He enclosed, with the letter to the nun, a response to a request:

Ned O'Gorman is doing a mysterious and complex book for Random House, to which many have been asked to contribute bits and pieces. He asked me to define seven words. The definitions had to be "revolutionary" because the book is revolutionary thinking. I don't know how revolutionary I was in the seven words, but anyway here they are. They might throw your retreat into a turmoil. You can make a revolutionary retreat. I should have developed the one on war more, but have written so much on it I was fed up with the subject. . . . The first one on death is largely Rahner and existentialism and I think it is the best. The one on purity will make a lot of people sit up and some will reach for their anathemas. . . .[17]

John Eudes Bamberger, O.C.S.O., a trained pyschiatrist and priest who had been a counselor to Merton in the 1960s in Gethsemani, seemed to be commenting indirectly on the subject of the nurse during an interview in 1999 at the Abbey of Genesee, a Trappist monastery outside of Rochester, New York, where he was then the abbot. Bamberger had told Paul Wilkes, who compiled the book *Merton by Those Who Knew Him Best,* that "he [Merton] was not quite suited to be a hermit. . . . I think there's a lot of evidence for that. . . ."[18] I referred to that sentence in my interview, and asked him if he thought that the evidence had, in fact, come out eventually as he expected it would. "Oh, yeah I probably was referring to his trouble with that woman . . . but you know . . . a hermit . . . really . . . for the first time in his life after twenty-five years as a monk . . . if you have a real vocation you don't run away from it . . . and that's probably what I had in mind when I said that, in terms of evidence. I knew Merton himself, of course, was providing most of the evidence." Bamberger, although he says that he had not had a "particularly intimate friendship" with Merton, "thought the world of him . . . I still feel I owed a lot to him." He had been frank with Merton, however, and told him, "after he had been in the hermitage for a year or so . . . 'What are you doing out there? You are having too many contacts with people. It's not the right thing.'"[19]

The advice was evidently ignored, and Merton, even after the M affair was over, had rousing bourbon and beer sessions in the hermitage and in the fields and woods of the monastery with the likes of old friends Ping Ferry and Jay Laughlin, and new ones like the folk singer Joan Baez. Baez, asked what she remembered from her visit to Gethsemani, said simply that "the time I spent with Thomas Merton [in December 1966], we mostly laughed."[20] But he also had less impious visitors during that year, including Jacques Maritain, with whom he had had years of correspondence, the Sufi Master C. D. Abdesalam, and the Vietnamese Buddhist monk Thich Nhat Hanh. With Hanh, "a fine guy altogether. . . . We made a tape together for Dan Berrigan in which we do everything including sing, he a Buddhist Gatha, I a Cistercian Alleluia."[21] His writing productivity did not suffer in these times. His publications in 1966 included prose poems in *Raids on the Unspeak-*

able, published by New Directions, and, finally, the updated version of "My Argument with the Gestapo." The latter included, among many other perceptive short essays, one on the Brazilian poets. He particularly cited Jorge de Lima, whose works reminded him of Bob Lax's *Circus of the Sun*. Merton called de Lima "a mystic of cosmic as well as Christian vision. I wrote to Lax about him right away, when I discovered his great, incomparable circus. The same paradisaical humor, viewing the universe as 'play.'"[22]

Rice remembers from his 1966 visit how much Merton loved the privacy, and the proximity of nature, at the hermitage. On his return to New York, Rice sent Merton some of the records of Bob Dylan, who had become a favorite of the monk. Merton's description of Dylan's music is as insightful as that of a *Rolling Stone* reviewer:

> The Bob Dylan records Ed Rice sent finally reached me Thursday and Thursday night I played some of them. Rich variety of things. I like best the "middle" (so far) protest songs like "Gates of Eden" which is full of a real prophetic ardor and irony. And power! But the newest baroque obscenities, the dead voice, the noise of rock, the crowding in of new fashion, this is very intriguing too. Intriguing is a bad word. One does not get "curious" about Dylan. You are either all in it or all out of it. I am *in* his new stuff. His song "I want you" ran through my head all day yesterday in Louisville.[23]

Merton exchanged long and lively letters with the outspoken thirty-ish theologian Rosemary Radford Ruether from 1966 to early 1968. They covered, in blunt language, such subjects as sexuality, Teilhard de Chardin, monasticism (she said it seemed irrelevant), even the sensual aspects of manual work. In this posting he talked of his Catholic friends, including Ed Rice, and then got in some hard licks about his own unhappiness with some aspects of Catholicism.

> I am simply browned off with and afraid of Catholics. All Catholics, from Ottaviani to Du Bay, all down the damn line. There are a few Catholics I can stand with equanimity when I forget they are Catholics, and remember they are just my friends, like Dan Berrigan and Ed Rice and Sister Mary Luke and a lot of people like that. I love the monks but they might as well be in China. I love all the nice well-meaning people who go to Mass and want things to get better and so on, but I understand Zen Buddhists better than I do them and the Zens understand me better. But this is awful because where is the Church and where am I in the Church?

. . . I'd be perfectly content to forget I'm Catholic. I suppose that is bad faith, because meanwhile I continue in a monastery and a hermitage where I am content with life and the institution is supporting me in this. . . .

. . . I do wonder at times if the Church is real at all. I believe it, you know. But I wonder if I am nuts to do so. And [am] I a part of a great big hoax?[24]

I cited those words in my interview with Bamberger, and these, from another Merton letter, in 1967, to Ruether: "I am a notorious maverick in the Order and my Abbot considers me a dangerous subject always ready to run off with a woman or something so I am under constant surveillance." Bamberger's response was that "well, there was that side to him . . . this out of control, angry side, he sort of cultivated that . . . but at the same time if you read his later letters to her [Ruether] he turns on her and defends monastic life,"[25] as he does indeed in this statement: "Honestly, your view of monasticism is to me so abstract and so in a way arbitrary (though plenty of basis in texts can be found) that it is simply poles apart from the existential, concrete, human dimension which the problem has for us here."[26]

It may be that Merton had never encountered a Catholic woman as brassy and smart as Ruether. A theologian at Howard University at the time, she expressed skepticism about monastic life in several letters from 1967: ". . . monasticism, no longer today standing for radical Christianity, has indeed lost its soul"; and later, "No wonder the young monks left—they left, not because they lost their vocations, but hopefully because they found them and knew that they would not be expressed in that corner of 'this world' which calls itself 'monastery.'"[27]

Years later, in a preface to the publication of the full texts of the letters between her and the monk, she wrote, "What I was looking for in initiating this conversation was neither a confessor, nor to be his confessor, but a genuine Catholic intellectual peer, and with whom I could be ruthlessly honest . . . I was trying to test . . . what was the crucial issue, for me, at that time: whether it was, in fact, actually possible to be a Roman Catholic and to be a person of integrity."[28] The letters between the two are as cogent today as they were then, and Ruether, now at the Graduate Theological Union in Berkeley, California, continues to tilt with the church, while staying in it, as a columnist for the *National Catholic Reporter.*

Bamberger feels that Merton's health problems, which had been "pretty much in the background," worsened during his hermit period of 1966 and 1967, and that this was "significant," presumably with respect to his obstreperous moods at that time.[29] He groused to Lax, "I am like to go to jail in a huge fight with seven publishers, much woe, black eyes all over. Why did I not years ago make my way to Patmose where the poets are happy?"[30]

Lax was, indeed, very happy on his various islands—Lesbos, Kos, Kalymnos, Patmos. He sometimes took the long ferry rides to Piraeus and Athens, for practical needs like seeing the dentist—and he went back to Europe every year or so to visit with friends in Paris, or to stay with Bernhard Moosbrugger, his publisher, in Zurich, or to join me at a space congress. He had many visitors on the islands, probably more than he wished to have since he treasured his solitude so much. Oona Sullivan once said that Lax had the solitude that Merton wanted. His devoted nieces, Marcia Kelly, with husband, Jack, and Connie Brothers, with husband, Bill Bolger, and grandniece Cammy Brothers, visited him periodically. Old friends from New York—Emil Antonucci, Judy Emery—made the trek occasionally. Emery became editor of one of Lax's last journals, *Peacemaker's Handbook*. Ed Rice went twice, the first time taking some great photos of Lax against the columns of the Acropolis in Athens. He described Kalymnos as "Endsville. . . . Every Greek island has a temple or a monastery or something picturesque. Kalymnos has nothing. No tourists. They had two B-class hotels the first time I was there. The second time I stayed with Lax. They speak a dialect, which Lax learned. It's like learning English by going to Appalachia."[31]

The Lax–Merton correspondence in the 1966-67 period was rich with absurdities. Snippets:

July 10, 1966, Lax ["Sam"] to Merton ["Most dear Pandolf"] from Athens:
    One does not write because of cinemas. One is engaged to perform (arf, arf) on the films. Travelling (in a bus) to all parts of Greece with the headless director. Today is Meteora, tomorrow Delphous, next week the very plains of Olympia . . . but there is no script. No one has any idea of what we will do amongst the monks.

July 15, 1966, Merton ("Cassidy") to Lax ("Revered Postum"):
    Ahah, I knew all along you were with the film. As to the script, pay no attention whatever there is no script. . . . Just show the monks of meteora knocking off their derbies with custard pies and go "POW" on the screen once in a while.

. . . I have now the sprained ankle. I am all tore up in the joints.
I am a veritable orthopedic case rent limb from limb by the drs.
. . . I got a new Buddhist meditation book all about bare atten-
tion and clear comprehensions and all the works I learn to float.
What does a growing boy care for disks and bumps if he can float,
tell me that?

November 4, 1966, Merton ("Captain Nemo") to Lax ("Frost-
nip"):
Here I sit in the big silences and nothing speaks but the gas
heater which clucks and chunks but gives out the big heat, for
because of the burse and the bump I no longer chop the log or
fell the pine. I just sit here looking at the snow and wishing hard
for some whiskey but there is none. I live a flawed existence. I am
utterly without rapport.
. . . Also was here Maritain, very fine, very noble, back from
the old days when there used to be people. We sat in the wood
and lamented the loss of people and I took five million pix on a
camera borrowed from Picasso but I don't know how it comes up
the prints.

July 23, 1967, Lax ("Lefty") to Merton ("Wingy" [Manone, a
great jazz trumpeter they used to hear in New York]), from Patmos:
Just before it fell apart, my typewriter made up a batch of these
& said I shld snd them.
[Enclosed were 18 strips like this]:

TTTTTTTT
NNNNNNNNNN
XXXXXXXXX
NNNNNNNNNN
TTTTTTTT

The loss of old Columbia friends had begun to strike Lax, Merton,
and Rice cruelly when, at the end of 1965, Bob Gerdy, who had been
one of the *Jester* stalwarts, was found dead on the street in Manhattan.
"He drank himself to death," Rice said. A brilliant writer, Gerdy had
been on the *Jester* staff, along with Lax and Merton, when Rice was
editor-in-chief. He had earlier been editor-in-chief himself. At his death
he was a senior editor of the *New Yorker*. Described by Merton when
they first met as a "smart sophomore with the face of a child and a lot

of curly hair on top of it,"[32] he had been one of three Jews present at Merton's baptism—the others being Lax and Freedgood. He later converted to Catholicism but it did not stick. It was Gerdy who influenced Merton to take the course on St. Thomas Aquinas that he himself had taken in Columbia graduate school.

In 1967, and into early 1968, the tragedies mounted. Next to go was Ad Reinhardt, who succumbed to a heart ailment. By this time a renowned abstract expressionist, Reinhardt had sometimes made drawings for *Jubilee* and regularly attended the magazine's wine and cheese parties, which is where Millie and I met him. I recall him as stocky and jovial, but he must have had his dark and contemplative side. One of his black paintings hangs prominently in the Princeton University Art Museum, often baffling viewers who try to discern the subtle stygian rectangles. Merton said Mass for him after hearing of his death from Sister Thérèse, who had sent him a news clip of the obituary. "I wrote at once to Lax out in Greece," he told her. "Poor Ad. I had been thinking about him a lot lately, wanting to see him again. . . . He was really a stupendous person. One of the very smartest and best, and there was a great deal packed into that painting of blacks on blacks." He added, somewhat gratuitously, a jab at mass audience Catholic writers, "The Catholic writers in this country who are most significant seem to me to be people who write as marginal or unusual Catholics, and do not speak for the mass of our brethren (that is probably one reason why they are good!)."[33] To Lax, Merton's epitaph on Reinhardt was poignant, "Reinhardt he died. . . . Last Wednesday he die with the sorrows in the studio. . . . Don't say in the clips how he died, maybe just sat down and give up in front of the black picture. . . . Tomorrow the solemns. The requiems alone in the hermit hatch. . . . The clean oblations all round thunder quiet silence black picture oblations. Make Mass beautiful silence like big black picture speaking requiem."[34]

Lax wrote back promptly,

oy oy
sad for old
Reinhardt
very sad for
old Reinhardt
oy oy[35]

Merton coveted his own black on black Reinhardt painting, which hung in his hermitage. Millie and I saw it once when Brother Patrick Hart took us there in 1997. It had been stained by kitchen vapors over the years—Brother Patrick said that John Howard Griffin stayed there while working on Merton's biography (he died before finishing it). He would sometimes fry eggs in the kitchen and some of the grease would splatter all over. The painting was cleaned, and is now locked up in the monastery vault and has been appraised at $1.1 million.

Merton's journal reveals eerie premonitions of his other friends' deaths. In September 1967, he wrote that "Ed Rice sent a long obituary of Ad Reinhardt from the Times. Poor Ad. I wonder if any of our bunch will live much beyond sixty. I don't have much confidence in Slate or Freedgood doing so after the way they looked (tired, overworked, overwrought) this year."[36] Then he wrote Sister Thérèse, "I wish I could get Slate, that lawyer, moving on the estate business. With Reinhardt—who seemed the most indestructible of us all—gone, the others could go like that. And Slate and Freedgood are . . . living rather wildly, burning everything out: not that they drink because if they do it's impossible. But they are very busy and crazy. Sy was down here and cracked up a Hertz car and nearly ended up in lawsuits with everybody from the State on down."[37]

The demise of both Slate and Freedgood came shortly afterward. Slate, a prominent New York lawyer who had made several visits to Gethsemani to consult with Merton on his will, died, also in September, of a heart attack on his fifty-fourth birthday; and Freedgood, who had been a senior editor of *Fortune* magazine, burned himself to death when he dropped a lighted cigarette in a chair in his eastern Long Island vacation home after a lot of drink. When Slate died, Merton cabled the news to Lax in Greece, and wrote his widow, Mary Ellen, a warm note. She replied with descriptors of her husband that seem to have characterized all of the Columbia buddies, "I share your pleasure that you and John had met and laughed this past Spring. . . . John was especially special-extra funny, extra tormented, extra kind, extra bedevilled."[38] An example of Slate's humor is his comment to Merton after receiving a copy of *Mystics and Zen Masters*: "I will read [it] with much interest inasmuch as I am both a mystic and a zen master. Incidentally, I mean to write a piece about what I call Zen Capitalism, the motto of which is Double Your Money or Double Your Money Back."[39] Lax remembers that Slate was "one of the best of the Columbia gang at keeping things together. Everyone hung around Slate's room. Once someone said something about a guy who had left the room, and Slate said, 'No more of that, if that happens again we're through.' Later, when he was a corporate lawyer for Pan Am he would phone from someplace like Chicago and he'd bark for three minutes and he'd hang up. Only he and Merton and I could speak that language. Rice didn't talk at all. I once told my sister in Olean that Rice was hungry and she said, 'How do you know?'"[40]

Merton phoned Anne Freedgood on January 21, 1968, when he heard of Sy's death. "Poor Sy!" Merton wrote in his journal. "Mass for him yesterday (Library Chapel) and today (hermitage). I remember so many things: Sy and Rice at my baptism; the time we rented the house in Woodstock for the summer and didn't go—a good thing. . . . Brama-chari. Sy's place in Long Beach, the brothers and uncles. That crazy paper we started. . . . Sy trying to teach me Judo on a sandbar in the lagoon behind Long Beach. . . . Last year he was here looking terrible in his fur hat and bandaged face and I knew he was finished. Yet he was full of ideas and plans. We made a voluble, profane tape. Talked of his analysis. . . . And death, which he had very much on his mind. It must have been tough on Anne to cope with all his drive and all his despair."[41]

Although communications with the friends from college days had been sporadic, Lax, Merton, and Rice kept in touch with all of them, and missed them when they had not been heard from. For example, Lax complained to Merton at the end of 1966: "i never hear from slate either, though i write a cajoling note every Christmas to himself & his wife. they never send any jokes in return . . . he never writes to his poor old college buddy-roops.

"reinhardt does. every once in a while he puts on his old raccoon coat & looks up his friends. & rice has taken to wearing his psi u [fraternity] button night & day. i can never forget the old days myself. . . ."[42]

Lax wrote a poem, inspired by Reinhardt, that is in his Columbia archive:

> I'm beginning to think
> r was wrong
>
> not r, but an idea i had
> of him that i practically
> worshipped
>
> that said life was the
> opposite of art
>
> & art was the opposite
> of life
>
> & proud of it

but i think life
has something
to do with art

& it's just a matter
of finding

the special point

at which the
two of them
get together[43]

The year 1967 also brought the end to *Jubilee*, which Rice, Lax, and Merton had been involved in for some seventeen years—since its conception and planning in 1950. Merton had worried often about the magazine's, and Rice's, welfare. When, in mid-1967, Rice's financial woes were peaking again, Merton tried to buck him up:

> I'm sure something will turn up to make life more bearable on Jubilee but undertaking a thing like that I suppose you have to expect that kind of jazz: just as in becoming a monk one has to expect to be pushed around unreasonably. . . . No use getting sick of everything. It comes up like bile but don't let it affect you if you can help it. Me I get the same about various things too. Just the depression of living under constant absurd attrition [referring, presumably, to the departure of some of the monks]. Fortunately I have the woods. Peace.[44]

In the last years of its life the burden of keeping the *Jubilee* staff enthusiastic must have been heavy on Rice. Frank Monaco, one of the brilliant staff photographers, recalled that the washroom had a sign: "St Rita [the saint of impossible miracles] can't help you."[45]

Merton once asked John Eudes Bamberger, his fellow Trappist, to stop in to see Rice at the *Jubilee* office in New York. "I remember what Rice was having for lunch . . . he had an apple and a sandwich on his table . . . and he told me to tell Father Louis to stop writing so much. Merton's response was, 'Well, he's got a good point there,' then he laughed and he went his own way." This was ironic because Rice was continually dependent on having Merton write for *Jubilee*. "He was one of about fifty people who were asking him to write for them," said Bamberger, who was, himself, a *Jubilee* admirer. "I thought [the magazine] was great. . . .

It was an important contribution to the Church. It took Catholicism out of the ghetto, made it more intellectually respectable."[46]

Before *Jubilee* died, Rice had looked frantically for help from other publishers. The Rice archive at Georgetown University has numerous documents dealing with possible bailouts. One is a staff memo by Father Comber of *Catholic World*, published by Paulist Press. He told of having received a phone call from someone who said Rice was trying to sell *Jubilee*, then having dinner with Rice and reviewing the magazine's history. "He's tired, feels that the only future for Catholic magazines is merger into one significant publication—too many little ones around, advocates *Jubilee* merger with *Catholic World*, has Father Cotter of Jesuit *Sacred Heart Messenger* as consultant."

The memo states that *Jubilee* had 16,000 paid subscriptions after 15 years (down from some 35,000 at its peak). *Catholic World* had 10,000 after 100 years. Comber and Rice felt, unrealistically, that they could get 25,000 individual subscriptions at $10 and "20,000 bulk" [probably back-of-the-church sales, at a substantial discount, like 40 percent]. The memo said that Rice indicated that "his salary need was $17,000, his managing editor needed $7,000, and there were three other editors requiring $6,500, $6,000 and $5,500. Payments to artists and contributors were $12,000, and miscellaneous other costs were detailed, including printing at $90,000." Even recognizing the forty years of inflation, those costs are astoundingly low. Rice wanted coverage of the $27,600 mortgage on the brownstone at 168 E. 91st St. in Manhattan, then in *Jubilee*'s name. He also wanted some $68,000 in current bills paid, and said he owed a friend $11,500. Rice said that "he would keep going a year or two if this deal didn't go through."[47] The deal did not go through, and he was unable to hang on for another year.

"I had put some of my own money into the magazine in its last year," Rice said in a 1996 interview.

I did the editing from a house we bought on E. 91st St., helped by a loan of $17K from Ann Light [a staffer], who had money from a pharmaceutical company and who later died an alcoholic. I sold the brownstone for $35K. I lost money but not a significant amount. We owed maybe $100K at the end. We were even harassed by the fire department. Suddenly there would be a dozen fire engines outside the building. They would come in and tell us that our wainscotting and wood panels were against the law, maybe they were looking for graft.[48]

The very last issue of *Jubilee* under Rice, in June 1967, contained, ironically, an article by Merton, "The Death of a Holy Terror," about

Frère Pascal Bourgoint, a maverick French Trappist whose life was not unlike that of Merton's own.[49] Pascal, who died in 1966, was a friend of Jean Cocteau, himself the godson of Jacques Maritain, and was the hero of Cocteau's *Les Enfants Terribles* (published as *The Holy Terrors* by New Directions). A painter, Pascal had "abandoned the Parisian art world" and, at forty-two, had become a Cistercian monk at the Abbey of Citeaux. Shortly thereafter, he went to work in a leper colony in Cameroon, and he died there. Merton's article gives him a platform for his views on the need for monastic reform. "Frère Pascal was one of many, very many, monks who have been plunged into suffering self-questioning and conflict in the monastic crisis of the past ten years." Merton wrote that "[m]any of them have left—whether to go forward along the line of their monastic vocation, or to go back and start over again on some other track. This is a sign that the forces of vocational charism and spirit which the institution seeks to 'contain' (if not in some cases actually to suppress) are still very much alive. This of course is part of the same crisis of institutionalism and of authority which rocks the entire Church, as the Reformation finally works its way completely to the heart of Roman Catholicism." Think of it: those prophetic words by Merton were written almost forty years ago! He ended his piece with a plea for monastic renewal: ". . . monasteries must face the problem that, in their present state, and with their present aims, they cannot provide a lifetime vocation for any but a few specially constructed people. It does not have to be that way, and monastic renewal will surely demand some examination of new and more flexible ways of relating to the world of today and to the people in it."[50]

Rice held talks with Justus George Lawler, editor of *Continuum*, about beginning a *Jubilee* partnership starting with a September 1967 issue "now that all of the major points have been settled," but the talks broke off.[51] He then turned to a German book publisher, Herder & Herder, but the negotiations soon became nasty. In a long letter to the director of the company, known in Germany as Verlag Herder, headquartered in Freiburg, Rice accused the New York representatives of having "committed injustices and unsavory practices" and asked for an impartial meeting. Herder & Herder acquired *Jubilee*'s assets but, says Rice, reneged on an arrangement allowing Rice to keep the 91st St. brownstone, assume the building's mortgage, and pay Rice a salary.[52] These requests were not honored, but evidently by this time Herder & Herder had the upper hand over a cashless *Jubilee* and simply took over the building and the magazine, to begin with a proposed September issue. Oona Sullivan remembers that "the staff was locked out and we weren't even permitted to take our belongings, I lost a pair of shoes, a few books—no great loss but I regret having to leave a painting from a friend that was very valuable to me. The Herder & Herder people were brutish. We called them Nazis. To remember that a gentleman like Ed Rice was caught in their clutches makes me ill even today. But at the end the *Jubilee* spirit prevailed. One of our contributors, the painter Alice Wadowska, came by with a bottle of wine. So we sat around in Ed's office, opened up the bottle and drank to the future. Well, it was great fun, intellectually stimulating, and spiritually broadening. The ending was sad, but I wouldn't have missed a day of all those years."[53]

"What killed Jubilee," Sullivan said, "was the open talk of subjects like contraception, which triggered a lot of letters and some parishes refused to keep the magazine in their book racks. Atom bomb OK but condoms no. . . . We did a Children's Missal. Can you imagine if we had printed it? They would have thought we were Unitarians."[54] At the end, on August 3, 1967, a letter went to all subscribers from "The Editors of Jubilee"—although it almost certainly was not written by them but by the new owner, Herder & Herder. It included some upbeat, unrealistic sentences indicating that there were plans for a commemorative issue at Christmas time.[55] A letter dated the same day went from Robert E. Rambusch, the noted church architect, to Frank Schworer of Herder & Herder, New York, stating that the "change-over and handling of it appears to reflect little credit on this organization." Rambusch asked that his name be removed from *Jubilee*'s masthead as a member of the advisory board. A few days later, on August 9, Rice wrote to Werner Linz of Herder & Herder's New York office that he had resigned as of August 3, and that his name and those of Sullivan, Robert Lax, Richard Staub, Frank Monaco, Jane Gibson, and Margery Rice were not to be used in connection "with the September issue or any future issue." The letter was acknowledged by Herder's head in Germany, a Mr. Dornreich, on August 18, who extended wishes for good luck to Rice. Rice, in turn, acknowledged that letter but, on August 29, apparently still awaiting some response to his demands, wrote, "I am still awaiting your interested intervention." There is no letter of response in the fat folder on the subject in the Rice archive at Georgetown. There were no July or August issues of the magazine, and then—on the second page of the September issue, which still carried the masthead of the Ed Rice staff—there appeared an unsigned statement titled, "A Message." It apologized to readers for the missing issues and promised a continuation of the *Jubilee* quality. It had sixty-four pages, looking quite robust, and indicated that the office was now at the Herder Book Center, 232 Madison Avenue. There was a major article by Harrison Salisbury titled "The Church and North Vietnam." The next letter in the Georgetown file, dated September 12, comes from Jane Gibson, who protested the use of her name and two of her movie reviews in the September issue, and asked for $70 compensation. Also protesting was Sullivan, who complained on September 15 that Herder & Herder had given readers the impression with the September issue that the magazine had merely been relocated.

It is likely that the Rice file at Georgetown on these negotiations is incomplete, and so it is not clear what was transacted over the period, but there continued to be letters, such as board member Edmund T. Delaney's claim to Herder & Herder on September 14 that they had not been authorized to use his name on the masthead, and there is correspondence as late as January and February of 1968 about a Herder & Herder person rifling the *Jubilee* bookkeeper's files. Rice felt that Herder & Herder's tactics had been "ghoulish." Herder & Herder, with Justus George Lawler as editor, published the magazine with the *Jubilee* title through the rest of 1967 and for the first three months of 1968, skipped April, May, and June, and ran a final August–September issue, containing mostly cartoons, with a statement titled "A Fond Farewell." The statement indicated that the magazine was being merged with *U.S. Catholic* and given the name *U.S. Catholic and Jubilee*. Purchaser was the Claretian Fathers from Chicago, with Rev. Robert J. Leuver listed as editor. The *Jubilee* add-on was actually kept until January 1972, when it was dropped, but the magazine had really been dead for five years by then.

One subscriber, Helen Stewart of Los Angeles, mourned the end, writing sadly, after an article on the "sale" had appeared in the *National Catholic Reporter* on August 16, 1967, that "[m]y personal Christmas list for gifts has consisted almost entirely of annual subscriptions to *Jubilee*, mainly among non-Catholics. . . ." *Sic transit gloria.*

Merton's comment on the magazine's demise, to Sister Thérèse, was that "Ed's trouble with Jubilee has been very sad. He absolutely did not make a fortune. They cleaned him out of the last cent he had and left him with seventeen years of hard work and nothing to show for it. But Jubilee was certainly a good magazine."[56]

Rice's woes were large. "My marriage to Margery broke up after twenty years, but things had been going down hill for ten years. . . . Margery said she was going to make life hell for me and she did. She had a boy friend who didn't want to marry her. I left the church."[57]

He would soon go on extended travel. "It was tragic about the way Ed was taken over by the Herder people," wrote Merton to Sister Thérèse. "But he is well out of it now. And off to Asia somewhere." In the same letter he told the nun that Rice had sent him the manuscript for "Journal of My Escape from the Nazis," which he had been holding, and that it would be probably be published in the next year.[58] He also reported that "I am still waiting to get everything about my estate legal and ship shape. The dreadful thing that happened was that my old friend and lawyer John Slate just died, and Ad Reinhardt died only a few weeks before him. I'm looking around for another lawyer. Nothing definite has been done at all. I sent Lax a telegram in Greece about Slate and the Western Union people called back to say Lax had left Kalymnos and there was no forwarding address. I hope he is all right! With the nonsense in Greece [this was the period when the Greek colonels had taken over the country] he might be in jail or something."[59]

Lax must have left Kalymnos temporarily, probably to take a boat and train to Belgrade, Yugoslavia, where he met me around that time at another space congress. A few days before the congress started he had written me, "Kalymnos delegation is on its way & will meet you with bazuki band at Belgrade airport Saturday."[60] Although naturally shy, he would strike up friendships at these congresses with oddball scientists, and—over the years—with some of the Russian space experts who were then very standoffish toward most Westerners. But they were fascinated by this raffish-looking American poet in scruffy cap, clodhopper shoes, and oversized sweater—who seemed so different from the other Americans at the congress—mostly aerospace engineers from NASA, Lockheed, Boeing, MIT, Princeton, and other centers of high tech work. The Russians might have thought at first that Lax was a CIA plant, but eventually they took a liking to him and some of them still remember him warmly. He had become enthusiastic about the professional sessions at the congresses on such subjects as the search for extraterrestrial life and space law. Once again we had wonderful walks and talks and he introduced me to the local specialties, thick bitter coffee and the very special Slavic yoghurt.

Although Merton, the career contemplative, would, ironically, never achieve the solitude that Lax experienced, his hermitage gave him much more peace than he had before, even though John Eudes Bamberger feels that "he lived best, I think, and was happiest when he was novice master and had half time in the hermitage and worked with the young people. . . ." Merton had the full-time job of novice master for ten years, until 1965, the last five while he was in the hermitage. "The Abbot let him go out there [to the hermitage], and you see that way he had more balance. He participated in the community, the services . . . and it seems to me that's when he was at his best."

After that, felt Bamberger, he spoiled the intent of the hermitage, by such doing such things as

having picnics . . . we didn't do that . . . it's not what he went
out there to do and it wasn't in keeping with the monastic spirit,
although I always felt that he was special and he deserved special treatment but there are some things . . . there are limits . . .
and I said people were talking about him . . . and that hurt him,
because . . . he liked to be liked. I didn't want to hurt him but . . .
I think that's what friends are for . . . he sort of lost his way for
a while. He got depressed. You could see . . . I ran into him one
day in the woods when we were both out walking, completely by
accident. . . . I could see that he was depressed . . . well that can
happen to anybody but . . . on the other hand, I only saw he had
a very real gift for prayer and for solitude but he also needed the
community.[61]

Bamberger feels that it is significant that Merton's health was not up
to par during the hermitage years. It is certainly the case that the monk
made numerous journal entries, or mentions to correspondents, about
his ailments. In December 1967, for instance, he wrote Sister Thérèse,
"Due to bursitis & the operation which did not turn out completely
successful—I have to rest my arm & do a minimum of typing. . . ."[62]
The ailment must have been bothering him for some time because more
than a year earlier he had complained to Sister Thérèse that he had been
getting cortisone shots for it.

With Slate gone, Merton turned to the Louisville lawyer, John Ford,
to take over the preparation of the will. Sister Thérèse, who typed it,
made her first and only visit to Gethsemani in October or November
1967, after Merton wrote her, "The Abbot is away now, but I am sure he
will have no objection [to her visit], and as I said he is about to retire. At
least it is pretty sure he is. So we may well get a few significant changes
around here, and things may open up somewhat. But it is still impossible for me to go anywhere, although I get all kinds of invitations, even
one last August to come to NY and meet Cardinal Koenig and discuss
his work with atheists etc."[63] Sister Thérèse must have worked on the
will with dispatch because a few weeks later he thanked her for sending
a copy to him and told her:

do not send the final version here because the more copies exist
the more complicated things are, legally, when the thing has to
be settled. I have only two, one for me and one for the lawyer or
wherever it is to be filed. Tuesday finally we signed the whole Trust
agreement and I think it is pretty intelligently worked out so that
everything will make sense. . . . There is yet to be an official policy

for the various collections, but the rule of thumb is that what is not yet published has to be restricted (all permissions to copy etc from the Trust) and what has been published can be consulted freely with ordinary library rules, and permissions to quote in print are cleared through the trust.[64]

It could have been that one of the provisions of the Will was to include a modest stipend to Lax, maybe the dividends from Grosset and Dunlap stock that had been owned by his grandfather.

Important transitions were about to occur at the monastery in this period, including the election of a new abbot. Merton sniffed the changes and wrote Sister Thérèse, "Things have been a little rough here. The situation is not altogether healthy. A kind of atmosphere of triumphal pseudo-change. It is bound to backfire when the young ones find out that in spite of appearances there is really nothing happening at all, only a game of musical chairs."[65] But it proved not to be musical chairs. A few months later, a new abbot was elected to succeed Dom James. Apparently Merton himself had been a possible, although unwilling, candidate—and surely a long shot for the position. He wrote in his journal, "The fact is that the community is full of half-sick people, immensely vulnerable, wasting their lives in petty, neurotic machinations. . . ."[66]

The new abbot, Flavian Burns, would make a huge difference for Merton, who told Sister Thérèse that he was "[a] very good man—the best we have—years ago I spotted him for a future Abbot. Young, alert, solid. Pray for him & us."[67]

****

Lax, Merton, Rice, and Ad Reinhardt all served as editor-in-chief of Columbia's humor magazine, *Jester*, at one time or another during the 1936–1939 period, and all four were talented cartoonists. Examples of their work can be seen in the first five illustrations.

Lax depicted Hitler bemoaning the fate of Little Orphan Annie as paper's headline reads "Jews Beaten." *Columbia University Archive*

The Christmas cover in 1939, as World War II began, showed Mussolini, Hitler, and Franco cradling bombs while following the Star of Bethlehem. The cartoonist, unidentified, was probably Rice. *Columbia University Archive*

Most issues included one or more of Merton's scantily clad cuties. Caption for this was, "Now toin around, and tell me more about Brahms!" *Columbia University Archive*

Ad Reinhardt article satirizing fraternities showed a student rushee in a quandary. *Columbia University Archive*

Lax illustrated a Merton piece on beards in *Jester*. *Columbia University Archive*

Drinking and women were often a part of Merton's Columbia years. *Columbia University Archive. Photographer unknown*

Jester editors: Tom Merton, art editor; Bob Lax, editor; Ralph de Toledano, managing editor. *Columbia University Archive. Photographer unknown*

Gethsemani, 1949. Merton, eight years a monk, is ordained. Lax, Giroux, and Rice were present. *St. Bonaventure University, Friedsam Library Archive. Photographer unknown*

Lax and Millie Harford at L'Eau Vive, a
Catholic retreat house in the former manse
of Madame Pompidou outside Paris, 1953.
James Harford

Ed Rice took a number of photographs of
Merton, including this one, during a 1966
visit to Gethsemani.
Copyright Edward Rice III

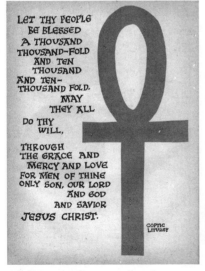

Jubilee's artwork was consistently
imaginative, thanks to Rice.
James Harford

Rice in *Jubilee* office. The magazine, which he
founded and managed from 1953–1967, won
numerous prizes, but was always cash-poor.
Rice Georgetown University Archive

Merton with nuns and monks, including Jean Leclercq, second from left, just prior to his accidental electrocution in Bangkok, 1968.
Merton Center, Merton Legacy Trust

Merton's grave in Gethsemani.
James Harford

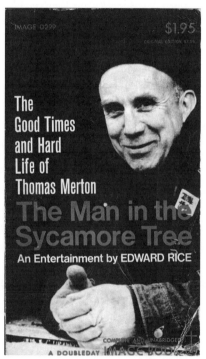

Edward Rice's 1970 biography of Merton evoked controversy as too hastily prepared and left an impression that Merton was headed for Buddhism, but the book was highly praised by Lax and by friends who had known the monk from before Gethsemani days. *Cover photo by Edward Rice. Copyright Edward Rice III.*

VI. R. Lax

here isa bird iam send you
from Patmose

FOR   black
AD   black
REIN-   black
HARD T   blue
         blue
         blue

         black
         black
         black
         black

         blue
         blue
         blue
         —

An issue of *Voyages* included a Lax cartoon with a characteristically brief message for publisher William Claire. *Copyright Voyages*

A Lax poem dedicated to his friend, the artist Ad Reinhardt, whose paintings were often black and blue. *Copyright Voyages*

Lax's friends would often get short poems, designed on postcards, like this one on a space travel theme. *James Harford*

Lax counseled
many visitors on
his Greek islands.
Here he talks to
fifteen-year-old
Jimmy Harford on
Kalymnos, 1970.
James Harford

. . . . and Jimmy's
mother, Millie
Harford.
James Harford

Lax was fascinated
by space science
and often accompa-
nied the author to
space congresses.
The Russian atten-
dees, such as Yuri
Zonov, here with
Lax and Millie Har-
ford at a congress in
Lausanne in 1984,
were much taken by
him after realizing
he was not a CIA
agent.
James Harford

Rice married
Susanna Franklin,
right, in 1990.
Millie Harford
is on left, in
Rice's home in
Sagaponack.
James Harford

1990 gathering at
Tuxedo Park summer
rental of Marcia and
Jack Kelly. Lax,
Marcia, and Rice in
front row. Millie
Harford, Judy Emery,
Susanna Franklin
Rice, Jim Harford in
rear.
Jack Kelly photo

Rice in 1996
showed the effects
of Parkinson's
disease, which
became very
debilitating after
Susanna's tragic
death three years
earlier.
James Harford

Thomas Merton at Gethsemani.
Photo by John Lyons.
Copyright Merton Center, Merton Legacy Trust

Lax, ageing visibly, held forth for visitors from his bed in his Patmos house in May 1997. *James Harford*

Merton's longtime friend and secretary, Brother Patrick Hart, O.C.S.O., holds a "black on black" Ad Reinhart painting that hung in the monk's hermitage for years and is now in the monastery archive.
Patrick Hart. Abbey of Gethsemani

8

ODYSSEYS

*Lax, Rice, and Merton More Deeply into Eastern
Religions; Rice Travels; Merton Outraged at
Vietnam War, Disillusioned with Vatican II;
Final Meetings at Gethsemani;
Merton's Death in Bangkok*

In the 1960s all three protagonists—thirty years into their friend-ship—had begun to deepen their interest in Christian and other mys-tics, and intensified their study of Asian and Orthodox cultures and religions. For Lax this was largely passive—meditating, thinking, writ-ing poems, and reading, while developing a discipline for practicing yoga. He had a routine for many years of doing carefully orchestrated breathing rituals followed by therapeutic swims, except for the winter months, in the warm waters of his Greek islands. His reading had long included the writings of St. John of the Cross, St. Theresa of Avila, and now he was investigating mystical tomes such as Mircea Eliade's *Ten Thousand Years of Milarepa*, about Tibetan Buddhism's most famous saint. He recommended it enthusiastically to others.

Merton was much more active in his investigations. As far back as 1951 he had written eloquently about the Christian mystics in *The Ascent to Truth*, an impressive piece of research and comment that became a 342-page book very likely read by both Lax and Rice. It ends with seventeen pages of valuable biographical material on Christian mystics: besides the sixteenth-century Theresa and John of the Cross of Spain there are the fourth-century St. Gregory of Nyssa of Asia Minor; the twelfth-century St. Bernard of Clairvaux of France; the thirteenth-century St. Thomas Aquinas of Italy; the fourteenth-century Blessed John Ruysbroeck of Belgium; and the seventeenth-century Blaise Pascal of France.

Never one to underplay his main point, Merton led off the book with an apocalyptic prologue, all too relevant even today: "The human race is facing the greatest crisis in its history, because religion itself is being weighed in the balance. The present unrest in five continents, with everyone fearful of being destroyed, has brought many men to their knees."[1] The subsequent text is dominated by an exposition of the thinking of John of the Cross, covering some one hundred pages, beginning with a fascinating account of the rigorous environment in which the saint was educated at the University of Salamanca. He was one of a "dozen Carmelites, who lived tucked away in a little corner called the College of Saint Andrew" for whom "any signal breach of discipline would mean for them ten days in the convent jail cell on bread and water, with the prospect of a return to their house of origin if the offense were too often repeated."[2]

While John of the Cross continued to be a major figure in Merton's mystical thinking, he became more broadly interested in other non-Christian contemplative philosophies. In 1960 he told Ed Rice that he intended to write some book reviews of works on Zen under an assumed name. In a letter signed "Jess Stacey" [a jazz pianist hero], he said, "Have Zen books. Will have to write surreptitious reviews in invisible ink, but will do my all."[3]

Rice's interest in Eastern thinking was manifest in the 1950s and '60s in his choices of material for *Jubilee*. One of the most substantive articles had been Merton's 1961 piece titled "Classic Chinese Thought."[4] It called out perceptively the immensely important influence that China, India, and Japan, and their beliefs, would be exerting on the world in the coming years. He urged colleges to begin teaching courses in Asiatic thought and religion. He objected to what he said was a prevalent cliché that Confucianism, Taoism, and Buddhism corresponded "in some way, with Catholicism, Protestantism and Judaism in America" whereas "there is not the faintest resemblance between the ancient religious situation in China and America's." Most *Jubilee* readers probably got, in subsequent paragraphs, their first exposure to the tenets of the Oriental religions. "Confucianism," he pointed out, "is less a 'faith' than a sacred philosophy," and, as the early Jesuits believed, "it should not be impossible to remain essentially a Confucian and yet to become a Christian, since Confucianism is nothing more or less than natural ethics in a very refined and traditional form: the natural law expressed in a sacred culture."

The founder of Taoism, Lao Tzu, a mystic, says Merton, had, as an ideal of society, "the small primitive state consisting of nothing more than a few villages . . . a philosophy that would have worked fine in the Garden of Eden, and if Adam and Eve had stuck to the Tao there would have been little difficulty for the rest of us to do so." Surely this would have been copasetic also for Lax, Merton, and Rice, who espoused the simple lifestyle anyway. Merton did not deal with Buddhism in this essay, remarking that, while it "has been the most important religion in China, for it brought the masses a definite message of salvation," it does not belong to the classic period of Chinese philosophy, with which the essay dealt.

He merely touched on Zen in the essay, pointing out that it enabled one to arrive at a state of *satori*, "or the explosive rediscovery of the hidden and lost reality within us." However, Zen, including Zen Catholicism, emerged in the mid-sixties as a subject well worth Merton's further examination, and out of that feeling came the 303-page *Mystics and Zen Masters*.[5] "Far from being suspicious of the Oriental mystical traditions," he wrote in that book, "Catholic contemplatives since the Second Vatican Council should be in a position to appreciate the wealth of experience that has accumulated in those traditions." He cited contemporary Catholic scholars like R. C. Zaehner, who had written in *Jubilee* about Buddhism,[6] and whose research, Merton wrote, "now enables us to evaluate these other traditions more correctly," and Dom Aelred Graham, whose *Zen Catholicism*, said Merton, is an example of writing that shows that "Zen has something to say not only to the curious scholar, the poet, or the aesthete, but to the ordinary Christian who takes his Christianity seriously."[7]

Some "ordinary Christian[s]" must surely have found themselves over their heads shortly after turning past the Merton quote cited above. It is interesting that the Zaehner book even gave Communism a paean, though quite conditionally, pointing out that Marxism never found its real center, but rather tried to establish Stalin as the center. Merton also called attention to a source of further enlightenment, a book by Father Heinrich Dumoulin, a Jesuit who spent years in Japan, titled *A History of Zen Buddhism*.[8] "This book makes it possible for the average Christian student to advance, with a certain amount of security and confidence, into a very mysterious realm.[9] Possible, but not so easy. Dumoulin explains patiently that Buddhism "ranks among the world's great religions," and that, like Christianity, its "basic trait . . . is its striving for otherworldly salvation." The rest of the book is an intellectual struggle, challenging in establishing the notion that mysticism should be considered as "all efforts of man to elevate himself to a supercosmic, supersensory sphere which he experiences immediately" and that "Buddha, and those who followed him, saw in mystical enlightenment the 'vehicle of salvation' that carried them beyond this world to the 'other shore.'"[10]

Paul Tillich, the noted Protestant theologian, wrote an essay for *Jubilee* entitled "A Christian-Buddhist Conversation"[11] that bears close reading today, particularly as more and more Catholics become interested in Buddhist concepts. Tillich referred to "the common problems . . . with respect to the secularization of all mankind" that each religion faces and how a dialogue between them could be of benefit to the consideration of those problems. He had had personal experience in dialogue with scholarly Buddhists in Japan and maintained that the dialogue must deal first and foremost with "the question of the intrinsic aim of existence—in Greek, the *telos* of all existing things . . . and not with a comparison of the contrasting concepts of God or man or history or salvation . . . in Christianity the telos of every*one* and everything united in the Kingdom of God; in Buddhism the telos of every*thing* and everyone fulfilled in the Nirvana." Merton, Lax, and Rice would each delve deeply into Buddhism in their personal lives in subsequent years.

Hinduism came up for analysis in *Jubilee* periodically, as in the May 1963 issue that began with an instructive editorial comment: "Hinduism is the only major religion that stands as a separate unity independent of Christianity. (Buddhism and Confucianism are a-religious, and Islam is an offshoot of Judaism and Christianity.)"[12] The same issue carried a report by Dom Bede Griffiths, a Benedictine monk, which cited the view of the Hindu Vinoba Bhave, then the head of a national movement called *Sarvodaya*, based on nonviolence, which was aimed at transforming India by the development of a village economy. No easy task, and certainly Bhave's words were tough talk for the average *Jubilee* reader, although they seem painfully relevant to today's agonies over the hatred and violence of some Islamic fanaticists. He maintained that [Griffiths's interpretation of his words] "only by building up the spiritual force of non-violence among dedicated people . . . we can hope to overcome violence. Such people will need the spirit of martyrs. They must be prepared to suffer and die, and what is perhaps more difficult, to surrender home and family and their most cherished liberties, even religious freedom. This is a challenge few Hindus or Christians are prepared to accept, yet it may be one which Hindus and Christians can work out together."[13]

In the same issue came an analysis of Hinduism by R. C. Zaehner, an Oxford expert on the religions of the East.[14] It was not easy reading, but it is a very useful primer for Catholics. "The Catholic Church (though not the major Protestant churches)," wrote Zaehner, holds that man, made in the image and likeness of God, according to Genesis, had that image "marred but not wholly effaced by original sin: the Spirit of God still inheres in the soul of fallen man. Hinduism claims that this same Spirit of God can be experienced here and now" and that "the soul cannot die, because its true home is not in space and time, but outside them; therefore the soul is unaffected by birth, death or any of the vicissitudes of mortal life."

Zaehner went on to write that "[t]he Hindu technique devised thousands of years before Christ, and still used, to achieve the transcendence of the soul is called Yoga; the transcendental state itself is called *moksha*, meaning 'release, liberation, emancipation, deliverance or salvation' of the soul from space, time, causation and all that contributes to human mortality." It is likely these are the kinds of words that Lax, Merton, and Rice mused on when they came from the mouth of Bramachari thirty years earlier, during the days at Columbia.

At the beginning of 1967, Rice—who would write nine books himself on mystic sects—sent Merton a book on Hinduism (the title not identified in Merton's acknowledgment letter). The overcommitted monk wrote back, "I haven't touched it yet but will let you know more about it when I do."[15] It was unrealistic for Merton to expect that he would get any less busy as he tried to balance book, essay, and letter writing with prayer and meditation. However, he probably got to it eventually as his interest in Eastern thought was growing, and so was his conviction that more people, especially Christians, should be reading about it.

Unfortunately, some of his writing on the Eastern religions—admittedly a tough subject to deal with—is difficult to follow. He is not so clear, for example, about what Zen is exactly: "the Zen tradition absolutely refuses to tolerate any abstract or theoretical answer . . . the question probably has no satisfactory answer. . . . Zen simply does not lend itself to logical analysis." Many things Zen is not, he goes on. It is not a method of meditation, not a kind of spirituality, not a religion, not a philosophy, not a system of thought, not a doctrine, not an ascesis. It seemed that he was then going to clarify what it *was* by writing it is a "way" and an "experience," a "life," but all that goes up in smoke when he adds, "but the way is paradoxically not a way." Enough of that. How about its relationship to God? Merton says that Zen is "perfectly compatible with Christian belief" but also says it is not "news from the Father who sends His Son into this world, but awareness of the ontological ground of our own being here and now, right in the midst of the world." Not much help to me. Suffice it to say that Merton bought Zen wholeheartedly—go read him yourself, and good luck.[16] The book, only eighty-four pages, contains excerpts from *Mystics and Zen Masters*. There are introductions by the late George Woodcock to Merton's thoughts on not only Zen but also on Taoism, Sufism, varieties of Buddhism, and Hinduism. For this reader, Woodcock's primer was easier to understand than Merton's text. He writes, for example, that "Zen aims at the intuitive grasp of the truth of enlightenment as the direct seeing of one's "original mind" (which is Buddha), and places a greater spiritual value on meditation than on scholarly knowledge, doctrine, ritual, particular scriptures, or the performance of good deeds."[17]

Wilfrid Sheed cites William Blake as one of the original sources of Merton's interest in Buddhism, as he was for another Columbia "beat" from a later generation—Allen Ginsberg. "Each," Sheed wrote, "was jolted toward mysticism by reading Blake in the Columbia bookstore. Each, with gregarious appetite, had swallowed more of the 20th century than he could handle, and suffered heavy internal bleeding from it, and each came back by way of Indian wisdom to the simple exuberance that builds tree houses and pulls daisies. Call it coincidence, but it didn't happen at Michigan State."[18]

The "Indian wisdom" that Sheed cites came to Merton, as well as to Lax and Rice, from their exposure to Bramachari Mahanambrata in the Columbia days, as mentioned earlier in this book.

It was not just Buddhism, however, but all of the Eastern sects that fascinated Merton. In 1967, , he had had as visitors at Gethsemani both the Sufi master C. D. Abdesalam and the Buddhist monk Thich Nhat Hanh. Abdesalam may be the "Hindu" that John Eudes Bamberger met in Merton's room. "After the session I told him, politely," Bamberger told me in an interview, "'You sounded like you were a Hindu. You went too far,' And he said, 'Well, you've gotta go along with those guys.'"[19] Bamberger's feeling is that this was one more case of Merton allowing his broad-ranging interests too much latitude.

The influence of Aldous Huxley on both Lax and Merton, back to Columbia days, seems to have stuck in later years. In particular, these words of Huxley's continued to ring true for the two friends:

> It is impossible for the mystic to pay attention to his real relation to God and to his fellows, unless he has previously detached his attention from his animal nature and the business of being socially successful. But he cannot detach his attention from these things except by the consistent and conscious practice of the highest morality . . . and if I want to have even the smallest knowledge of God as it is possible for human beings to have, I must be as good as it is possible for human beings to be. Virtue is the essential preliminary to the mystical experience.[20]

Back in 1958, after having read an article by Huxley in the *Saturday Evening Post*, Merton had invited the philosopher to Gethsemani, telling him that "Victor Hammer and his wife at Lexington, would gladly bring you over." He told Huxley in the letter that he wanted to know more about "genuine mystical experience," perhaps engendered by drugs. He said he was "interested in Yoga and above all in Zen, which I find to be the finest example of a technique leading to the highest natural perfection of man's contemplative liberty."[21]

Although he never made it to Gethsemani, Huxley wrote a remarkably detailed reply a few months later on his experiments with drugs such as mescaline and lysergic acid that had been used on alcoholics and "victims of assorted neuroses." He said that 70 percent of the victims had a "positive" experience. Huxley himself had taken both mescaline and lysergic acid multiple times and they

helped me to understand many of the obscure utterances to be found in the writings of the mystics, Christian and Oriental. An unspeakable sense of gratitude for the privilege of being born into this universe. . . . Finally, an understanding, not intellectual, but in some sort total, an understanding with the entire organism, of the affirmation that God is love. . . . There seems to be no evidence in the published literature that the drug is habit forming or that it creates a craving for repetition . . . the experience is so transcendentally important that it is in no circumstances a thing to be entered upon light-heartedly or for enjoyment. (In some respects, it is not enjoyable; for it entails a temporary death of the ego, a going-beyond.)[22]

There is no evidence that Merton did any experimenting with these drugs, either before or after entering the monastery. But his interest in the mystics stayed at a high level. His fascination with Zen Buddhism had been derided during a 1956 stay at St. John's Abbey in Minnesota by the psychiatrist Gregory Zilboorg. Zilboorg impugned an article that Merton had written on neurosis in religious life, accused him of serious emotional problems, and claimed that the monk, in an account of the meeting of the two by Anthony Padovano, was "guilty of dialogue with Zen Buddhism that did not have conversion as object."[23] The accusations seem unjust, even cruel, when one reflects on the monk's own comments on the healthy state of his emotions only months after the St. John's experience.

Lax seconded Merton's interest in Zen, having written, "Am in receipt of your thoughts on Zen. . . . There shd be more Zen in the world & less strife and confusion."[24] More orthodox thinking was occupying Lax's mind in these years, however, as he continued to have success with his poetry. He had developed a relationship with BBC radio that resulted in several on-air readings. One, in January 1967, was for the BBC *Poetry Now* program, for which Lax, and several other voices, read his poem *DRAMA*. Then, in October 1968 he did an hour-long reading of his poems.

Merton was writing letters at his usual pace and taking on new correspondents. Jim Forest "was astounded at Merton's speed at the typewriter," having once looked over his shoulder as he answered a letter Forest had handed him. "It was a fine letter, on monastery letterhead, that would have taken me hours to write. . . . I had a glimpse of his concentration—like one sometimes sees in a newsroom."[25]

He had written Rosemary Radford Ruether in March 1967

> One of the things I love about my life, and therefore one of the reasons why I would not change it for anything, is the fact that I live in the woods and according to a tempo of sun and moon and season in which it is naturally easy and possible to walk in God's light, so to speak, and through his creation . . . monks are, and I am, in my own mind, the remnant of desperate conservationists. . . . The contemplative life, in my way of thinking (with Greek fathers, etc.) is simply the restoration of man, in Christ, to the state in which he was originally intended to live.[26]

Toward the end of 1967, however, Merton had seemed to be getting mentally and spiritually tired. Bamberger feels that it was, in fact, his "worst year."[27] It was a period when, for instance, he wrote in his journal, "I am sick of responding to requests for articles for this or that collection" and then getting no follow-up, and he mentions as examples, "Msgr. Robert Fox and his East Harlem picture book. Ned O'Gorman. Even Ed Rice's thing on monasticism. I must write him about it."[28] He was unhappy about "the laxity of my own life this past year—and worse still in 1966."[29] He was being mentioned as a possible candidate for abbot, and took pains to make it unequivocal that he was not in the running. A postcard from M, a week later, months after the affair had ended, made him think that he felt "less real, somehow, without our constant communication, our sense of being in communion (so intense last year)." But he reflected, "Anyway, that's all over. In a month I'll be 53, and no one in his right mind would get married for the first time at such an age. Yet, this afternoon I wondered if I'd really missed the point of life after all. A dreadful thought!"[30]

He expressed his disillusionment with Vatican II and religious life. "The whole thing is sickening. The mechanical, cause-and-effect, official machinery of Catholicism. Dreadfully dead, putrid."[31]

But only a few weeks earlier he had experienced a very satisfying several days with a group of contemplative nuns.

All of them—or almost all—real contemplatives, and were really human. . . . I have never before had such a sense of community with any group . . . we ended up singing "We Shall Overcome" with a sense that our own revolution was well under way![32]

. . . they are what they are not just *in spite of* the communities to which they are committed, but because of them. I am completely confident in the contemplative orders once again. There is a lot that needs changing, but our life is fundamentally one of the soundest and most healthy things in the Church, and I am sure has all kinds of promise.[33]

His buoyancy persisted, as he wrote in his journal two days later,

I remembered their happiness, especially when they were at Mass in the hermitage. . . . Really, it was wonderful to have them here, to have such a perfect mutual understanding, such an atmosphere of unity and sense of realistic purpose: for once possibilities were not only hopeful but even realized, to some extent![34]

Merton's own fluctuations of mood did not inhibit him from counseling his friend Ed Rice. Rice must have written, probably in 1967, of a spiritual crisis, probably stemming from his loss of *Jubilee* and his breakup with Margery. Merton's counsel, under the salutation "Octobri viginto" was to

Go where you like: go back to the hell you are trying to get out of, and fail that way: or else go to some other religion where, eventually, you will be asked the same kind of submission, and then you will refuse again. . . . You will be very fortunate if you can return to the sacraments soon. . . . In order to get out of that hell, you have to want God to exist. That is stating it as nakedly as possible. If you find yourself unable to do this, the next best thing that can happen to you is for you to get forced so far down into a living hell that it becomes essential for you to want God to exist, or you will be destroyed, unable to live, burst like a hanged man. . . . I am saying all this because it is a plain description of the problem I myself was faced with, and I believe you would rather have me tell you straight, what I think, without any doubletalk. Your letter was a good letter, and demanded it. And I am not making any joke when I say stop in a Church some time and pray for me.[35]

This was the beginning of the period of Rice's perambulations, and the start of a seventeen-year separation from the church. His finances were precarious as he got modest sustenance from freelance writing assignments while paying alimony to Margery, who wrote him angry letters protesting that he was missing his court-directed payments of child support. His children, Ted and Chris, were going to expensive schools, Chris to Choate. One of his New York friends, Dick Dresselhuys, asked other friends, including us Harfords, to contribute $100 each "to help get him out of a financial jam . . . [writing that Rice was] hard hit by alimony problems after coming back from Vietnam and Southeast Asia in December 1967 and divorce ensued. [He was] Freelancing and writing a book every two years but [had to pay] annual alimony of $9,400 at first—less later—and $5,000 for kids' education & med expenses, and $6,500 for lawyers."[36]

Rice's travels, sometimes on assignment for the United Nations and the International Red Cross, took him in 1967–1969 virtually all over the world. There are letters in his Georgetown archive from Cuba, Guatemala, Calcutta, Iran, Trinidad, Tibet, Barbados, Turkey, Vietnam, India, Mogadishu, Ankara, Nairobi, Addis Ababa, Tripoli, and Tunis. While in India he looked up Bramachari and was somewhat disillusioned that the ascetic monk he had known in the 1930s had seemed to him to have become as "fat and earthy as many an American bishop."

He wrote mostly warm notes home to Margery in his early travels in 1967. After the breakup, however, there are sensuous love messages to one or the other of his Indian amours. None of these affairs culminated in marriage, although Rice claimed that it was considered seriously several times. I once asked him how he became so interested in India. "My favorite uncle, Jay Becker, my mother's brother, spent 10 years in India, having gone there at 18 in the rubber business. He married an Australian girl, Dawn Bailey-Fischer Becker." Rice's fascination with India led him, eventually, to write a book about India's young people,[37] and to edit and provide photos for a book on the Indian mind.[38] He also wrote, in the late 1960s and early '70s, magazine articles on such diverse subjects as rich Catholics ("High on the Harp," for *Status* magazine,1969); Vietnam ("The Human Face of Vietnam," in *Sign*, February 1968); glaucoma, cholera, yoga, travels in Pakistan, Arab refugees, Tibetans, renewal of the liturgy in Asia, the Christian-Hindu dialog, and Thomas

More. He proposed numerous books to publishers, only a few of which were accepted. Among the apparent turndowns were biographies of Mark Twain and Herman Melville, a novel called *Moon Goddess,* and books titled *Tibet* and *Women's Liberation in Asia.* He actually did get published biographies for young adults of Margaret Mead and Robert Louis Stevenson, and *Marx, Engels and the Workers of the World.*

Merton's surging interest in Eastern religions seems to have been apace with his discomfort about the way that Catholicism was developing in the United States. He had written Lax in early 1967 that

> I am truly spry and full of fun, but am pursued by the vilifications of progressed Catholics. Mark my word man there is no uglier species on the face of the earth than progressed Catholics, mean, frivol, ungainly, inarticulate, venomous, and bursting at the seams with progress into the secular cities and Teilhardian subways. The Ottavianis was bad but these are infinitely worse. You wait and see.[39]

His letters to Rosemary Radford Ruether in these months carried the same critical tone:

> What bothers me theologically (I am not enough of a theologian to be really bothered by theological problems) is the sense that, when you go back into the history of the Church, you run into a bigger and bigger hole of unconscious bad faith, and at that point I get rather uneasy about our dictating to all the "other" religions that we are the one authentic outfit that has the real goods. I am not saying that I want to be able to mix Christianity and Buddhism in quantities to suit myself, however. Far from it. I think you got me wrong on that.
>   . . . I have had a monumental struggle with monasticism as it now is and still disagree violently with most of the party-line policies. I am a notorious maverick in the Order and my Abbot considers me a dangerous subject, always ready to run off with a woman or something, so I am under constant surveillance.[40]

A few weeks later he once again lit out at the monastery in another letter to Ruether:

> Yes, the monastic life here is an idol.
>   Provisional solution: the people are not idols, they are real, they are my brothers though they are also for the most part idiots (my Karnap friend [Sy Freedgood?] told me last week, without any opposition from me, "you live among idiots").[41]

Even for the outspoken Merton that passage seems outrageous, and he would surely have softened his view in dialogue with other outsiders. But, the Merton journals in this period were harshly critical not only of the church but, as the war in Vietnam heated up, of U.S. policy in Southeast Asia:

> I think the world of the U.S.A. in 1967 is a world of crass, blind, overstimulated, phony, lying stupidity. The war in Asia gets slowly worse—and always more inane. The temper of the country is one of blindness, fat, self-satisfied, ruthless, mindless corruption. . . .
> . . . Catholicism itself is to me more and more of a problem. Not a theological one—it is on the level of culture and psychology. American Catholicism—the American Catholic mind and consciousness. The American Catholic Spasm! Again, aggressively, a forbidding, combative stance, now legalist and more pseudo-liberal (the liberal publicist itch). The whole thing revolts me.[42]

If the abbot had read those entries one would think that Merton might well have been asked to leave the monastery. He had, in fact, been forbidden to write about the war for publication. What seemed to sustain him was his growing intellectual involvement in the East and maybe the prospect that he would soon get to go there. Although he had genuine interest in Buddhism, however, it does not seem to have been at the expense of his commitment, wavering though it may have become, to Catholicism and to the monastery.

He began to speculate, in early 1968, about what his future might be in the monastery, where he might go if it were logical for him to leave, and whether or not the possibility of attending the conference on Buddhist-Christian dialogue in Bangkok was realistic. One option, among numerous others, was apparently Chile, from which he evidently had received an invitation. "For instance if I am completely silenced here, and if the Chile foundation wants me very badly, should I pull up stakes and go there?" he wrote in his journal.[43]

A few days later he had second thoughts about his community.

> I realize how seriously I misjudged the community the other day—saying they were all conservatives and wanted security above all. They voted [on a new Abbot] with courage and imagination and their option was for openness, growth, greater freedom, real progress.[44]

It is likely that the increasingly strong possibility of going to Bangkok improved his optimism.

Thinking too of the meeting in Bangkok—the AIM Meeting of
Asian Superiors in December to which I may or may not go. What
sense can monastic renewal and "implantation" in Asia have if
the (Christian) monasteries are implicitly identified with Western
power? Dom Leclercq sees this of course. Utility of the meeting
could be in clarification of this problem first of all.[45]

His occupation with Zen continued at a high level with the completion of the manuscript for *Zen and the Birds of Appetite,* in February 1968, the first of four books that would come out in that year.[46]
His definition of Zen, however, is still not easy to fathom, as in this
introductory paragraph, "Zen enriches no one. There is no body to be
found. The birds may come and circle for a while in the place where
it is thought to be. But they soon go elsewhere. When they are gone,
the 'nothing,' the 'no-body' that was there, suddenly appears. That is
Zen."

In May he dedicated "For Robert Lax" a new book of anti-poems,
Cables to the Ace, subtitled *Familiar Liturgies of Misunderstanding.*[47]
Lax acknowledged his copy with this from Olean:

Ho, ho, ho
   Guess what is fall from the sky? fables mit dedicajio! boccaccio
table with electrifying telegram! . . . all over the house electrifying
cables! at every turn is edification & joys. . . . This is no joke: these
are absolutely earth-shattering indictments . . . will make the birds
fly up from the swamps with a new wild cry.[48]

The book has an upbeat prologue, "I am the obstetrician of good
fortune. I live in the social cages of joy." Although only sixty-pages
long it has eighty-eight segments, and they are mostly very obscure to
this reader. He ends with an admonishing epilogue that says, "All you
have to do is dance a little and you will attract the infinite toy atten-
tions of the elite." In 1984 Lax remembered, in a letter to Rice, that
"Merton was pleased when somebody said that Cables to the Ace was
like Rabelais."[49]

Two other major publications absorbed much of the monk's time
and energy in 1968, but Merton saw neither of them in final published
form. One was *Monks Pond,*[50] some 349 pages of poems printed on
the abbey's offset press (Merton wrote Jonathan Williams that the
monastery should "put out something besides cheese ads for heavens
sakes").[51] Merton had written Lax about his plans for *Monks Pond* in
late 1967:

Imagine great flames inspiration outburst crash wap zap bowie gonna start a magazine. . . . Four (4) issues only. Wham. Zap. Bop. Blap. No $$$$ involved. All for free. . . . Four (4) collections poetry prose from friends only or from anyway people. Only problem not to shock monks with four (4) letter wdz. Must be dirty words all in French or Eyetalian. . . . Send proses poetries send anything but above all collaborate to dig up and find old Reinhardt statements letters manifests and anything Reinhardt and also Slate. [Signed Harpo][52]

Lax's quick response from Olean, signed "Happy," was equally flamboyant and enthusiastic.

Four issues is just right. Every issue we will pack with trenchant articles, mordant satires, poignant inquiries from the pencil of Simone de Beauvoir, Andre Breton, Guillaume Apollinaire.

Manifestoes from the mimeographs of alas poor Reinhardt will make up the major portion of the work in what is to be called either the Offset Follies or the Duplicator Blues of 1968.[53]

In the final publication, there were poems by Merton and some of his closest poet-friends—Lax, Van Doren, Ernesto Cardenal, John Wu, and dozens of others, including Jack Kerouac and Czeslaw Milosz. Sister Thérèse is represented by three poems, one of them about Lax, titled "You Sing From Islands." Merton said it was "one of your very best" and remarked that Lax was going back to Greece because "He can't stand it here."[54] An excerpt from her poem, apparently about meeting Lax:

You sing from islands—
Manhattan, and you came into my summer
lightly as Mogador
in the 'circus of the sun'
while a marvelous music sang
through all our conversation.[55]

Lax's three poems in *Monks Pond* include one of his "black white" classics—in this instance thirty-nine "black" and thirty-eight "white" spaced around a single page. He sent it to Merton in a letter that describes it as a "faultless black & white poem. sail this poem on mondt's pond. see if ladies don't fall over cold. all ladies go crazy for black & white monks poem."

Here, in the same letter, is Lax's take on his own concrete poetry:

friends. is db like qp? why? endless funs in all part of monkhaus.
new waves of precision in the noosphere. teilhard don't 'low no
pdqb here. (no p no q, no coconut b.) then how coma X look so
much like a k? endless fun in the omniverts.
 anyway, I send you results of this tireless research. this little bit
is only the beginning. in patmos under the noses of the poleeks
[police, who constantly harassed Lax during this period, thinking
he was an American spy] *i compose many more, whole books for*
the here too is concrete's most ingenious: a large x made of x's
(according largely with theories lucretius, see his astonishing de
natur' artifax); a large circle made of circles; large triangle pretty
much the same. large & black is the big thing in concrete. no odes
to nightingale spelled upside down. many more concretes possible
on old typewriter. unheard of thousands. ever notice how b looks
like p, how d like q, how q again like b. well turn a b upside down
& try it on q. fun for your *bafflement of the censors. tomorrow,*
yes, tomorrow i will send these bks. we will bind up the whole
groaning world in a nest of concretes, every wound will have its
word, every crucifixion its acrostic, every niche, a backward let-
ter. for every byzantine battlement, a pile of b's and t's.[56]

Concrete poetry, alas, posed a huge problem for publishers, and Lax
especially would suffer from it always. Jay Laughlin put it this way in
a letter to Merton:

 The problem about doing Concrete poetry in the Annual is to get
 it set, unless the author can supply his own pasteup. It costs a fortune now to get tricky word and type layouts set at a composition
 house, and the regular printers can't handle it.[57]

The other big Merton opus of 1968 was *The Geography of*
Lograire,[58] a 153-page book that he mailed off to Laughlin in September. He felt it was one of his most important pieces of work. Not
everyone agrees. John Eudes Bamberger, for example, does not think
it will stand up long term, whereas he feels that much of the monk's
other writing—he calls out, for example, *SSM* and *Sign of Jonas*—will
be read "for years to come." Ed Rice, though, wrote enthusiastically
about the book in a letter written in the 1970s to a literary agent. It
[*Lograire*] is, he wrote, "crucial for an interpretation on Merton's life
and thought . . . [but] has not been given its due because of its incredible complexity. . . ." He advises the agent to put a text of the poem in
front of her "as we discuss it . . . the poem is simply astonishing, the

language stunning, the imagery innovative and probing. Somehow the poem manages to indict and celebrate the human condition at one and the same time."[59]

Sister Thérèse Lentfoehr, who also liked the poem, told Rice that Merton said *Lograire* is an adaptation of the real name, *Des Loges*, of the French lyric poet François Villon, but it also describes Merton's hermitage, which was surrounded by forest. The word "loges" refers to small cabins used by foresters—Merton was at one time the chief forester of the monastery.

Michael Mott, who called *Lograire* Merton's best volume of poetry,[60] quotes from the *Restricted Journal*, "Writing this [*Lograire*] is most fun for me now, because in it, I think I have finally got away from self-consciousness and introversion. It may be my final liberation from all diaries. Maybe that is my one remaining task."[61] It is bizarre that Merton gave so many such intimations that he might have been reaching the end of his life. This stanza from one of the poems in *Lograire* reveals his bitterness about the ways of his adopted country:

> At this precise moment of history
> With Goody-two-shoes running for Congress
> We are testing supersonic engines
> To keep God safe in the cherry tree.
> When I said so in this space last Thursday
> I meant what I said: power struggles.[62]

Lax liked the poem, too. He told Merton that he was "Happy all the time with Geog. of Lograire. remembering every image like I seen it in films."[63] Years later, in 1982, Mott wrote Lax,

> I think it took T.M. a while to see his way to the kind of freedom he shows in Lograire . . . he identified this in some of your poems that came out in Jester and in Ad's paintings. And of course it has everything to do with risk taking. My own feeling was that it was a long time before he became a good critic of his own work.[64]

Merton's final seven months of 1968—the last of his life—were very hectic. After he got permission in May to accept the Bangkok invitation with the proviso that he give retreats at Cistercian monasteries in Indonesia and Hong Kong, he arranged, through Dom Aelred Graham and the latter's friend Harold Talbott, to meet with the Dalai Lama when he reached Dharamsala.

First, however, he visited Christ in the Desert in New Mexico and

Our Lady of the Redwoods in California. Lax had tried to get him to divert on his way west to a poetry seminar he was giving at General Beadle State College in South Dakota—"visit General Boggles Bison herd. Stop by for haiku lesson in Indian Badlands"[65]—but that was not realistic. The seminar had been laid on by an old friend from L'Eau Vive days, Jerry Lange, then a professor at the college. His readings were a smash hit. "Everyone knocked out of their seats," he wrote to Emil Antonucci.

First time since blizzard of '12. Big reactions, esp. from hardest sections to hit: faculty squares who don't like visiting medicine-men & tough students down on whole system. I guess "Goodbye" was the real show-stopper (& I can't see why) but everything worked. Like espc., zowied, zowie—The Hospital, & The Watcher (knocks me over every time)—& had them all jumping out of their seats. Big Flowers still a steady winner. Violin—a favorite specially with freshman cats & swingers: Love & Death socko with older, quasi-pot crowd. Thought (Beautiful) split the campus right down the middle. Affable dumbs didn't get it at all—anyone smart enough to get it thought he'd done it himself & wanted to kill non believers.[66]

Merton's report to Lax on the Redwoods visit—signed Uncle Charlie de Gaulle, was classic, and the experience must have been wild:

Some groovy Zulu nuns! Dancing in the kirk (for terce). . . . Is full bodied flavor of Christian novitiate wines smacking the tongue. Abbess played the guitar and me bongos. . . . Tomorrow I get to play bongo drums while serving the modern mass. Forget all the rosaries! Wingy Manone & his Mazz Madness.

He would be off the next day to San Francisco's Chinatown and then to New Mexico:

Ho Ho Ho. Dull New Mex. No dance no nuns. Just dull days desert monks making pumpernickel on red hot sand [at Christ in the Desert]. Then back in a trice to loathesome Kentucky.

The letter revealed once more how much he was casting about in his mind about where he might end up after the Asia trip:

I am thinking to get permission from new abt to live here on desolate pacifica in small white house twenty miles from no place

only seagulls. Groovy nuns bring health soup once a week. . . .
Ideal for hermit new home. . . . Live in small white haven & write
small poems each one describing over and over again one small
seagull.[67]

A few days later he wrote Lax [signed Billy the Kid] that "In San
Francisco I was live for one night in the City Light bkshp hospitalities
of Cardinal Ferlinghetti."[68] Ferlinghetti was more or less poet laureate
of the beats in those days.

One of the earlier harbingers of Lax's recognition was a special issue
devoted to him by the poetry journal *Voyages*, in 1968. In his introduction, the publisher, William Claire, says,

> the poetry of Robert Lax is just beginning to take hold in the
> minds of many people on both sides of the Atlantic, and among
> those who are curious about the role of the artist with private
> vision of his own. Robert Lax's vision of the world is unspeak-
> ably beautiful and ever new, ever today or tomorrow: a continual
> searching, a kind of voyage that never ends, but is always just
> beginning.
>
> . . . If one really believes, with all attendant nuances that,
>
> this
>
> bread
>
> is
>
> bread
>
> as Robert Lax does, then faith, which he has in great abundance,
> is often both wonderously and mysteriously present. Such faith, in
> God, in life, bears repetition, and becomes, in his poetry, a rep-
> etition of line, which somehow does not become repetitious. His
> constant re-discovery of what has always existed—can only lead
> to reprise, a restatement of theme . . . like the sun, Robert Lax has
> just begun.[69]

Denise Levertov, herself a famous poet, was one of the few peers who
knew Lax's work from earlier years. In the same issue of *Voyages*, she
gives a rhapsodic review of *Circus*. It is, she wrote, "quite apart from
the others [the review was abstracted from one that also covered the

poems of Gilbert Sorrentino, LeRoi Jones, and Paul Blackburn]. For one thing he is a Catholic and the radiant security of his faith appears in his work as a serenity of tone. . . . One might feel Lax's book too much ignores the world's anguish, if it were not full of a gentleness, a tenderness, that is not smug. The kinship here is with St. Francis' *Canticle of the Sun.*" Then, in a *Postscript, 1968* she wrote,

> Robert Lax's work of recent years saddens me sometimes because I believe so deeply that the mainstream of poetry is aural—sonic— not visual; and I found in "Sunset City" and others of his earlier poems such especially impressive examples of the sonic. Yet, among his "concrete" poems, I rejoice to note, there are important examples of a concretism that is sonic, not visual: I am thinking particularly of "Sea/Sun/Stone" in which the repeated words, when the poem is read aloud properly, bring about in the imagination a more profound sense of their meanings till by the end of the poem we are hot with the sun on stone and our eyes [did she mean ears?] are filled with the susurrations of the sea and our eyes with its dazzle.[70]

Recognition continued to mount modestly in the late 1960s. In London, George Macbeth, producer of the BBC's *Poetry Now,* carried Lax's *DRAMA* with several voices in January 1967, and in October 1968 did an hour-long production of a Lax reading. His poem "Kalymniad" was published by Ron Schreiber in *31 New American Poets* (1969); and Lax poems appeared in Emmet Williams's anthology of "Expanded Poetry"; Richard Kostelanetz's anthology of word-image poems; George Plimpton's Viking Press anthology of poems and prose; and, as mentioned above, James Laughlin's *New Directions Annual.*

In a letter to Antonucci in May 1968, Lax mentioned the possibility of the much-discussed publication of the Merton–Lax letters:

> here is one . . . illegible xerox from Merton (not his xerox, one here made by the snow elves) where he talks in undecipherable languidges forbidden by st. paul to the following effect: that he has had a jesuit copy off all the new letters from him to me & back & that once again he thinks we could make a million bucks by publishing them off on our washington press. (well, maybe the jesuit would want to set type for it, & press the blocks). anyway he says maybe we could get Santa to pay some of the expenses (man in red suit in california & sent me a check just before Christmas)

& that Merton would gather some more from the chipmunks & that then when he had a book we could sell it by little grey dusty men on the staten island ferry. . . .

The letter must have been written in New York because in it he tells Antonucci that "jim harford called & wanted me to come & walk around a beach in jersey with him & his wife this weekend. don't think i can. . . ." These days, he said, he spends "all day indoors except for walk to post box. do breathing exercises every morning, nearing levitation. most of day spent walking through vapors, settling down near 5 p m to letters, poems or dream bk."[71]

He sent William Claire a price list of his poems, revealing the difficulty of getting any substantial income from his profession. Both his classic, *Circus*, and his *Robert Lax New Poems* were priced at $1.50.[72] While income generally was paltry, "[e]very day is jiu-jitsu over expenses," he wrote Antonucci.

In the middle of May 1968, after a short visit in Colorado with Beverly Burford, the now-divorced wife of his friend Bob Burford, who had hired Lax to work on *New Story* magazine in Paris in the 1950s, he headed for what became his last visit to Merton. The old friends had good talks and walks, but the days were not as peaceful as they would have liked, having been shared with such events as a picnic put on by the monk's dear Louisville friend, Tommie O'Callaghan, and her family: ". . . exhausting in the very hot weather." He worried about what might happen to Lax. "I don't know if he should return to Greece. Kalymnos seems to be the only place he likes anywhere. I don't blame him. But also I don't trust a police state sustained by the C.I.A."[73] The visits and the picnic "have been a drag no matter how much I like Lax, Jonathan Greene, Ron Seitz, Dick Sisto, etc. I just need to have long periods of no talking and not special thinking and immediate contact with the sun, the grass, the dirt, the leaves. Undistracted by statements, jokes, opinions, news. And undistracted by my own writing." In the same journal entry he gave more evidence of his serious interest in Zen: "fell on the bed in a stupor, slept an hour, got up and said Office, read a few Zen texts in Spanish in Cona Franca and finally some Rene Char (which Jonathan Greene left with me) which I very much enjoyed again."[74]

He wrote Mark Van Doren that Lax had brought with him "innumerable cans of tuna fish and several pints of whiskey, the latter being more practical than the former. We had great conversaziones and took a lot of pictures (mine not yet printed, will send some if any good)."[75]

In the same letter he evidenced his excitement about the forthcoming trip, writing to his old professor in language as colloquial as that he used with Lax and Rice.

All sorts of places I am supposed to go to if I don't faint from delight at the mere thought. Since I hop from Singapore to Darjeeling, and have a meeting there with various swamis gurus etc, I hope to sneak into Nepal. Then maybe a bit more of the top of India. Then Thailand (if not Burma, hard to get into, but may manage), then Indonesia (a monastery of ours there) then Japan, then home. Maybe. If they can get me home, I should say. This doesn't begin until October but at the moment I am itching with vaccinations and expectations and being photographed for the passprops and phonographed for the pesthouse and airlifted to the quarantine and divided up into computers. If I survive I may manage to get to a country where they don't even have roads. And where if you ride its on an ox or not at all. Or a yak. or an eleflamp. All this because of a meeting of dull Abbots in Thailand, but who would not go to a meeting of Abbots for all those secondary gains?[76]

In August Merton gave a final denouement to his romance with M: "Today, among other things, I burned M's letters. Incredible stupidity in 1966. I did not even glance at any one of them. High hot flames of the pine branches in the sun!"[77]

In the same month Lax gave Merton a heads-up that Rice would be visiting him in Kentucky, reporting as well on Rice's assessment of the sad state of religious architecture.

rice, on the other hands is hopping across the country in a rattly but amiable folkswagon, hopping out to photograph each architectural disaster; sisters of mercy cathedral, rabbis of mercy synagoguumm, zen temples, baptist hutches, holy igloos, vats, ghats, druid mounds.

his thesis follows: there is no religious architecture anywhere. (will stop by soon in gethsemani for the clinchers.) no, no,: he will stop on his way back home, about september 5, he says, & will write you. let him take plenty of pictures. he must be about the world's best picture-taker.[78]

Lax made mention again of the prospects for publishing a selection of the wacky Lax–Merton "ladders."

again about the ladders, shld we send the ladders to random house? do you know a girl there named alice mayhew? is alice mayhew really her name? (i don't know her) but i could send them, or you could.[79]

The two would have trouble finding a publisher for some years.[80] Merton wrote Jay Laughlin, "It is not certain yet that Unicorn will do the antiletters. First the edition will have to be subsidized, and then Lax would like if possible a commercial publisher—for obvious reasons. I don't know what will eventually happen, but I doubt if a commercial publisher will take it. And don't feel that would be desirable, really. . . ."[81]

Merton's preoccupations in this period began to be dominated by the prospective trip to Asia. He thought even of some more unusual possibilities for his return itinerary, writing to Lax that

> Was I come home from Asias the wrong way (all around the block) I wd stop and see you a Kalympops and we cd smoke up the remaining opium but I come back, if ever, the other ways with much Zens and roshis and bossus and stomping on the burlesques of Honolulu etc.
>
> I got one last idea just one last idea for a place for a quiet life and no dam disturbances and less police state. The Leper Colony on Molokai. Serious. It is on a point that can only be reached by helicopter. And all the nice lepers scare shit out of tourists, guaranteeing peace and quiet.
>
> Think it over. It may be where I end up.
> [signed] Daddy Damien[82]

The ailment-plagued monk complained of bursitis in the jaw ("it hurts when I eat") just before the visit from Rice. Besides the friendship they brought, each of Merton's visitors seemed especially welcome for having a fresh supply of spirits. "Is coming Old Rouse in a moment of figments with his gins," he wrote Lax.

> After that the deluge.
> Next wk I am in the flights. I am off. I am done.
> I am off first to the apaches for the dance of confirming the
>   suspicion.
> I am then off to the kayaks for the ball of obfirming the
>   mission.
> I am then off to the Coats for the stamps of permission.
> I am then off to the moats for the lamps of the perception.
> I am then off to the bikkhus (Buddhist monks) with a cigar
>   and a cigarette.

It is until Sept 30 the addresses: c/o W. H. Ferry Box 4068
    Santa Barbara Cal 93103.
It is until Oct 15 the address Redwoods Monaster
    Whitethorn Cal. 95489.
After that it is bikkhus too numerous to mention of which
    I send after. . . . Like until end Nov I think is always
    likely American Express Calcutta.
Is big introductions to the Dalai Lama no kidding.
Is going to have to drop the gins and learn to meditate.
And to levitate.
And rope trick . . .
And dawncing all around the funfairs with Sakyamuni
    Buddha. . . .

No kidding about Molokai—is possibles. If I don't end up in some
Dalai Lama permanent bush in Nepal I maybe return to Molokai
in May. Is questionable???[83]

That last sentence makes it clear that he was still uncertain about
where he might be going post-Asia and would welcome Lax's advice.
Lax, in a subsequent letter told him to "Work out with Rice a couple
of lively steps for the (wow) Dalai Lama. (Like what are *his* views on
infinite regress & the post toasties theory of history.) Tell him our problems frankly & ask him what his are. Don't pull any punches with the
bikkhu."[84]
    Merton had written Lax the day before, "Around here all is a vote for
Wallace and rifle clubs, irresponsible Kentucky mafia shooting up the
woods all day and all night. . . . I go down to the monkshops and find
out if is sighted Rice in his Volkswagen."[85] Rice showed up on September 6, driving a "battered blue Volkswagen," having traveled through
Salt Lake City, Denver, Christ in the Desert in Abiquiu, New Mexico,
St. Louis southern Illinois, New Harmony, Indiana, where there was a
Shaker establishment, and "for the last two days doing a story on a blind
seminarian in Louisville." He showed Merton some vivid pictures he had
taken of "beautiful, though starving people" in India, Cuba, Vietnam.
"We had supper together in the hermitage, and after that his Volkswagen wouldn't start though we rolled it until it went all the way down the
steep hill. We left it at the bottom."[86] It might have been at this supper
that Rice showed Merton a photo of a young Vietnamese mother and
child horribly scarred by napalm dropped by an American airplane. Rice
would later write that Merton "looked at it a long time, wondering not
only about the tragic burns on the two victims, but what had happened

to the interior sensibilities of the young American men who could drop such a weapon without an apparent thought of the consequences."[87]

The next day the two had dinner together with the French Benedictine monk Dom Leclercq, and Merton's new abbot, Flavian Burns, then went out to see the fish hatchery in the lake in Rice's now-rehabilitated VW. They talked of the Orient, and Merton revealed that he had been reading "a long report on a preparatory questionnaire for the Bangkok meeting. . . . In my opinion, I don't think Christian monasticism, as we now know it, has much future in Asia. Merely wearing saffron robes won't do much good."[88]

Merton's travels toward Asia began in earnest after a last Mass in the hermitage chapel with Patrick Hart and several others on September 9. Then he was off to Albuquerque, and then to Abiquiu, New Mexico, where he made another visit to Christ in the Desert and had a meeting with Georgia O'Keeffe, to whom he promised to send *Monks Pond*, *Conjectures*, and *Chuang Tzu*. Then came a fiesta on an Apache reservation. Off to Chicago, he visited the Poor Clares, then he headed for Alaska by way of Tokyo and Seoul.

Alaska produced more speculation on a future hermitage. After a visit to the Convent of the Precious Blood in Eagle River, where he put on a worksop for the nuns, he wrote in his journal that "I feel they are eager to have me settle here."[89] A few days later, after climbing a mountain behind the convent, he wrote, "I have no hesitation in saying Eyak Lake seemed perfect in many ways—for a place to live."[90] Forays to Valdez, Anchorage, and Yakutat, a former Russian penal colony, were followed by Seattle, San Francisco, then back to the Redwoods monastery and then Santa Barbara.

In the latter place he visited his old friend Ping Ferry at the Center for the Study of Democratic Institutions, where he gave a talk that was taped. "What I'm going to do this morning," he told his audience, is give you some kind of account of the mischief I expect to get into in Asia . . . if I get back without dying of dysentery I'll give you an account of what happened." One of his remarks to the group was, "If Catholics had a little more Zen there would be a lot less trouble with things like, say, birth control."[91] He thought that one of his destinations in Asia—a "summit meeting of religions" scheduled for Darjeeling [put on by the Temple of Understanding]—could produce results of "critical importance" to the exchange between Eastern and Western religions, although "not in terms of official dialogue" but rather in "communicating on a deep pyschological level. . . . This is what I hope to get into, carried by a force a little more than me. What will come of it? Maybe nothing."

He barreled around the San Francisco area for the next week, meeting such varied personalities as Suzanne Butorovich and her family—

she the young girl who had corresponded with him and would attend his funeral at Gethsemani; John Cogley, the *Commonweal* writer; Czeslaw Milosz and wife. He participated in a three-day conference at the Redwoods monastery on the contemplative life with the nuns of Immaculate Heart of Mary, did some tourism, and was off on October 15 from San Francisco for Bangkok.

We left the ground—I with Christian mantras and a great sense of destiny, of being at last on my true way after years of waiting and wondering and fooling around. . . . May I not come back without having settled the great affair. And found also the great compassion, mahakaruna. . . . I am going home, to the home where I have never been in this body. . . .[92]

After two days of touring, and Mass in a big, somewhat dilapidated church—maybe a cathedral—he headed for Calcutta and from there wrote his first letter to Lax. In his journal he had described the city as having "the lucidity of despair, of absolute confusion, of vitality helpless to cope with itself."[93] To Lax he wrote, "No Bramachari as yet. . . . Bramachari very effective in making monks never find him again. . . . Here I am sitting in crazy airplane office plucking daisies & saying Kathmandu yes, Kathmandu no. [signed] Salaams, King Victoria."[94]

In another, longer, letter to Lax, also from Calcutta ("Calicutok") signed "Uncle Tim," undated, but probably a few days after the first one, Merton reported that Lax's letters were waiting for him when he arrived, and said, "Is everywhere jovial Lamas who acclaim me the chenrezigs and the reincarnation of the Dops of Lomzog or the Mops of Jopsmitch. . . . I am discovered to be the mahayana bootsrtap attemptjing to escapt from its own bottle." He must have been disappointed that he had received no letter from Abbot Flavian Burns "premitting estencion of le voyage—voy Age—until the midts of Europas. Thus I dunno what cometh with the posts of Easter but any3w ay (wow) I bear in mente the winds of spring from Tokyop wafting the passengers to Athens and Mount Arthritis." He was still hoping to get to Greece after the Bangkok conference.

There was still no sign of Bramachari: "The real Bramachari has vanish and is still in the movies." He had seen a Bramachari movie poster but "the man in the pictures looks more like Edward G. Robinson."[95]

He gave an adlib talk in Calcutta—discarding the formal paper he had prepared for the conference on world religions, which had been scheduled for Darjeeling but moved because of floods in that city. Sponsored by the Temple of Understanding, based in New York, the conference was termed a "Spiritual Summit Conference" and it involved, as the Temple newsletter described it, "close consultation" among "30 distinguished leaders of 10 world religions—Buddhism, Christianity, Confucianism, Islam, Judaism, Hinduism, Sikhism, Baha'i, Zoroastrianism, and Jainism."[96]

In the talk he represented himself in a way that might also have described his friends Lax and Rice. "Thus I find myself representing perhaps hippies among you, poets, people of this kind who are seeking in all sorts of ways and have absolutely no established status whatever," and a little later, "And so I stand among you as one who offers a small message of hope, that first, there are always people who dare to seek on the margin of society, who are not dependent on social acceptance, not dependent on social routine, and prefer a kind of free-floating existence under a state of risk. And among these people, if they are faithful to their own calling, to their own vocation, and to their own message from God, communication on the deepest level is possible."[97]

Meanwhile Lax was on his way back to Kalymnos, stopping in Marseilles, always one of his favorite cities. When he got back to Kalymnos he reported to Antonucci that it was "Winter here with all kinds beautiful storms. Also, alas. Earth-tremors—six at least that have rocked the cradle since I got here. . . . Writing quite a bit. Sent off 75 pages—prose—poems yesterday—regular mail—so may take a month. Took nice trip by caiqui to Patmos & back. Nice there too, but for sparky people. No place like Kal."[98] A few days later he mentioned in another letter to Antonucci, "merton: new couple of letters from india, zowie."[99]

Lax wrote two more letters to Merton before the monk's death, only one of which was received. It was from Kalymnos ("Calimpost"), written on December 5. It acknowledged receipt of Merton's letters from Calcutta, commented whimsically about the locals suggesting that he was a reincarnation of a holy man, and urged him to come home via Greece:

> yours is arrive from calcitraps where is all hupp hup with the Gang
> . . . is it truly Calbooza, crown of the orient, pearl of bengalis & hindustanis. is it all as they say an enchanted city with university gardens & parks, leftover bobbies, invisible rope-trick, guided tour to the osalisque? . . . is it the rival of capetown for beauty, of vancouver for enchantment, or is it, as they more truly say, the very hash-smokes of the orient?
> . . . am glad you have been recognized by the lama committees & guru-watchers from every side of the Gung as the Mops of Jops & the boomstrikes of Lompzog.
> . . . tell the abt you must come through here for easter; even for Christmas. Byzantine Christmas; coptic new year. happy hours with byzantines and copts. plenty of each: on every corner, a byz-

antine, in every bush, a copt. come soon for the celebrations &
later we go to Mount Arthur.[100]

The letter that Merton never got was dated December 8. In it Lax
acknowledged that he did "receive by tidal wave your Asian Letter & I
am happy with all the encounters,"[101] presumably referring to Merton's
meeting with the Dalai Lama and other holy men. The monk had had profound experiences—in New Delhi, October 28-31, and in Dharamsala,
November 1-8, including three sessions with the Dalai Lama. He then
went back to Calcutta, November 11-12, where he got a "completely new
impression: greater respect for this vast, crumby city. There is a kind of
nobility in its sordidness. . . ."[102] On he traveled to Darjeeling, "a much
finer place than I expected—a king of places, full of Tibetans, prayer
flags, high in mists, wonderful mountains, all hidden as we came up
the wretched road along which there have been some seventy bad land-
slides."[103] There he encountered Kanchenjunga, "dim in the dawn and in
haze, not colored by the sun but dovelike in its bluegray. . . ."[104]

Still musing about a long-term destination for himself he saw a book-
let before Mass in the Loreto Convent about La Salette, in the French
Alps, where Lax had spent some time, and he wrote in his journal,
"Maybe after all I shall go there."[105]

The photos of Merton on these travels—even though he suffered
sometimes from a cold and from the polluted atmosphere and was often
fatigued—show him looking healthy and affable—as with the picture
in the *Asian Journal* of him with the Dalai Lama. In his autobiography
the Dalai Lama says that he and Merton met on three consecutive days
for two hours each time.

> I could see he was a truly humble and deeply spiritual man. This
> was the first time that I had been struck by such a feeling of spiritu-
> ality in anyone who professed Christianity. Since then, I have come
> across others with similar qualities, but it was Merton who intro-
> duced me to the real meaning of the word "Christian." . . . I called
> him a Catholic *geshe* (accomplished Buddhist scholar). We talked
> about intellectual and spiritual matters that were of mutual inter-
> est and exchanged information about monasticism. I was keen to
> learn all I could about the monastic tradition in the West. . . . For
> his part Merton wanted to know all he could about the Bodhisattva
> (aspiring Buddha) ideal. He also hoped to meet a teacher who
> could introduce him to Tantrism (a yoga practice leading to
> divine ecstasy). Altogether, it was a most useful exchange—not
> least because I discovered from it that there are many similarities
> between Buddhism and Catholicism. So I was extremely sad to

hear of his sudden death. Merton acted as a strong bridge between our two very different religious traditions. Above all, he helped me to realize that every major religion, with its teaching of love and compassion, can produce good human beings.[106]

Later Merton met with another Buddhist leader—Chatral Rimpoche:

the greatest rimpoche I have met so far. . . . We must have talked for two hours or more, covering all sorts of ground, mostly around about the idea of dzogchen [perfection] but also taking in some points of Christian doctrine compared with Buddhist: dharma-kaya [thought] . . . the Risen Christ, suffering, compassion for all creatures, motives for "helping others"—but all leading back to dzogchen, the ultimate emptiness, the unity of sunyata [a refinement of emptiness] and karuna [compassion], going "beyond the dharmakaya" and "beyond God" to the ultimate perfect emptiness. He said he had meditated in solitude for thirty years or more and had not attained to perfect emptiness and I said I hadn't either. . . . He told me, seriously, that perhaps he and I would attain to complete Buddhahood in our next lives, perhaps even in this life, and the parting note was a kind of compact that we would both do our best to make it in this life. . . . If I were going to settle down with a Tibetan guru, I think Chatral would be the one I'd choose. But I don't know yet if that is what I'll be able to do—or whether I need to.[107]

By all odds Merton's most profound experience on the trip was at Polonnaruwa, in Ceylon.

I know and have seen what I was obscurely looking for. I don't know what else remains but I have now seen and have pierced through the surface and have got beyond the shadow and the disguise. . . .
    . . . The whole thing is very much a Zen garden, a span of bareness and openness and evidence, and the great figures, motionless, yet with lines in full movement, waves of vesture and bodily form, a beautiful and holy vision.[108]

In jarring contrast was Colombo, the capital of Ceylon, where, "Everywhere there are police and military, very aggressive, with sharp fixed bayonets or machine guns even. Ed Rice had told me something of this but I had forgotten."[109]

While in Darjeeling Merton got word from Lax that the poet Emmett Williams wanted some of his poems for an anthology of concrete poetry.[110] A few days later Lax repeated that he hoped the monk would come to Greece. Then, in his journal, exemplifying his continued unsettledness, Merton speculated wildly on various routes that might take him to or through Moscow, India, Athens, Tokyo, Anchorage, Amsterdam, Switzerland, "then back to England for Wales and Scotland. What about the letter from the man at Orval [a Cistercian abbey in Belgium] about the old Grandmontine priory that is falling into ruins? . . . at Puy near Chevier in the Indre [an eremetical order in Grandmont, France?].[111]

Merton spent his longest period of time in Asia in Darjeeling—almost two weeks, November 12-25. During that time he discussed with his friend Harold Talbott the idea of setting up "a good Tibetan meditation center in America, perhaps in New Mexico, in some indirect connection with Christ in the Desert."[112] Many such initiatives have taken place in the decades since Merton died.

His death, on December 10, 1968, twenty-seven years to the day since entering Gethsemani, seemed absurd—an electrocution from touching a defective fan after getting out of a shower following a lecture at the Bangkok conference. The news hit the West like a bombshell. The headline on the front page of the *New York Times* the next day read, "Thomas Merton Is Dead at 53; Monk Wrote of Search for God." It was written by Israel Shenker, one of the paper's most eloquent journalists, who termed Merton "a writer of singular grace about the City of God and an essayist of penetrating originality on the City of Man." Mark Van Doren wrote in a longhand night letter to the abbot that, "He was one of the great persons of our time or of any time. I shall mourn for him as long as I live." To Lax Van Doren wired: "Tom dead in Bangkok. The Abbot just telegraphed me—no details. I never felt so bad. I'll never get over it. And I know you won't."[113]

Lax and Rice, though deeply shaken, took the news stoically, as if their friend's fate might have been predetermined. Neither made it to Gethsemani for the funeral, held on December 17. The Mass was celebrated with "chanting of the funeral liturgy by the monks," wrote Brother Patrick, before, "At dusk under a light snowfall, his body was laid to rest in the monastic cemetery beneath a solitary cedar tree."[114] "The most moving of the many cables of sympathy," Brother Patrick later told me—"from such people as Coretta Scott King, Claire Booth Luce and Ethel Kennedy—was Bob Lax's one word message, 'Sad.'"

It was ironic that the monk who had written so angrily against war, including the Vietnam War, had been flown back to the United States in an Air Force jet that also carried the bodies of American soldiers killed in that conflict.

Rice did not make it to the funeral because, he told me, he was dead broke at the time. He gave Sister Thérèse Lentfoehr another reason: "It seemed like too much of a traumatic experience. I went to the Mass at St Patrick's [held on December 30] but for a long time I had to block out the fact of Tom's death."[115] Mark Van Doren was at the St. Patrick's Mass, too, and wrote Lax that the celebrant, Father Ford,

> looked terribly ancient, but his voice reached the whole audience, which filled the cathedral. Afterwards we saw him for a minute, then went to Schrafft's for lunch with Bob Giroux and Ned O'Gorman. We talked much of you—did you hear us? Did Merton hear us? Maybe. For some reason I felt better when Ned suddenly blurted: "I'll miss that cat." Probably the best way to talk about him. Yet only one way. America asked me to do a piece about him, and I made it up mostly out of his last letter to me (July), talking with great joy about the trip he was to take. Heartbreaking now, and yet because it was so funny—almost like his letters to you—it somehow preserves him without loss. Loss, though! God.[116]

In the *America* piece, Van Doren wrote,

> I have never known a mind more brilliant, more beautiful, more serious, more playful. The energy behind it was immeasurable, and the capacity for love. . . .
> . . . the man never seemed to be tired; or if he was, he said so in language so laughable that I knew the lightning still played beyond the clouds. Soon he was back in his stride: writing endlessly, book after book; keeping up with the affairs of the outside world—but for him it was never outside, and he knew more about it than most of us did; maintaining contact with his innumerable friends; reading everything within reach; praying for mankind, whose manifold miseries he knew at first hand and lived with daily; performing his offices at the monastery, and when he was free from those, retiring to his hermitage in the woods; and always, always dashing off those letters. . . .[117]

When Rice visited Lax on Kalymnos a year later, almost on the anniversary of Merton's death, the two talked little about him as they walked the island, as if there was nothing more to add. As Lax wrote Sister Thérèse, "We hardly mentioned our friend, but we knew he was with us (& kept the best of our jokes for him). I know he's with you, too, as he is with me, here. May we all stay together, as he longed for us to, both here and in Heaven."[118]

****

9

LAURELS

Merton's Corpus Grows Post-Mortem;
Lax's Poems Hailed; Rice Writes a
Controversial Merton Biography

In early 1969, both Lax and Rice considered how to put their recollections about Merton, and their grief, into writing. Lax told Emil
Antonucci that he had composed a poem about his friend "on one of
first sad nights" with a "dedication sort of along with it. . . . Someone
says i shld write a bk (or maybe just an article) about him. Don't know
whether it's just what to do (or just what not to) for holding the old
mind together. Anyway, we'll see. Bleak nights & days, but like I say,
still moving along." He never wrote either the book or the article, but
here is "A Poem for Thomas Merton," which Brother Patrick Hart feels
is the most moving written tribute the monk got at his death:

> sin
> gu
> lar
>
> star
>
> sin
> gu
> lar
>
> cloud
>
> sin
> gu
> lar
>
> hill

sin
gu
lar

cloud

sin
gu
lar

star

sin
gu
lar

hill

one
cloud

one
star

one
hill

one hill

one cloud

one
star[1]

A few days after writing the poem Lax moved into a new house on Kalymnos. "great, great. you should really visit," he wrote Antonucci. "looks at sea, is dry, high; even seems solid."[2]

The new digs helped him to get himself together, even generate inspiration to write. "Moving zammo into abstract poems & concrete/abstract photos—where, like you say, familiar object becomes unfamiliar."[3]

While he loved the house and wrote uninterruptedly there, he had to confess to Antonucci that the working conditions were hardly optimum at first. He was "all the time writing, writing. no light at night but oil lamp and imaginary crocodiles: run, run, run."[4] His concrete poems had always posed problems for publishers, even for willing ones like James Fitzsimmons, who in 1963 had printed the long "Sea & Sky" in *Lugano Review* but now told Lax that he couldn't handle his "day book-diary poems" [the Kalymnos Journal] because "if, to save space, we printed it as we would have to, in two or three parallel columns, the linear quality, and some of the simplicity/limpidity, would be lost."[5]

Another project—the publication of Lax's letters to and from Merton, which the monk had tried fruitlessly for several years to bring to reality—moved to the front burner, although it seemed a more difficult challenge without Merton's intercession. "Me, some day will write Harvard Library about Merton letters—(them & a couple of other people). Also wrote banker friend St Louis to ask about private grant (or even a low-interest loan)."[6] He must have had no response because success with getting the letters printed would not be achieved until nine years later.

In the meantime he sought literary sustenance from a classic source for writers over the years: a Guggenheim fellowship. He had failed in a try for a Guggenheim in 1962, supported by a "glowing" letter from Merton. Now, in 1969, he would try again. In what might be a draft of what was actually mailed he wrote that a grant would allow him "to continue work in progress on a new long poem [the Kalymnos Journal]: to devote my entire time to it for the period of a year. I should prefer, if possible," he wrote in the application, "to live in Greece, on the island of Kalymnos, where the poem was begun and where the mountains and sea, the rocks and (sparse) olive groves have become for me a familiar landscape."[7]

Besides the boiler-plate material on his education and past jobs he listed a powerful set of references—not only William Maxwell, Denise Levertov, and James Laughlin, but Padraic Colum, John Ashbery (who told him that he had applied for a Guggenheim for twelve straight years before finally getting $7,500), Mrs. E. E. Cummings, and Marianne Moore. I was proud that he included Millie and me with his more personal references, along with Ed Rice and Sister Thérèse. Paul Spaeth, guardian of the Lax archive at St. Bonaventure, thinks that it was this application which drew from R. C. Kenedy of the Victoria and Albert Museum the statement that Lax's *Circus of the Sun* is "in all probability, the finest volume of poems published by an English-speaking poet of the generation which comes in T. S. Eliot's wake."[8]

The writing in the Guggenheim application seems offbeat for a formal document, which is why I suspect that the copy I have is a draft. But maybe these were the actual words submitted, since writing a dry document was not in Lax's bones. In any case, it is a lovely summing up of his persona:

a large part of my writing career has been devoted to trying to stay alive in order to write. (by "write" of course i mean to write seriously and from the heart in the way one believes one should write.)[9]

He then gave "a detailed account of his career as a writer." Although it covers some material already found in this book, the repetition—in Lax's signature words—carries a special charm:

I wrote poetry in high-school and continued writing it in college and after. My first poems, some lyric, some satirical, were published in the New Yorker magazine in the early 1940s, and at the same time I went to work there as contributing and assistant poetry editor. I continued to write on the side of various jobs (as editor, screenwriter, college instructor—all listed above in my application form) for the next ten or fifteen years, contributing occasionally to literary or learned magazines (Furioso, The American Scholar, the Quarterly Review among them) and publishing under the aegis of Journeyman Books and the Hand Press (see list below) a few small books. At last I completed a longer and more unified work, the Circus of the Sun, a sequence of poems, mostly lyrical, which play with the circus as a metaphor for the whole of creation. This was the first of my works to receive any critical notice. It was read with considerable enthusiasm by Stuart Gilbert [whom Lax describes in another paper as "James Joyce's friend and exegesist"] in Paris, and by E. E. Cummings, Mark Van Doren, Thomas Merton (by Robert Lowell, too, I believe) in America. Denise Levertov wrote a most enthusiastic piece about it in the Nation and I received a further word of cheer from Miss Marianne Moore.

I continued to work slowly on the side of other jobs, publishing what for me was a revolutionary volume called New Poems. It was translated into Spanish by Ernesto Cardenal and excerpts from it appear in his extremely [that word scratched out] selective Antologia of North American Poetry published in Madrid in 1963.

These poems in a fairly stark new style (which seemed to have invented itself from life in the city). New Poems was not warmly received by the older generation of critics in America but it brought me into lively contact with a whole new generation of writers to

Europe and America, and with those in literary movements who tended to adopt my work (and sometimes republish it) even before I had known of their existence. John Ashbery, then in Europe, included new poems of mine in an anthology, <u>Locus Solus</u> of which he was editor. Ian Hamilton Finlay (Scotland) republished one of these in POTH, and Edwin Morgan, another Scotch poet, read still another on a BBC Third Program. Aram Saroyan, then scarcely out of school, wrote me a letter of gratitude and appreciation, and Denise Levertov continued to show a friendly interest in my work.

In 1962 I decided to leave New York and editorial jobs behind, to go to (almost any) small Greek island, to continue my work as a poet in a new style, in the hope of being fed, if necessary, by ravens (It hasn't yet come to that. I have managed, up to now, to live meagerly and to write, in fact, rather copiously). But a moment of crisis approaches. (So far, no ravens have appeared.)

In 1965 during my first year on the island of Kalymnos, I wrote a new long poem (this is a still more drastically simplified style), called Sea & Sky and (in a moment of temerity) sent it to James Fitzsimmons, the editor of Art International and the then new *Lugano Review*.[10] His first reaction was one of bewildering indifference, but on second or third reading he decided to devote an entire issue of his new magazine to it (117, mostly blank, pages long). An expensive venture and one for which he received more abuse than gratitude. positive reactions to the poem were again slow, but they have been steady, and steadily mounting in enthusiasm.

without going into detail, i'd say that i should like to live in greece for a year (even for two)—meaning at least a year or two more than i already have [supposing that this application was prepared in 1969, he had already been in Greece for seven years]—and to write poems there. what poems? the ones i've been preparing to write, the kind i've been writing all my life.

why in greece: because i feel that the landscape here is properly classical, properly stripped of all that is not essential, all that is not universal. it is ready-made for abstraction and for concrete, exact, particular abstraction.

i'd like to live in greece, too, because i now do know the language well enough to converse with people at almost every level of society, including the level that most interests me on this island: that of the fishermen and sponge divers. these are people, mostly unlettered, and who, even though they have sometimes traveled widely in terms of miles in the modern world, are really in mind much like the ancient dorians, their forebears, neither simple nor unimaginably complex, but interesting in their responses to a modern man of the cities.

but i am not here as an anthropologist, but as a poet and whatever in the daily life here feeds my spirit, feeds me more particularly as a poet.

—technically my interest of recent years has been in the syllable. i have seen it as the unit of which poems are made much as, until recently, at least, the atom was seen as the unit of physical matter. i have been interested, that is in the syllable, not in the line, not in the word, but in syllables and in rhythmic groups of syllables, which perhaps should be called lines but which as i use them rather resemble chains, vertical groups of syllables (usually common words of striking universal significance—cut into syllables and arranged in rhythmic and semantic grouping—after the manner of poets of all time, but in vertical arrangement, rather than horizontal. the reason for this verticality is to present the eye of the reader—the ear, too, with one syllable at a time—the syllables of which the word, the words, and which the poem is made

————

although most of my writing has been in the lyric vein, my reading is more often in the epic (and rhapsodic) my favorite poets (& writers) being: homer dante joyce chaucer rabelais (vergil, blake and lucretius)

Concise statement of my project [what follows are excerpts— maybe these were alternatives from which Lax would later make choices]:

to write poetry, exploring further the syllabic structure of our current vocabulary and its implications in poetry as to rhythmic effect, visual image and meaning

a disentanglement, slow and patient of the soul's own inner & eternal song

to attempt a thoroughgoing and radical reform of the present (most loved modes) of english american and european poetry

to discover beneath the traditional modes of poetry a firmer, more universal foundation for the (eternal) & recurrent modes of poetry

writing career:

among the other dreams that haunt me i suppose is that of being able to make something that will stand, something that will last

to rise in the morning and find himself in a blessed city, and to

live in it through the day, and indeed through all the days of his
life.

the work of the poet is to make that dream real, at least in
words, at least on paper

i have admired ancient writers for the weight of their words, the
simplicity and strength of their expression. homer, dante, david of
the psalms, basho (of the haiku) being among my favorites.

of modern writers james joyce and st john perse seem most
admirable

(& blake and isaiah among the timelessly prophetic)

(i have not stopped here to do reverence to vergil, but if dante
revered him he has been forever revered.)

the way of using words in all of these poets has been stated by
the psalmist david: "the words of the Lord are pure words: refined
seven times."

and this refinement can be to no other purpose but ultimately
to the Lord's

for we do not refine to achieve a base metal but only to attain
a pure gold.[11]

I never saw a turndown letter in Lax's various archives, but I do
know that his application was rejected. He kept up his writing faithfully in those years. One example from 1969 is a poem, unpublished,
that he sent to Antonucci on a 3" x 8" piece of cardboard:

War/Peace

mmmmm

rrrrr

mmmmm

rrrrr

rrrrr

mmmmm

rrrrr

mmmmm

mmmmm

rrrrr

mmmmm

rrrrr[12]

Without help from the Guggenheim fellowhip, funds were hard to come by, and so he was especially grateful to get money from home, as when his Olean neighbor Mary Davis sent him $150, writing him that she loved "Singular Star," the Merton encomium.

Vital to his survival was his devoted friend and publisher of Journeyman Books, Emil Antonucci, who worked out of his apartment in Brooklyn. An undated letter to an unidentified recipient in the Lax archive at St. Bonaventure University—it could, actually, be a paragraph from the draft of the Guggenheim application—gives testimony to Antonucci's importance.

> In the meantime I've continued to write, and I believe quite confidently, to develop. Emil Antonucci (without whose heroic, self-sacrificing & inspired cooperation, i could scarcely have brought one work to fruition) has continued to publish what I have written, at his own pace, & by his own means. Next planned for publication is a collection called Selected Poems a representative selection from my works both short and long, published and unpublished.
>
> In the meantime, I continue to work on a new long poem which I hope will be wider and deeper, longer and better made than any I have attempted so far. (It is for help in completing this work—in Greece—that I am now seeking Fellowship funds.)[13]

Antonucci himself would finally make the trip to Kalymnos, in 1971, evoking this acknowledgment of his importance from Lax after the trip. "It really was great, your being here. Pulled everything into place; have been feeling fine since."[14]

Although he seemed pleased with Kalymnos Lax continued to check out other islands. In one ten-day period in 1969 he visited Patmos, Ikaria, and "from there by friendly dolphin to fournos, really small, obscure, sea-locked island, surrounded that is by wild waves that nobody wants to go out on." Body warmth, quiet, and possible accessibility to at least some level of medical attention were always priorities for Lax, and Fournos did not measure up on all counts. "if it weren't (very likely) to be cold in winter & really inaccessible if you had any needs, i'd like to stay here," he told Antonucci. "the air really quiet (except of course, for a family from piraeus with iron lungs and a stereo transistor who live right down the hall from me in this hotel)."[15] Fournos was dropped from the list of prospects. Kalymnos stayed on it.

He was writing vigorously on what became his *Kalymnos Journal*. ". . . not all immortal prose, but it's coming along; more and more nonselfconscious aspects & dimensions of mine (or somebody's) life & place i live; . . . this island's brought my appetite back for life, climbing around hills, seeing new rocks and stuff. kal is great . . . but you get into ruts about where you eat, who you eat with and where you parade for the evening . . . gleeks . . . got about 20 million extra ways of staying calm than we have."[16] At one point he told Emil about an idea he had for a film, but no other mention was made of it:

full color movie: screen full of red—screen full of blue—screen full of white (is that possible?) screen full of black (is that?)—screen full of yellow etc. then variations—both fast & slow—but nothing on screen at any one time (whether for 25 seconds, or one second) than one pure color, to be followed (semi-predictably) by another—just as strong & pure. . . . For background music wild noise: peruvian whistles & congo drums—or native tiger yells—but a different set of wild noises for each color[17]

Winters in Kalymnos could be bone chilling and discouraging to the creative urge, as on a day in February 1970 when he wrote Antonucci of "hail outside the window, rock breaking thunder, big lightning; first time like this all winter. small electric stove inside, all ok. haven't been able to get near typewriter for one or two months . . . all i do is take walks walks; work piling up in all directions." Encouragement from home was a tonic, particularly praise from his dear older sister, Gladys. "Gladio crazy about jrnl & she doesn't really throw her hat in the air unless she means it."[18]

He did a reading for the U.S. cultural attache at the embassy in Athens that "made everybody happy." He got laughs especially for

The Maximum Capacity
of this room
is 262 people

262 people

The Maximum Capacity
of this room
is 262 people[19]

He became conscious of the importance of having his works properly archived after Columbia University asked for his Merton letters. He told Antonucci not to send them yet but that it might be a good idea to give them something, like his Van Doren letters, "just to get a collection started."[20] The Lax archive in the Butler Library at Columbia is now well established and may be almost as complete as the one at St. Bonaventure University in the Friedsam Library.

He asked Antonucci to look at the pictures that Rice had taken during his recent visit to Kalymnos. A wonderful one of Lax, wearing his trademark cap and riding a bike, would, years later, become the poster picture advertising his very successful *Abstrakte Poesie* reading, organized by Thomas Kellein in Stuttgart (1985) and then the cover photo on *33 Poems* (1987). Another, which Rice snapped of Lax in silhouette at the entrance to the Parthenon, would become the cover shot of a special issue on Lax of the poetry journal *Voyages*, in 1968.

When not writing, meditating or walking he was mostly reading, including the books by Merton that came out after his death. He particularly admired *Zen and the Birds of Appetite*, "in which he pins old Suzuki to mat in 3 Japanese flips."[21] Lax could have been referring to Merton's statement in *Zen* that "Dr. Suzuki has not mentioned one of the main actors in the drama of the Fall: the devil."[22] While Buddhists believe in the concept of such a personage as the devil, it appears very little in Zen.

Kalymnos got so hot in the summer of 1970, "i couldn't even address an envelope," that Lax went off to a cooler place, Leipsos, his occasional escape island, about twenty-five miles away.[23]

In August he met the whole Harford family at the Athens airport —Millie and me and our children, Susan, sixteen, Jimmy, fifteen, Jennifer, eleven, and Christopher, seven. He joined us at a rooftop banquet in the King George Hotel where I gave a lecture on the American space program. Two days later, after we had toured the Acropolis and other Athens sights, he went with us on the jam-packed island-hopping ship, the *Knossos*, for the seventeen-hour overnight sail from Piraeus to Kalymnos. All night we had to fight for sleeping space in one of the lounges with a bevy of crones—the kind of withered ladies in black dresses and kerchiefs who appeared famously in the death scene of the film *Zorba the Greek*. The mild-mannered Lax proved to be a tiger in repelling the aggressive women.

The family still remembers the ten-day stay in Kalymnos as one of the most peaceful and beautiful of our many vacations together. Children of those ages might be expected to have short attention spans, but they were engrossed by Lax, whose calm talks over thick Greek coffee, lemon soda for them, in the town square or under the grape arbor at our tiny pensione in the little village of Myrties on the waterfront, looking over the bay to the tiny, practically uninhabited island of Telendos, seemed to center them. Our rooms cost an unbelievable $10 a day for the whole family, including simple meals—mostly fresh fish or roast lamb, tomatoes, onions, feta cheese, bread, red wine. We would take long walks by the sea or in the hills, picking figs and cactus pears along the way. Son Christopher, who celebrated his eighth birthday there, and I rowed over to Telendos one day, looking down through a glass-bottomed bucket to see what we had been told was a city that had sunk after a volcano eruption hundreds of years in the past. Did we see anything? Well, maybe those vague and shimmering shapes below were once buildings. Memorable in particular were the sunsets over the hills of Telendos, their profile shaped like a giant face with a big nose.

Here is a poem from *Voyages* depicting Lax's Kalymnos:

what
is
this
strange

dis-
in-
teg-
rat-
ing

sand
?

what
are
the
moun-
tains
made
of
?

the
mount-
ains
arch
their
backs

like
angry
cats[24]

Afternoons on Kalymnos we would visit Lax in his whitewashed apartment up long, winding stairs from the town. His talks with teens Susan and Jimmy were particularly warm, gentle, and philosophical about life's vicissitudes. His kindnesses to the two youngest—Christopher and Jennifer—were treasured, so much so that when they both, separately, had professional burnout from high-intensity jobs years later they revisited him, by then on Patmos, and came home renewed. Jimmy, when in his twenties in the late 1970s, spent several days with Lax wandering the streets of little Spanish towns such as Rondo, during one of the poet's trips to Europe.

All was not tranquility for Lax, however, in Kalymnos. I remember his face blanching when once, in a restaurant, I kidded him about the menacing photo of the Greek dictator on the wall. He hushed me quickly, apparently in fear of the Greek undercover men who had been hounding, and routinely searching, his house and opening his mail. They could not believe that he was not an American spy.

Some modest financial reward came to poet Lax in 1970 when Antonucci landed a grant from the National Endowment for the Arts for *Fables: Robert Lax* [thirty-two unnumbered pages including Antonucci's marvelous drawings].[25] One fable was titled "therapist":

A man came to me with the
following problem:

"My mother-in-law, he said, "de-
spises me; my creditors once friendly, are now all over me; my wife
threatens to leave me tomorrow unless I put the children in a better
school; my employers criticize
the tone of my work for what they

call a failure of nerve. What
do you suggest I do?"

I turned a somersault for
him & he felt better.

Lax was becoming more and more the hermit. He turned down a
request from a U.S. Information Agency program officer who phoned
him from Athens asking him to go on tour, "to places like Pakistan."[26]
Then he told Antonucci that his old friend from Paris days, Padre
Tomas, wanted him to come for a visit, but he "probably won't go
unless it turns out he really needs somebody fast."[27]

Jay Laughlin sent him Merton's newly published *Asian Journal*[28] in
1973. It is interesting that Lax, who had read practically everything
Merton wrote, called it the

best book of Merton's I've read: he's most himself, most keen &
observant, witty, lost, (found) erudite, enlightened, clean, natural,
free, mature, & whatever qualities else are good in man & in
Merton.

his books are good, but obviously can't all be best. the fragmen-
tariness of this doesn't get in its way. he hits so hard & so well at
each stroke, that each is complete in itself. (best of all, for me, is
that he is so recognizably himself.) . . . it is not what merton taught
his asian friends or what they taught him, for me, that matters, but
who merton is & who they are, that shines through every page of
the book, & tells us more than any treatise on samadhi can. [29]

While Lax had been settling with reasonable ease into his writing
in Kalymnos, Rice, in 1970, was arrested for participating in a protest
of the Vietnam War. Then, only two years after Merton's death, he
completed the first biography of his monk-friend, and it was controversial. "Idiosyncratic," one reviewer called it.[30] Another described it as a
"grotesque reconstruction of Merton."[31] Titled *The Man in the Sycamore Tree (MIST)*,[32] some Merton devotees, as well as Gethsemani
colleagues, felt that it was impulsively written, published opportunisti-
cally, and gave erroneous impressions of the monk's disposition toward
his future, seeming to imply that he was headed for Buddhism. Rice
was, in fact, rather flip on the subject of Merton's interest in Buddhism,
at one point in *MIST* telling someone that he was writing "a book
about an Englishman who became a Communist, then a Catholic, later
a Trappist monk, and finally a Buddhist, at which point, his life having
been fulfilled he died."[33]

The flippancy aside, Rice thought it not extraordinary that a Catholic monk might have Buddhist leanings. He said once that "Christianity was greatly influenced by Buddhism, including the idea of monasticism which came from third century Buddhism. Plenty of documents on this."[34] In a paper that he had prepared for delivery in Calcutta only weeks before he died, Merton himself wrote, "I need not add that I think we have now reached a stage of (long-overdue) religious maturity at which it may be possible for someone to remain perfectly faithful to a Christian and Western monastic commitment, and yet to learn in depth from, say a Buddhist or Hindu discipline and experience."[35] Rice's theory, as stated in *MIST*, is that

Merton was searching not for a religion—which he had—but a discipline of a different color and intensity from the Trappists'. He turned to Zen Buddhism. To Merton, Zen was not the slippery, one-upmanship game that Zen became for many Westerners, but a mature, demanding, responsible and rock-hard discipline that was the antithesis of Western thinking, which, he believed, had become too stratified, too codified and "logical" to the exclusion of true thought.[36]

Rice says that Merton spent "five or six years in meditating on the works of Chuang Tzu," who lived in the fourth and third centuries B.C. He annotated Chuang Tzu's works and then did a book of translations. Chuang Tzu would seem to be an unlikely inspiration for the Trappist since he "did not believe in any creator God, or any God at all in the Western sense. But he did believe in an underlying Tao, Way or One, from which the Heaven and Earth derived. This One transfused everything in the universe from the lowest to the highest."[37] On the other hand Merton identified closely with the Chinese philosopher's view that "[p]eople should abandon concern for fame, power and wealth and follow a simple life. They should distrust ethical and political schemes and follow their instincts."[38] Rice avers that Merton's

studies of Buddhism had gone far beyond Chuang Tzu when he died. His essays—and those published were already considerable—were only the beginning of what had promised to be years of work and meditation on the massive body of Eastern thought and philosophy. Merton saw Buddhism not in the limited, passive terms which brings its dismissal by Western philosophers (and this has been one of the faults of Catholics particularly) but as a dynamic and creative force which had been the way for millions of people for longer than Christianity had existed. He did not try to "baptize" Buddhism as the average Chrisitian might. . . . Buddhism had its own very valid and true existence, and he was trying to shed the restrictions of the Western mind in reaching out for it.[39]

John Eudes Bamberger wrote a very critical review of *MIST*, emphasizing what he thought were particular errors and distortions. As to Rice's interpretation of Merton's inclination toward Buddhism, for example, Bamberger wrote:

In this talk [to a group of nuns in Calcutta], far from approaching interiority in the Buddhist manner, he takes a wholly Christological perspective, and urges the nuns in the warmest terms to adhere to their traditional spiritual values and practices and not be influenced by the present excesses of the West.
    . . . Instead of allaying the rumours concerning the spirit in which Merton visited the East, Rice has added to the confusion. He has lost an opportunity to do his friend an important service which would have meant a great deal to him personally and to the meaning of his work and life. Merton was a deeply spiritual man, a rich and complex person, who ever remained deeply human with all the lovableness and all the suffering and all the weakness that that implies.[40]

Bamberger felt that Rice was off base, also, in his characterization of the relationship of the monk to Abbot James Fox. In the review he wrote,

Obviously, these [the relations of Merton with his community and abbot] were very complex. . . . But the picture of Merton living in an atmosphere of literal observance, of authoritarianism and of unrelieved austerity with an inadequate diet in spite of his bad health, and of a "constant state of tension" between the abbot and most of the monks that undermined life in the community—such a picture is not a portrait which enables us to understand the milieu in which Merton's personality developed but is a caricature which suggests that he grew in opposition to his milieu, rising above an unbearable situation by the force of his genius and character.
    Like all good caricatures, this one has a good deal of truth in it. But it is so distorted that it is quite misleading.[41]

Before reading this I had gone to see Bamberger in 1999 and asked about his recollections of the monk's relations with his abbot. Merton, he said, had a gift for contemplative prayer and a love of solitude but he needed to be part of a group and he needed a strong superior. . . . Dom James was extremely patient with him. . . . He told me that when he [Merton] starts traveling he'll get in trouble, that he was too free a spirit.[42]

I asked Bamberger if Merton confided in him since he was a psychiatrist. "Sometimes, and at the deepest times," he responded, "and frankly I was edified. Some of the things I can't talk about. One of his deepest problems, when he spoke about it, one of the lowest points in his life, I came away edified. I've never seen anybody who was so low who could still laugh at himself, and he did."

Earlier in his book review, Bamberger called *MIST* a "frankly journalistic account" by "one of his [Merton's] college friends." I pointed out to him that this was an unfair putdown since Rice was far more than a mere "college friend," having been a colleague at Columbia on *Jester* magazine, and for fifteen years on *Jubilee*, as well as a thirty-year correspondent and sometime Gethsemani visitor. Also, a remark Bamberger made that the photos and sketches of Merton in the book were mostly from the Columbia days was inaccurate since well more than half were Rice's own superb photos taken of Merton at Gethsemani.

Bamberger conceded to me that he had probably overminimized the friendship, but he stuck with another objection to the book—Rice's intimation that Merton had not planned to come back to the monastery after Bangkok. Bamberger cites Merton's letter of November 9, 1968, to his abbot (by then, Dom Flavian Burns) in which he stated that "the abbot will want him to return to Gethsemani where, slowly and patiently, he will work out his future, 'praying to know God's will.'" Bamberger agreed with Rice that Merton could have remained a Gethsemani monk even if he were to move to another "small, monastic foundation, perhaps with one or two other members of Gethsemani, in Alaska or some other place."[43] As for another possibility that Merton had mentioned—going to Nicaragua to establish a hermitage near his old friend Ernesto Cardenal, by then working with the Sandinistas— Bamberger told me, "Ernesto is a wonderful person, with high motives . . . but look who he got tied up with . . . a government producing tyrants [the Sandinistas]." Bamberger also put down still another invitation that the restive Merton considered seriously, from Dom Gregorio Lemercier, prior of a monastery in Cuernavaca, Mexico. "I visited Lemercier's place. The whole thing was closed down. He had left. It would have been a disaster and Rice had mentioned it as if it would have been a real possibility."[44]

Years later, in 1981, Bamberger seemed to be sideswiping at Rice when he wrote, in a preface to Henri Nouwen's book on Merton, that "he [Nouwen, although he met Merton only once] has understood the central motivation force of Merton's life: meditation and prayer. He has seen this more truly and profoundly than some who, while claiming to be intimate friends of Merton, have altogether missed the point of his work and life through lack of feeling for his vision of God, humanity and the cosmos."[45]

Another criticism of the Rice book, by a professor, characterized it as a "bitter misrepresentation of a man of his monastic community that is in many ways calculated, irresponsible, sensational and quite unworthy of both the man and his community. . . ."[46]

Closer to home, and certainly more painful to Rice if he had read them—which he may not have—were Mark Van Doren's comments to Bob Lax on the book. "I'm not sure what I think of it. Much new information (to me new), and many ideas about Tom that I'm glad to see stated, true or untrue; but something about the book bothers me. I guess it's Rice's omniscience about Merton, as if he and only he had all the answers. Jay Laughlin can't abide the book. I can, but still I'm bothered."[47]

Jim Forest was disappointed also in *MIST*, feeling that Rice was

gunning for the Church and was ready to use Merton as a club . . . he crudely caricatured Merton's relationship with his abbot. In the last part of the book he failed to note that Merton in Asia was still saying Mass and praying the rosary. Many readers came away with the notion that Merton's final conversion was to Buddhism. It's a myth that still lives on.[48]

Lax, however, praised the book extravagantly in a letter to Rice. "I really think it is great, great, great . . . hard hitting where it ought to be, true, funny & everything. (The spooks who don't like it have obviously got vested interests somewhere.)"[49] It must be said, however, that the gentle poet seemed always to be copious with his praise of the writings of both Rice and Merton, whatever they were.

Merton's Columbia and *Jubilee* pals found Rice's blunt, candid style in *MIST* refreshing, and they surely must have chuckled at the use of Merton's nude sketches from *Jester*. Merton became apologetic about those drawings in later years, once calling them, in a letter to Sister Thérèse, who had been digging into the Columbia archives, "those inane pictures. Well, I deserve punishment."[50] Jim Knight, who wrote a piece called "The Thomas Merton We Knew," which can be accessed on the Internet (www.therealmerton.com), is one of the Columbia gang who thinks Merton has been wronged by many who have written about him. He was "a different man, and monk, from the saintly person of pre-fabricated purity that has become his image these days. He was a real person, not a saint; he was a mystic searching for God, but a God that crossed the boundary of all religions; his was not a purely Christian soul. He developed closer spiritual ties than Church authorities will ever admit to the Eastern religions, Hinduism as well as Buddhism." Knight quotes Rice as saying, "the Church has wronged him, and continues to wrong him, by glossing over, by evading the universality of his thought. The Church wants to obscure his basic human nature, his reaching out to other people in a desire to create a common bond, not necessarily based on religion."[51]

Very complimentary toward *MIST* was a reader who wrote Rice, ". . . how glad I am that this kind of book has been written about Thomas Merton. Ever since his death I have been irritated by the fact that we Catholics—I am myself a convert, at least in part through reading *The Seven Storey Mountain*—will quite effectively bring about the eclipse of this man by making of him, as with Belloc and Chesterton before him, a 'Catholic writer'—that, in effect, the real man, the poet, the highly inventive thinker, the brilliant essayist, would be entirely lost behind the 'party line' of parochial boosterism."[52]

Besides his own thirty-year friendship, Rice's research for *MIST* drew on many other sources, including the memories of Lax and Sister Thérèse Lentfoehr, the nun who had served on Rice's *Jubilee* advisory board, had transcribed many of the monk's writings, and who had corresponded with him steadily and intimately over several decades. This is from a letter he wrote to Lentfoehr nine months after Merton's death:

I'm sorry I lost touch with you, but somehow I was snowed under, trying to keep Jubilee going, and then it was lost anyway. Since Herder got it, I've been doing free-lance writing and photography, mainly for the United Nations. Now I've just started a photographic book on Tom Merton. I have pictures going back to the Olean period, and I've taken a number on my various visits to Gethsemani. I know you have a big collection of Mertonia, and I wonder if you can supply me with the names and addresses of certain people, whom he mentions without identifying. One is his guardian, the English doctor. The others would be his aunts who are said to be living in Babylon, Long Island. Then there is that very tragic situation that occurred in his Cambridge days. You and I had discussed this once briefly, when I was living on Bank Street.

There are rumors about it now, and I was wondering what should be done about them. This of course, is private between us. It's something Tom and I never talked about, but on the other hand Bob Lax and I have several times, and we believe the people to be dead. Do you know about them?

I am taking a brief trip at the end of October [he didn't make the trip until December] to see Bob Lax (he is still living in Greece) and then I will come back and finish the book. Anything you can do for me—names, background information about some of these people—would be most welcome.[53]

Sister Thérèse's response is not in the archives, but she must have answered in some depth, although she probably avoided comment on Merton's paternity at Cambridge. Rice's thank you reveals the professional writer's sense of competitiveness with Merton's official biographer, John Howard Griffin, who died without completing the work [it was picked up by Michael Mott, whose book *The Seven Mountains of Thomas Merton*, written twelve years after Rice's, was broadly praised, and who had an unsatisfactory interview with the very guarded Rice in the course of his research]. Before he died, Griffin wrote a journal while researching the Merton biography, and in it charged that Rice, in *MIST*, "manages to get a great deal of incorrect material and speculation down on paper, but is nevertheless fascinating. Again and again he makes contentions that Merton rebuts in his own private diaries, and more or less leaves the impression that Merton told him these things."[54]

But the fact is that Rice had gotten much of his material on Merton from his own relationship with the monk and his writings, and he had striven mightily to be objective and thorough in his research. Here is an excerpt from one of his letters to Lentfoehr:

It was such a pleasure receiving your letter. It contained some helpful information. The question of the mother & child is still a puzzling one. It was common knowledge when Tom was at Columbia—apparently he boasted about it, or had spoken openly, and my friends from that time all know about it. Sooner or later Griffin is going to hear some of the rumors. I always wondered how you had heard about it—I remember your telling me there were two [illegitimate children] and I replied only one, as far as I knew. It would be nice to have it cleared up, to avoid distortion. I wish I could follow Tom's trail, from France to England and then to America. Unfortunately I am limited to the American scene. It would be interesting to learn more about his life as a school boy. However, I have material that Griffin is not likely to get.[55]

MIST did not bring Rice much income, although it had three print-ings and was republished, by Image, Doubleday's religious imprint, as a paperback in 1972. It was a difficult period for Rice. His divorce from Margery had occurred in 1969, and he needed work. "I thought I'd send you the enclosed resume," he wrote Millie and me and other friends, "as I am looking for a job. Unfortunately I fell behind in my alimony payments and was brought to court by my ex-wife. . . . The Court ordered that I give up freelance work and take a regular job. . . . If you have any ideas where I can find a nice, fat, well-paying job, please let me know." That the letter was pro forma in order to satisfy the court that he was looking for work is confirmed by this P.S. added to my copy of the letter: "Jim—this is for laughs & the record. The ex Mrs R is being a bit vindictive. Hope to see you and Millie soon."[56] He had no intention of taking a salaried job and kept plugging away at his books and magazine articles. But he was, indeed, on hard times.

The photographs he had taken on his travels, as well as for *Jubilee*, have great value and deserve to be catalogued carefully and displayed in muse-ums: there are many striking portraits of Merton, as well as of famous personalities like Jacques Maritain, Dan Berrigan, Mother Teresa, Hans Küng, Christopher Dawson, Karl Rahner. There are also beautiful shots of simple holy men and women, starving children with beatific smiles, sick old people, devoted nuns, gory surgical operations, bathing in the Ganges, lovely Indian women of high caste, priests, monks, lamas, war protesters, hippies, cholera victims, napalmed babies.

After his marriage ended, Rice lived in New York on East 89th Street, where Millie and I dined with him several times; he was a very good cook, specializing in Indian and Indonesian delicacies. Then, in 1972 he bought the dilapidated house of a potato farmer and moved it to a lot in fashionable Sagaponack, Long Island. It cost him $21,779, plus $8,500 to move and to build a basement and septic tank. The house and property, inherited by son Chris on Ed's death in 2002, are prob-ably worth well over $1 million.

Rice's prolific free-lancing in the the late 1960s and early 1970s was eclectic—such as an article in *LOOK* that termed Calcutta the "Worst City in the World"; one on elegant Indian ladies for *Town & Country*; two pieces for *Sign* magazine—one on Hinduism, and one on "The Human Face of Vietnam"; and one titled "High on the Harp," about rich Catholics, for *Status* magazine. He wrote on assignment for various publications and organizations, including the UN, on world diseases—glaucoma, leprosy, and cholera. Other articles published or proposed were on travels to Pakistan, Arab refugees, yoga, renewal of the liturgy in Asia, Christian-Hindu dialog, Thomas More, and the

Orthodox Church in the United States. Some of this writing he did during a month at the MacDowell Colony in New Hampshire, where, he wrote Lax, "the only sound is the dripping of the icicles."

Not long after *MIST* was published, Rice thought seriously about a second Merton biography that would treat his friend's interest in Eastern thought, especially Buddhism, more substantively. In 1972 he outlined what he had in mind to his agent.

> I've been thinking again about the possibility of a second Merton book—a kind of Zen Merton, which would put the last six weeks of his life in India and Thailand against the background of his very pronounced Buddhist "conversion." Some of the reasons are as follows:
>
> 1) After publication of The Man in the Sycamore Tree I learned of a number of people who were with Merton those last six weeks. There are also several with whom he spent some time in preparation on the West Coast. Most of the people in India are either Tibetans or Hindus. I also know of one American (and there may be others) who served as a guide and assistant in his Indian travels. Two or more of the Tibetans are now in the States, and I know of others, including those at the Dalai Lama's center north of Delhi and those at the lamasery at Darjeeling. I have also met Indians in Calcutta who talked with him; one of them says that "Tom was very, very Buddhist in his thinking." Then there are the various Thais and Americans in Bangkok, where he died, and other people, like an Indonesian scholar whom Merton had talked to.
>
> 2) Merton left behind an Asian journal which cryptically covers his travels, his experiences, his new influences and his reactions. New Directions is supposed to have published it last year but is said to be having trouble in deciphering his notes, most of which refer to obscure works. Some of the books he had been reading are quite esoteric and are unknown in America. At least one that I know of is a heavily sexual, sensual manual on tantric yoga which centers around the worship of the goddess Kali.
>
> 3) I have received a number of letters from people who knew Merton at various times and have information which has not been published. Some of it is trivial, of course, but some is important.
>
> 4) My own thinking, experience and exposure to the East is far deeper and broader than when I wrote the biography. I think I can put Merton into a more interesting perspective.
>
> 5) I am most likely going to Asia again within the next year and will be able to follow up the various leads. I think that the

Official Biography is not likely to have much or any of this material unless the author knows of these people I have mentioned and can spend the time interviewing them. What is more obvious is that my own point of view is certainly going to be much different from his (more engaging, entertaining, perceptive, more in tune with the East, whatever you wish) because each of us sees Merton in different contexts.

I haven't followed any of the new leads because I am not able to spend time on them unless there is a chance of a book. I would be unable to do more than a brief outline now without devoting a lot of time to research, and that is impossible without a commitment from a publisher. But on the basis of the (critical) success of my biography, I would hope that some of the preliminaries could be skipped.

I am confident that there is a good second book in Merton, not as a "Catholic," but as a seminal figure in the current easternization of the West—that is, the Zen Merton, the Buddha Merton, Merton the Avatar of the Bodhisattva. Such would be the theme. It has been interesting for me to see that the aspects of Merton that people wrote me about were not the Christian ones but the eastern.

This doesn't have to be a big book—perhaps forty thousand words, with a handful of pictures. It would be written not for the pious Catholic, but for the pious eastern audience, which, I suspect, is a good one. As a final word, I don't think the editor who says that "Merton is finished, we've had enough of Merton," knows that the phenomenon is only beginning. Merton the Trappist has been buried, but Merton the Buddha is just starting.

Hope this interests you.[57]

Rice was correct, of course, in pointing out that the interest in Merton was only beginning. An undated paper in his archive, probably prepared for the same agent, not long after the above letter, consists of 197 double-spaced, thirty-line pages from what must have been the working manuscript for the second book. Toward the end he wrote:

Thomas Merton summed up an era. If one wishes to know where the Western world was in the second half of the twentieth century, Thomas Merton offers considerable enlightenment. He showed us our spiritual potential in the midst of our secular endeavors. He made holiness equivalent with a life that seeks to be whole, honest and free. He taught us that it was possible to be truly religious without being formally religious. He proved that contemplation could occur in the throes of restlessness and that it was permissible to be fully human.

Merton was part of the great Catholic tradition and yet seemed not to be confined by it. He saw in that tradition the capacity for a comprehensive synthesis of human thought but he protested against institutional tendencies in the Catholic Church toward fascism. He observed that claims of infallibility and an insistence on mandatory celibacy would destroy its authority. He loved the liturgy and community life which Catholicism made possible, the spiritual tradition and sense of mysticism it encouraged, the humor and humanity which shone through its sometimes rigid structure. He was Catholic to the core because he would not allow Catholicism to particularize or parochialize him. He was against the Church "as established and worldly," against all in the Church which was "dirty" and "demonic." He defined fidelity as the capacity to condemn the lie in the Church, the refusal to canonize its sinfulness. But he also saw the beauty and splendor, the sincerity and love that the Catholic tradition could inspire.

. . . I am not giving in to an ingenuous, admiring expression of friendship when I rank Merton with the Fathers of the Early Church and those of the Middle Ages. . . . His humanism explains why his message, as did theirs, has found so great an audience.

. . . The human journey is always a circle. The universe does not go out forever in one direction but bends back on itself. The planet on which we live is a globe so that all our pilgrimages are already homecomings. There is really no way out. No one is ever lost. They merely return by different paths. There is a paradox in that—one built into the fabric of the Gospel message; the goings forth are ways in which we remain near the ones we love. How the Zen Buddhists would appreciate that puzzle. Thomas Merton never left us. The journey goes on.[58]

Unfortunately the agent, evidently not persuaded that a second Rice biography of Merton would sell, failed to pursue a publisher.

In about 1974 Lax sent Millie and me—and probably others—a 129-page, double-spaced "Sec 1" of the manuscript of the Kalymnos journal, which begins in Kos in 1964 and ends in Kalymnos in 1973. A portion of the journal was eventually published by James Laughlin, who—urged by Merton—had long wanted to put some of Lax's poems in *New Directions*. "If you have any poems which are more 'horizontal' than the one you sent me last year," he wrote to Lax, "I'd love to have a look, for I've always wanted to see you in the Annual one year. But we do have this terrible space problem now, which cuts down badly on certain types of poems [like Lax's that often used one word or one syllable or even one letter per line]."[59] Laughlin put an excerpt from the Kalymnos journal into his 1975 *Annual*. Perhaps so as to justify to his readers the selection of the little-known Lax in a volume that also contained such poets as Robert Lowell, Gregory Corso, and Lawrence Ferlinghetti, Laughlin identified him in the notes as "A lifelong friend of the late Thomas Merton." Here is an excerpt:

> it was good to get back to Kalymnos, which, the way I
> live in it, is not just my island, it's myself. we
> arrived at three in the morning and i walked up the hill
> with a bag of old books and old clothes in each hand.
> my cat came out to meet me a hundred yards from the
>   house,
> and circled around my legs all the way to the door.
> luckily there was a can or two of milk in the kitchen,
> enough for both of us.
>
> mist on the
> mountain
>
> grace to the
> mind
>
> suddenly the floodgates are open: rivers of
> memory from all times of my life, rush-
> ing together into the sea[60]

It was about that kind of poetry that Mark Van Doren wrote, "The poems put—oh, what life into the sea, the sun, the birds, and finally the sea again, always the sea, the sea."[61]

The Lax poetic creations continued in the 1970s to be experimental, spare, humorous, perceptive. The noted *New Yorker* writer William Maxwell made this comment to Lax in a letter in 1974: ". . . liked the Angel and the Little Old Lady so much that I had to get up and walk around after I read it." Another time he wrote, on *New Yorker* stationery, "I put my feet on my desk and read your book of fables from cover to cover, with delight. . . . I will now take the book home and read it aloud to my family." Still later he wrote, "I like your poems even better in longhand. The words are all so short and they look as if they

were about to flap their wings and fly off into the sky, like herons."[62]
Maxwell was right on the nose when he later wrote Lax, "I assume that
what keeps you in Greece year after year is not sightseeing but a full
heart, the soul let out of its straitjacket."

Also in 1974, R. C. Kenedy, the English poet who had written the
laudatory appraisal of Lax on his application for a Guggenheim fellowship, wrote twelve dense pages of analysis of the Lax genre that
included these remarks:

> Lax's subjects are the most highly charged and symbolic units of
> our western experience. His choice of them is, obviously, not acci-
> dental . . . he lists truths which hint at the religious mysteries of
> our still-changeless rites, performed as they are throughout Chris-
> tendom's churches and cathedrals every Sunday. The wine—which
> is not wine; the bread which is no longer bread. . . . [63]

Rice once told me that he thought Lax had the life of solitude that
Merton really wished for. Lax described his own thoughts on his soli-
tude and his writing habits to a friend and fellow poet, the late William
Packard:

> I've often thought of sitting at the typewriter [to write a poem] as
> being sort of like a piano player . . . like Art Tatum . . . warming
> up before he actually begins to play. And the journal sometimes
> has been like a warming up process in that way.
>   . . . I never try to make myself write. I do it when I enjoy it.
> Sometimes if I don't feel like writing, I do feel like drawing. So I
> draw.
>   . . . You really need to be alone during a good part of the day.
> The isolation itself brings things to the surface that otherwise
> remain hidden. You get to know yourself as a writer when you're
> alone.
>   . . . I'm happy if I can be alone and can be left to writing,
> drawing, reading, thinking, taking walks. That is the sort of life
> I enjoy.
>   . . . I never felt like an expatriate . . . I do feel an ever increas-
> ing affinity with the Greek people, and I'm pretty sure it would
> influence my writing. . . . I get the feeling that Greeks, and island
> Greeks in particular, have all the qualities that we've come to asso-
> ciate with human beings we've encountered in life and literature;
> they have them in a high degree, and always in kinetic form. Some-
> thing is always happening here that gives clear, clean testimony to

the human quality of the person or people involved in any action. Any gesture that's made or word that's passed, in a public place, in a café or in the street, will be seen and understood in all its dimensions by whatever witnesses are at hand. If it's funny, it will be understood and laughed at; if it's worthy of comment, it will be commented on and often, penetratingly. In that sense, almost every moment that passes here is a moment of Greek Drama. The chorus is always on hand to make its observation.

The chorus . . . has been standing here since the Age of Pericles. . . . [64]

One of the most eloquent praises of Lax's poetry came in 1978 from the poet-critic Richard Kostelanetz, who, ironically, inserted his plaudits into a negative, and some poets think unfair, review in the *New York Times Book Review* of *The Collected Poems of Thomas Merton*.[65] "It was commonly joked," wrote Kostelanetz, "that Merton, having taken the vow of silence, then wrote tons of garrulous prose. His poems are similarly verbose, generally more prosy than poetic, and undistinguished in both language and idea. . . ."[66] Kostelanetz then pointed out, parenthetically, in a kind of afterthought, that Merton's *Cables to the Ace* "is dedicated to his [Merton's] college classmate Robert Lax, whom I regard among America's greatest experimental poets, a true minimalist who can weave awesome poems from remarkably few words. Though a survivor, Lax remains the last unacknowledged —and, alas, uncollected—major poet of his post-60's generation."[67]

He was not uncollected by friends in those days, however, including us Harfords, who treasure their published Lax and their private Lax from as far back as the 1950s. Well qualified to appreciate him was the writer Leonard Robinson, a *New Yorker* colleague whose interview of the Cristiani family originally triggered the *Circus* poem. He wrote in 1976 from the MacDowell Colony that "your letter lit up our house like big Christmas candles." It motivated him to make this tribute:

yes

fine spirited Lax a
singing hickory

o Kalymnos o Kalymnos

in Greece, of
all places, a
small island,

nothing like Euboeia.
a pearl, with
blessed Lax there.
in the Aegean

yes, Kalymnos, we
say yes.[68]

The following year Robinson, having picked up a copy of Lax's *New Poems*,[69] wrote from San Miguel de Allende in Mexico, "How entirely beautiful your lines are! I can understand why you went to Greece—they are like the lines of a Greek temple."[70] Then, after reading the Kostelanetz tribute, Robinson wrote, "Patricia & I waltzed around the living room of our adobe hut in celebration of how good you are—a beautiful waltz that would have made Nancy Flagg green with envy even at the height of her tremendously slinky dancing days."[71]

A few months earlier, Alex Eliot, an art expert who had been a friend since *Time* magazine days, and who—with his wife, Jane, housed Lax when he first went to Greece in 1962—wrote him, "I'd love to do something to help spread your poems around for they're the finest crystals of enlightenment now being formed anywhere within my ken."[72] These dear friends must have helped sustain Lax's spirits in the years when he was not being accorded the recognition that he would later acquire. Eliot, for example, kept up his praises, writing in 1979 about *A Catch of Anti-Letters*, the zany correspondence of Lax and Merton that was batted about by publishers for years before it came out just after Merton's death: "what comes through . . . is pain, gallantry, and wit, plus a terrific insight every so often. To call this book poignant would be an abysmal understatement. It taps the funnybone and lightens the mind, yes, and then like zazen meditation it may fill with healing hurt."[73]

Lax's correspondence with the gallivanting Rice must have helped the two fill the emotional hole left by the loss of their friend Tom Merton. It is remarkable that Rice took on some of his most ambitious travel at a time when his vision was getting worse and worse. A 1979 letter from his opthalmologist says that he had "less than 20/200 vision in both eyes and is therefore legally blind."[74] Nonetheless he took on strenuous journeys to write articles and research his upcoming books. He summarized several trips for Lax:

November 21, 1979, from Pakistan
Happy Birthday—Eye-ran and Pakistan giving us white folks a hard time [it was only days after the American hostages were

taken from the U.S. Embassy in Teheran]. . . . I had planned on about two months or so in India and Pakistan but now envision myself one jump ahead of a bunch of howling fanatics running down Chandi Marg for safety. So I may arrive in the islands sooner than planned. Only Allah knows . . . I am plumb wore out from trying to finish too many books in too short a time.

February 4, 1980 from somewhere in India
Got as much done as might be done, considering weather (94°+), wogs (600 million) & Delly Belly (frequent). Hope to take off from here on Feb 20 for Athens. . . .

Will probably go to Istanbul, Kenya from Athens, & then to Kalymnos, say mid-March. . . . Getting plumb wore out on these trips. They sound glamorous to stay-at-homes but you know the problems. But I seen things you wld never find in books . . . from here looks as if President Peanuts [Carter] might have us in another police action. Save Democracy in Pakistan.

February 10, 1980, from Baroda, India
My old bones creak. Longing for western chit-chat. Also for a street that isn't full of sacred cow-plop. (We got goats, too, here in Baroda.) And a meal that doesn't burn out my insides.[75]

Some friends aped Lax's style in writing to him, like the late poet William Packard, a professor at New York University, editor of *New York Quarterly*, who had tried, unsuccessfully, to get Lax on his editorial board.

dear
boss

at
a
recent
editorial
meeting
inside
my
head

it was
decided

you
should
be
on
our advisory
board

how
about
it

duties
slight
just
judge
one
issue
poems
every
100
years[76]

There were dozens of friends on Lax's complimentary list for copies of his books, including us Harfords, who were always proud to see the inscription, "Jim, Millie, Love, Bob," sometimes decorated by little yellow suns. The list included his many relatives and such a disparate group of friends as—besides his publishers and those identified in the correspondence above—Nancy Flagg Gibney, Ned O'Gorman, John Slate, Mogador (of the Cristiani family), Ad Reinhardt's widow, Rita, C. K. Williams, R. C. Kenedy, Howard Gold, Dick Dresselhuys, and others. He paid for the copies, writing one of his publishers, David Kilburn, "And yr money all gone on yr list And my money gone on my list. . . . Tried panning the bathwater for gold dust & got back ache."[77]

His letters in the late 1970s from Antonucci, signed with names such as "The Hulk," "Bobo," "Rufus," sometimes described "frantic efforts" to get the Lax poems displayed in places like Rizzoli's on Park Avenue—"almost threw us out the door [Lax's devoted niece Marcia Kelly was with him]." Successes were savored: ". . . the guy at Books & Co—hottest book store in town, a sort of rich Gotham Book Mart—liked the poems, took five copies of everything." Antonucci was always on the prowl for financial support and had to tell Lax that his own effort to get a Guggenheim fellowship had failed, just as Lax's had, "The Googly Heimers zapped me too. . . ."[78]

Lax had many Greek friends, some of them sponge fishermen who took dangerous voyages to the coast of Africa to dive for their product. They, and the Kalymnos townspeople, addressed him affably as "Petros" when he walked the streets or patronized the stores. He also formed friendships with a number of visiting westerners, like the American poet C. K. Williams and his Parisian wife, Catherine Mauger. Although he would win a raft of poetry awards in the 1980s and then the Pulitzer Prize in 2000, Williams was not especially well known when he was on Patmos for four weeks in 1973. He had had two books published and well received, and several of his poems had been printed in the *New Yorker* and other journals, but at times he would experience the "commonplace slump"[79] that seems periodically to afflict most poets.

He described one of those slumps to Lax in a letter from 1977, acknowledging what must have been a boost from Lax. "Your words meant, and mean, very much to me. You were right, though, in speaking of how awful I must feel—it's been terribly depressing. I've written nothing for a year except dubious prose sketches that'll probably end in the wastebasket and still am utterly uncertain about which way to go now, whether to go at all . . . the music is just silenced and facing a blank sheet of paper has become so painful that for the first time since I started writing, I don't even bother. . . ."[80]

It may be that comments like this from Lax in a letter of 1979 helped raise Williams's spirits: "I hope you'll write more like FLOOR. It rocked me as only a poem—real one—can. It kept me awake that night, and stayed with me for days to follow," and later in the same letter: "what i really like is your own unfaked but complete, compassionate gaze. i know, and anyone can feel, that it's not an attitude, it's your being, and that's what gives the poem its life. (and does to all your work.) it's also, I'm sure, what makes them so hard to write."[81] Williams today says that he "loved Bob, and admired him in many ways, but I never thought of him, as did some who knew him, as a fount of unique wisdom; he was a good friend, and a poet, which meant we shared a lot in our vision of the world, and that was what was essential in our relationship."[82]

Favorable critical attention to Lax's work picked up nicely in the late 1970s. N. Deedy, in *Commonweal*, wrote that "Lax's poetry is atypical, iconoclastic, dependent on the imagery of the eye as much as that of the mind. He deals in inks of varying colors, in word arrangements, in jottings, a single sentence, a single line of verse."[83]

In these years Lax would read occasionally for the BBC and also do well-attended readings in European cities, sometimes accompanied by Tessa Weigner, the daughter of Bernhard Moosbrugger's partner, Gladys, on jazz piano.

By and large Lax's publishers had become accustomed to indulging his one-word, one-syllable, or even one-letter lines with remarkable forebearance. Good example is the publication *Hanging Loose 29,* which included Lax's "One Island,"[84] and which went on for twenty-one pages, most of them repeating a few words like

cir
cle

of
brown

cir
cle

of
blue

For three consecutive summers in the late 1970s Lax took the long trip to the United States from Greece. Not wanting to fly, he would take a train across Greece, then a ferry to Brindisi, then a ship to America. Emil Antonucci would meet him at the pier in New York, and they would head for the New York State Park for Art, "Art Park" for short, on a 280-acre piece of land in the town of Lewiston, just downstream from Niagara Falls. With that location it got a good number of visitors. The two were artists in residence, paid modestly well for poetry readings and filmmaking, and put up in a nearby motel. There the two came in contact with Anthony Bannon, now director of George Eastman House in Rochester, who was a filmmaker occupying adjacent space, where he would film the Park's events with a Super 8mm camera, incorporate the footage into a 16mm camera, and show them. Every day, Bannon remembers, Lax would write poems on the spot and Antonucci would illustrate them for presentation to the passers-by. The Park also had performers—poets, dance troupes, theatrical groups doing touring versions of such shows as *The King and I,* and sometimes featured stars like Joan Baez or the Beach Boys.

Bannon, who had originally been put in touch with Lax by Merton, once asked him to do a poem for the *Buffalo News,* where he was the Sunday arts editor. He told Lax that the poem would be published in an edition of 350,000 in the Sunday paper that "would likely wrap fish the next day or be blowing in the wind . . . but he made this incredible poem about newspapers called 'Black Metal.' It's germane to newspapers because it deals with the elements, the metal that created old hot type . . . black metal black wood white metal white wood. . . ."[85]

Lax gave Bannon an interesting account of his writing style:

[I] carry small notebooks to record poems, thoughts and journal entries. Later I transcribe portions from these that seem to be the most worthwhile. Some of my longer pieces are written out in a single sitting or two. The first draft is almost always the finished product. Time and solitude are key elements in the production of my work.

In my work I'm talking to myself as clearly as I can about things that matter to me. If I've spoken clearly to myself and someone reads it and finds that it is meaningful to them, then I am happy. Curiously enough this is what has happened over the years.

The whole idea of non-violence, what Gandhi called *ahimsa*, is of prime importance to me. I try in my poetry to make it a kind of a song that evokes a picture of this peaceable kingdom.

I think that my poems *Sea and Sky, Circus of the Sun* and *21 Pages* are good illustrations of what I want to accomplish. In the coming year I hope to complete more of this work.[86]

Rice, meanwhile, kept up his writing at an incredible pace through the 1970s, although he experienced several more rejections. In 1973 he edited a book on contemporary Indian yogis, swamis, and gurus (*Temple of the Phallic King*), and in 1974 Doubleday published *John Frum He Come*, an account of a cargo cult in the South Pacific, a subject that had been of interest to Merton.

The résumé he sent to potential publishers, written in the third person with a dollop of mischief, recapped his language capabilities:

Athough he has been accused of being "only semi-bilingual," Edward Rice, as the result of a classical education and some fifteen years experience in wandering about five continents can carry on macaronic conversations not only in his native dialect (which he speaks with fluency) but French, Spanish, Italian, Portuguese, German, Russian, Hindu and Urdu, and even classical and medieval Latin. He has survived a week in Damascus on five words of Arabic, and reports that the words nem and iggen solve all problems in Hungarian. He can read the street signs in Hellenic, Cyrillic and Devanagari, and scientific summaries in Inter-Lingua.[87]

Also for "young adults" he wrote about growing up in a Third World country (*Mother India's Children* [Pantheon, 1971]); the religions of

Judaism, Christianity, Islam, Hinduism, and Buddhism (*Five Great Religions* [Four Winds Press, 1973]), and his personal view of India's great river (*The Ganges* [Four Winds, 1974]). The latter two had some of Rice's most striking photos of the Indian people, and the Ganges book had absorbing asides on history, archeology, and geology.

All of that writing was prelude to some seven years of work in the 1980s—after an even longer period of travel in Asia and Africa—on the creation of what would become, in 1990, his *magnum opus*—the life of Captain Sir Richard Francis Burton.

****

10

MERTON MOVEMENT

Merton Chapters Formed Worldwide;
Books by Lax and Rice Praised;
Rice Remarries, Then Loses Susanna

Although Thomas Merton was long a household name in Catholic circles, the explosion of Mertoniana in the 1980s was a phenomenon. His forty-some years worth of books, journals, letters, and poetry sold even more briskly than when he was alive. The market was fed by many thousands of new readers, the formation in 1987 of the International Thomas Merton Society—which now has thirty-nine chapters all over the United States and ten in foreign countries, including Russia—as well as a Merton Center, a Merton Foundation, Merton seminars and conferences, the *Merton Annual, Merton Seasonal,* Merton scholarships, and field trips to his birthplace in France, his prep school and university in England, his monastery in Kentucky, and his Olean and New York city haunts. There is even a Thomas Merton high school curriculum that has been adopted by some 200 U.S. secondary schools and 250 parishes.

Recognition of Lax and Rice was building as well, if not as spectacularly. *Circus of the Sun,* Lax's best-known work, was republished in 1981 as *circus zirkus cirque circo,*[1] with marvelous photos of clowns, acrobats, and horses taken by Lax's Zurich publisher, Bernhard Moosbrugger. It included parallel translations from the English into French, German, and Spanish—an ambitious undertaking, but it was represented artfully. Catherine Mauger, wife of C. K. Williams, worked on the beautifully nuanced French translation for months "off and on." Fredi Kuoni finished the German translation only, as Lax put it, "after a two, nearly three year struggle," and, while it is not known how much time it must have taken Ernesto Cardenal, Merton's friend from Trappist days, to do the Spanish *fragmentos,* the work must have been done in 1979 while he was serving as Minister of Culture for the Sandinista rebels in Nicaragua.

More sadness came to Lax in 1980 with the death of his old flame, Nancy Flagg Gibney. Her husband, Columbia pal Bob Gibney, had died in 1973. Four years later, in 1977, she had written Lax inviting him to visit her in St. John, where he and Reinhardt had spent happy, if somewhat dissolute, months in the 1940s. But the poet-hermit was not about to renew a romance at sixty-two. He declined the invitation and wrote Rice that St. John "seems very far away." In the same letter he said that "old Harford said he came out to see you & that you walked him all over the island at 5 in the morning. (if i ever get out there, we've got to think of something else to do.), he says you making your own yoghourt. . . . All I'm doing here, besides swimming, is writing same old poems—they are either getting better, or I getting crazier thinking so. . . ." By now he was "pushing new white beard, to the knees."[2]

It's certainly true that in those years Rice was in great physical shape. He felt robust enough even to make suggestions for Lax's dietary, exercise, and medical regime, citing his own recent rehabilitation from back problems. It was exercise, he maintained, that cured his backaches "after having spent $60 to see the doc and got no help." He urged his friend, somewhat righteously, to get seven hours sleep, citing a

> big study, 25 yrs, one million people . . . no smoking, easy on alchohol, moderate diet &c . . . cut down on protein yes protein . . . once American cure-all, especially animal protein. More carbohydrates like breads, beans, vegetables, seeds, nuts, fruit . . . drink too much very bad . . . couple of glasses of wine a day with meals . . . don't eat meat except abt once a month when I get an urge, and then find my memories of it are false . . . Eggs—big move here not to eat eggs but sensible people say that you need eggs and eat them instead of meat. . . . About fish. Eat small ones. Big ones full of chemicals from pollution.[3]

Lax would usually be called on whenever and wherever commemorations of Merton occurred. He prepared a long poem for the departed Trappist for a Merton/Maritain symposium in Louisville in 1980. Maritain was the philosopher-professor who had been Merton's friend and correspondent. The poem was not read, although Lax was there—it might have presented too big a challenge for the sponsors. Although a touching tribute to his dear friend, the poem is a classic example of Lax's obliviousness of the economics of typesetting, layout, and printing. Titled "Harpo's Progress," it took up sixteen pages when eventually published, eight years later, in the *Merton Annual*. The beginning segments:[4]

HARPO'S PROGRESS

Notes Toward an Understanding of Merton's Ways

There was a hermit who lived in the woods. He spent his days and nights in prayer, and in peaceful works that gave praise to the Lord. Though his spirit rested always in the heart of his Creator, his hands and feet were seldom idle, and neither was his mind. It might be said that the things he made were useless (he didn't weave baskets, he didn't make shoes), or if useful, only to the spirit: only to the soul in its journey toward God.

What were his works? Tracts, translations, poems, fables, drawings, photographs, dancing and drumming. So many works and all of the spirit? So many works, and all from a single source, toward a single end.

whom would he have gotten along with
in history?
with rabelais?
surely
with donne?

yes
with blake?

yes, yes
with augustine?
surely
chaucer, shakespeare?

yes
louis armstrong?
yes

Commenting on Merton's musical sense, Lax told me once, during a long walk along the shore of Lake Lausanne: "When Merton played hand drums on the hill in Olean it was like he was communicating with Bramachari in India. Somehow he found drums in a convent he visited in California [in 1968] and had the whole place rocking. He even played piano as a percussion instrument."[5]

Rice's travels in Asia and Africa in the late 1970s enabled him to author a prodigious quantity of articles for magazines, for the UN, and eventually for his best-recognized work, a life of Sir Richard Francis Burton, which would not be published until 1990. The expeditions were not without peril, however. "Once, in Somalia," he told me, "I was taking a picture of an old woman feeding goats when a young man came out of a thatched hut, pulled a knife from his sarong and tried to stab me. I had a bodyguard, though, and he saved me. Another time, in the Arabian desert, I was photographing—again an old woman—and a Bedouin chief wanted to execute me because it was against tribal law to take pictures of women—I was stupid to even try it but the scene was so exotic I couldn't resist. This time a UN person accompanying me persuaded the chief to just confiscate the roll of film."

Millie and I would admire his doggedness when we visited him in Sagaponack in the late 1970s and early '80s, banging away on an old manual typewriter, several hundred words a day, every day of the week. He would break for a cup of tea or a glass of wine when we arrived, and offer us some of his own freshly baked Nam, a deliciously light Indian bread. He taught Millie how to make the bread and taught me how to make my own yogurt, straining the curds through cheese cloth. We helped him tend his apple and pear trees and the vegetables that provided him good nutrition in summer time. But the Long Island winters were severe; he had nothing but a pot-bellied wood stove for heat, and his life was hard. Getting sufficient food was a drain on his meager income. Because of his failing eyes he had to give up driving a car and so a bicycle became his transport. He was in excellent physical condition though, having conceived, and constructed with pick and shovel, a huge—maybe thirty feet in diameter—circular trench with a three- or four-foot-tall monolith of wood, salvaged from the sea, sticking up in the middle. He called it Sag Henge. His explanation as to how it signaled astronomical phenomena was too abstruse for us. He would claim that it arrived from outer space one starry night but the fact is that he dug it mostly himself, although my son Jim and I spent many an hour helping him. "It's part of my psyche to do strange things," he told me. "It took me three years to dig."[6]

His financial situation was not healthy, though. He spent the first three months of 1981 in India, using most of $2,700 he had received in book advances. His files for that year show tiny royalty checks, as reported by his agent, Phoebe Larmore: a total of $121.08 for three books—*Man in the Sycamore Tree, Eastern Definitions, Mother India's Children*; $41.92 for *The Ganges*; and two checks, one for $16.18 and another for $292.40, for *Marx, Engels*. It was not easy to live on that kind of income. In the same year, he told Larmore, he had made "three trips to the table" for glaucoma operations.[7]

In September of 1982, Millie and I met Bob Lax in Zurich, where he was staying with his publishers, Bernard Moosbrugger and Gladys Weigner. One afternoon, on the quai next to the Fraumeister cathedral, we had a quiet coffee, and we talked a lot, Bob offering gentle advice, as people walked by, some looking happy, some morose. "Some people are in the light, some are in the dark, and some in a kind of gray. Keep trying to work towards the light. Don't try to convert or confront people. Just shine."[8]

That year the Congress of the International Astronautical Federation was held in Paris, and Lax was there with bells on, ready to take over once again as photographer for the report on the sessions that I made annually for the National Aeronautics and Space Administration. He did a good job, although once again he had trouble fighting other photographers for position during the ceremonial events, like when the astronauts and cosmonauts met. We found time for lovely walks around Paris, and after the sessions we drove to the vacation home of the family of one of my colleagues at the American Institute of Aeronautics and Astronautics, Mireille Gerard, in Mescher, in the Medoc country, on the Gironde north of Bordeaux. It was a peaceful and memorable experience. We visited the nearby twelfth-century church in Talmont, which jutted into the sea. It was one of the stops on the pilgrimage route to Santiago de Compostela. Mireille's parents fed us splendidly—I especially recall huge platters of smelts and sardines, and copious amounts of the local red wine that they had bottled themselves at a vineyard across the river. One afternoon Bob read to me, and I taped, his poem "Searching," later published as *21 Pages* by Moosbrugger. It was wonderful to hear the poem in Lax's own sonorous voice. He then asked me to read the poem and I found it embarrassing to play it back after having heard him deliver the same passages so beautifully.

It must have been in early 1983 that Rice was seeking a Vatican annulment of his marriage to Margery and had asked Lax for written documentation in support of the request. Lax wrote back, "I sent about 15 pages of dream-scenario to the Inquisition. I hope it will do some good. Couldn't remember any facts, but gave them impressions. The longest thing I've written since the Prophet Elias."[9]

Doping out the Rice–Lax letters on the subject is very difficult, but what does come through is how tortuous the proceedings for annulment were in the church in those years. Rice was supposed to "see the Inquisition last week but due to blindness did not read the letter clearly & went to the wrong place & never had the grilling." Getting to the annulment office in New York, he complained, was a three to four hour "schlepp. . . . My sister [Carol McCormack] is so upset by the whole thing, apparent hypocrisy of Church at this point all the red tape and the loopholes and so on, she is ready to join god knows what crowd, the Chinese perhaps."[10]

I should have been more tenacious in querying Rice in his last years about his efforts for the annulment, but he was not forthcoming on the subject. His son Chris remembers only that his mother got a Mexican divorce in 1969. Sister Carol's memory is that the annulment eventually was authorized, but she does not recall the date.

In 1982 and early 1983 Rice and Lax had spirited correspondence about a possible film on Merton. The effort seemed to have been trumped, in 1984, by *Merton, A Film Biography*, made by Paul Wilkes, but although the latter was well received, Rice was unhappy with it, and with the way that Merton's life was being portrayed by numerous others. He wrote Lax, "I got an awful feeling of frustration, plus sadness, at the way these people going (Michael Mott, Tony and Theresa Padovano, Wilkes, DiAntonio, Hobbel &c &c). No one seems to have read Mutton, just looking for a quick summary from someone else. . . .

"Perhaps we really shld get started on a film. Say, take five years, go slowly, let Harford raise $100,000 each from five rich men who otherwise wld put the money into condos."[11] Rice apparently got into talks with some slick businessmen about the idea. "One of the hustlers," he wrote Lax, offered him "one G . . . just to keep me from selling it to someone else." Lax was enthusiastic about the film idea and wrote Rice that he, too, thought that I should get involved, although he offered an approach that was as offbeat as it was unrealistic. "I just wrote Jim Harford to get up some bucks for a Merton & Coltrane film." Rice did ask me to help him raise funds for the project, so I said I would do my best, but I failed him.

Lax had promised Rice that he would send him notes, letters, and tapes for the film from Thessalonika where he had a one-month "no-job" as a writer in residence at Anatolia College.[12] Time went by as Rice worked on other projects. Then, in October 1984, Lax and Millie and I met in Lausanne, Switzerland, at another space congress, and Lax must have heard from Rice about a renewal of his interest in making the film. On one of our walks along Lake Geneva he said, "Rice ought to continue the way he's going . . . no commentary, just non-intensive footage of people. . . . He's got a vision there—jazz Merton liked, his jokes from his letters to us—and in the last few years he's reread Merton's books . . . you know, Millie and Jim, what questions you want answered, so that ought to be included."[13] A happy memory for Millie and me is going with Bob to the Circus Knie outside of Lausanne. The ringmaster knew him and put all three of us in front row seats. Lax's knowledge of circuses was still encyclopedic. I found a letter from 1974 in his archive to a "Mr. Zimmerman" that is virtually a compendium of circus books and circus troupes from many countries.

A few months later, in January 1985, Rice prepared a draft of a film treatment and sent me a copy. It builds a mood at the start that reflects Merton's deep interest in Eastern mysticism, as well as Rice's familiarity with the subject from his own travels. The first page:

Behind titles are scenes of Indian pilgrims approaching the cave complex at Mahablipuran. The Lingam temple is silhouetted against the sky, water laps at its foot and along the sand. After the titles, cut to back view of a figure seated in the lotus position

(Sound of OM, long drawn out and increasing in intensity)

Cut to Indian dancer, feet pounding on the temple stones, anklets jangling. Cut back to the figure and then to the dancer &c. Shots become quicker and shorter.

(Music, drums, clash and jangle of dancer's ornaments)

(OM & music alternate, each becoming louder and stronger)

Screen darkens and goes totally black. A few quick, very animated shots of Bangkok exotica—alligators in the canals, street scenes, movie posters, signs in Thai script, swaying palm trees . . . &c

(We hear the noise of a jet plane)

A flash of electrical sparks

The screen goes blank, then we open on a single shot of M; the camera moves in and we see his face very close

(Sound: Ellington music)

The forty-some pages of script that followed cover the Merton story from early life to final denouement—the death of his mother; school in France; playing rugby at Oakham in England; the death of his father; the Cambridge period when Merton indulged in—Rice quotes from SSM—

"an incoherent riot of undirected passion" resulting in the birth of an illegitimate child; the "intellectual awakening" but "hard drinking and womanizing" days, and the *Jester* magazine experiences at Columbia; the influence of Huxley and Joyce; the intrusion of the Spanish Civil War and the first Nazi initiatives; the appearance of Bramachari; the writings of John of the Cross and William Blake; baptism into Catholicism [with Rice as godfather]; his 1939 and 1940 dissipations with Lax, Rice, Freedgood, Jim Knight, Nancy Flagg, and others while the camera pans the mountains and the cottage at Olean; his entry into Gethsemani; his outrage at World War II and Vietnam; his prayers, including his meditations, with a quote from a letter to a Sufi friend in which he described a "direct seeking of the Face of the Invisible"; very discreet mention of the affair with the nurse—the script reads, "In the distance a young woman whose face we never see," accompanied by a song from Joan Baez; the trip to Asia, "the home where he had never been in this body . . . seeking mahakaruna, the great compassion"; a sequence with the "forest monks" in the caves of Sri Lanka, which Rice's script calls the "major passage in his spiritual life" and indicates, in caps, "THIS ENTIRE SEQUENCE HAS NOT BEEN INVESTIGATED BY ANYONE" [I asked Merton's secretary, Patrick Hart, what this was all about but he was unable to offer an answer]; and, finally, as the camera shows Lax in silhouette—a photo taken by Rice—the script reads, "On a remote Greek island, Bob Lax, who had expected to meet Merton in Greece, heard the tragic news of his friend's death. He wandered along the waterfront and worked out the words of what he called 'The Star Poem.'" The last page of the script instructs the camera to cut to Rice's own photo of Merton at the pond in Gethsemani while the OM sound is heard.

Lax fed Rice with ideas for the film: "Stuff I think we should include: zen drawings, girly angels; lots of photos, his and yours, background music from his record collection. My sister in Florida has all our old Beiderbecke records, Ellington, King Oliver. . . . He had a lot of John Coltrane records at his hutch when I was there." He went on to suggest that the script refer to Merton's "loud zen piano" and his playing of the bongos. "I used to think he could communicate with Bramachari through it. . . . Glad you mentioned all those influences on [him]. . . . I think you're right—Rabelais meant a lot to him. (To all of us.) I didn't realize then that that's a fairly rare influence. Nobody talks about him, as far as I know, even in France (except in the schools). But I think he's wonderful, and Merton did too."[14]

The amount of Merton material coming out in these years was overwhelming even Lax, who wrote Rice from his temporary artist-in-residence job at Anatolia College in Thessaloniki:

Rocco:

. . . Mr Moto got me surrounded: biography, m quarterly, & commonweal. wilks book coming [the Paul Wilkes book came out that year from Harper & Row as *Merton by Those Who Knew Him Best*, including a good portrait of a bearded and be-capped Lax and a lengthy interview]. victor kramer too. did you ever meet him? Daggy journal says you'll have an article in next one. Hope you do. Send xerox of that and the long one when you can.

What I hang onto through all of it is Moto's unqualified endorsement of Chuang Tzu. And vice versa. Q: did you see a book of letters from M to Ping Pinckney Ferry? Good and quite relaxed. Think you should see it . . . all the new stuff makes me think that the bix beiderbecke, eddie foy jr, wampus baby star picture I had in mind wouldn't have any takers, except you & me & harford if we did it right. everyone else wants a book about "tóm."[15]

Unfortunately, under my own pressures of work involving U.S. aero-space, I had limited time for trying to raise money, but I made several passes at possible supporters. What had seemed to be a promising inter-view with an executive of ABC-TV, which might have been a sponsor, went nowhere, unfortunately, as did my talks with a wealthy Catholic from Houston, and a priest who made Catholic films in Los Angeles.

Lax was paralyzed by Rice's insistence that he participate in the film. I, too, had urged him to take a crack at a script, and he wrote back, "How's a type-Z like me going to write about a type-A like Merton. It's like having a turtle write about Halley's comet. Still, I'm trying."[16]

The subject of the film would come up once more when Millie and I met Lax in Stockholm at the October 1985 International Astronauti-cal Congress. He was once again serving as paid photographer for my report on the technical sessions for NASA—and, once again, he missed a key photo, of the King of Sweden opening the Congress. While we stayed at the classy headquarters hotel in town, he bunked in a stu-dent hostel on a ship in the harbor, arranged by two young Swedish TV actors who had befriended him on the beach during their vaca-tion on Patmos. In those days Lax, seventy years old, was still fit to travel, although he could not abide airplanes. He had taken trains from Athens to Hamburg via Munich before reaching Stockholm, and he would probably entrain to Zurich to see Moosbrugger, then go back to Greece—by train to Ancona, Italy, boat across the Aegean to Patras, and another train to Athens. We had a great time with him and the young Swedes and their girl friends—long walks and talks, aquavit, herring. In one of our walks he told us, "What I like about talking to myself is I have a captive audience."[17]

When Bob and Millie and I took a day off from the congress for a ferry ride to the island of Waxholm, not far from Stockholm, we talked again about the idea for a film on Merton. "It's hard to portray this guy who draws Zen pictures, plays bongos, entertains novices, and is also serious about the church and its attitudes, especially the American church. He likes what the council did but selling the American church on what the council said is not easy. As a churchman he has something to say to the U.S. hierarchy. He felt obliged to talk, but he was forbidden as a Trappist because monks aren't supposed to talk about that."

Millie asked, "What about his feelings on East-West thinking?" "Yeah, Rice won't even do the picture unless that's in it. He wants to see Buddhism, Sufism, Christianity, Judaism merge by uniting them into one person. He did that himself through grace. You don't merge these things by interfaith conferences. He had this total understanding. Merton seems to have been *there* when those Buddhist texts were written."

Millie again: "What I'd like to know is how he made the leap from jazz to Zen?"

"From jazz to Zen? No leap."

"I mean when he was young."

He was running around but he was writing poems. He didn't write poems until his senior year. I told him about three words, and he started writing poems. He knew all sorts of things even in his senior year. He didn't know that he didn't have to read a lot of books. Bramachari came along and told us to look into our own roots. Jewish for me. Christian roots for him. Anything he did he did quietly but thoroughly. When he did get into the church he sort of recapitulated the history of Christianity—the Bible, the psalms, Job, all of the mystics, the Orthodox saints, always getting to the point where he could teach what he learned. This wanting to be a saint needs clearing up. He didn't mean a plastic saint; he knew the world needed saints. He knew it would involve lots of work, sacrifice; that's why he needed to go to a strict monastery with lots of discipline. When I first knew him at Columbia he had in mind training for the diplomatic service, studying Chinese, Chinese philosophy, so he was already half into things like Zen. He worked his way back, studied the whole history of Christianity, and began to see the relationship between the Christianity of the early fathers and Zen. He wrote to the Japanese, Suzuki, met him in New York, and Suzuki told him he was the one guy in the West who understood Zen. What Merton saw in Louis Armstrong was Zen. He was playing John Coltrane when I saw him at the hermitage. He didn't like *Seven Storey Mountain* afterwards because it seemed to take him out of the world—people liked that but not him. He got mad at America, and he was down on Christian optimism because it seemed to worship consumerism when you get right down to it.[18]

How would we show all this in a film? It would have been difficult, but when I reread Rice's script these days I get a renewal of my feeling of guilt for not having come up with the funding needed to produce it. It really should be made, even now. Although the Wilkes film stands up very well, and was rereleased in 2004 on DVD with an extra hour of excerpts of Merton Foundation programs that feature men and women who knew the monk, Rice's film would have portrayed a quite different and very interesting Merton, though it may very well have polarized viewers, just as *The Man in the Sycamore Tree* did.

Without support for a Merton film Rice turned back to work on the Burton book, although the huge scale of it sometimes caused him to look for diversion. He was feeling "crotchedly and feeble" when he wrote Lax in praise of some of the poet's works that had just arrived. "Magnificent," he called them. "So nice to see well printed, well designed volumes. Spent the afternoon reading them rather than working on Burton. Well worth it. Like the one with goat's blood, a subject rarely broached these days, though when I used to do chi-chi pieces for Town & Country I would always submit an expense voucher for '1 Goat sacrificed at kalighat for well-being of magazine. They always paid it.'" He was angry with Anne Freedgood, wife of the late Sy Freedgood, who had been his and Lax's and Merton's friend. She was his editor on the Burton book for Random House. "The Widow F," he called her in a letter to Lax, "needs a Hindu-Muslim-Buddhist hex on her. . . . You asked if she has seen the MS—yes, gave her 715 pgs abt a year ago, which she returned in ten days—not enough time to have read it—muttering abt cutting, cutting, cutting, and that is all I have heard since. Now up to abt 1200 pp. But all that cutting talk comes out more like, dare one say it?—castration."[19]

It was around that time that a wonderful turn in his life occurred with the appearance of one Susanna Franklin, who would become his most fulfilling love. One weekend Susanna accompanied Judith Emery, a Manhattan writer who was also Lax's friend, on a visit to Rice's home in Sagaponack, and the two, recalls Emery, "hit it off immediately." A divorcee in her early forties, mother of two, and a baptized Catholic with some American Indian heritage, she and Ed became devoted to each other.[20]

Their courtship continued and then—it must have been the day after Thanksgiving in 1985, Emery thinks—Ed became ill during a visit to Susanna's house in New Jersey. She insisted that he be taken by ambulance to New York Hospital, where he had a quadruple heart bypass. Susanna visited him daily. He recuperated nicely, and their companionship blossomed.

Lax, meanwhile, got one of his earliest showcases in Germany when Thomas Kellein, curator of the SOHN gallery in Stuttgart, discovered his poetry while organizing a show of the works of Ad Reinhardt, and decided to feature readings of Lax poetry as well. A wonderful poster for the exhibit—ROBERT LAX ABSTRAKT POESIE, Staatsgalerie, April 20–May 26, 1985—featured a photo of Bob on a bicycle that had been taken during Rice's visit to Kalymnos—and for which Rice got a much-needed fee. The event drew a very appreciative audience and made possible a reunion with Ad's wife, Rita, and their daughter Annie, both with new husbands. An enthusiastic review in *Stuttgarter Zeitung* called out Lax's "unceasing search for truth in human life" and his "dialogue with God." The exhibit included copies of the eighteen editions of Lax's long-dead *Pax,* whose purpose, said the review, "was to disseminate, in Thomas Aquinas spirit, the idea of eternal peace . . . distributed without profit, it mostly landed in the trash cans." Well, copies of *Pax* are rare but some are in the Millie and Jim Harford treasure chest and virtually all of them are in the archive of Lax at St. Bonaventure. There were also some of Lax's inimitable drawings, which the review describes as "One of the surprises. . . . The sovereignty of the sketches reminds us of Joseph Beuys, whereas the female figures recall deKooning. It is striking to find out that the sketches were done in the 1940s, which were mostly lost in the following years. But even these few remaining samples, as well as the poetry of the artist, show the genius."

Another review, in *Stuttgarter Nachrichten,* subtitled "Text and Pictures of a Stubbornly Unknown: Robert Lax," had a perceptive analysis of the poems and of Lax's reading style.

> It moves in an acoustical imaginative realm. When reading, his voice does not betray emotions. . . . Lax does not claim to be artsy or to present a challenge, and through this simplicity creates art of an almost unbearably high standard . . . [the text of] the structure of the poem "Black and White" . . . depends on being recited aloud. Robert Lax's challenge is the introduction to meditation.

The 12-minute séance might create impatience . . . meaningfully unintentional minimal shifts happen again and again. . . . When reading, Lax beats the metre with his foot, for breaks and for silence. Who listens, wakes up, and listens differently. It is a text that leads away from the self. . . . Lax writes in a vertical manner, structures his texts into text-images, symmetrical orders and structures. From the extreme reduction of the material he creates multiple meanings beyond the ornamental. Wit hovers between the lines, so to speak.[21]

The long-loyal publishers of Lax's work, Emil Antonucci and Bernhard Moosbrugger, had a fine showcase for their Lax books, and Moosbrugger was given the opportunity to show the Lax films *New Film* (1969) and *Shorts* (1971).

When he got back to his Greek island hermitage Lax told Rice that he was writing again, "Rocco, i've been back about a week, mostly sleeping and swimming. feel good again; have refound the typewriter and a chair to put it on. i asked the landlord to build me a table for it two years ago. he keeps saying: sure thing, right away." Although Lax's objectivity, as Rice's dear friend, can be questioned, his sincerity in praising the new paperback edition of *The Man in the Sycamore Tree* comes through strongly in the same letter. The book had

just arrived and looks great. i'm reading, rereading it now: best book ever written about Moto, and one of the best about anyone . . . what is good is that if you had written just for yourself, or for you, me, Moto & Freedgood, as a memory book, you couldn't have stuck more closely to the pertinent facts. as far as i've read, there's no time spent in talking to an imaginary reader. these are the things you'd want to say to yourself or a couple of friends.[22]

Rice must have told him about Susanna because, at the end of the same letter he wrote, "it's great to hear about you and Susanna, had had no idea of what she was like, now want to hear more. being good tempered sounds best of all so far. can see no reason (this late in the world) for hanging around with anyone who isn't. anyway it all sounds good and hope it will be. . . ."

Susanna's presence was a needed palliative for Rice, who continued to have problems with Anne Freedgood. She criticized the Burton manuscript as "long-winded and rambling," and she probably had a point, because Rice's 800 typed pages, which he had cut down from 1,200, had grown back up to 1,060.

He was no doubt cheered by another Lax letter that went into more detail on why he liked the new paperback *MIST*, and also gave testimony on why Merton's life was important:

> i've read every word, parenthetical, italicized and straight, picture captions too, and studied the pictures . . . and think it's tremendous. hadn't realized what a good driving jazz trumpet style it has, until now, how well it moves along, holds together and makes socko if ultimately unnameable point. great book, and absolutely no one else on the planet could have written it. the photos are wonderful too, and work perfectly to confirm whole story in text and captions. in your long hard life in the picture-book business how often have you seen that happen? the guy you're talking about is the one in those pictures (including the passport picture) and they're the only ones I've seen that get him right. all those people who were trying to get pictures of his halo missed his face. what you can see in all the later ones is strength and struggle, just like the captions say.
>
> the transitions, forward jumps and back flashes are all great too. and the way you come into and out of it where you need to. it'll be good if the film has that feeling too. (i haven't reread the scenario since i got here, but will now.) you also wrote it as though you knew he was going to read it and would approve. everything you say about him is said right in front of him, and right in front of everyone.
>
> that makes it honest testimony: no gossip & sidelights, just pertinent facts.
>
> what comes out of it is that he's remarkable, not for idiosyncracies, or even for talent but for the actual (cosmic) significance of his life. (& when you look closely, of every minute of it.) it makes us realize the significance of our own lives (everybody's) too and reaffirms any belief we have in the importance of our own decisions.[23]

Back once more came Lax to the International Astronautical Congress in October 1986, this time in Innsbruck, Austria. While Millie and I enjoyed his company, he again gave a lot of time to talks with the Russian delegates, renewing his friendship especially with Yuri Zonov, then a specialist in earth resources satellites, who probably had a dual role in the Soviet spy satellite program. Their talks never got into the technical, but stayed with poetry, Zonov being a Pushkin devotee, as were most Russians. Zonov was one of the few Soviets whose English was fluent enough to talk poetry with Lax and he recalls that

Bob did send me a book of his poems some years ago, the ones that consisted of single words. I tried to figure out what they meant and how to read them but then gave up and decided that the author himself should read them out because they might be like some music, and he is the only man that knows how to extract it for the listener. Of course over the years . . . through our passing meetings I developed my image of Bob. In my mind's view he appeared to me as an extremely kind man, not fit for the ruthless world, very close to my impression of what a saint might be. Even his face is closer to the image I have of what Christ might have looked like than he is depicted in the paintings. Look at the Milan shroud—I find resemblance between the two. As we say in Russia for the deceased: "may the earth lie on him lightly" [a kind of Russian "may he rest in peace"].[24]

That December Lax went to Zurich for a hernia operation and stayed for three months, moving from the home of Bernhard Moosbrugger and Gladys Weigner after the operation to stay at a theological seminary in Lucerne. He wrote the Harfords from there, "[I] Walk three hours a day by the lake & sit around panting the rest of the time. . . . As I walk I write poems & jokes in notebook and will send some soon."[25]

Rice got mad at Lax in 1987 when, after hatching an idea to do an oral history of people who knew Merton he discovered that Victor Kramer, editor of the *Merton Annual,* already had one underway, and Lax had been one of the interviewees. Rice fired off a hurt letter to his old friend, telling him, "Now I been going around like some dumb innocent, pushing Harford to raise money, writing letters to rich old ladies, when it has already started and you are a contributor. At least you could have told me. . . . I feel like some damn flatfooted horse's backside."[26] Lax was contrite, but it was unreasonable of Rice to have expected that Lax would refuse a bona fide interview about his old friend Merton.

Who would publish the Burton book was still up for grabs as 1988 began. "Have told my agent," Rice wrote Lax, "I can't work with the WF [Widow Freedgood]," whose "hatchet job" he was having to re-edit. He said that someone at Harper & Row was interested but wanted to see "the works not just an outline." Complicating his situation was the fact that Susanna was in depression, possibly because of an asthma condition that plagued her: ". . . acting miserable," he told Lax, "Send her a card."[27]

Lax complained back to Rice about his own problems with publishers. He could get neither copies nor sales figures for *A Catch of Anti-*

Letters, which had come out ten years earlier, in 1978. "Publisher used to send me monthly reports saying No Sales: none. Later when I wanted copies they said it was out of print. Do you think they put its feet in concrete and dropped it into the river?"[28]

An upbeat letter, dated Good Friday 1988, from his old friend Alex Eliot had lyrical things to say about Lax's *33 Poems*,[29] which had come out the year before. "Now at last the public aspect of your poetry breaks through the stony ground to spread its shady fragrance, blossom, bloom, and slowly fructify in what is doubtless the best way."[30] Among the poems in it is one that has been read often by the Harfords at family gatherings, and was chosen recently by Garrison Keilor for one of his radio shows:

> "are you a visitor?" asked
> the dog.
>
> "yes," i answered.
>
> "only a visitor?" asked
> the dog.
>
> "yes," i answered.
>
> "take me with you," said
> the dog.[31]

Rice was stung by a review (1988) in *America* of two new Merton books by the Trappist M. Basil Pennington. The reviewer, George Kilcourse of Bellarmine College, contrasted Pennington's view that Merton was "monastic to the core" with what he called "[o]pportunists like Ed Rice and Charles Kinzie [who] have persisted in grotesque deconstructions of Merton."[32] Rice's letter to George Hunt, editor of the magazine, demanding a retraction, never got an answer, nor did mine in support of his protest. It seems that there was, and is, a large group of Merton devotees who find it difficult, even today, to allow for the monk's humanness. On the other hand, Rice's closeness to the Merton that few people—other than Lax—knew as well as he, and his candor in recalling the monk with all his fallibilities, made him prey to the Merton hagiographers.

It was an especially difficult period for Rice. Susanna was often ill. He wrote Lax that she had a "new lung infection, should be in hospital but trying to stick it out at home," where the winter living conditions were mean ordinarily, but even more so when there was, as he reported, a "cold wave down from Alaska." He was constantly troubled by the use of his Merton photos without permission. Even his old Columbia classmate, Robert Giroux, was excoriated. "I am getting a real shafting from Giroux," he wrote Lax. Giroux had claimed that a Rice photo of Merton was "in the public domain . . . since it was not copyrighted." It was copyrighted in 1966, 1970, 1972, and 1985, Rice maintained. Feeling beaten down, he signed his letter, "Battered and Bruised White Old Man."[33]

With the Parkinson's disease afflicting him worse, his sight failing, and worried about Susanna's health, he got nasty to some correspondents who asked his cooperation. In October 1989, he told Lax, "My sight is so fragile that I can read and work only during daylight hours. My work day ends with sunset, so the winter months are miserable"; and, in the same letter, said that he had turned down what was a straightforward request from David Miller of Stride Publications, Devon, England, to contribute to a compendium of articles about Lax. Angrily he asked Miller, ". . . what is your competence to edit a book of the type you propose . . . Who are you? Who is your publisher? What else have you written or edited?" The book that came out, edited by Miller and Nicholas Zurbrugg, was titled *The ABC's of Robert Lax,* and is a very valuable, if modestly designed paperback, that includes no less than forty-eight mostly short pieces about Lax, by authors such as Jack Kerouac, C. K. Williams, Denise Levertov, Susan Howe, Mark Van Doren, Nancy Flagg, Alexander Eliot, Ian Hamilton Finlay, Emmett Williams, Brother Patrick Hart, and a couple by Lax himself. Whether with his permission or not, it uses a humorous excerpt from an interview Rice did with Lax, dating to *Jubilee* days. Lax, it seems, with his penchant for economy with words, even rewrote some chapters from the Bible. When published, readers remarked about how good the "translation" was. "What is it?" they asked. "We said it was still in progress."[34]

* * * * * * * * * * * * * * * *

11

Ups, Downs, Requiems

The recognition of both Merton, post-mortem, and Lax, still productive on Patmos, kept going up in the 1990s. Rice, too, had success but experienced serious personal setbacks as well.

Merton's following kept soaring as his books sold well; more International Thomas Merton Society branches were formed; more scholars analyzed his work, and—what is very significant—his views on the importance of Catholic-Buddhist dialogue helped to spark a whole new movement. Just weeks before he died, Merton, following a meeting on November 16, 1968 in India with Chatral Rimpoche—"the greatest rimpoche I have met so far"—said:

> The unspoken or half-spoken message of the talk was our complete understanding of each other as people who were somehow *on the edge* of a great realization and knew it and were trying, somehow or other, to go out and get lost in it—and it was a grace for us to meet one another.[1]

A few days later, in his concluding words to the Bangkok conference on December 10, he had signalled an alarm and placed the responsibility for heeding it on the monastics: "we find ourselves in a crisis, a moment of crucial choice. We are in grave danger of losing a spiritual heritage that has been painfully accumulated by thousands of generations of saints and contemplatives. It is the peculiar office of the monk in the modern world to keep alive the contemplative experience and to keep the way open for modern technological man to recover the integrity of his own inner depths."[2]

Merton had written for years of the importance of dialogue with Buddhists, and so had Lax and Rice. But a practical step leading to what the monk referred to above as "a great realization" had been made possible only three years before, on October 28, 1965, with what, wrote Pascaline Coff, O.S.B., "Karl Rahner, one of the greatest theologians of this century [termed] one of the greatest enactments of the Second Vatican Council,"[3] namely, *Nostra Aetate*, the *Declaration on the Relationship of the Church to Non-Christian Religions.*"[4] "In this document, for the first time in her history, the Roman Catholic Church, publicly proclaimed that truth is to be found in other religions."[5] *Nostra Aetate*, in fact, encouraged, among other initiatives, the very conference that Merton was attending when he died. It was, wrote Coff, "a watershed beginning for East-West intermonastic dialogue. . . . From his place beyond, he no doubt has had an influence on all that has transpired from then until now. . . . Indeed it has been said," and Coff quotes Simon Tonini, "His [Merton's] death had the same effect of the seed, which in dying produces much fruit."[6]

The seed gave flower to another Asian conference, sponsored by a new organization, the Aide Inter-Monastères (AIM) in Bangalore in 1973. Then an action was taken by the Vatican that gave official responsibility for continuing the dialogue to the Benedictine monks and nuns. The authorizing paper was a 1974 letter to Benedictine Abbot Primate Rembert Weakland from Cardinal Sergio Pignedoli, the president of a special secretariat that had been created in 1964 to promote the church's relationship with other religions, urging that the monastics "pursue" the goal of becoming a "bridge and contact-point" for cooperation with "persons of other faiths."[7]

Developments were rapid-fire after that. Still guided by the Pignedoli paper, the new AIM convened two groups of monks and nuns in 1977—one in Petersham, Massachusetts, another in Loppem, Belgium. AIM's North American Board for East-West Dialogue eventually took the name Monastic Interreligious Dialogue (MID), and that name has stuck for its U.S. component. The European monastics chose the name Dialogue Interreligieux Monastique (DIM) and began to develop their own program.

Meetings of MID ensued—first in 1980 and 1981 in Boulder, Colorado, the latter attended by the Dalai Lama, who had so graciously received Merton in 1968. Then came exchanges of Christian and Buddhist monks and nuns in 1982, 1983, 1985, 1986 (the latter included a visit with the Dalai Lama at his home in Dharamsala, where Merton had met him in 1968), and 1988. After this last one, held in the United States, Pope John Paul II met the Tibetan monastics as they were returning to India, adding one more important blessing to the movement. The pace picked up with gatherings in 1989 in Newport Beach, California, and in 1991 in Tesuque, New Mexico. At the latter, in an action that surely would have heartened Merton, a press conference, which included the Dalai Lama, was held on nonviolence and the incompatibility of religions and war. Exchange visits and MID meetings took place each year up to a landmark meeting in 1996, an account of which was published in *The Gethsemani Encounter*,[8] appropriately honoring Merton at his monastery. Sister Coff summarized the history of the movement in "How We Reached This Point: Communication Becoming Communion." After a humorous recap of the trials that the principals had endured, she ended her talk with a paraphrasing of one of Merton's own admonitions:

> After many mountains, caves, harrowing jeep rides, monsoons, landslides, soldiers, a one-eyed man/woman-eating mountain lion, giant spiders, hungry mice, and months of travel to monasteries and convents on both sides of the globe, we are here now at the Abbey of Gethsemani with His Holiness the Dalai Lama, MID Board members, advisers and contact persons from our monasteries—twenty-five strong—with twenty-five Buddhists, also strong, for a historic dialogue on the spiritual life. . . . We are at the "point" where, based on a long and rich history of friendship, Thomas Merton's prophecy of communication becoming communion may be realized. And at what better place than here at Thomas Merton's own spiritual home?[9]

During a memorial service for Merton in the Gethsemani choir, the Dalai Lama said, "I always consider myself as one of his Buddhist brothers," and, "the impact of meeting him will remain until my last breath."[10] At the same service, James Conner, O.C.S.O., once an assistant novice master with Merton, closed his tribute with a quote from his Gethsemani colleague's own Calcutta remarks, "My dear brothers and sisters, we are already one. But we imagine we are not. And what we have to recover is our original unity. What we have to be is what we are."[11]

Since the pivotal conference in 1996 the MID/DIM program continues with promising results, which can be tracked by a communications medium unknown to Merton, the Web site www.monasticdialog.com. A second Gethsemani Enounter occurred in 2002, on the theme "Transferring Suffering," and, in 2003, thirteen Christian nuns gathered with sixteen Buddhist nuns and one Hindu nun as "Nuns of the West" to talk about how spiritual values can be sustained in the secular culture of the United States The next initiative will be to develop a dialogue with Islam.[12]

While it was much less dramatic than Merton's explosive recognition, Bob Lax got appreciably more attention in the 1990s as well, and not just in Europe, where his readings, especially on BBC, had long generated audiences. Lax archives were created at both Columbia and St. Bonaventure, where there are also Merton archives. In 1990 Lax was given an honorary doctorate by St. Bonaventure, the university in his hometown, Olean, and he was made the university's first Reginald Lenna Visiting Professor.

His stature in the United States took another upturn in 1992 when Columbia's Rare Book and Manuscript Library staged an exhibit of his works, which included books, individual poems, and thirty-two "broadsides." The author of a press release announcing the exhibit must have felt obliged to pre-educate visitors who might have been puzzled by the abstract qualities of Lax's poetry:

> [C]oncrete poetry blurs the distinction between poetry and graphic art. It was inspired as much by the abstract paintings of Piet Mondrian as by Japanese Haiku poetry. . . . Among concrete poets who employ a minimalist style, Mr. Lax is one of the most admired practitioners. His poems often form a slim vertical image on the page, such as in "red red blue," commissioned in 1990 for the exhibition. The words red, blue and yellow are scripted, each in its color, in two slender columns. Mr. Lax's work has been strongly identified with the painter Ad Reinhardt, who was his friend since they were students at Columbia College in the 1930's. His 1968 poem, "For// AD//REIN-//HARDT," is another example of using a few words, in this case, black and blue, to create a slim column.[13]

Back on Patmos, Lax had neighbors doting on him, and he continued to be busy with his daily writings. "i keep filling up notebooks with one-liner jokes & hope someday to copy them into a book," he wrote Rice. "the rest of the time i spend running fish to the cats who come to the door. all strays, but if you feed them enough, they get to look pretty good."[14]

When he wasn't writing he was meditating, praying, or reading. One of the books he was reading reveals the same interest in Eastern religions that Merton and Rice had. It was Rice's *Eastern Definitions*, a 433-page tome that Doubleday had published in 1978 and which, even today, stands as a valuable encyclopedia of terms used in Hinduism, Sufism, Buddhism, Islam, Zen, Tao, the Sikhs, Zoroastrianism, and other Eastern religions. He also told Rice about the other books at his bedside: *Ten Eastern Religions* and *The Wisdom of Chuang Tzu*. "Sometimes," he said, he looked at the *Philokalia*[15] and "the big one you sent me about the Kabbala. Why do i like all these things? I think because they give you a variety of answers to all the questions you asked yourself when you were about three years old. & which somebody (audibly) inside me keeps on asking. i hardly ever read Tom Swift anymore."[16]

A big success for Rice during these years was the publication and acceptance of his Burton book. It is probable that Anne Freedgood's tough recommendations on cutting the text had been in order because, when it finally came out, not from Random House, which finally rejected it, but from Scribners, it had been edited down to 522 pages. Rice, then seventy-two years old, must have made most of the cuts himself because the late Ned Chase, who took over the editing for Scribners, said that it required very little editing, that his "total confidence in Ed" led to his judgment that it would be a good book.[17] It was.

The title was *Captain Sir Richard Francis Burton.* The subhead, which ran for two full lines across the front cover, no doubt helped the sale: *The Secret Agent Who Made the Pilgrimage to Mecca, Discovered the Kama Sutra, and Brought the Arabian Nights to the West.* While the first printing was for only 5,000 copies, it got a front-page review in the book section of the *New York Times* by the noted writer Anthony Burgess, who had himself been a Burton fan. Burgess called Rice's "telling of the tale . . . first class." It shot into the top ten on the *Times* best-seller list, stayed there for ten weeks, and sold more than 58,000 copies, providing Rice with the first bonanza of royalties he had ever experienced. No more did he have to get his heat from a wood stove. He bought a gas furnace and other amenities for his creaky old house and generally spruced it up. In a promotional chat with Bryant Gumbel on the NBC Today program, Rice growsed, "I worked just as hard on all those other books as I did on that one." His friends had thought he would never finish the book. In fact, it took him almost ten years to write, and he claims on the flap that the background knowledge came from ten long trips over a period of eighteen years, "to India, Pakistan . . . Nepal, Iran, the Arab countries and Israel, often using Burton's books [written in the late 1800s] as a guide." He told an interviewer that "when I read his books I knew what he was writing about, what the places looked like, how the streets smelled. Everything."[18]

Susanna Franklin had been an important figure in the negotiations with the publisher, as well as a steadying influence on Ed generally. A letter in his file, on her stationery, imprinted "Corporate and Domestic Legal Mediation, 381 Sagg Main St., Sagaponack [Ed's address]" shows that she made sure that business details were handled adequately, in this letter demanding $5,000 from a publisher for translations of some Spanish material. She would later help Rice win a suit against his old Columbia classmate, Robert Giroux, of Farrar, Straus & Giroux, for

using one of Rice's Merton photos without permission. He got, he wrote
Lax, "twelve times what Giroux first offered as a compromise." In the
same letter he said the Burton book was selling better than expected
and that he would need, "besides the agent, a business manager, who
in turn gets a lawyer who brings in an accountant, so already there is a
small business going and lord knows what happens to the author."[19]

Ed and Susanna were married at a private ceremony in the
Southampton town hall—not even Rice's children were there—on
March 6, 1990, the same year that *Burton* came out. The dedication is
to her. Their short life together was blissful, notwithstanding Susanna's
periodic illnesses. Millie and I had happy visits with them several times
in Sagaponack, and I remember one lovely October weekend when Ed
and Susanna and Millie and I went to Tuxedo Park, New York, for
a reunion with Bob Lax, who came down from Art Park in Buffalo
and was staying with his niece Marcia Kelly and her husband, Jack, at
their elegant vacation rental. Marcia, with her sister Connie Brothers
a veritable watchdog on Lax's health, finances, and general well-being
for many years, also had as a guest Judy Emery, who had several times
visited Lax in Greece and also coproduced a film on him. It was a lovely
weekend—good walks, good talks, good food and wine.

But back went Lax to Patmos, where the traffic of visitors to his
house on the hillside escalated more than ever. One visitor was Victoria
Lowe Allen, daughter of Jacques Lowe, the *Jubilee* photographer and
later a Kennedy family photographer, and Jillen Ahearn, who had been
one of the *Jubilee* volunteers in the 1950s. Victoria told me, "My parents were divorced when I was four. When I was a kid I used to stare
at one of the photos in our hallway full of photos—it was of a striking man with high cheekbones holding a kitten in his lap. Years later
I found out he was Bob Lax, my godfather. I had no contact with him
until I was in my thirties. Then I wrote him, and in 1990 or 1991 my
husband, Julian Allen, who was a water colorist, and I went to Patmos
and spent two weeks with him." Both Jacques Lowe and Julian Allen
have since died. The Lax interlude, while memorable, did not—evidently—ignite spiritual renewal. "I have no religion," Victoria said, and
that is the case with her mother, as well.[20] Both, it seems, had become
alienated from a Catholicism that seemed irrelevant to their lives, as it
has become in recent years to so many cradle Catholics, including three
of the four offspring of Millie and me.

Lax, who had always been in decent physical shape, following a yoga
and swimming regime and a spartan diet, began to slip back physically.
He wrote Rice in 1991, "I'm just getting back on my feet after long trek
through Europe. Stayed pretty well till I got to Verona . . . then suddenly

klonked. Back-ache like knives: couldn't sleep, couldn't pull myself out of bed in the morning."[21] He thought he was beginning to have some rheumatism. In that year he had also traveled to Louisville to participate in a commemoration of Merton, who had entered the monastery fifty years before. At the conference, which was attended by the Berrigan brothers, among others, he did not give a paper, although he had written one. "It was a paper on silence, I observed it," he cracked.[22]

Rice was encountering major problems of his own in 1991.

His photography, of which he was justly proud, came under harsh criticism from Paul Quenon, one of Merton's fellow monks, who wrote in the *Merton Seasonal*, "It seems to have been Ed Rice's practice to annoy his subjects until they were feeling quite vulnerable (his portraits of Jacques Maritain are a case in point), and then snap the shutter. Something of the irate comes through in his portrait of Merton on the hill in front of the monastery. . . ."[23] It was an undeserved remark since the Maritain and Merton portraits have been praised by many others as of high quality and sensitivity. It so incensed Rice that he wrote Quenon, "This statement is unfounded, nasty and malicious" and demanded "an immediate retraction and public apology by means of a letter published in the next *Merton Seasonal*." He never got the retraction, even though he said he was "tempted to turn the matter over to a lawyer, as such a statement as yours harms my ability to earn a living as a photographer."[24]

In the next year came an even more severe blow to his photography, as well as to his family pride. He had entrusted his elder son, Ted (Edward Jr.), a gifted professional printmaker and photographer living in Santa Fe, with some four hundred negatives of his photos of Merton from 1939 to 1968. They were to be catalogued for making prints as needed for future works. When Ed asked for them to be returned, Ted told him he would have to pay $15,000. Ed was so upset by this that he prepared a paper—perhaps drafted by Susanna—that read, "Legal Notice: Warning of Stolen Archival Photo Negatives." "Any use by Ted Rice, his heirs or assigns, including but not limited to the sale, reproduction, or publication of these negatives or prints made from them, shall be considered fraudulent and subject to appropriate legal action."[25] It's not known to whom the notice was sent, or if it was sent to anyone, but the estrangement of the two lasted for some time.

Lax, hearing of the impasse, wrote "Rocco" [Ed]: "Terrible story about poor ole Ted. Hope my godson Chris [Rice's other son] isn't acting like that . . . wish we could surround him, like that boy in Waco, move in before he sets fire to the house or treat him sweet & calm for about 5 years & then ask him gently to hand things over." That strategy, unreal as it was, became moot when Ed and Ted reestablished relations some years later, and, when Ed died, he left the negatives to Ted in his will.

Still ahead was the worst of all of Rice's sufferances. His happiness with Susanna, then at its peak, came crashing to an end on June 24, 1993. On that night, Susanna, who had bad asthma, suffered an attack in the small hours, and, rather than wake Ed, began driving herself to the hospital. Evidently she got dizzy or passed out, lost control of the car, collided with a utility pole and was killed instantly. It devastated Rice, and he was never the same. Symptoms of Parkinson's disease, which had already begun to affect him—he had been diagnosed some years earlier—got progressively worse. He told the writer Mary Cummings, "We were going to do a lot of books together but she got killed. That was when I went to pieces."[26]

Lax, knowing how important Susanna had been to his old friend, wrote immediately:

> . . . terrible news. I can't even imagine what you're going through at this moment. But I know and you must too how important it is to go slowly and quietly through the dark time & wait for some light.
>
> Keep at work, if you can, and take good care of your health. it isn't just for you: every one of us needs you. And all of us know it.[27]

Millie and I wrote Ed that we had had a Mass said for Susanna, and we tried to get him to go with us to Olean to visit Marcia and Jack Kelly and spend some time at the nearby Franciscan retreat center, Mount Irenaeus, but he was essentially unmoveable in those days.

Rice continued to work on his books every day. But his energies were never the same, and his productivity was way down. He hired a housekeeper, Dollin ("Dolly") Jagdeo, a devoted and competent woman whose great-great grandfather had migrated from Calcutta to Trinidad and whose father's mother was "Calalou," a mix of Negro and Spanish. There was a shortage of labor in Trinidad, and so the British brought people from India as indentured servants. African and Indian music became Caribbean music. An attractive, calm, olive-skinned, plumpish lady, she always wore colorful saris. Ever pleasant, she was able to keep smiling through Rice's increased crankiness as his ailment got worse, and she was strong enough to help him move about, take him to the bathroom, cook his meals, clean the house, put him to bed, and even cultivate his garden and harvest the fruit from the trees.

Lax's letters helped Rice's spirits, and—from thousands of miles away on Patmos—would sometimes offer advice, albeit usually unrealistic.

"Awful about error in dose & consumption. Hope better now. Wish you could get to Princeton more often. Could you rent a well-heated hutch down there so you'd be near Chris—and the Harfords? . . ." Rice's son Christopher, Lax's godson, a successful businessman, and his wife, Liza, and their two children were by then living in Princeton, where we Harfords had lived for some forty years. Millie and I would make periodic three-hour trips up the New Jersey Turnpike, over the Verrazano Bridge, out the Belt Parkway, Southern Parkway, and Montauk Highway to Sagaponack to visit Ed. Chris made the same trips much more often, monitoring Ed's health and the attentiveness of Dolly, who really needed little monitoring. She was spelled sometimes by one of her own relatives, but she was the constant, and surely she deserves time off in Purgatory for her ministrations to the ill, deteriorating, and often irascible Ed Rice.

And there were bad setbacks, one of which sent Ed to the hospital in 1995, producing this sympathetic note from Lax:

> hope you're back by now & feeling better. Someone out there should know the right treatment for P's [Parkinson's disease]. I've asked Marcia [his niece] . . . to see what she can learn . . . I wish you had a neighbor like the one I've got here. Stops by to see me once or twice a day—doesn't talk—leaves a plate of whatever she's cooked for her family, & moves on.[28]

The International Thomas Merton Society, founded in 1987, held its biennial conference in Olean in 1995. Although Lax and Rice were unable to make the event, some four hundred attendees of the growing ITMS included in their program a visit to the cottage on the hill outside of town once owned by Lax's brother-in-law, Benji Marcus. It was where he, Merton, Rice, and friends had held forth in beat style in the summers of 1939 and 1940. Many pictures were snapped of Lax's niece Marcia Marcus Kelly, a living link to the three friends, in front of the house.

The Lax–Rice letters in this period were not only a report on doings but, at times, pure whimsy. In longhand came this terse note, sometime in 1996:

> i still
> > keeping head
> > > above
> > > > water

followed by a typed letter:

this feels like first spring day on the island, which doesn't mean warm: am wearing overcoat as i write. haven't written to anyone, or hardly to anyone since i got back here just before Christmas [that may have been the last trip out of Patmos except for his final return to Olean just before he died in 2000]. too cold most of the time, and too floored by the number of unanswered letters, some of them dated '94 (and most marked urgent) . . . you show up in a number of my dreams too (pretty often in some connection with merton) & always in good situations.

oona sullivan said she'd been out to see you and that you were doing pretty well. . . .

i do keep writing, anyway: mostly by flashlight and into a note-book next to my bed. i keep reworking the same three jokes . . . grove/atlantic is doing a collection (mostly of old stuff but also quite a bit of my marseille journal) this spring.[29]

letter from nicholas sheetz (at georgetown) says that you & chris had given and sold him some things this year. does he pay like a man? says he wants things from me too, but i don't even know what to send him.

Lax long had a penchant for asking his friends "Whatever happened to . . ." questions (fill in Rochelle Hudson, Bubbles Schinasi, Judge Crater, Wingy Manone). This time he asked Rice, in longhand:

what

ev
er

hap
pen
'd

to

Booth
Tar
king
ton

?[30]

Millie and I stayed for two weeks in a bed-and-breakfast in the fall of 1996 in Water Mill, a few miles from Sagaponack, and almost every day we visited Ed. Our son Jim, then forty-one and working in Manhattan as a computer graphics specialist, came out for one weekend.

We observed that Sag Henge, his huge astronomical excavation, badly needed work. We had sweated and grunted to carry away wheelbarrows full of dirt when it was first dug years earlier. Now we concentrated on removing the weeds and young saplings that had grown up, a task that the ailing seventy-eight-year-old Rice was no longer up to. The Parkinson's disease was getting worse.

His writing capacity, however, was something else. He had three books going—one called *Cities of the Sacred Unicorn*, a report on a lost civilization in western India, in the Indus Valley, which Ned Chase was prepared to edit for Scribners, another an autobiography that would include some of his best photos. "I have ten or twelve thousand, I could put a thousand in the book," he said. The third would be *Blind Ed's Bread Book*, which would capitalize on his superb ability to bake Indian breads of several varieties. He had quite a few visitors, such as his longtime friends Mary and Bradford Kelleher, who also knew a lot about Merton and the *Jubilee* days. They came out from their apartment in Manhattan or from their home across the Island in Cutchogue. Another faithful visitor was Mary Cummings, a writer from the area, who—despite her slight frame—manhandled Ed into his bed or his wheelchair as needed. She brought Ed's Columbia confreres up to date on his colorful career with a fine twelve-page article, using some of the pictures from his Eastern travels, his shots of Lax and Merton, and reproductions of his paintings, in the Columbia alumni magazine in 2001.[31]

Even inside the house Ed wore a floppy khaki rain hat with green band, his tortoise-rimmed glasses often askew. His chin flesh sagged, and his face was heavily wrinkled. Dolly puttered about the kitchen and prepared delicious meals, like the one we were served on this visit of lamb shishkebabs, Indian bread and salad, with red wine accompaniment.

Since Ed could no longer make it up the ramp that was built especially to help him get in and out of the house, he never went out any more. A friend from Ed's parish in Bridgehampton regularly stopped at his house to give him the Eucharist, the highlight of his day. He also got visits from the parish priest, Father Callan, whom Millie and I met and who well remembered *Jubilee*. At Immaculate Conception Seminary in the period from 1955 to 1961, he said, they were told that the Bible was all they needed for salvation, but, in fact, they all "devoured" *Catholic Worker* and *Jubilee*. "Anything to put some life in those dogmatic theology courses."[32]

Big Foot, Ed's cat, had died the previous year at an advanced age. "I found him under the bed," he said sadly. "West Indians don't like cats—they think the devil is in them—so [in deference to Dolly] I don't have another one."[33]

Ed talked freely about the effects of his Parkinson's disease. "Your handwriting starts shrinking, gets smaller and smaller, your voice slurs. I get weak and take drugs for two days then I get reactions and have to stop." He moved back and forth from a hospital-type bed in the living room to his bedroom bed, and took a drug called Sinemet—$100 for ninety pills. He had been taking Paxil, but it gave him a bad reaction after two days when depression and nausea set in. It took a week to flush it out. Dodo [Dolly's sister] came in and rubbed his feet. He sometimes got bed sores. Our daughter, Jennifer, who had come up from Philadelphia to stay with us, and who had a remarkable way with Ed on previous visits, rubbed his feet and asked him, "Are you on a spiritual journey?" "No, I don't have a spiritual journey, I'm just getting from one journey to the next. . . . I was away from the church for seventeen years, since 1967, then I went back, started riding my bike to church. Now I can't get there, but I get the Eucharist. Don't need anything else. I haven't been in a church since Susanna died, but I'm still a Catholic. I find things like confession hard to accept though. I can't bring myself to tell some priest anything." His irreverence toward the established church flowed over to a cynicism, unfair really, about the Trappists, maybe deepened by self-pity over his illness. "They made a lot of money on Merton's writings," he cracked. "They used to sleep on boards, got two robes a year. They were lean fellows who worked in the fields. Now they are fat, jolly monks who like a bottle of wine."

Millie and I went upstairs to take pictures of some of Ed's paintings—a whole roomful covering the period from 1936 to about 1993, when his ailment reduced his productivity. The work is startlingly good, influenced, he says, by Russian icons. He gave Millie two of his paintings, which now grace our living room wall, one of them a stark black silhouette of the parents with whom he had had such an ambiguous relationship—Freudian implications apparent. Desiring to pay honor to another artist-friend from the Lax–Merton–Rice past, we drove out to Springs, about twenty miles west of Sagaponack, to see Green River cemetery, where Ad Reinhardt is buried. We found his gravestone—a white tablet with coins, shells, even a dollar bill on it, near the graves of Elaine de Kooning, Stuart Davis, A. J. Liebling, and Jean Stafford.

Back in the house we found Ed rolling around the bed from the medication. He said that he took it every four hours, and is particularly weak until he takes another dose. The sickness, he said, is very discouraging because it is irreversible and debilitating, giving him nausea, dizziness, and mental confusion. On this day Millie and I left him so he could be bathed, as he was on Monday, Wednesday, and Friday mornings by a Dominican nun from a nearby community. He also had a nurse three times a week, but his rock was still the twenty-four-hour-a-day presence of Dolly or Dodo.

During this stay we interviewed Rice's former editor, Anne Freedgood, Sy's widow, who had given Ed such a difficult, probably justified, time over the editing of *Burton*, before rejecting it when she was an editor at Random House. Although a resident of Manhattan, she had a house in Bridgehampton, only minutes away from Rice's home. Anne, Bryn Mawr '38, said that many of her friends and classmates joined the Loyalists in Spain in that period, as had some of the friends of Lax, Merton, and Rice at Columbia. Anne met Sy after he was already divorced from his first wife, Helen Ehrlich, who later married the folk singer Burl Ives. Ehrlich had been reponsible for getting Bramachari to come to Columbia, where he slept in the Lax/Freedgood apartment.

Anne told me that "Sy was very amused when Merton 'took to the church' and had no sympathy for his entry into the Trappists . . . didn't understand why he joined." Nonetheless, the two maintained a correspondence, and Sy, while an editor at *Fortune*, visited the monk at Gethsemani at least twice. A large sheaf of Freedgood–Merton letters is in the Merton archive in Louisville, although some of the original Merton letters are in the possession of Anne's daughter, Judy, in New York.

Anne had blunt opinions about the writing talents of Lax, Merton, and Rice, made credible by her credentials as a former editor at Random House, Doubleday, Harcourt Brace, and Morrow. The poetry of Lax, who used to stay with the Freedgoods sometimes when in New York, she regarded as "so-so." She thought Merton's writing "extremely good." As for Rice, whose *Burton* she rejected, his *Man in the Sycamore Tree*, she thought, is the "best book on Merton." And she gave Rice credit for the fact that "the church is changing a lot in ways that started with *Jubilee*." Like many of Merton's New York area friends she wondered what would have happened if the monk had not died. "Was he going to stay in the Far East? Was he going to say what he really thought about religion?" she asked, the implication being that she didn't think much of any religions herself. She is one of those who ponder the nature of Merton's death, even assessing the far-out possibility that he might have done himself in, perhaps in anguish over his growing convictions about the validity of Far Eastern religions while still being revered by Catholics.[34]

At the end of the 1990s two eloquent paeans to Lax's poetry were published in the United States. One was in a book devoted entirely to him and his poems by James Uebbing, who contrasted Lax's poems and style with that of Merton:

[H]is early verse, like Merton's, clearly shows the power that the Church held over his imagination. For Lax, however, the doctrinal and aesthetic elements of Catholicism do not become a part of his craft: although there is an unmistakably religious framework surrounding such poems as "Jerusalem," for example, one would look through Lax in vain for something as overtly Catholic as the rhetoric and imagery of the English mystics. . . . In Lax's work Christianity does not intrude itself as either a social or a cultural force, and since (in literary terms) this is practically the only existence it has been granted in our day, it is likely that we may overlook it altogether.

It is the core of his work all the same, and as it provides the only coherent context in which Lax can be read, we ignore it at our peril.[35]

On the cover of the Uebbing book was a striking portrait of Lax on a hill in Patmos, taken some years earlier by Richard Avedon. "I had fallen a couple of days before and knocked out a tooth . . . he was into backgrounds and he found this place on the island that looked like Ireland . . . he got his film crew to carry me up the hill so he could take the picture."

In 1997, Michael McGregor, in the journal *Poets & Writers*, gave the Lax style a scholarly analysis. He wrote, "Long before there was something called 'concrete poetry' he [Lax] was stripping away the adjectives and adverbs, paring down his vocabulary, using only those words he thought he could definitely define. . . . His poetry became a kind of meditation or music, something pulse-like, primal and profound. It was more suited to the winds and the waves and the traditional way of unpretentious Greek islanders than the frantic, clamoring dissonance of New York City. . . ."[36]

Bob took many photos of the fishermen, pictures that Francesco Conz, a professional photographer, thinks are "chronicles of an artist's meditations. . . . His subjects are people who look into the lens of the camera without the slightest embarrassment, people . . . in harmony with their way of life."[37]

My daughter, Jennifer, recalls from her 1996 visit with Lax on Patmos that "[y]ou could ask anyone where 'Petros' lived—the name the locals gave him—and they would point out his house, or simply say, 'stay here, he'll be walking by soon.' The residents considered him one of them, and often gave him gifts of prepared meals, or fresh-caught fish, which he gave to his cats."

Jennifer stayed about five weeks on the island, enough time to observe him often in his daily habits, and to prepare some foods for him.

> He had no teeth so I would mix stuff in a blender—like all the constituents of a Greek salad. He liked that. . . . He went to the market himself sometimes for fresh fish for the twenty-some cats he fed. Once, when he got home, he noticed that one of the fish was still flopping. He put it in a bucket of water and salt and dumped it back in the sea. . . . He would not kill flies or spiders. He would catch them in a cup against the wall and release them outside. But in the cold weather he would not release them at all because he was worried about how they might fare in the cold.

> He told me he could never have kids. He wouldn't ever let them cross the street. And I was responsive to his advice to just take my time when I went shopping for vegetables and feta cheese. So when the Patmos natives elbowed ahead of me I just waited. The store people ignored me at first but on the third day or so they realized that I was going to be patient, what I wanted was feta, and they would get it for me and pay polite attention to me, as they did for Bob.

Millie and I visited Bob a year later, in May 1997, and we found him to be noticeably more fragile. He was, after all, almost eighty-two. There were wisps of white hair on his otherwise bald head. It was a bit frightening when he opened his mouth to reveal only a few teeth. He had long had trouble with his teeth. They were his main reason for his rare visits to Athens. His small apartment was part of a white-washed house high up on the hill at the top of a circuitous stairway up from Skala. He had a grand view of the sea from his living room window or from his front porch, but he didn't often leave the house to see it. The porch was a mess of cat food bits, fish bones, and other debris. Inside was a small kitchen, a big living room–bedroom where he slept, ate, talked to his guests. An adjoining room was packed with books on shelves, boxes of books, piles of letters, many unanswered. Some years earlier he had mailed Millie a large box of them and asked her to keep them, which she did before sending most of them, eventually, to his archive at St. Bonaventure.

Also present during this visit were his longtime publisher, Bernhard Moosbrugger, and Bernhard's partner in Pendo Verlag, Gladys

Weigner. They had driven all the way from Zurich in a Volkswagen and were staying near us in the Hotel Skala. They had driven first to Padua, then Venice, then by boat to Patras in western Greece, then through beautiful "green country" until they reached traffic-choked Piraeus and got on the same ship we had taken, the Rodanthi. We didn't know they were aboard. Millie and I slept some in our modest cabin for the overnight fourteen-hour trip, while Bernhard and Gladys slept on lounge chairs or in the VW.

One of our first talks with Bob occurred on Monday, May 19, at about five in the late afternoon. It was in this year that I had decided to write this book, and so I taped our conversations. Here is an excerpt:

Harford: Can you comment on the popular conception of Merton?

Lax: A lot of (people) leave out the possibility of his sense of humor, so when they hear how devout he was, and read articles and see the kind of canonization people have done of him, they get their own idea of what a saintly person should be. Most of them lack a human touch, sense of humor, which was essential.

Harford: When you read the correspondence that you had with him and read his books, and as Millie said the other day, you perceive the sense of joy that he had in the early years in the monastery, and later when he gets to be frustrated, you wonder was he just frustrated or was he, at the end, disillusioned by, in a large sense, by the monastery, the Trappists, Catholicism.

Lax: I don't really think he was disillusioned in the large sense. I think he was bugged by human beings in certain positions in the monastery. Probably after the original enthusiasm it may have come as a shock to him that these were human beings, and not always very pleasant ones, but he knew enough not to be too surprised or too shocked about that either. He never wrote me a letter that wasn't funny. I mean no matter what, he'd never say, "Honestly, Bob . . . it's gotten too much for me [he chuckles]," any of that sort of thing.

Harford: His engagement with Buddhism . . . where was he going with that?

Lax: I think he was heading toward a . . . maybe this is it . . . a kind of transcendent vision which included all the legitimate religions and saw where they all came together at a real point, and so he wasn't switching from one to another or anything like that he was just finding how they resembled each other in all their best points.

He could probably see that all of them were trying for something. He knew that there was a central thing which has to do with love or compassion or something like that, that all of them are talking about in their own way.

Harford: Well, I take it that you too have this feeling about the transcendency of religions?

Lax: I guess my feeling is more and more that it does have something to do with [chuckle] . . . life. Life [little self-conscious murmur] is doing its best in this world to perpetuate itself in all its forms, and heaven is probably cooperating with it in every possible way and would like it if life cooperated with heaven [more chuckles].

Harford: Yesterday, a Sunday, we went up to the Apocalypse cave and arrived in the middle of the liturgy. A group of young boys, with varied vocal abilities, were singing with gusto. I would have been ready to leave after standing for an hour and a half on the hard stone. . . . [Lax laughs]. The priest comes out from whatever the Greeks' word is for sacristy only once in a while. I say to myself, "This time he's going to end it . . ." [Lax ho hos] but no, he goes back in again. Millie, with much greater devotion than I, was up in the front row totally absorbed, lighting candles. I guess . . . I really am often skeptical. Even though I don't think I have missed more than fifteen or twenty Sunday Masses in my life, I am perpetually skeptical about the authenticity of my own religion and even about God. "What about you?" I ask him. Is it [your belief] always strong?

Lax: Well, I think it. . . . I don't know, I hear skepticism recommended by a lot of quite pious people, and I think that's the right idea, too. I don't know how to describe it beyond that. But I think you gotta use your noodle in all this too, as much as you can. You weren't given that for nothing.

Harford: Well, do you pray?

Lax: I pray every day. I read some psalms every day, but I don't think that's the center of my spiritual life. It's just something you do, it's more like training, it's more like . . . to remind you of what you're up to in general.

Harford: What *is* the center of your spiritual life?

Lax: Well, let's see. It's that life is meant to be good, meant to be a blessing for all of us, and it's a blessing we should share just as far as we can.

Harford: You say that in spite of all the troubles in the world . . . Serbia . . . Croatia . . .

Lax: Yes, you don't have to go to Croatia to see the kind of troubles that people have with each other . . . any two people, if they don't have some consideration for each other . . . can be beasts [laugh].

Harford: But life is meant to be good?

Lax: It's meant to be good . . . I think we're evolving toward a realization that life right from the beginning was meant to be good and that if we cooperate with it as far as we can it will be good and will get to be better and better and that most of the things we talk about doing in heaven we can do right here on earth if we get to be sufficiently considerate of each other.

Harford: That's a very optimistic view. Have you seen any movement toward it?

Lax: Yes, if I didn't I would be discouraged. Every time I've seen anyone who acted like a *mensch* . . . that's a Yiddish word that means a good guy, a realistic one . . . in most cases he gets treated like a *mensch,* too.

Harford: Is that why you seem to admire people like Teilhard de Chardin?

Lax: Yes, I think that whole idea of evolution that he has—we *are* evolving—is worth thinking about.

There were five of us—Millie and I, Bernhard and Gladys—in Bob's living room during this conversation, plus John Beer, the former

Princeton University graduate student who was helping Bob catalog his papers before sending them to the archive at St. Bonaventure. We sat around a little table while Bob assumed the lotus position on the bed. He had a three-inch grizzled beard. Although it was stifling in the room, he wore a knitted black hat. The windows were closed. He was evidently oblivious of the heat and the awful smell from the fish, the dust, the cats. It was dark in the room, although there was glorious sun outdoors. On the walls were a crucifix—over the bed—and a photo of Bramachari, drawings by friends and by kids, a poster of the Marx Brothers' *A Day at the Races*. I counted sixty-five photos and other items on the walls—including James Joyce, Dalai Lama, St. Jerome, Harpo, Chico, and Groucho Marx, a reproduction of Seurat's circus painting, a Picasso sketch, Rice's silhouette painting of the photo of Lax in the Parthenon on the Acropolis that was on the cover of the journal *Voyages*, Jack Kerouac, St. Thérèse of Lisieux, Allen Ginsberg, four rabbis. "Nice crowd up there," said Bob, noting my interest in the wall pictures. When he saw me focusing on the rabbis he said, "Who knows where they're going and what they'll do next?"

Millie took notes as she watched Bob and later wrote this poem:

You with a hole in your sock

Inside your feet move like fins, swaying from
    side to side

Your legs bend and fold

    like a card table collapsing

Your right arm waves extending way out

Your right hand punctuates your words

Or lifts your navy wool cap

    as though to let a poem escape

Placing the navy cap on your knee

    lets your bald head breathe

Leaving a few white wisps to radiate like smoke

At breakfast that day Millie and I had the chance to talk with Bernhard and Gladys, looking out at the sea under the vine-covered terrace at the Hotel Skala, about how their relationship with Lax began, and about Pendo, their publishing house, which succeeded Emil Antonucci's Journeyman Press in publishing Bob's poetry. It seems that they met Lax in Paris in about 1954 at a party given by an American woman—possibly Theodora "Teddy" Bergery, who had been a student of Bob's at Connecticut College and who had paid his air travel to Europe on several occasions. Through Lax they got involved with *Jubilee,* then only one year old. They had gone to New York seeking foundation support for their concept of a "supra-national magazine of peace, understanding, love, with good pictures and 'nothing negative.'" Since *Jubilee's* concept was close, they began working for the magazine. The idea for Pendo, which is Swahili for love and understanding, came in the 1980s from Laurean Rugambwa, who was the first black cardinal. Bernhard once photographed him, and Gladys wrote the text for a story on him in *LIFE* magazine.

The publication of Lax's poetry by Pendo, which goes back to 1981 and includes some eighteen books,[38] has been subsidized, Bernhard says, by "wealthy Swiss friends." Each Lax volume was printed in one thousand copies, and an average sale was about seven hundred. It has been a profitable enterprise only in its psychic satisfaction. But it has produced a treasure of Lax poetry.

Bernhard was a bit redder and puffier than when Millie and I last saw him, some years earlier in Zurich. He walked a bit old. Gladys looked fine. Bernhard would pass on, alas, a few years later.

Millie and I eventually had a long talk with John Beer. It seems that Jennifer Harford, when she was here in 1996, realized that Lax needed a research assistant to catalog his works. She let everyone know about this. Niece Connie Brothers thought of John, who had spent ten days with Bob in 1995, having come over at his own expense from the Iowa University Writers Workshop, where Connie worked. He had not been finding it easy to get a job as a writing instructor, and so the idea of working with Bob was attractive. Jennifer, Marcia Kelly, and others were able to get several people to put up $1,000 each, including Millie and me, and St. Bonaventure covered the rest up to $10,000.

Beer, soon to be twenty years old at the time of our meeting, comes from Auburn, New York, graduated in 1991 in philosophy from Princeton, and wrote a senior thesis entitled "Philosophy of Psychology"— how people characterize things. He had now sorted all but two of about thirty boxes of Lax's writings. He had already sent four or five boxes to St. Bonaventure, where Paul Spaeth, director of the Friedsam Library, which has both the Merton and the Lax archives, has catalogued them. Columbia University's Rare Book and Manuscript Library already has much Lax material in its archives, mostly from the 1950s and '60s, but some of it, including the Ad Reinhardt and Jack Kerouac letters, seems to have been misplaced, causing dismay to the whole Lax retinue. Bob said that Thomas Kellein, who published *33 Poems*, "threw up his hands when he discovered how badly those thirty-two boxes or something of mine at Columbia have been sorted." "We get the sense that all the stuff at Columbia has not been logged in terribly well," said Beer. Even the Bibliothèque Nationale de France in Paris lost some valuable Lax material—photos that had been left with a researcher who had planned to publish a collection of Lax pictures. "We gave them to her," said Beer, "and she gave the six best to the curator and he lost them."

Beer's usual day was to get to Lax's house around 3 P.M. and stay until 9:30 seven days a week. He handled correspondence every couple of weeks and typed manuscripts from Lax's longhand. It was a big job. He said he still faced an eight-year backlog.

He was excited, as Lax was, about work the two were performing on an oratorio, based on Bob's "Black White" and "Red Red" poems, which was to have a chorus and numerous solos, and was expected to be staged in Geneva in September with Vincent Barras as producer. There are nine people in the chorus, three soloists, a conductor. The funds to support it were to come from "somewhere." Beer said the idea

> was prompted by hearing Richard II on the radio . . . we had listened to that . . . and afterwards we talked about how it would really be fun to pick out lots of the color poems—black white red blue poems and Bob sort of had the idea that a chorus of people would read these poems in a certain order . . . we would start out simply and then get more complicated and then in the middle it would again get simpler and maybe more and more dark would come in and then it would get very dark like a dramatic climax . . . and that was sort of the idea we started with and . . . we put it together . . . I guess all along Reinhardt was in a way a kind of guiding spirit. . . .

"How long will it take? Millie asked.

"We've only read it with one voice," answered Beer, "so we don't really know . . . but when I read it from start to finish it took about an hour."

"Then it will be a real theater piece. It will be staged," said Millie.

"It will be staged. But with the oratorio you will have three separate groups of three to five people so there will be nine to fifteen people on stage. There is one soloist who comes out of each group to start . . . it starts with the soloist saying, "Black, black, white, black, black, white" and going on from there and everyone comes in with the black white thing. When I read it it sounds good to me."

"It would be nice to have some music with it," I said.

"I think that if it's spoken right it won't need it," said Bob. "Music could interfere with it."

"Speaking of music . . . your idea, which you had described to Merton I think, of having the 'Juggler of Notre Dame' put on with Mogador as performer, that was a terrific idea," I said.

"A terrific idea and somebody . . . one of Gladys and Bernhard's friends with a radio station in Strasbourg or somewhere—really wanted to do it but it collapsed somehow," Bob replied. "He had me do a treatment . . . I sent it to him . . . but then he just . . . disappeared . . . yeah I think it is a good idea. . . . maybe some day . . . I don't think Mogador could do it . . . he might have a grandson who could."

"The oratorio sounds like a really ambitious work," said Millie.

"Yes. And a second idea," said Bob, *Conversations with Artists*, will be twice as long." Beer went farther into it:

> It would be about ninety minutes and I think much more complicated. Same idea as the oratorio . . . very sparing in its vocabulary. *Oratorio* uses just colors . . . nine words throughout . . . black, white, red, blue, green, yellow, orange, purple, gray. There are more words, I think twenty, in *Conversations with Artists*. It includes objects like tree and rock and door and clouds . . . but it's the same idea . . . you have three groups on stage and three soloists and they're all based on poems like red cloud and blue cloud. . . .

"What does it have to do with conversations with artists?" I asked. "I thought you meant made-up conversations with guys like Reinhardt. . . ."

"Yeah, well," said Bob, "there's a title of a book that I can't remember the author of, from the Renaissance, called *Conversations with Artists*—Victoria Colonna and Michelangelo talking. It does have things like red zag blue zig—things like that—there are more images in it than just colors . . . so it felt like just the right title for us."

"The colors become symbols of emotion?" Millie asked. Bob offered a somewhat complex explanation:

> People have written to me after listening to readings, especially people who are, you know, doing art of their own, and they say that it wakes up images . . . of whatever red means to you if you

let it echo through you. . . . I mean when you've heard it enough times you don't just think of other things that are red and of all the associations that a word like red can awaken in you, slowly, in a fairly, we hope, painless way. You hear it and what you're listening to is not just the rhythm and the repetition, but there's sort of a hidden metaphor in it. You're not saying red fire and you're not saying all of the other things that might be red, but all those things are sleeping in your mind somewhere and they'll wake up as they hear this . . . that has been apparently the effect on people who've liked the readings . . . some people thought it was like a meditation and they've asked me if I'm into meditation and others would ask if I'm interested in music because, if it comes across at all, it comes across with that kind of association . . . and I don't know how I arrived at it. I guess I do, because I've wanted things to be as telegraphic as possible. . . . I'd rather have two words than five on most things. . . . I always thought that metaphors were essential in poetry. A word like red in a sense is a metaphor, a metaphor for all the things that are red or associated with red . . . the simplest form of a metaphor if you like that I could come upon . . . the fact that it's one syllable helps, too.

The next day, as we continued the interview on a less complex track, I asked Bob how many poems he might compose each day.

If you call them poems it might be ten a day or more. It's a bunch of them. I've been calling them momentaries. I used to write a journal and now it's not a journal it's a momentary . . . you write down what comes to you at the moment.

I fill one of these little notebooks in three to four days, sometimes two weeks. John copies them on the computer and then we send them in a big envelope to Paul Spaeth at St. Bonaventure.

I asked him to read one or two of the most recent momentaries and he picked up the little notebook:

he seems to be getting along with himself a whole lot better than he used to. . . .

give all the voices in you a chance to speak their mind. . . .

"When the momentaries go to Paul Spaeth, Lax said, "the original blue book goes with them, and John keeps the computer printout." Was there a certain time of day when he did the writing?

No, it's like . . . all day, really, and all night too . . . a lot of it by flashlight . . . but I don't get up and write if I don't feel like it . . . If I'm awake enough to turn on the flashlight I do it . . . but . . . otherwise I say, "Come back later."

"Are you sometimes too tired, and then miss having fixed an idea you wished you had written down?"

"Sometimes, yes . . . I used to persecute myself about it more than I do now, but most of the thoughts will come back and sometimes in improved form, and they go right down on the page, into syllables already because I'm used to doing it."

"I think that's such a gift you have . . . you don't have to scratch out," said Millie, and I added, "Then each day is different. You don't write, say, from two to three in the morning like the pope?"

"I used to do things like that when I first came to Kalymnos, and at various times in my life, but not at this point."

"So when you add it all up, is it a couple of hours a day, or just a matter of minutes, doing this?"

"Well, it's more like twenty-four hours . . . it really is . . . it's what happens except when I'm shopping, and then I usually take a pad down in case there's something I think of along the way."

"You *do* go down shopping?"

"I used to and I hope to be doing it again."

"Well, tell me about that, have you not been well enough to go down shopping, and are you coming back from being unwell?"

"Oh, yeah."

"We talked to Marcia and she said you were fine."

"Well, that's a family tradition for one thing."

"Everybody's fine?"

"Everybody's fine, right. But she's concerned enough to be calling to find out if I need any medicine. I don't feel very bad either. I feel better now than a couple of weeks ago, when . . . coming up the hill . . . even with the stick . . . [a lot of pauses] . . ."

"Is it because you have some kind of bug?"

"No, it's this heart . . . the thing that I'm wearing this stocking [elastic one, on his leg] for . . . irregular heartbeat."

"Are you getting attention from a properly qualified cardiologist?"

"Yeah. I think I'm getting pretty good attention on it, not so much locally but at least up in Athens I went to a good medical center."

"When was that?"

"Last month [that would have been April]."

"Last June and again in October," interjected John Beer, indicating that Bob was months off on his guess about the date of the last trip to the doctor in Athens, an indication that he was unaware of time passing.

Millie commented on a letter she was reading from Bob's mail, with his permission. "This is so touching and so sweet. It's a Christmas song, from a young man that Bob met, by chance, in the marketplace."

"I think he either wrote the song," said Bob, "or translated it, but still it's nice and it's a nice letter, too." Millie read an excerpt: "When my life pushes me around and everything seems to be upside down I see you coming to the marketplace, wideawake, open to every inner and outer possible movement, taking one step after the other, just one step after another, not rushing, not hesitating. . . ."

"He's a German . . . from Hamburg. We had some good conversations about . . . spiritual things and . . . I think he had gotten a lot of spiritual advice in very formal terms and so he was saying, 'How do you pray this or how do you pray that . . . and what do you do in situations like that . . . I remember one of my answers was, 'You say, Help!'"

At eighty-two, Bob's impact on total strangers was still profound.

"Can you mention anyone that you correspond with in some sequential way," I asked him. "They write and you write back."

"Most of that has just broken down . . . maybe Rice and not very sequentially even with him."

"You're just not writing anybody?"

"Hardly . . . I haven't even thought of why. Usually if I'm feeling like writing, I'm feeling like writing in my notebook."

Beer reminded him, "You're getting out like ten letters a month."

The next day, Bob made his first venture down the hill since we arrived. His face color was healthier; he had his false teeth in; and he used the cane only sparingly. He wore his cap, not the knitted hat he'd been wearing in bed. Lots of people hailed him, including one gray-haired old timer who had had a stroke and was being wheeled by his plump wife. "Used to sell peanuts," Bob said. The motor bikes were roaring by us, and each time one approached, Bob would go a few feet into the nearest café until they had passed.

Bob had a Ukrainian lady, whom we had not met, who cleaned his house, and she was due that day. He said he'd ask her to clear the entrance terrace, which is a mess from the cat food, the fish heads, and the cats themselves. Yesterday Bob had the window open for the first time, a relief from the stale air.

On the next Saturday morning [May 24, 1997] we once again appeared at Bob's apartment, which was clean from the Ukrainian lady's work and the smell not so bad. Bob turned down, gently, our offer of some of the raisins and powdered milk that we had brought with us from home—"not good for me." He turned on the BBC to hear Angela Wood, author of children's books, recite. He listened to her every day, as well as to an 11:10 Jewish program. Then, the news—on this day about changes in the Iranian government.

Bob seemed to save everything, and I spotted, on the cluttered table, a 1976 postcard from me reporting on an evening of oldtime jazz that Millie and I had enjoyed the previous year at Preservation Hall in New Orleans. "The jazz musicians," he said, "remind me of Kalymnos sponge fishermen—no talk, just blow good music . . . what gives me great pleasure is seeing things well done—by musicians, carpenters, fishermen, acrobats . . . Rice on Jubilee, Merton on drums. . . . I overlook moderately poor stuff."

Millie said, "Speaking of your effect on people, when we were together in Stockholm at the space congress in 1985, you were trying to teach me how to write, and you said, 'What you do, you get a little book, and you write down your thoughts . . . ' and the next thing I knew you bought me a little book."

"Imagine that . . . good!"

"And in it, you wrote a poem. Here is the book."

"Wow."

"It says 'For Millie and Jim, Love Bob. 14th of October, Stockholm '85.'"

"Oy, vey [softly]."

Millie read the words:

> The world is not a world
> The world is a flower
> The flower is not a flower
> The flower is a world
> The world is a flower
> The flower the world
> The world the flower
> The flower the world

"Was that the one you wrote?" asked Bob.

"No, YOU wrote that. Then I tried," said Millie.

"Yes!" said Bob.

"And it was kind of like what you were saying was a prayer, and I said, 'Help me to help myself to help YOU,'" responded Millie.

"Ooh, good! Yes, you see?"

"Aren't you a good teacher? And then you wrote . . . we had this little conversation. You said:

> Purify the inner light
> Purify the inner light
> The inner light is purified
> The inner light is purified

"Then I wrote (she showed Bob a page)"

> Emotions, like fevers, fluctuate.
> Sorrow, joy, fear, despair
> Run their course until they stop
> And only love is there

"Whoa. That's good . . . beautiful . . . lovely."

"I keep trying. It shows how you influence people, how you have the patience and the encouragement to say, 'You can do it.'"

"Yes, because I believe you can. Oh, that's good."

That afternoon we got into a heady conversation about evil, an "absence of good," as Augustine put it. Bob held forth.

Plato says that whatever one does he thinks is good. Manicheism is a heresy that says the world is divided into good and evil forces. I once wrote a story for *Jubilee* on Piccola Casa de la Divina Providencia in Turin. It was for boys and girls up to high-school age who had been rejected by all the hospitals, a whole city inside a wall. It had been founded at the end of the nineteenth century by Giovanni Cartalango, who saw one person who needed help, then two, then a whole city. Some religious order runs it now. When I went there to do the article, I was with a priest who told the nun at the door that I was a friend of Merton's, and she cried. Anyone who knew Merton stirred her to tears. That school was doing pure good.

"The point," Bob said, "is that maybe something can be done to deal with evil even in a place like Princeton. Start with anyone in Princeton, and his little brother will come along."

Bob said there is a room full of voices. Listen to all of them—maybe there is something good, it helps you to understand the others. It doesn't help to call it evil. Don't call it anything until you listen to it. Fulfill your real vocation from the most high. Martin Buber wrote about all these things in *Jubilee* in the 1950s. Bob said we should get Martin Buber's collected Hassidic sayings (*Ten Rings* [Citadel Press, 1995]). Merton also loved Meister Eckhart (*Meister Eckhart, Selected Writings* [Penguin Press, 1994]). He also cited *Meditation Words to Live By* (Eknath Easwaran, Nilgiri Press, Box 477, Petaluma CA 94953). We should also read, he says, about Dame Julian of Norwich. "Merton gave up on John of the Cross when he came into contact with Julian."

"I woke up last night," Bob said, "to this dream phrase still in my mind: 'Exploiting ethnic rivalries for short-term political gains.' I didn't think I had phrases like that going on in my head. I've been listening to the radio too much. He paused as he looked at the pages of his notebook and read what seemed to be random sentences that might have occurred to him in the middle of the night:

> Who is the world's gentlest human being?
> Number one candidates: Saint Francis,
> Maimonides

7 pt"When John sends a copy of the word processor text to St. Bonaventure's, and keeps one copy, does he also send a copy of the word-processed text to Bernhard?"

"We're more likely to wait until John has shaken it down into a publishable work, and then we send it to Bernhard."

"Bernhard has published fourteen or fifteen of my books starting around . . . maybe 1960? I think he has done one every year."

"That would be more than thirty."

"Then maybe it didn't start in 1960 [he laughs]. The dates are all on the books and in the bibliography." [Pendo Verlag's publication of Lax books actually started in 1981 with *circus, zirkus, cirque, circo*, and totaled eighteen through 2001.]

"Was Bernhard an avenue to Overlook Press [which published *A Thing That Is*, edited by Paul Spaeth, in 1997, and would publish *Circus Days & Nights*, also edited by Spaeth, in 2000]?"

"Definitely. Bernhard would take my books up to the Frankfurt book fair every year, and one man who would always pick them up was Peter Mayer, publisher of Overlook Press.

The conversation became more philosophical and Bob said, "I think that the whole universe is so alive that it's as though there was a roomful of angels. . . . I mean we are living sort of unconsciously in a universe that's wide awake, conscious. And we're being invited to join up with it and we hope to at some point but our regular level of consciousness is so . . . primitive, so low geared that to talk about the real state of affairs means you're obliged to talk about angels . . . you know, something that different from what we're used to, but it's all there to be discovered if you give yourself a chance to discover it, and I think the way to give yourself a chance is to sit still, like . . . either in some sort of formal meditation or, however you can, in a conscious attempt to tune in to the rest of the universe. And it's . . . creative."

"You do that?"

"Formal meditation, yes, every day, for a half an hour."

"At some appointed time?"

"Yeah, well 'appointed time' meaning right after I pull down the elastic socks, which I should do first thing in the morning [light laugh]."

"So it's a morning thing?"

"It could be, but according to the book I'm trying to follow it should be in the evening too. I've been doing it now for three or four years."

"What book?"

"It's called *Meditation.* I'll find it for you in the other room. Author is Eknath Easwaran, a Hindu but came very young to America, lives in California. Connie has studied with him. He's a very good man to know about. . . . You ought to be able to get his book from the library or through Connie or Marcia."

"So you're being guided by his ideas . . ."

"Yeah, it's a very simple routine that he recommends. It sounds so mechanical that you resist it at first, but I've done it now for three years whether I'm traveling on trains or wherever. I do it for half an hour anyway."

"Does it have any OMs in it?"

"No OMs. Any prayer you like. But he gives a St. Francis prayer and you just repeat it slowly over and over but, you know, not to knock yourself out . . . over a period of half an hour. . . . Lord make me an instrument of thy peace . . . over and over . . . if you find yourself going to sleep or forgetting the words start at the beginning again. It's like everything else, like the walk to town from here, which I do every day, or used to do every day . . . it changes . . . the meaning of the doors change for you . . . the meaning of the stairs change for you . . . you're doing it every day with the same routine but you have different feelings about everything you see. The same is true of the St. Francis prayer, when you say it that many times different things about it come out, different ways of approaching the whole. . . . I mean one way you can do it, for example, is the way we might read the *Oratorio* or might read a poem . . . boam, boam, boam . . . thinking of yourself as reading a poem. Another time you might be . . . I've only recently started turning it into a telegram . . . just in the interest of . . . still you're watching every word and every idea. But you have different approaches to it, and it has different feelings. For example you might say, 'Lord make ME an instrument of thy peace,' or you might get a little removed from it and think of St. Francis saying it, 'Lord make ME an instrument of thy peace, . . .' and so on . . . the process changes in many ways, but the feeling at the end of it, what's desirable about it, is that it does get you into . . . we'll call it a contemplative state, that is, call it the state that a baby is in when he's left alone and nobody goes gootchy, gootchy, goo. He's sitting there and he's taking in what he sees in front of him. Slowly, and at his own pace. He's confident because his mother is nearby and nothing to fear. If it thunders he looks up at his mother and she says, 'It's nothing," and he goes back to the state. That's about the state, I think, those exercises leave you in. And it's a state I wish the whole of humanity was in most of the time. I think beautiful things would flower if it were like that.'"

"You used to do breathing," I say. "You taught me . . . to put a finger on one nostril, inhale, then switch the finger to the other nostril and slowly exhale, thirty seconds, and suck in your belly while exhaling. . . ."

"I just got a letter from a friend the other day sending me some Hindu pictures . . . he said he'd run into that exercise, he wanted to tell me about it . . . I've done it . . . lately I've stopped doing it . . . he says not to combine it, not to try the meditation and breathing exercises in the same moment . . . he doesn't say not to do breathing exercises, but anyway I still like those exercises and I still do them."

"Good . . . well, you have to be in a place like this to even have it occur to you . . . I think it's a great thing to slow down . . . there's a positive reason for doing it, not just to get away from all the bad effects of charging around. . . . I think slowing down does get you back to what I think of as your natural state and the state we were created to be in. It's a fairly slow-moving meditative state. I always liked stories about giants because I always think of them as moving very slowly, and I like the kind of people I see who are big, like the ones you saw . . . they're big, they're graceful at the same time but they do move slowly . . . that always inspires me . . . little and busy doesn't do a thing for me."

"I don't know how you include me as a friend because I'm not one to move slowly."

"We wouldn't be friends if we weren't supposed to be . . . and certainly I think there's enough about both us that we do share."

"Well, we've had many good laughs together."

"I've said this a lot of times, but I can say it again to you. You're one of the few people I've met since college that I think would have been part of our gang at college."

"That's a nice compliment. I'll give you one back. Sometimes, late at night, I will play a CD of Muggsy Spanier's 'Relaxing at the Touro,' or Thelonius Monk playing 'Blue Mist' . . . it's what I call three o'clock in the morning music, and there aren't too many people that I would like to have with me listening to that music because they are liable to interrupt, but you wouldn't interrupt right in the middle of one of Muggsy's solos. I've had friends come over to hear that music and they TALK."

"Bob," Millie asked, "are you on a schedule of any kind? Do you just wake up when you wake up?"

"I do just wake up when I wake up . . . usually at six. I wake up a couple of times during the night regularly, once probably at three and probably at five, by six I'm about ready to do the meditation.

"Let's see . . . first the meditation, then there's a medicine. . . . I take a herbal heart medicine after which you can't eat for another fifteen minutes, and after all that I start breakfast. Because of this diuretic that I take I'm supposed to take things like apricots or bananas, things like that have, I guess, potassium in them, and things like organic peanut butter, and sometimes egg white with oil and bread."

When Millie and I were back home we got a report on the September 6-7, 1997 performance of the *Oratorio* in Geneva. The Geneva newspaper, *Le Courrier*, quoted Lax—in characteristic understatement, "I don't like to use a lot of words to fill a page." The article remarked that the nine voices in three groups, chanting mostly "Black" and "White" "in solos, duos, trios, or by all the voices" evoked the music of one Morton Feldman and the black paintings of Ad Reinhardt. In the finale other colors come slowly into play—"Blue" "Red" "Yellow" "Green" "Orange" "Purple" "Grey." It ends "in a mosaic . . . reduced to just one voice." Vincent Barras, who occupied the podium during the performance, called Lax "une poète inclassable," largely influenced by Catholic mysticism.

Back in the United States, Millie and I had more visits with Ed Rice, who was quite frail but had periods of recovery. Jennifer had by then become a part of the research team for this book, having already made a major contribution with her visit to Lax in 1996, and now she went to see Rice as well. Here are excerpts of her taped conversation with him in April 1998. The first interview was in the morning, when he was "not always good," needing time for his pills to take effect. Jen went right to the heart of Rice's relationship with the Almighty:

Rice: The point is that God wants to strip you down until it's just you and him. That's all you need, really. All the things that God takes away from us, all the things we lose, we really don't need them. In the universal equation it's just God and yourself. I think that's what's happening to me, I'm meeting with God. He's there and I'm here. It's like a house call.

Jennifer: You're getting house calls from God?

Rice: They wonder about me in the local church. It just awes them that I'm Thomas Merton's godfather—this great figure in *our* parish. And then they see me, and I'm nothing. They're all nice people and we get along but whether or not God is in the parish. He's already sent the advance material—really a publicity release.

Jennifer: You were interested in Hinduism. How do you think it relates to Catholicism? What's the same about it?

Rice: We're all the same religion when it gets right down to it. The Vatican doesn't want to admit it. We're all concentrating on the divine. God's there. The Hindus pray, and the Christians pray. It's the same way, way down.

Jennifer: What disturbs me in the Old Testament is when the Pharaoh wants to let the Jews go but God keeps hardening the Pharaoh's heart. Do you think everything is a gift from God, even the hardening of our hearts at times? Why would he do that?

Rice: We don't know. . . . We'll never know what he knows . . . we can't . . . then he's not God. I'm inclined to leave it alone. He told us we shouldn't be killing animals . . . we shouldn't kill anything . . . he told us over and over again but we go on killing. . . . He gives us a beautiful Earth, and we destroy it.

Jennifer: You'd think a God who is omnipotent would know that we are going to muck things up. Why did he give us this world if he knew we were going to destroy it?

Rice: I don't know. Lax is right in many ways. He's trying to get peace . . . he doesn't get much help. A lot of tension. Counterculture. Children. Frustrated. Lax sees what's there and nobody else wants to see it.

Jennifer: There is a priest I like who says that he has never heard one authentic sin. Do you think there is no such thing as sin?

Rice: There definitely is sin, deliberate sin. I know people who want to hurt somebody else. . . .

He then jumped to the subject of what he thinks of as a deteriorating civilization:

Rice: It's all going down the drain.

Jennifer: How do you think it's going down the drain?

Rice: Because all the old institutions are disappearing. They were founded just to get civilization off to a start. We have mathematics and literature. These things weren't known before the birth of Christ, the Sumerians, people like that. Without any apparent reason we have a high degree of civilization. We couldn't have had computers without the Babylonians and the Indus Valley people. They gave us mathematics, the concept of zero, the x, the unknown, and now it's all going to be destroyed. All these computer things we see on TV have no relevance; it's just to get us over the ground until the new world comes. And the new world . . . it's a different world.

Jennifer: What will it be like?

Rice: When my two grandchildren can think in complex mathematical terms you know we're in a different world. We never knew anything like that before. I don't know if Lax knows or not . . . apparently Merton was just learning it and he understood it immediately. I don't understand, and I'm not going to bother with it.

Jennifer: I can tell you that Lax has a little computer, and he looks at it and goes "Wow." It can center all of his lettering . . . so you guys are on the edge of this civilization. . . .

Rice: I liked the old Catholic Church . . . the church has become chaotic and confused . . . needs nuns with lots of spirit. . . . I'd like to see the church continue in some dynamic way . . . it's a great institution . . . but they squeezed out some of their best . . . like Dorothy Day . . . birth control . . . I'm for it . . . and abortion . . . I'm against it . . . are shattering the church, keeping the church from doing what it should be doing. Marriage is an important

social institution, you need homes, places for children to grow up
. . . the pope ought to go out in the desert, build a house with his
own hands, let the monsignori run the institutional part.

Two months later, in July, Millie and I made it once again to Sagaponack. It was a beautiful day with a nice breeze, but Ed wore the wool
serape that he bought in Buenos Aires in the 1960s and kept the door
closed, so we couldn't enjoy the breeze. His mind and his tongue seemed
much slower than they were on the previous visit. Dolly lifted him to
take him to the bathroom, and when he came back he put the serape on
again and went into detail on his Parkinson's disease:

It's like there are a lot of little BB holes in the brain . . . the damn-
dest sickness—there are three people who live around here who
have it. He put his head down on a pillow on the table; his speech
gets slower as the medication wears off.

Then he reflected on *Jubilee*, conscious of the importance of getting
me to know the facts so that this book would be accurate, even though
much of what he told me on this day I already knew:

A lot of people don't realize that I started *Jubilee*. They think Lax
started it, although some people credit O'Gorman. Lax wasn't
even in the United States. He would send notes with little scribbles
on them saying, "Great idea, Rocco." He was very good, though,
at keeping me together when I had problems. Lax found a book on
the communitarian, anarchistic movement, "All Things in Common," by Claire Huchet Bishop. It had an influence on the *Jubilee*
concept. Merton had a big impact on *Jubilee*, a lot more than
people realize. He probably sent in a hundred contributions over
time. Other people who were important: Peter McDonnell, Bob
Reynolds, Peter White. Reinhardt did a number of drawings.

I commented on the beautiful art in *Jubilee,* and Ed said he took an
Oriental art course as a lecture course at Columbia and it "spilled over
into *Jubilee*." He once again went over his recollections of starting the
magazine. Then he said, wistfully, and exaggeratedly, "*Jubilee* became
a refuge for the homeless and dispossessed."

Dolly prepared a nice lunch of curried lamb, tomatoes and lettuce,
beets, which Ed consumed as ravenously as Millie and I. He said he was
trying to regain some of the 70 pounds he had lost—down from 190 to
120. He eats "everything," said Dolly, and Rice proved it by consuming

all of the Haagen-Dazs ice cream we were served for dessert. During our talk Ed twitched a lot, pulled on his sagging neck skin, squirmed and wiggled, and wound his arms around his neck. His skinny legs showed splotches of of red and purple.

Like a lot of other Catholics these days, Rice was mad at the pope. "What the pope thinks makes no difference. Most Catholics go the way their conscience tells them to go. In the early days the Christians led their own lives with little reference to the authority in Rome. I have this image of two big circles—one with the pope in it, the other with people doing what they want." About his own sons he said: "Neither of them are in the church. Ted became a Tibetan Buddhist. Chris grew up a hard-core Republican and has evolved into an independent Democrat. Liza, Chris's wife, takes their children to the Presbyterian church in Princeton, where they have a nice program of kid's activities."

"The young people, even though they don't follow the Catholic Church, believe in social justice, even in Princeton," Millie said. "It's the Eucharist that holds the Catholic Church together." "That's what keeps me there," said Rice. "It's interesting, though, that the only good things being done out here are being done by Catholics . . . feeding programs for migrant workers, for example. The Protestants spend their time organizing socials."

Almost a year later, in April 1999, we were in Sagaponack again. Although Ed was still working away at *Cities of the Sacred Unicorn,* he seemed very frail and was quite cranky toward Dolly and Dodo. He was dressed in a green baseball cap, Indian shawl, baggy navy blue sweat pants, white sweat socks, and a white sweater. He took a dopamine pill, and when that wore off he began to squirm. He reminisced about his childhood, recalling that when he was about fourteen he packed a suitcase and got on a bike to leave home, crossed the river in a ferry to New Jersey, wanting to go to Chicago, but a cop stopped him and he went home. He jumped around in subject matter, musing that "I'm not spiritual but I'm being used in some way," then expressed the thought that the Catholics and the Buddhists were going to get together, then told us he was trying to make peace with Margery. He reminisced that he and Margery had been married in the rectory of St. Patrick's Cathedral, and that neither Lax nor Merton was there—Merton being in Gethsemani and Lax in Europe. He talked about his favorite writers—Joyce is number one; but he also likes Hemingway, Fitzgerald, Graham Greene, Evelyn Waugh, Kafka. He missed having Van Doren as a professor.

Two people from a "Save Ed Committee" visit him each week. His right eye is the "good" eye. He has no vision at all in the left eye. "I know this house," he says, "but when I go to a different environment, like the supermarket, I know I'm blind."

Later that year I interviewed Jim Forest, one of the few people still alive who knew all three of this book's protagonists, at his son's home in Red Bank, New Jersey. He was on a lecture tour with a brutal schedule for the next few weeks, meant to raise funds for his Orthodox Peace Fellowship in Alkmaar, The Netherlands. He asks fees of $1,000 for each appearance. Jim was fifty-eight years old at the time of the interview, somewhat portly, with a scruffy, greying beard and thinning hair. He has been married four times. He seems healthy and is certainly affable. We talked about Catholic–Orthodox relations. He hoped the pope would make a "real symbolic gesture" toward the Orthodox community, like giving the icon of Our Lady of Kazan, which was originally in the cathedral in St. Petersburg, back to the Russian Orthodox Church [that has happened]. "The Roman Catholic Church should show in action its respect for the Orthodox Church—like recognizing married priests in the Orthodox churches in the Middle East . . . the difference between the letter of the word and action is enormous . . . don't blame the pope . . . he says positive things and the cardinals pay no attention." He cited the experience of trying to get the pope to meet in person with Nobel Prize winner Adolfo Perez Esquivel of Argentina. The pope wanted to, but his staff wouldn't think of it. They didn't want to offend the hierarchy in Argentina.[39] They did meet, however, in 1980, and Forest wrote of the meeting in *Commonweal* (April 22, 2005).

A wonderful volume of tributes to Bob Lax came out in 1999.[40] It included reprints of old ones from the likes of Jack Kerouac, Denise Levertov, C. K. Williams, Mark Van Doren, Nancy Flagg, Emmett Williams, Emil Antonucci—and newer ones from Paul Spaeth, William Packard, and Nicholas Zurbrugg and David Miller. The latter two served as editors of the volume. The paragraph from C. K. Williams, written years earlier, was eloquent in analyzing Lax's poems:

> And he will not use degraded spiritual terminology to describe himself or his work any more than he will allow it or any semblance of it in that work. "Black and white," not "good or evil" or "life and death."
>
> The integrity of Lax's spiritual attempt is awesome. A renunciation, a series of renunciations, of falsehood, of sham, of any sort of pretence—even of relative "meaning" or traditional verbal music. It is an asceticism, and, like any such, may be misinterpreted as a mere system or aesthetic, but it is important to recognize how inspiring the task he has set for himself can be for us.[41]

In his last year on Patmos, in late 1999 and early 2000, Lax had a young American couple, Rebecca and Michael Daugherty [she an artist, he a writer from the Iowa workshop where Connie Brothers, Bob's niece, worked], helping him. Then, when Michael's father became very ill, the two returned to the United States, and a new helper, Sarah McCann, a Princeton University graduate who had also been with the Iowa writers group, took over for a few weeks. Bob was delighted that she could speak Greek and therefore was able to read the labels on his medical prescriptions. At first Sarah faced a difficult situation:

> He was wary when I arrived. Mike and Rebecca had left suddenly and I think he was unsettled and distrustful of me. But when I said my mother had worked in a pharmacy for years I was a star. I could get him out of bed to move his legs . . . some days he seemed discouraged with his own body . . . within the first week he knew I was a capable person and I cared about him.[42]

Eventually, she remembered, his spirits improved; he took walks with his friend Niko Eliou, and he even "made jokes, subtle and outlandish." But he could be finicky, insisting on having his pen and paper in the right place, the windows and doors latched, and "quiet during dinner but not during dessert." Sarah tried to get him up from bed, where he spent most of the day, for breakfast and dinner. He wouldn't budge for lunch. He did no reading except for one quote per day from the Easwaran book. He still did some writing during the night, interrupted sometimes by a spot of yogurt and honey. He no longer went for a swim, but he would sometimes pace the alley.

"He loved his cats," Sarah recalls, "especially the blind one named Homer. He spoke to them as he walked. His bookshelves [were] neatly categorized: reference/language, friends, Merton, religion/philosophy/art . . . [he] wanted me to read Mircea Eliade. . . .

"He would get a container of lunch from the woman in the store he patronized but he wouldn't eat a well-meaning neighbor's gift because he was sure it was salty."

Sometimes Sarah would get him into substantive conversation, as when one evening she asked him if he considered himself an American. He said that his passport said so, but the next morning he said the question "kept him up all night." He said that he loved the Constitution, that it was "better than any other political document, fabulous, philosophic, beautifully written," and he really considered himself from Olean and Manhattan.[43]

Comprehending his own growing frailty, in April 2000 Bob telephoned his niece Marcia in New York and and asked if she and her husband, Jack Kelly, would come to Patmos to help him move to Lucerne, where, he thought, he would like to live in the seminary he had stayed in years earlier. Marcia and Jack got to Patmos on May 22 and decided that they would take Bob to Brussels for rehabilitation—he had stomach flu and a swollen knee from a fall and needed a wheelchair. Lucerne was rejected because Bob would have had to walk to meals. An invitation from Bernhard and Gladys to have him stay upstairs in their home in Zurich was declined. Forty-three stairs to mount. A veritable odyssey began in mid-June, starting with, as Marcia described it, a "perilous descent from the hilltop." The regular ferry to Piraeus would have involved stairs and so was rejected. Connie Brothers got wind of a luxury cruise ship, replete with jazz band, no stairs, which would go directly from Patmos to Civitavecchia. There they boarded a wheelchair-accessible van, also arranged by Connie, for the trip to Rome where Cammy, Connie's daughter, joined what she called the A-team— Marcia, Jack, Connie, Niko, and Ulf Knaus, an Austrian painter who had been living on Patmos [he later sold to St. Bonaventure a painting based on a Lax poem]. Then came a bullet train to Brussels, where, at the Clinique Deux Alice, Bob had a reunion with Sarah, who remembers that he said "hello, dear" to me, "gave me a fabulous smile, and we talked the whole first day. . . . He told me about his New York days with the magazines, E. B. White, and 'his girl' Nancy Flagg. . . ."[44]

Bob stayed for a month at the Clinique, where a friend who was a layman in the local Jesuit community, Olivier de Kerchove, was especially helpful, and where he was tended each evening by a young former Carmelite nun who spoke French to Bob. But, recalls Jack Kelly, "Complete examinations by competent physicians, x-rays, cardiograms, blood tests, revealed nothing." It was then that Marcia asked Bob if he would consider going home to Olean. "No . . . I won't fly." "If you didn't have to fly would you consider it?" "Yes, I'd like that." Plans were quickly hatched to go to Southampton to catch the Queen Elizabeth 2.[45]

Marcia and Jack flew home to prepare the Olean house, but Olivier, Niko, Sarah, and her writer–boyfriend, Lewis Robinson, boarded the ship with Bob. Sarah's memories of the voyage are not happy ones:

He was not the same. He was in bed all day, quiet, maybe thinking, but his mood not the same. I have seen many elderly people lose themselves a bit when they leave their familiar surroundings. This seemed to happen with Bob. Perhaps he was just meditative. . . . He seemed to me depressed or contemplating his place in the world. He was unhappy with his body . . . it was betraying him. He looked at his legs and asked why they were so thin. He wanted someone in his room always. One of us would keep him company during the day and Olivier would sleep there at night. He had changed so much from when I left him in Greece and I felt awful that there was nothing I could do to ease him. We were just company.[46]

She does remember that "[o]n July 23 at 9:40 A.M.," he made these jottings, jumping subjects in characteristic Laxian style: "Better to see what I have seen than to be remembered for what I see. Better to know what I know than to be remembered for what I know . . . breathing habit of staccato exhaling . . . ship's spec gave horsepower of engines: 'enough horsepower to make Ben Hur.'"[47]

Once in Olean, at 215 Madison Ave., which had been the home of his sister, Gladys Marcus, and her husband, Benji, Lax hardly stirred from the big bed that looked out on a lush, green backyard—in such contrast to the parched soil of Patmos. He received some guests, and some phone calls were put through by the vigilantly protective Marcia. He heard from Rice, and from Jim Knight, another old Columbia friend from the 1930s, to whom he said, "I'm in the family house and I'm very happy here."[48]

Only a few weeks later, "On September 26, the feast day of St. John, he passed over early in the morning, quietly, gently, unhurriedly," as Jack Kelly described it.[49]

Deeply touching at the end of the funeral service at St. Bonaventure on September 29, the eve of Rosh Hashanah, was a soulful, wandering tenor saxophone solo by Richard Simpson, whose classes Bob visited when he was Reginald Lenna Professor at St. Bonaventure. It was a Billy Strayhorn piece, and Lax, Merton, and Rice would have loved it. Burial in the friars cemetery was "on a knoll, looking across the valley to the university where your writings, full of wisdom and humor, are kept safely, nearby are the friars happy with your company, with a bench to sit on for those who visit. . . ."[50]

A few weeks later, on November 18, a memorial Mass took place at Corpus Christi Church in New York, where more than sixty years earlier Bob had witnessed the baptism of Thomas Merton, with Ed Rice the godfather. Father Raymond Rafferty, who said the Mass, pointed out the baptismal font for the large representation of old New York friends—*Jubilee* alumni such as Ned O'Gorman, Oona Sullivan, Jacques Lowe; Joe Rush from the *Catholic Worker*; Chris Rice and family, most of the Harford family, Marcia and Jack Kelly. Especially memorable were the intonements of psalms in Hebrew by a cantor with a splendid voice. Among the eulogies was one by O'Gorman, who extemporized that "Bob's poetry and his life seem to me . . . to be a symbol of what it is to be a Man . . . to be a Jew . . . to be a Catholic . . . to be a solitary . . . to be the most convivial and glorious of men . . . finding in the church and in God . . . and in the street . . . and in Greek life . . . the very essence of what it is to be the redeemed child of a difficult and possible presence of God."[51]

Ed Rice was too ill to attend the Mass, but I recounted for the gathering an anecdote that he had told me: "Lax once gave a reading in the *Jubilee* office, and afterwards people crowded around him and put questions to him. Somebody asked him about heaven, and he said, 'I'm looking forward to the time when I meet Jesus face to face.' I muttered to myself [said Rice], 'How will anybody tell them apart?'"

Most of the group stayed on for hours, partaking in Greek pastries, stuffed grape leaves, olives, wine, ouzo, and retsina laid on by Marcia.

Less than a year after Lax's death, Rice would also succumb—of complications from his Parkinson's disease—at eighty-two on August 18, 2001. As with Lax's funeral Mass, Rice's was joyous—everyone singing "When the Saints Go Marchin' In" before heading back to the Sagaponack house for vittles and a keg of beer. The priest who said the Mass, Monsignor Ronald Richardson, recalled that he had been greatly influenced by *Jubilee* as a young seminarian. Some of the magazine's staffers at the funeral—Oona Sullivan, Wilfrid Sheed—were no doubt proud to hear that. Ed's one-time editor Anne Freedgood was there. She would die of complications from Alzheimer's disease that same year, at eighty-five. Also present were the friends who had cared for or looked in on Ed in his last months—Dollin Jagdeo, Pat Farrell, the writer Mary Cummings, Didi Hadik, Mary and Brad Kelleher, and four Harfords—Millie and I, Jimmy and Jennifer. The Rice family turned out in full—Chris and Liza Rice and their two children from Princeton, Ted Rice up from New Mexico, Ed's brother, Donald, and his wife from a nearby Long Island town, his sister, Carol McCormack, and daughter from Pennsylvania, and—lo and behold—ex-wife Margery.

* * * * * * * * * * * * * *

12

LEGACY

Impact of All Three on a Troubled American Catholicism

Lax, Merton, and Rice can't claim credit for the prolific growth of rebel organizations that have sprouted up among lay Catholics in the United States since the sex scandals first exploded in 2002. All three had passed on by then. But they surely would have been pleased at the apparent vitality of these groups, especially in the light of the anemia of the church. One wonders what they might have had to say about the general mess that the American church found itself in. They were not "I told you so" people, but they did tell us so, again and again, registering their discontent over hierarchical arrogance and disregard for the laity; the neurotic preoccupation of the church with human sexuality; the playing down of religious women, and women in general; the hostility toward even opening up issues like contraception, abortion rights, ordination of women, clerical celibacy, gay marriage, married priests, Catholic homosexuals; the timidity of many Catholic leaders to have real dialogue with Eastern religions; the lack of leadership in improving the dismal state of American Catholic music, art, architecture, literature, scholarship. All were their personal concerns—sometimes muted in their public writings but prominent in their letters to one another.

It is hoped that each of these deeply thoughtful men will witness—from their heavenly perches—a resurgence in the faithful of qualities to which they gave high priority—simplicity, love of God, and laughter, compassion for their fellow human beings. Their lives, conjoined by deep friendship and lively correspondence over decades, give us who read their letters and their works an unusual, if not unique, perspective. I, for one, had not encountered such a trio of thinkers before. Each, certainly, had a profound influence on my own life.

What about their effect on others? I once asked Lax what he thought that Merton was getting at. He answered, "He was trying to see the truth beyond all the masks—that's a Christian idea. St. Paul says, 'Now we see through a glass darkly, but at the end we will see Him face to face.' One of the reasons that Merton," said Lax, "got deeply interested in Buddhism was because the Buddhists, too, wanted to 'get out of the temporal world of illusion into the world of truth. They think you go through life after life until you are born as a human being and if you don't have too much bad karma accumulated you may be able to arrive at Truth, Enlightenment, Buddhahood, and I think Merton had arrived at that hope—he wrote this in his *Asian Journal*. Another monk, a lama, told him that he should 'go for it' in this life. Not long after he visited Polonnaruwa in Sri Lanka he said he had seen through the mask—and a few days later he died. What you felt he had seen was a perfect passivity . . . receptivity."[1]

In his last letter to the Benedictine Jean Leclercq, just a few months before his death, Merton wrote, "The vocation of the monk in the modern world, especially Marxist, is not survival but prophecy."[2] It was this conviction that motivated the man who was perhaps the most famous Trappist of all time to deliver many harsh judgments on the materialism and bellicosity of his adopted country, as well as the Roman Catholic Church. "His criticisms of the United States and the culture of his day are acerbic and in the spirit of the prophets of old," wrote Archbishop Rembert G. Weakland.[3]

What of the overall legacy of these three men? Who is listening these days to what they had to say about their church? What impact have their writings, their lives, had on American Catholics, on the general populace? In the case of Merton the impact is powerful, if not totally acceptable to church authorities. Monsignor William Shannon, a leading Merton scholar and author of a number of books on the monk, states that he "gave us a whole new way of understanding spirituality. Contemplation, before Merton, was for elite people—St. John of the Cross, St. Theresa of Avila—but Merton made it important for all of us. It enables us to go beyond, to a deeper way of having contact with God. He literally changed the direction of Catholic spirituality." Shannon's own life was changed appreciably. "Merton made us realize that just being quiet in the presence of God was a meaningful way of praying." Whereas Shannon used to go on retreats and be given points to reflect on, he began to spend twenty minutes each morning in silence, first emptying his mind. "You are already in the presence of God, but it's important to be aware of that . . . you are in God yourself."[4]

Lax, too, spent time each day—or in the middle of the night, meditating on God silently. The catalog for an exhibit of writings and photos by Lax held in Basel, Switzerland, in early 2005, printed in both German and English, called him a "Dichter und Prophet der Langsamkeit," which might be translated as "poet and prophet of slowing down." Although slowing down was not characteristic of either Merton or Rice, reflection certainly was, and the ideas of all three were ratified, to a great extent, by the recommendations of Vatican II—too many of which, unfortunately, were ignored or cancelled by latter-day church leaders. But their impact goes beyond even that epochal council. Thousands of non-Catholics and Catholics identify with Merton, his spirituality, his humanity, his vicissitudes, and—in the end—his steady proclamation of faith in God. Those descriptors apply as well to Lax and Rice. And surely, the fifteen years—180 issues—of *Jubilee*, in which all three men had strong hands, bear reexamination by scholars and others who want to fathom the era and compare it to contemporary times. All one needs to do is review the body of the magazine's articles from 1953 to 1967 to realize that, as Anne Freedgood put it, "The church has changed a lot in ways that started with *Jubilee*." An impressive scholarly test of that thesis was made recently by Mary Anne Rivera in a Ph.D. dissertation for Duquesne University. She concluded, in a well-documented, 322-page study, that the "Second Vatican Council, its spirit, structure and mission reflected much of *Jubilee*'s outlook: the primacy of liturgy in the life of the Church, the concepts of authority, responsibility and collegiality among the faithful, and the concept of Christian culture in dialogue with the world."[5] Through the magazine, Rice, Merton, and Lax were intent on no less than jogging the church into reforms of the way the Mass is conducted, the way the congregation sings, the way the Catholic schools teach art, literature, and intellectual thought, the way that Catholics interact with people of other faiths, as well as to recognize their obligations to oppose war and to help the poor and oppressed.

It was a tall order, and looking back on Vatican II, although it conjures up good memories of the way in which some of those objectives were realized, it also evokes the painful realization that many opportunities for the transformation of Catholicism were not taken. *National Catholic Reporter* editor Tom Roberts, leading off a special issue on *Vatican II: 40 Years Later,* in October 2002,[6] wrote that "the council lives and continues to reform the church and its members." But the subsequent text does not support unmixed optimism. Garry Wills, in the very next pages, wrote that "the initial euphoria has worn off, and the initial panic [presumably among those not wanting change] has turned to hope that some return to the past is still possible. Episcopal collegiality has been baffled. Consulting the laity seems a joke. . . ." Still, he asked,

"Does all this mean that the movement launched by the Second Vatican Council has foundered? No more than we can say that the civil rights movement failed, or that feminism is dead. . . . Catholics live in a different world since the council." He continued:

> On a superficial but striking level, the identifying marks of the past are missing—gone are fish on Friday, confession on Saturday, and compelled church attendance on Sunday. Gone are the trademark 10-children Catholic families. Gone is the sin-driven mentality of the past. Gone, for most, the condemning or shunning of gays. . . .
> . . . [a Lilly Foundation survey in 1997 reported that . . . "over twice as many young Catholics are attending college as attended in 1970 . . . [they are] getting married four or five years later than in 1970, having two-career families, bearing children four to five years later, using contraceptives . . . marrying non-Catholics. This puts in a whole new light such matters as premarital sex, birth control, abortion, divorce and remarriage."]

In spite of these factors, wrote Wills, the council's stands on many issues were not followed up. "Episcopal collegiality could not be more strikingly repudiated than by the 1998 *motu proprio Apostolos Suos,* which said that no act of a national conference of bishops could be binding unless it were a) voted for unanimously, and b) subject of papal approval. This was a castration of the conferences." If unanimity had been required, Wills continued, "the statement that the Jews had not killed Christ would have failed because of the 188 council fathers who voted against it." He cited other reverses from Rome since Vatican II: The bishops no longer control local liturgies, numerous drafts of a statement on women from the American bishops have been turned down, and several university theologians have been hamstrung. John Paul II, Wills thinks, was behind these actions because, although "an impressive man, in some ways a great one. . . . He showers favor on those who share his paranoid concerns." But, he concluded, "the young people in general belong to a Vatican II generation, not the Pope John Paul generation. . . . Vatican II lives."[7]

Writing for conservative Catholics in the same issue was George Weigel. He argued that "intellectuals seduced by power" had dominated the discussions in the post–Vatican II years, that the council had not been about power but that John XXIII had "imagined a new Pentecost, a fresh experience of the Holy Spirit to prepare the church to enter its third millennium as a vital evangelical movement, offering the

world the truth about itself—which is the story of salvation history."
Weigel is

> indebted to Vatican II for the renewed liturgy (despite the literary
> and musical gaucheries that still plague us); for a new relation-
> ship between the church's people and the church's pastors; for the
> impetus it gave to Catholic social doctrine (a far more humane
> proposal for the human future than utilitarianism or Islamism,
> the other two global proposals now on offer); for the place the
> council created for lay people like me to contribute to the church's
> life, thought and public witness. The man history may one day
> know as John Paul the Great is indisputably a product of the
> Council, and like many millions of others, I am immensely grate-
> ful to Vatican II for that.[8]

If *Jubilee* were alive today it is very likely that Wills's convictions
about the council would receive more space than Weigel's.

The magazine would likely agree with Weigel, however, about the
"musical gaucheries that still plague us." *Jubilee*'s passion about church
music is memorable as the debates go on. Forty-five years after the eloquent plea in the magazine's November 1959 issue by Dom Ludovic
Baron, O.S.B., for Gregorian chant and later letters from readers, we
read this by John L. Allen Jr. in the *National Catholic Reporter*: "For
all those who romanticize about a 'golden age' of sacred music prior to
the Second Vatican Council, for all those who would banish any melody
but Gregorian chant from the Mass, the Catholic church's top musician
has a simple message: Get over it."[9] He goes on to quote "top musician," Monsignor Giuseppe Liberto, the "maestro of the pope's own
Sistine Chapel choir," as saying, "Any kind of guerilla action against
Vatican II doesn't produce good fruits. . . . The councils are by now
untouchable." The monsignor doesn't want to throw out the chant—his
choir uses it regularly—but, as Allen writes, he wants "creativity, finding new musical wine to pour into new liturgical wineskins"; and that,
he says, is a "work largely yet to be done." Amen, but what kind of
music is he talking about, and just where does one find it? Not in most
parishes, certainly! Allen doesn't get the monsignor to spell it out in the
article, except to paraphrase him in saying that "[h]e, too, has been disappointed by some of the more banal music written after the council."

Rays of hope for better music come from having heard it on retreats
at Benedictine monasteries like St. John's Abbey in Collegeville, Minnesota, Christ in the Desert in Abiquiu, New Mexico, and Mount Saviour, near Elmira, New York. I have struck up a correspondence with

a young nun, Sister Sheryl Frances Chen, a fellow Yale graduate and a convert, who is proud of the music at her Trappistine monastery on a fjord in Norway. And Millie and I count as a dear friend Sister Sheila Long, also a convert, who, after graduating as a music major from Mount Holyoke, went around Europe to find good Gregorian chant, and found it in a Benedictine monastery near Angouleme, France.

Sister Sheryl's and Sister Sheila's monasteries have both participated in East–West spiritual encounters, including those between Catholic monastics and Buddhist monks. Merton's deep interest in Buddhism, and what Catholicism can learn from it, is referred to on page 286.

The germination of Merton's interest in Buddhism into a substantial dialogue between Catholic and Buddhist monastics has developed since his death. It is bizarre, however, that largely because of his interest in Buddhism, Merton's name became embroiled post-mortem in a *cause célèbre*. In 2005 a project to write a new catechism of Catholicism was undertaken by a committee of the U.S. Conference of Catholic Bishops, headed by Bishop Donald W. Wuerl of Pittsburgh. The format was to include a profile of an exemplary Catholic as introduction to each chapter, with Merton chosen for chapter 1. Enter two conservative Catholics named Monsignor Michael Wrenn, dean of students at St. Joseph Seminary, Dunwoodie, New York, and a layman, Kenneth D. Whitehead, a former U.S. assistant secretary of education, who intervened that Merton was not a proper choice since he was a "lapsed monk" who had shown an inclination toward Buddhism in his last years. Besides, said Bishop Wuerl, young people don't even know who Merton is.[10] That is a claim made ridiculous by the fact that a significant percentage of the continuing sales of *The Seven Storey Mountain, The Sign of Jonas,* and many other Merton books is accounted for by young people. A good example is the Trappistine nun mentioned earlier in this chapter—Sheryl Frances Chen, O.C.S.O., of the Tautra Mariakloster monastery in Norway—who told me that her reading of those books while a student at Yale had a great influence on her conversion to Catholicism and her choice of a monastic vocation. *Sign of Jonas* especially made its mark on her, and she is even thinking of translating Merton into Norwegian. "I liked *Sign of Jonas* even better than *SSM,*" she wrote me, "because it told of Merton's novitiate and was even earthier. I was fascinated by all that went on in the cloister. I could also see that Merton's sense of humor had survived intact. I also think that manual labor has been the Cistercians' saving grace. Merton had the gift of being able to capture the spirit of all this in his writings." She is not uncritical of Merton, however, feeling that some of his writings are "dated."

That remains my concern with applicants who still come into the [monastic] life because they've read Merton's books. The order has changed dramatically in the last 35 years. Are the people coming now attracted to something that no longer exists? Or coming for the wrong reasons? There's a passage in SOJ that I used to use for a second nocturn reading. Merton describes the time he was watching a flock of sparrows when a hawk swooped down and picked off the slowest sparrow. He said contemplative prayer should be like that—going straight to its target. I still love that image. Anyway, I still think someone needs to do what Merton did, again, only with the modern order in mind.[11]

Merton would certainly have pushed harder for changes in the contemplative life of the church himself if he had lived another few decades. He wrote in his journal that "the Message of Contemplatives—dutifully printed in the Osservatore, with the usual picture of a monk with his hood up and his back to the camera—has been totally and utterly forgotten—dropped into a well of silence as if it had never been. . . ."[12]

How the contemplatives will fare under Pope Benedict XVI is conjectural. John Paul II, God rest his sainted soul, seems to have paid little attention to the monastics while concentrating on other subjects dear to the hearts of Lax, Merton, and Rice: opposition to war [all three would have loved Pope John Paul II's criticism of President Bush over the Iraq catastrophe]; on helping the poor and oppressed; on criticizing the materialism of capitalist nations.

But while not getting much attention from the Vatican, the monasteries themselves have substantially improved the sophistication of their techniques for attracting adherents. An enterprising e-mail from the Benedictines in England recently called attention to a Web site that is aimed at attracting "pre-vocations to all religious orders." Response so far from the "target audience . . . men and women from 20 to 35" who are to be invited to spend a weekend a month for nine months in a house at Worth Abbey in West Sussex is "encouraging." Abbot Christopher Jamison of the Benedictines feels that "Catholics should stop lamenting the decline in religious vocations" and "start asking what are we doing to create a culture in which everybody sees that God is calling to them in different ways."[13]

They have a long row to hoe. The decline not only in monastics but in priests and nuns, churches and schools, generally is devastating. David Gibson, a convert, covers in his book *The Coming Catholic Church* the collapse in vocations to the priesthood. These numbers seem to belie the optimistic subtitle of Gibson's book, *How the Faithful Are Shaping a New American Catholicism.*[14]

The failure to deal with the sexual scandals among priests—covered up for years—has greatly exacerbated the problem. Gibson quotes Tom Beaudoin, a young professor of theology at Boston College, as saying that the church is experiencing a "Catholic Watergate," and "only honesty, frank discussion, a truly adult church, and changing our Catholic family dynamics will get us out of it."[15]

It will take that and more. The feeder lines—Catholic schools and churches—are closing by the year. Some forty to fifty churches will close in the archdiocese of Newark in the next five years, says the Associated Press.[16]

Rice told Lax, waggishly, what he thought Merton might have done about these crises, in a letter of 1983: "if the Old Boy had got to the Vatican first thing he wld have done wld be to install Pope Joan as his consort."[17] Not only was Merton concerned about the fate of women in the church, he was blunt about the need to reengage young people. Here is what he wrote Lax on the subject in 1966:

> No, it is no joke, we must *win the teens.* Or else we are sunk my dear Bish. The chanceries must fold and the curiales must crawl away under the rug if we fail to win the teens. It is the greatest crisis of the moment. Buckets of trinkets and this alone will win teens says Bishop . . .
>
> It is your beard that will pack the pews with teens. Never forget this for an instant.[18]

I find myself cautiously optimistic about young people in the church. I sensed a rise in idealism among many young Catholics during the final days of John Paul II, and it was very impressive to note the enthusiastic participation in World Youth Day in Cologne, Germany, in 2005. Is it not realistic to ask that these young people—and why not include retired old people like my generation—take leadership positions in carrying out the huge social, ecumenical, and humanitarian tasks that the world so achingly needs? Think of it: Pope Benedict XVI has at his disposal a two-thousand-year-old structure of neighborhood centers ideally suited to these tasks—the worldwide parishes of the Roman Catholic Church.

* * * * * * * * * * * * * * * * * *

Sources

Abbreviations of Main Archival Sources
for *Merton and Friends*

AJ   Thomas Merton, *The Asian Journal of Thomas Merton*. New York: New Directions, 1973.

Biddle   *When Prophecy Still Had a Voice: The Letters of Thomas Merton and Robert Lax*. Edited by Arthur W. Biddle. Lexington, Ky.: University Press of Kentucky, 2001. Copyright © Merton Legacy Trust and Robert Lax Estate.

CGB   Thomas Merton, *Conjectures of a Guilty Bystander*. New York: Doubleday, 1966.

FFA   Thomas Merton, *Figures for an Apocalypse*. New York: New Directions, 1948.

HGL   *The Hidden Ground of Love*. Edited by William H. Shannon. New York: Farrar, Straus & Giroux, 1985.

IM   Thomas Merton, *The Intimate Thomas Merton: His Life from His Journals*. Edited by Patrick Hart and Jonathan Montaldo. San Francisco: HarperSanFrancisco, 1999.

LCU   Robert Lax Papers, Rare Book and Manuscript Library, Columbia University.

LSBA   Lax Saint Bonaventure Archive, Friedsam Library, St. Bonaventure University.

LTL   Thomas Merton, *Learning to Love: Exploring Solitude and Freedom (1966-67)*. San Francisco: HarperSanFrancisco, 1997.

MBTWKHB
       Paul Wilkes, ed. *Merton by Those Who Knew Him Best*. San Francisco: HarperSanFrancisco, 1984.

MBA   Merton Bellarmine Archive.

MCU   Thomas Merton Papers, Rare Book and Manuscript Library, Columbia University.

MIST   Edward Rice, *The Man in the Sycamore Tree*. New York: Doubleday, 1970.

MLT   Merton Legacy Trust.

Mott   Michael Mott, *The Seven Mountains of Thomas Merton*. Boston: Houghton Mifflin, 1984.

MZM Thomas Merton, *Mystics and Zen Masters*. New York: Farrar, Straus and Giroux, 1967.

OSM Thomas Merton, *The Other Side of the Mountain: The End of the Journey (1967–68)*. San Francisco: HarperSanFrancisco, 1998.

RGA Rice Georgetown Archive.

RTJ *The Road to Joy*. Edited by Robert E. Daggy. New York: Harcourt Brace Jovanovich, 1989.

RTM Thomas Merton, *Run to the Mountain: The Story of a Vocation (1939–41)*. San Francisco: HarperSan Francisco, 1995.

SFS Thomas Merton, *A Search for Solitude: Pursuing the Monk's True Life (1952–60)*. San Francisco: HarperSanFrancisco, 1996.

SLML Thomas Merton and James Laughlin, *Selected Letters*. Edited by David D. Cooper. New York: W. W. Norton, 1997.

SLMVD
     Thomas Merton and Mark Van Doren, *Selected Letters*. Baton Rouge: Louisiana State University Press.

SOJ Thomas Merton, *The Sign of Jonas*. New York: Harcourt Brace, 1953.

SSM Thomas Merton, *The Seven Storey Mountain*. New York: Harcourt Brace Jovanovich, 1948.

ZBA Thomas Merton, *Zen and the Birds of Appetite*. New York: New Directions, 1968.

Lax, Merton, Rice Publications

Lax Publications

1955 *Tree*. New York: Hand Press.
1956 *The Juggler*. New York: Hand Press.
1958 *Oedipus*. New York: Hand Press.
      Question. New York: Hand Press.
      12 Poems. New York: Hand Press.
1959 *Circus of the Sun*. New York: Journeyman Press.
1961 *A Problem in Design, a Fable for the New Year*. New York: Hand Press.
1962 *New Poems*. New York: Journeyman Press.
1966 *How Does the Sun's Ray Seek the Flower?* New York: Journeyman Press.
      Sea Poem. Scotland: Wild Hawthorn Press.
      3 or 4 Poems about the Sea. New York: Journeyman Press.
      Thought. New York: Journeyman Books.
1969 *Three Poems*. New York: Journeyman Press.

A Poem for Thomas Merton. New York: Journeyman Books.

1970 *Fables.* New York: Journeyman Press.

1971 *Able Charlie Baker Dance.* East Markham, U.K.: Tarasque Press.
Another Red Red Blue poem. New York: Journeyman Press.
Black & White. New York: Journeyman Press.
An Evening at Webster Hall. New York: Journeyman Press.
4 Boats, 3 People. East Markham, U.K.: Tarasque Press.
A Guide for the Perplexed. New York: Journeyman Press.
A Moment. New York: Journeyman Press.
Mostly Blue. New York: Journeyman Press.
Red Circle—Blue Square. New York: Journeyman Press.

1973 *Wasser/Water/L'Eau.* Zurich: Pendo Verlag.

1974 *Circus Black—Circus White.* New York: Journeyman Press.
"Does the grass fear the dark. . . ." New York: Journeyman Press.
More blacks & whites. New York: Journeyman Press.
Pictures of Reality. New York: Journeyman Press.
Star Dialogue. New York: Journeyman Press.
13 Poems. New York: Journeyman Press.
"Try to see the air. . . ." New York: Journeyman Press.

1975 *Black Earth—Blue Sky.* New York: Journeyman Press.
Poèmes de Collines. Translated by Catherine Mauger. New York: Journeyman Press.

1976 *Color Poems.* New York: Journeyman Press.
Red Blue. New York: Journeyman Press.

1978 *A Catch of Anti-Letters, with Thomas Merton.* Mission, Ks.: Sheed Andrews & McMeel.
Selections. X-Press & Joe DiMaggio Press.
A Suite for Jiri Valoch. Falkynor Books.

1979 *Color.* Florence: Exempla.

1981 *circus zirkus cirque circo.* Zurich: Pendo Verlag.
10 Poems. Edited by John Landry. Patmos Publication.

1983 *Episodes.* Zurich: Pendo Verlag.
Fables. Zurich: Pendo Verlag.

1984 *Cloning for Yellow.* Seedorn Verlag.
21 Pages. Zurich: Pendo Verlag.

1986 *Journal A.* Zurich: Pendo Verlag.
New Poems 1962/1985. Edited by Heinz Gappmayr. Aachen: Ottenhausen Verlag.

1987 *Spark & Flame.* Frankfurt: Kuntsverein.

1988 *33 Poems.* Edited by Thomas Kellein. Edition Hansjorg Mayer, 1987. New York: New Directions.
Journal B. Zurich: Pendo Verlag.

1989 *The Light/The Shade.* Zurich: Pendo Verlag.

1990 *Journal C.* Edited by David Miller. Zurich: Pendo Verlag.

Red, Blue, Yellow. Piesport: Edition Hot.

To the Sea = à la mère: poème et variation. Robert Lax & Frédérick Leboyer. France: Livre à Livre.

1991 *Psalm.* Exeter, U.K.: Stride Publications.

Psalm & Homage to Wittgenstein. Zurich: Pendo Verlag.

"*White dark, black dark. . . .*" Edinburgh: Morning Star Publications, Edinburgh.

The Rooster Poems. Edited by Judith Emery. Exeter, U.K.: Stride Publications.

1992 *Mogador's Book.* Edited by Paul Spaeth. Zurich: Pendo Verlag.

1993 *Journal D.* Zurich: Pendo Verlag.

1994 *Dialogues.* Zurich: Pendo Verlag.

1995 *27th and 4th.* Exeter, U.K.: Stride.

Notes. Zurich: Pendo Verlag.

Xiliamondi. Exeter, U.K.: Trombone Press.

On & By Robert Lax, Gerhard van den Bergh. Zurich: Pendo Verlag.

1996 *Circle.* Eschenau: Summer Press.

Love Had a Compass. Edited by James Uebbing. New York: Grove Press.

Journal E Hollywood. Edited by Paul Spaeth. Zurich: Pendo Verlag.

1997 *Journal F Kalymnos.* Edited by John Beer. Zurich: Pendo Verlag.

More Scales. Eschenau: Summer Press.

Sleeping Waking. Edited by John Beer. Charleston, Ill.: Tel-Let.

A Thing That Is. Edited by Paul Spaeth. Woodstock, N.Y.: Overlook Press.

36 Poems. Edited by John Beer. Westerly R.I.: Ring Tarigh.

1998 *Dr. Glockenspiel's Invention.* Exeter, U.K.: Apparitions Press.

1999 *Aug 30/98+Sept 29/98.* Eschenau: Summer Press.

The ABCs of Robert Lax. Edited by David Miller and Nicholas Zurbrugg. Exeter, U.K.: Stride.

The Hill = Der Berg. Edited by Paula Diaz. Zurich: Pendo Verlag.

Red Blue. Eschenau: Summer Press.

Robert Lax Multimedia Box. Edited by Hartmut Geerken & Sigrid Hauff. Munich: belleville Verlag.

sea & sky. HMB Siebdruck.

2000 *Circus Days & Nights.* Edited by Paul Spaeth. Woodstock, N.Y.: Overlook Press.

Earth & Sky. Edited by William Cirocco. San Francisco: Hawkhaven Press.

Moments = Höhepunkte. Edited by John Beer. Zurich: Pendo Verlag.

One Island. Oaxaca: Carpe Diem Press.

2001 *Peacemaker's Handbook.* Edited by Judith Emery and Michael Daugherty. Zurich: Pendo Verlag.

When Prophecy Still Had a Voice: The Letters of Thomas Merton and

Robert Lax. Edited by Arthur W. Biddle. Lexington, Ky.: University Press of Kentucky.

2002 *Room Full of Voices.* Edited by John Beer. San Francisco: Hawkhaven Press.

The Way of the Dreamcatcher, Lax Interviews, by Steve Georgiou. Ottawa: Novalis.

2004 *The Green Minnow.* San Francisco: Kater Murr's Press.

Merton Publications

1944 *Thirty Poems.* New York: New Directions.

1946 *A Man in the Divided Sea.* New York: New Directions.

1948 *Exile Ends in Glory: The Life of a Trappistine, Mother M. Berchmans.* Milwaukee: Bruce.

Figures for an Apocalypse. New York: New Directions.

The Seven Storey Mountain. New York: Harcourt Brace Jovanovich.

Cistercian Contemplatives, A Guide to Trappist Life. Trappist, Ky.: Abbey of Gethsemani.

Guide to Cistercian Life. Trappist, Ky.: Abbey of Our Lady of Gethsemani.

Gethsemani Magnificat, Centenary of Abbey. Trappist, Ky.: Abbey of Our Lady of Gethsemani.

What Is Contemplation? London: Burns, Oates & Washbourne.

1949 *Elected Silence* [British edition of *SSM* with foreword by Evelyn Waugh]. London: Hollis and Carter.

Seeds of Contemplation. New York: New Directions.

The Tears of the Blind Lions. New York: New Directions.

The Waters of Siloe. New York: Harcourt Brace.

1950 *What Are These Wounds? The Life of a Cistercian Mystic.* Milwaukee: Bruce.

1951 *The Ascent to Truth.* New York: Harcourt Brace.

A Balanced Life of Prayer. Lexington, Ky.: Abbey of Gethsemani.

1953 *The Sign of Jonas.* New York: Harcourt Brace.

Bread in the Wilderness. New York: New Directions.

1954 *The Last of the Fathers: St. Bernard of Clairvaux.* New York: Harcourt Brace.

1955 *No Man Is an Island.* New York: Harcourt Brace.

1956 *The Living Bread.* New York: Farrar, Straus & Cudahy.

Praying the Psalms. Collegeville, Minn.: Liturgical Press.

Silence in Heaven: A Book of Monastic Life. New York: Studio Publications.

1957 *Basic Principles of Monastic Spirituality.* Trappist, Ky.: Abbey of Gethsemani.

The Psalms Are Our Prayer. London: Burns, Oates & Washbourne.

The Silent Life. New York: Farrar, Straus & Cudahy.
The Strange Islands. New York: New Directions.
The Tower of Babel. New York: New Directions.

1958   *Life at Gethsemani*. Trappist, Ky.: Abbey of Gethsemani.
Monastic Peace. Trappist, Ky.: Abbey of Gethsemani.
Native Kerygma. Trappist, Ky.: Abbey of Gethsemani.
Prometheus: A Meditation. Lexington, Ky.: King Library Press, University of Kentucky.
Thoughts in Solitude. New York: Farrar, Straus & Cudahy.

1959   *The Secular Journal of Thomas Merton*. New York: Farrar, Straus & Cudahy.
Selected Poems of Thomas Merton. New York: New Directions.
What Ought I to Do? Sayings from the Desert Fathers of the Fourth Century. Translated by Thomas Merton. Lexington, Ky.: Stamperio del Santuccio.

1960   *Disputed Questions*. New York: Farrar, Straus & Cudahy.
The Solitary Life. Lexington, Ky.: Stamperia del Santuccio.
Spiritual Direction and Meditation. Collegeville, Minn.: Liturgical Press.
The Wisdom of the Desert. New York: New Directions.

1961   *The Behavior of Titans*. New York: New Directions.
The New Man. New York: Farrar, Straus & Cudahy.

1962   *Breakthrough to Peace: Twelve Views on the Threat of Thermonuclear Extermination*. Edited by Thomas Merton. New York: New Directions.
Hagia Sophia. Lexington, Ky.: Samperia del Santuccio.
New Seeds of Contemplation. New York: New Directions.
Original Child Bomb. New York: New Directions.
A Thomas Merton Reader. New York: Harcourt Brace and World.

1963   *Emblems of a Season of Fury*. New York: New Directions.
Life and Holiness. New York: Herder & Herder.

1964   *Seeds of Destruction*. New York: Farrar, Straus & Giroux.

1965   *Gandhi on Non-Violence*. New York: New Directions.
Seasons of Celebration. New York: Farrar, Straus & Cudahy.
The Way of Chuang Tzu. New York: New Directions.

1966   *Conjectures of a Guilty Bystander*. Garden City, N.Y.: Doubleday.
Gethsemani: A Life of Praise. Trappist, Ky.: Abbey of Gethsemani.
Raids on the Unspeakable. New York: New Directions.
Redeeming the Time. London: Burns & Oates.

1967   *Mystics and Zen Masters*. New York: Farrar, Straus & Giroux.
A Prayer of Cassiodorus, Stanbrook Abbey Press, U.K.

1968   *Albert Camus' "The Plague."* New York: Seabury Press.
Faith and Violence. Notre Dame, Ind.: University of Notre Dame Press.
Cables to the Ace. New York: New Directions.
Zen and the Birds of Appetite. New York: New Directions.

1969 *The Geography of Lograire.* New York: New Directions.
      My Argument with the Gestapo: A Macaronic Journal [original title,
      Journal of My Escape from the Nazis]. Garden City, N.Y.: Doubleday.
      The True Solitude: Selections from the Writings of Thomas Merton.
      Kansas City: Hallmark.
1970 *Opening the Bible.* Collegeville, Minn.: Liturgical Press.
1971 *Contemplation in a World of Action.* Garden City, N.Y.: Doubleday.
      Early Poems 1940–42. Lexington, Ky.: Anvil Press.
      Thomas Merton on Peace. New York: McCall Publishing.
1973 *The Asian Journal of Thomas Merton.* New York: New Directions.
      Boris Pasternak, Thomas Merton, Six Letters. Lexington, Ky.: King
      Library Press, University of Kentucky.
1974 *Cistercian Life.* Spencer, Mass.: Cistercian Book Service.
1975 *He Is Risen: Thomas Merton Sermon.* Niles, Il.: Argus Communica-
      tions.
1976 *Ishi Means Man: Essays on Native Americans.* Greensboro, N.C.: Uni-
      corn Press.
1977 *The Collected Poems of Thomas Merton.* New York: New Directions.
      The Monastic Journey. Kansas City, Ks.: Sheed Andrews & McMeel.
      Thomas Merton on the Psalms. Sheldon Press U.K.
1978 *A Catch of Anti-Letters,* with Robert Lax. Kansas City, Ks.: Sheed
      Andrews, & McMeel.
1979 *Love and Living.* New York: Farrar, Straus & Giroux.
1980 *Thomas Merton on St. Bernard.* Kalamazoo, Mich.: Cistercian Publi-
      cations.
      The Non-Violent Alternative. New York: Farrar, Straus & Giroux.
1981 *The Climate of Monastic Prayer.* Kalamazoo, Mich.: Cistercian Publi-
      cations.
      Day of a Stranger. Salt Lake City: Gibbs M. Smith.
      Introductions East and West. Greensboro, N.C.: Unicorn Press.
      The Literary Essays of Thomas Merton. New York: New Directions.
1982 *Woods, Shore, Desert.* Albuquerque: University of New Mexico Press.
1988 *A Vow of Conversation,* New York: Farrar, Straus & Giroux.
1989 *Monks Pond.* Lexington, Ky.: University Press of Kentucky.
      Thomas Merton in Alaska. New York: New Directions.
1992 *Thomas Merton Spiritual Master.* Mahwah, N.J.: Paulist Press.
1995 *Passion for Peace: The Social Essays.* New York: Crossroad.
      Run to the Mountain: The Story of a Vocation (1939–41). San Fran-
      cisco: HarperSanFrancisco.
1996 *Entering the Silence: Becoming a Monk & Writer (1941–52).* San Fran-
      cisco: HarperSanFrancisco.
      A Search for Solitude: Pursuing the Monk's True Life (1952–60). San
      Francisco: HarperSanFrancisco.
1997 *Dancing in the Water of Life: Seeking Peace in the Hermitage (1963–
      65).* San Francisco: HarperSanFrancisco.

Learning to Love: Exploring Solitude and Freedom (1966–67). San Francisco: HarperSanFrancisco.

1998   *The Other Side of the Mountain: The End of the Journey (1967–68)*. San Francisco: HarperSanFrancisco.

1999   *The Intimate Merton: His Life from His Journals*. San Francisco: HarperSanFrancisco.

2000   *Thomas Merton: Essential Writings*. Maryknoll, N.Y.: Orbis Books.

2001   *Dialogues with Silence*. San Francisco: HarperSanFrancisco.

2003   *The Inner Experience*. San Francisco: HarperSanFrancisco.
Seeking Paradise: The Spirit of the Shakers. Maryknoll, N.Y.: Orbis Books.

2004   *Peace in a Post-Christian Era*. Maryknoll, N.Y.: Orbis Books.

2005   *Cassian and the Fathers*. Trappist, Ky.: Abbey of Gethsemani.

Rice Publications

1942   *General Douglas MacArthur.*

1946   *Come Out Fighting*. New York: Duell, Sloan and Pearce.

1947   *Cats, Cats, & Cats.*

1949   *Murder, Inc.*

1961   *The Church: A Pictorial History*. New York: Farrar, Straus & Cudahy.

1963   *A Young People's Pictorial History of the Church*. 3 vols. New York: Farrar, Straus & Company.

1970   *The Prophetic Generation*. Rensselaerville, N.Y.: Catholic Art Association.
The Man in the Sycamore Tree. New York: Doubleday.

1971   *Mother India's Children*. New York: Pantheon.

1973   *Temple of the Phallic King*. Edited by Edward Rice. New York: Simon & Schuster.
The Five Great Religions. New York: Four Winds Press.

1974   *John Frum He Come*. Garden City, N.Y.: Doubleday.
The Ganges: A Personal Encounter. New York: Four Winds Press.
Journey to Upolu: Robert Louis Stevenson, Victorian Rebel. New York: Dodd, Mead.

1977   *Marx, Engels and the Workers of the World*. New York: Four Winds Press.

1978   *Eastern Definitions*. Garden City, N.Y.: Doubleday.

1979   *Babylon, Next to Nineveh: Where the World Began*. New York: Four Winds Press.
Margaret Mead: A Portrait. New York: Harper & Row.

1982   *American Saints & Seers*. New York: Four Winds Press 1982.

1990   *Captain Sir Richard Francis Burton*. New York: Scribner's, 1990.
Cities of the Sacred Unicorn. Simon & Schuster. (In progress at the time of Rice's death in 2001. He described it as "An account of the largest

and most enigmatic of the 'lost' civilizations of the past, the 5,000-year-old cities of the Indus Valley in Pakistan.") The manuscript is in the possession of Chris Rice.

Publications about Lax

1996 *Love Had a Compass.* Edited by James Uebbing. New York: Grove.
1999 *ABC's of Robert Lax.* Various Contributors. Exeter: Stride.
2002 *The Way of the Dreamcatcher,* by S. T. Georgiou. Ottawa: Novalis.

Publications about Merton

1970 *The Man in the Sycamore Tree,* by Edward Rice. New York: Doubleday.
1984 *Merton by Those Who Knew Him Best.* Edited by Paul Wilkes. San Francisco: Harper & Row.
       The Seven Mountains of Thomas Merton, by Michael Mott. Boston: Houghton Mifflin.

Publications by or about Lax and Merton Together

1978 *Catch of Anti-Letters: Thomas Merton and Robert Lax.* Mission, Ks.: Sheed Andrews & McMeel.
1996 *Hermits: The Insights of Solitude,* by Peter France. New York: St. Martin's Press.
2001 *When Prophecy Still Had a Voice: The Letters of Thomas Merton & Robert Lax.* Edited by Arthur W. Biddle. Lexington, Ky.: University Press of Kentucky.

Notes

Preface

1. What has become known as the Lax Box, actually titled *robert lax,* is a remarkable compendium in English and German of poems, photos, compact discs, lithographs, a videotape, exhibitions, readings, and a bibliography by Sigrid Hauff citing more than six hundred works by and about Lax, covering the period 1934 to 1999. Herbert Kapfer and Barbara Schäfer, eds. Munich: Bayerischer Rundfunk, 1999. ISBN 3-933510-29-5.

2. *Black/White Oratorio,* based on a poem by Robert Lax, composed by John Beer, was performed at the Bâtie Festival de Genève, Geneva, September 6–7, 1997.

3. Edward Rice, *The Man in the Sycamore Tree: The Good Times and Hard Life of Thomas Merton* (Garden City, N.Y.: Doubleday, 1970).

4. Edward Rice, *Sir Richard Francis Burton: The Secret Agent Who Made the Pilgrimage to Mecca, Discovered the Kama Sutra, and Brought the Arabian Nights to the West* (New York: Charles Scribner's Sons, 1990).

1: Seeds of Unorthodoxy

1. *SSM,* 178.
2. Murray Kempton, *Our Time: Some Ruins and Monuments of the Thirties* (New York: Simon & Schuster, 1955).
3. Merton, *Love and Living* (New York: Farrar, Straus & Giroux, 1955), 11.
4. Ibid., 13.
5. Jack Kelly, interview with Gladys Marcus, Olean, N.Y., 1986.
6. Ibid.
7. *SSM,* 17.
8. Ibid., 19.
9. Rice interview, October 30, 1996, Sagaponack, N.Y.
10. Phone interview with Carol Rice McCormick, December 12, 2001.
11. Interview with Robert Lax, May 17, 1997, Patmos.
12. *SSM,* 30.
13. January 25, 1940, *RTM,* 147.
14. *SSM,* 30.
15. Ibid., 33.
16. Ibid., 37.
17. Ibid., 58–59.

18. Ibid., 64.

19. Ibid., 73.

20. Ibid., 78.

21. Ibid., 81.

22. Interview with Dick Marcus, July 1997, Olean, N.Y.

23. Personal collection of Lax's high school classmate Rose Bialick Flynn, 1934.

24. *Newtown High School Yearbook*, 1935.

25. Interview with Lax, May 19, 1997, Patmos.

26. Interview with Rice, October 30, 1996, Sagaponack, N.Y.

27. Jennifer Harford interview with Rice, 1996, Sagaponack, N.Y.

28. *SSM*, l54.

29. *Columbian*, 1935.

30. *Jester* 38, no. 5 (1937–38).

31. Ibid.; Rice interview, October 30, 1996, Sagaponack, N.Y.

32. *Jester* 37, no. 2 (1936–37), campaign issue.

33. *Jester* (December 1938), front cover.

34. *Columbian*, 1938.

35. Ibid.; Rice interview, October 30, 1996.

36. *SSM*, 178–79.

37. Ibid., 179–81.

38. Ibid.; Rice interview, October 30, 1996.

39. Jacques Barzun, *From Dawn to Decadence: 500 Years of Cultural Life, 1500 to the Present* (New York: HarperCollins, 2000).

40. James J. Uebbing, *Love Had a Compass: Robert Lax Journals and Poetry* (New York: Grove Press, 1996).

41. Ibid.; Lax interview, May 19, 1997, Patmos.

42. Ibid.; Rice interview, October 30, 1996.

43. Longhand letter to Lax from Irwin Edman, undated, probably 1937 or 1938. Lax Columbia Archive (LCU).

44. Lax e-mail to Harford, September 23, 1999.

45. Merton journal, undated, MCU.

46. Lax, *Columbia Poetry 1938* (New York: Columbia University Press, 1938), 37–38.

47. Merton, *Columbia Poetry 1939* (New York: Columbia University Press, 1939), 60–61.

48. Aldous Huxley, *Ends and Means* (New York: Harper & Brothers, 1937), 1.

49. Ibid., 4.

50. Ibid., 5.

51. Ibid.

52. Lax memo, undated, LCU.

53. Merton memo, "Dr. M. B. Brahmachari: A Personal Tribute," October 1964, MCU.

54. Lax to Bramachari, May 8, 1993, LCU.

55. *SSM*, 140.

56. Interview with Soni Holman, New York, December 16, 1996.

57. Merton to Lax, June 17, 1938, Biddle, 3; MCU.

58. Merton to Lax, June 29, 1938, Biddle, 5.

59. Merton to Lax, July 29, 1938, Biddle, 7.

60. Lax to Merton, probably August 1938, Biddle, 9.

61. Ibid., 10.

62. Merton to Lax, August 11, 1938, Biddle, 11
63. Mott to Lax, March 24, 1982, LSBA.
64. Merton to Lax, August 11, 1938, Biddle, 12.
65. Ibid., August 1938, 13. "N. Flagg" is Nancy Flagg, who was more or less Lax's girlfriend, although she later married Columbia friend Bob Gibney and they moved to the Virgin Islands, where Lax and Reinhardt visited them.
66. Lax interview, *MBTWKHB,* 68.
67. *RTM,* 455.

2: Spiritual Hippies

1. Rice interview, October 30, 1996, Sagaponack, N.Y.
2. Stephen Lewis, *Hotel Kid* (Philadelphia: Paul Dry Books, 2002), 119.
3. Lax to Merton, April 14, 1939, Biddle, 17.
4. *SSM,* 237.
5. Walsh became a secular priest in the diocese of Louisville and is buried in the Gethsemani cemetery.
6. Merton to Lax, April 1939, Biddle, 17–18.
7. *SSM,* 237–38.
8. *SSM,* 238.
9. Ibid.; Rice interview, October 30, 1996. Zorina was a Hollywood starlet. The manuscript might have been sent to Lax years later when he was a screenwriter, but it was never produced and the manuscript has disappeared.
10. Ibid.
11. *SSM,* 240.
12. Conversation with Lax, Lausanne, Switzerland, October 14, 1984.
13. Jim Knight interview, October 30, 1996, Sagaponack, N.Y.
14. Nancy Flagg, "The Beats in the Jungle," *Art International* (September 1977): 56–59.
15. Ibid.; Rice intervew, October 30, 1996.
16. Ibid.; Knight interview, October 30, 1996.
17. Dick Marcus interview, July 9, 1997, Olean, N.Y.
18. Merton to Lax, July 14, 1939, Biddle, 19.
19. Merton to Lax, probably later in July 1939, Biddle, 21.
20. Valerie Larbaud (1881–1957) was a French anglophile who translated Joyce, among others, and who helped support the founding of Sylvia Beach's *Shakespeare and Company* in Paris. He also wrote poetry and some innovative prose, including the novel *Fermina Marquez.*
21. Merton to Lax, August 21, 1939, Biddle, 22. The movie starred Lawrence Olivier, Ralph Richardson, and Valerie Hobson. Weak in both action and romance, it is available as a digitally remastered video.
22. Lax to Merton, probably September 1939, Biddle, 24.
23. Merton to Lax, probably September 1939, Biddle, 25–26.
24. September 8, 1939, *RTM,* 20.
25. October 19, 1939, *RTM,* 61.
26. Ibid.; Rice interview, October 30, 1996.
27. Ibid.
28. Interview with Wm. Theodore deBary, February 14, 2003, Columbia University. DeBary is one of the few people still alive who was a friend and classmate of

Lax, Merton, and Rice at Columbia (Jim Knight is another). While recognizing their talents on *Jester* and *Jubilee,* and in later life, he regards their "early hippy" lifestyle at Columbia as unserious and "their pacifism [as] a vague abstraction"—while he and others were marching in antiwar parades, debating national issues (he was president of student government as a junior). DeBary is former provost of Columbia, longtime head of the Asian American Studies department, and still carries a substantial teaching load in his eighties.

29. Merton to Lax, October 17, 1939, Biddle, 29.

30. *RTM*, 129.

31. January 5, 1940, *RTM*, 130.

32. March 27, 1940, *RTM*, 158.

33. October 29, 1939, *RTM*, 72.

34. Merton to Lax, December 3, 1939, MCU.

35. *SSM*, 236.

36. Ibid., 236–37.

37. Merton to Lax, February 4, 1940, MCU.

38. November 20, 1939, *RTM*, 91. There is no evidence of a Lax autobiography in his archives.

39. Dorothy Baker (1907–68) was a writer and dramatist whose first novel, *Young Man with a Horn* (1938), supposedly the life of Bix Beiderbecke, became a popular movie.

40. December 14, 1939, *RTM*, 103. It's doubtful if Merton ever wrote to Saroyan, although he might have. Paul Pearson of the Thomas Merton Center says he did not keep all of his correspondence before 1962, and Brother Patrick Hart, who was Merton's secretary, says he threw away a lot of material prior to that date.

41. Merton to Lax, April 1940, *RTJ*, 155–56.

42. Merton to Lax, April 1940, Biddle, 52–53.

43. January 13, 1940, *RTM*, 33.

44. Rice journal, March 7, 1940, RGA.

45. Ibid.

46. Ibid.

47. Ibid.

48. Ibid.

49. Paul Wilkes interview with Lax, *MBTWKHB*, 67.

50. Lax, *New Yorker* (May 4, 1940): 28.

51. Lax, *New Yorker* (June 15, 1940): 21.

52. Lax to Merton, undated, LCU.

53. Merton to Lax, January 25, 1941, *RTM*, 480.

54. Lax, *New Yorker* (July 6, 1940): 18.

55. Merton to Lax, July 24, 1940, Biddle, 54

56. Mott, 162. This incident, writes Mott, was recorded in a January 30, 1965 entry in Merton's *Restricted Journal.*

57. Merton to Lax, December 17, 1940.

3: The War, the Monk, the Manhattanites

1. Rice interview, October 31, 1996, Sagaponack, N.Y. In spite of the defect—in later years he was diagnosed as legally blind—Rice became an excellent photographer.

His photos of Merton and of his travels to India, Africa, and elsewhere are of museum quality.

2. Merton to Lax, March 13, 1941, *RTJ*, 158.

3. *SSM*, 311–12.

4. In a *Catholic Worker* remembrance of Lax in January, 2001, 7, Tom Cornell wrote that he had been trying, in the 1950s, to get the Selective Service System to make him a conscientious objector by reason of his Catholic convictions. He didn't want to go to jail, and he wanted to fill out the application well so other Catholics would find it easier to be COs. He asked Lax for counsel. "He [Lax] had sought conscientious objector status as a Jew, arguing his claim from the Torah rule that fruit trees must be spared," and, says Cornell, "He had no heart for battle. . . . He sat there, and all he could say was he didn't know if he would do the same all over again, but again . . . he wasn't going to make my mind up for me, and he wasn't going to make believe the question was any less difficult than it is."

5. Lax to Merton, April 2, 1941, LCU.

6. Lax interview, May 1997, Patmos.

7. Lax journal, January 6, 1941, LCU.

8. Lax, "The Man with the Big General Notions," *New Yorker* (October 10, 1942): 18.

9. Lax to Merton, probably early 1941, LCU.

10. Lax journal, early 1941, LCU.

11. Lax interview, May 20, 1997, Patmos.

12. Lax to Merton, probably early 1941, LCU.

13. Lax interview, May 20, 1997, Patmos.

14. Lax to Merton, perhaps July 1941, Biddle, 79.

15. Lax to Merton, undated, LCU.

16. Ibid.

17. January 25, 1941, *RTM*, 480.

18. Lax journal, undated, LSBA.

19. Lax interview, May 20, 1997, Patmos.

20. Merton to Rice, February 24, 1941, MCU.

21. February 22, 1941, *RTM*, 313.

22. Lax to Merton, undated, LCU.

23. March 18, 1941, *RTM*, 323. It's not known what happened to the poem.

24. Merton to Lax, March 1941, Biddle, 71.

25. *RTM* 333.

26. Merton to Lax, April 5, 1941, Biddle, 72–73.

27. Merton journal, possibly April 1941, MCU.

28. Lax interview, May 27, 1997, Patmos.

29. Ibid.

30. Ibid. "Was the poet Langston Hughes?" he was asked. He couldn't remember.

31. Ibid.

32. Ibid.

33. Ibid.

34. Merton to Lax, Rice, and others, September 9, 1941, MCU.

35. *SSM*, 362–63.

36. *RTM*, 465–66.

37. *SSM*, 366.

38. *SSM*, 368.

39. Merton to Lax, December 6, 1941, Biddle, 84.

40. *SSM*, 377.

41. Jack Kelly interview with Gladys Marcus, 1986, Olean, N.Y.

42. Lax interview, May 1997, Patmos.

43. Merton to Lax, November 21, 1942, *RTJ*, 164–65.

44. Ibid., 167.

45. Lax to Merton, early 1942, Biddle, 93.

46. Lax interview, May 1997, Patmos.

47. Soni Holman interview, December 16, 1996, New York.

48. Ibid., Lax, May 1997, Patmos interview.

49. Ibid.

50. Lax journal, LSBA.

51. *SSM*, 408.

52. Van Doren to James Laughlin, February 26, 1944, SLMVD, 167.

53. Merton, *30 Poems* (New York: New Directions, 1944).

4: Literary Triumphs

1. The same document specified that his other securities be divided by his brother John Paul's widow, Margaret M. Merton, 61 Camden St., Birkenhead, Cheshire, England, and his guardian, T. Izod Bennett, M.D. Esq., "to be paid by him to a person mentioned to him by me in my letters"—the mother of his illegitimate child—"if that person can be found." She never was found. Bennett's address was given as 29 Hill St., Berkeley Square, London W1.

2. SLML, xviii.

3. Merton, "An Argument: Of the Passion of Christ," in *30 Poems: Poets of the Year Series* (New York: New Directions, 1944). Merton, at twenty-nine, was in quite distinguished company. Others in the series that year included Herman Melville, Conrad Aiken, Rafael Alberti, and Richard Eberhart.

4. Van Doren to Laughlin, March 10, 1944, SLMVD, 168.

5. *SSM*, 4

6. Merton to Lax, Easter 1945, *RTJ*, 168

7. Lax, *New Yorker* (September 29, 1945): 55

8. Note addressed by Lowell on December 12, 1944, to Lax at 315 E. Franklin St., Chapel Hill, N.C., LCU.

9. Lax journal, January 5, 1945, LCU.

10. Jennifer Harford interview with Rice, April 1998, Sagaponack, N.Y.

11. Ibid.

12. Lax interview, May 21, 1997, Patmos.

13. Ibid.

14. Eliot letter to Harford, 1997.

15. Lax interview, Patmos, May 21, 1997.

16. Lax, *Journal E Hollywood journal,* July 13, 1947 (Zurich: Pendo, 1996) 34.

17. Lax interview, May 1997, Patmos.

18. Lax to Merton, April 7, 1947, LCU

19. Merton to Lax, April 13, 1947, Biddle, 102.

20. *All Movie Guide,* Internet.

21. Lax to Merton, November 29, 1947, Biddle, 103–4.

22. Lax interview, May 21, 1997, Patmos.

23. Lax, *New Yorker* (March 16, 1946): 32. Between 1940 and 1954 Lax had twelve poems published in that magazine. Merton had two.

24. April 23, 1947, *SOJ*, 41.

25. March 1, 1947, *SOJ*, 27.

26. March 20, 1947, *SOJ*, 32.

27. April 25, 1947, *SOJ*, 43.

28. Thomas Merton, *Figures for an Apocalypse* (New York: New Directions 1947).

29. Ibid., 16–18.

30. Ibid., 33.

31. Van Doren to Merton, March 14, 1948, SLMVD, 183.

32. Merton, *FFA,* 111.

33. Van Doren to Merton, July 7, 1946, SLMVD, 180–81. "Duns Scotus" is in *Figures for an Apocalypse,* 48

34. *FFA,* 48.

35. Laughlin to Merton, SLML, 44.

36. October 17, 1948, *SOJ*, 131–32.

37. Rice journal, March 27, 1949, RGA.

38. Merton to Lax, November 24, 1948, *RTJ,* 170–71.

39. Merton to Lentfoehr, January 18, 1949, *RTJ,* 190.

40. Merton to Lentfoehr, April 26, 1949, *RTJ,* 191.

41. May 29, 1949, *SOJ,* 193–95.

42. Rice journal, 1949, RGA.

43. Merton to Lentfoehr, October 3, 1949, MCU.

44. Lax e-mail, September 11, 1999.

45. Phone conversation with Mogador, September 2, 1999.

46. Van Doren, *Autobiography of Mark Van Doren* (New York: Harcourt Brace, 1958), 300–301.

47. Lax interview, May 1997, Patmos.

48. Lax, *Circus of the Sun* (New York: Journeyman Books, 1959).

49. Lax interview, May 20, 1997, Patmos.

50. Lax journal, LCU.

51. Nancy Flagg, "Reinhardt Revisiting," *Art International* 22, no. 2 (1978): 54–57.

52. Nancy Flagg, *Lugano Review* (1972): 56–59.

53. Ibid.

54. Ibid.

55. Ibid.

56. Lax interview, May 20, 1997, Patmos.

57. Lax to Merton, October 1949, Biddle, 108.

58. Merton to Lax, November 27, 1949, Biddle, 110.

59. Rice journal, December 1, 1949, RGA.

60. Ibid.

61. Evelyn Waugh to Merton, August 28, 1950, MCU.

62. Rice, *MIST,* 88.

63. Bamberger interview, November 18, 1999, Abbey of the Genesee, Genesee, N.Y.

64. Ernesto Cardenal interview, in *MBTWKHB*, 35.

65. Lax to Merton, probably early 1950, Biddle, 113.

66. Rice journal, May 22, 1950, RGA.

67. Rice to Lentfoehr, undated, RGA. Rice would eventually put Sister Thérèse Lentfoehr on his editorial advisory board and publish some of her poetry.

68. Rice to Merton, from 58 Bank St., New York, June 23, 1950, RGA. I did not find this letter until Rice had died, so I never had the chance to ask him who the potential Jewish backer was. I rather think that his help never materialized or I would surely have heard of him. And Rice never did get to see Cardinal Spellman.

69. Merton to Lentfoehr, July 31, 1950, *RTJ*, 203.

70. Merton to Lentfoehr, August 19, 1950, *RTJ*, 204.

71. Undated Rice journal entry, probably mid-1950, RGA.

72. Merton to Laughlin, January 7, 1950, SLML, 65.

73. October 3, 1950, SLML, 79.

74. Lax to Merton, April 23, 1950. On small card, Biddle, 11.

75. Lax to Merton, probably early 1950, Biddle, 113–14.

76. Lax to Lentfoehr, July 1, 1950, LCU.

77. January 18, 1950, *SOJ*, 269.

78. Lax to Merton, September 23, 1950, Biddle, 114–15.

79. *Journals Early Fifties Early Sixties Allen Ginsberg*, ed. Gordon Ball. July 11, 1954 entry (New York: Grove Press, 1977), 78–79.

80. Merton to Lentfoehr, September 30, 1950, MCU.

81. Merton to Lentfoehr, undated, MCU.

82. Merton to Lentfoehr, October 31, 1950, MCU.

83. James Uebbing, "The Poet Who Fell Off the Map," *Commonweal* (April 19, 1996): 13–17.

84. James Uebbing, *Love Had a Compass* (New York: Grove Press, 1996), xiii.

85. Merton to Lentfoehr, May 28, 1951, MCU.

86. Merton to Lentfoehr, July 13, 1951, *RTJ*, 208.

87. Lax interview, May 21, 1997, Patmos.

88. Rice to a "Mr. Desmond," May 25, 1951, RGA.

89. Rice, draft of letter to Mrs. Moncure Burke, February 16, 1952, RGA.

90. Merton to Laughlin, September 28, 1952, SLML, 95.

91. Robert Lax, *New Yorker* (May 30, 1953): 47.

5: *Jubilee*'s Heyday

1. Jim Forest, October 1999, talk to International Thomas Merton Society, Oxford, U.K.

2. "Learning Made Easy," *Jubilee* (September 1953): 46.

3. Rice interview, October 30, 1996, Sagaponack, N.Y.

4. Ibid.

5. Merton to Lentfoehr, September 11, 1950, MCU.

6. Merton, "Bernard of Clairvaux," *Jubilee* (August 1953): 33–37.

7. Merton to Lentfoehr, May 20, 1953, *RTJ*, 213.

8. Merton to Lentfoehr, July 26, 1953, MCU.

9. Michael Mott, *The Seven Mountains of Thomas Merton* (Boston: Houghton Mifflin, 1984), 306.

10. Telephone interview with Bishop Wcela, November 20, 1996.

11. Rice to Sullivan, November 12, 1956, RGA.

12. Interview with Moosbrugger, May 27, 1997, Patmos, Greece. The article was "Bishop of the Favelas," by Gladys Weigner, *Jubilee* (January 1957): 21–27.

13. Telephone interview with Lowe, April 9, 1999.

14. Rice, memo to *Jubilee* advisory board, April 14, 1958, RGA.

15. Rice interview, October 30, 1996, Sagaponack, N.Y.

16. Ibid.

17. Interview with Jillen Ahearn Lowe, April 13, 1999, Sag Harbor, N.Y.

18. Richard Gilman, *Faith, Sex, Mystery* (New York: Simon & Schuster, 1986), 62.

19. Ibid., 143.

20. Ibid., 144.

21. Ibid., 145.

22. Ibid., 147.

23. "Worcester: A New Diocese on the New England Scene," *Jubilee* (February 1956): 6–17.

24. James Forest, talk to International Thomas Merton Society, Oxford, U.K., October 1999.

25. Merton to John Harris, June 20, 1959, *HGL*, 390.

26. Rice interview, October 30, 1996.

27. Wilfrid Sheed interview, November 4, 1996, Bridgehampton, N.Y.

28. Wilfrid Sheed, *Frank & Maisie* (New York: Simon & Schuster, 1984), 269.

29. Wilfrid Sheed interview, November 4, 1996, Bridgehampton, N.Y.

30. Interview with Peter White, November 6, 1996, St James, N.Y.

31. Ibid. I reread recently my own answers to a questionnaire that I received from *Jubilee* in 1962 asking about my attitude toward the church's teachings on birth control. I didn't think there would be a change, and there hasn't been, alas.

32. Rice interview, October 30, 1996, Sagaponack, N.Y.

33. Interview with Harbutt, October 7, 1999, New York.

34. Ibid.

35. Mark Van Doren, *Autobiography of Mark Van Doren* (New York: Harcourt Brace, 1958), 344.

36. Merton to Lentfoehr, September 1, 1954, *RTJ*, 217.

37. Lax to Lentfoehr, September 8, 1954, LCU.

38. Lax to *Jubilee* staff and friends, 1959, Harford files.

39. Lax, *New Yorker* (August 28, 1954): 75.

40. Thomas Cornell, *Catholic Worker* (January–February 2001): 7.

41. Interview with Soni Holman, December 16, 1996, New York.

42. Alfred Isacsson, unpublished letter to *Commonweal,* May 2, 1996, Harford files.

43. Lax, *The Scapular* (July–August 1963).

44. *Jubilee* (August 1953): 1.

45. "Young Congressman," *Jubilee* (August 1953): 44.

46. Interview with Harbutt, October 7, 1999, New York.

47. Merton to Lentfoehr, February 12, 1959, *RTJ*, 232.

48. Merton, "Notes on Sacred and Profane Art," *Jubilee* (November 1956): 24–32.

49. Alexander Jones, "The World's Best Bible," *Jubilee* (October 1956): 41–43.

50. Merton to Lentfoehr, September 29, 1955, MCU.

51. Merton to Lentfoehr, September 25, 1956, *RTJ*, 225.

52. Merton to Lentfoehr, May 26, 1956, *RTJ*, 223–24.

53. Lax to Merton, April 23, 1958, LCU.

54. Lax, *Circus of the Sun* (New York: Journeyman Press, 1959).

55. Merton to Milosz, May 6, 1960; *The Courage for Truth* (New York: Farrar Straus & Giroux. 1993), 68.

56. Merton, *A Search for Solitude* (San Francisco: HarperSanFrancisco, 1997), 360–61 (December 20, 1959).

57. Lax to Merton, probably 1959, LCU.

58. Lax interview with William Packard. undated. *The ABC's of Robert Lax*, 15.

59. Merton, "Boris Pasternak and the People with Watch Chains," *Jubilee* (July 1959): 16–33.

6: Vatican II: Before and After

1. J. G. Porter, letter to the editor, *Jubilee* (January 1960): 4.

2. Lax interview, May 24, 1997, Patmos.

3. James Harford, "Pole in the Middle," *Jubilee* (February 1965): 45.

4. James Harford, "Rational Beings in Other Worlds," *Jubilee* (May 1962): 16.

5. Merton to Milosz, November 9, 1960, *Courage for Truth*, 70.

6. Merton to Father Kilian McDonnell, January 13, 1960, *Thomas Merton School of Charity Letters* (Fort Washington, Pa.: Harvest Books, 1993), 1–7.

7. O'Gorman interview, December 17, 1996, New York.

8. Ibid.

9. Ned O'Gorman, "The Freedom March," *Jubilee* (October 1963): 17–21.

10. O'Gorman, "Helping Rome Decline," *Jubilee* (September 1962): 48.

11. O'Gorman, "A Wit at His End," *Jubilee* (June 1962): 48.

12. O'Gorman interview, December 17, 1996, New York.

13. Merton letters to Laughlin, March 18 and April 20, 1960, SLML, 153.

14. Merton to Lax, May 12, 1960, MCU.

15. Merton to Lentfoehr, November 15, 1960, MCU.

16. Lax to Merton, May 1960, Biddle, 194.

17. Wilfrid Sheed and Shirley Feltmann, "The Funeral Business: A Report on the American Mortician and the High Cost of Dying," *Jubilee* (November 1960): 30–35.

18. Wilfrid Sheed, *Frank & Maisie: A Memoir with Parents* (New York: Simon & Schuster, 1985), 268.

19. Wilfrid Sheed and Shirley Feltmann, "The Barclay Street Image," *Jubilee* (May 1960): 28–33.

20. Lax to Merton, December 20, 1960, Biddle, 210.

21. "St. Louis Priory," *Jubilee* (January 1960): 8–15.

22. Peter White, "Pascal," *Jubilee* (January 1960): 18–23.

23. James Milord, "Report on the Dog Ribs," *Jubilee* (January 1960): 2–3.

24. Sylvester Theisen, "Protestants and Catholics in Germany," *Jubilee* (January 1960): 26–27.

25. Donald A. Lowrie, "Berdyaev," *Jubilee* (January 1960): 28–31.

26. Joseph Nettis, "Religion in Russia," *Jubilee* (January 1960): 34–39.

27. Merton to Lentfoehr, December 5, 1960, MCU.

28. Merton to Rice, December 12, 1960, RGA.

29. Van Doren to Merton, December 2, 1960, SLMVD, 230.

30. Merton, "Chinese Classic Thought," *Jubilee* (January 1961): 26–31.

31. Merton to Lax, August 22, 1960, Biddle, 206.

32. Merton to Laughlin, March 3, 1961, SLML, 166.

33. April 5, 1961, SLML, 168–69.

34. July 1, 1961, SLML, 170.

35. Merton to Lax, August 22, 1960, Biddle, 206–7.

36. Merton to Laughlin, November 25, 1961, SLML, 187.

37. Rev. H. A. Reinhold, "Liturgy and Church Architecture," *Jubilee* (February 1962): 17–19.

38. Oona Sullivan, "The Addict's Fix," *Jubilee* (September 1962): 8–21.

39. Frank Monaco, "England's Latter Day Romans," *Jubilee* (August 1962): 12–19.

40. Frank Monaco, "Oxford Catholics," *Jubilee* (April 1963): 32–39.

41. Ruth A. Wallace, "Where Were the Women?" a paper given at *Present at the Creation: A Vatican II Reunion*, sponsored by the Association of the Rights of Catholics in the Church (Milwaukee, November 3, 2000).

42. Ned O'Gorman, "Opening the Council," *Jubilee* (December 1962): 10–13.

43. Merton to Rice, September 10, 1962, RGA.

44. Oona Sullivan, "Behind the Council," *Jubilee* (October 1962): 7–8.

45. Peter White, "The Golden Ring," *Jubilee* (December 1962): 42–44.

46. Bernard C. Pawley, "Vatican Observer," *Jubilee* (March 1963): 17.

47. "A Theologian to Be Thankful For," *Jubilee* (April 1963): 23.

48. Nicholas E. Persich, "Inside the Council," *Jubilee* (April 1963): 12–21.

49. Xavier Rynne, *Vatican Council II* (Maryknoll, N.Y.: Orbis Books, 1999).

50. Idem., "The Church, the Curia and the Council," *Jubilee* (June 1963): 36–40.

51. Merton, "A Martyr to the Nazis: The Prison Journals of Father Alfred Delp SJ," *Jubilee* (March 1963): 32–37.

52. Ibid.

53. Merton, "The General Dance," *Jubilee* (December 1961): 8–11.

54. Merton, "Religion and the Bomb," *Jubilee* (May 1962): 7–13.

55. Oona Sullivan, "Joyous Mystics," *Jubilee* (November 1962): 19–33.

56. Leon Paul, letter to the editor, *Jubilee* (January 1963): 6.

57. James Kritzeck, "The Koran," *Jubilee* (January 1963): 22–27.

58. Dom Ludovic Baron, O.S.B., "Gregorian Chant," *Jubilee* (November 1959): 27–29.

59. Ethel Thurston, letter to the editor, *Jubilee* (January 1963): 6.

60. George A. John Porthan, letter to the editor, *Jubilee* (March 1963): 5–6.

61. Beverley D. Tucker, letter to the editor, *Jubilee* (March 1963): 6.

62. Ethel Thurston, letter to the editor, *Jubilee* (May 1963): 5.

63. *SSM*, 401.

64. "The Ikon Guild," *Jubilee* (June 1962): inside front cover.

65. "The Ikon Guild," *Jubilee* (May 1963): inside back cover.

66. Rynne, *Vatican Council II*, 138.

67. Edgar Alexander, "A Final Testament," *Jubilee* (July 1963): 2–4.

68. Joseph Lichten, "Pope John and the Jews," *Jubilee* (August 1963): 4–6.

69. John Rock, M.D., "The Time Has Come" (New York: Alfred Knopf, 1963).

70. Wilfrid Sheed, "Catholics and 'The Pill,'" *Jubilee* (July 1963): 41.

71. Rosemary Radford Ruether, "Marriage, Love, Children," *Jubilee* (December 1963): 16–20.

72. Rev. Vincent M. Walsh, letter to the editor, *Jubilee* (March 1964): 4–5.

73. William Melvin Kelley, *A Different Drummer* (New York: Doubleday, 1963).

74. Merton, "The Negro Revolt," *Jubilee* (September 1963): 39–43.

75. O'Gorman, "The South," *Jubilee* (March 1964): 16–23.

76. Merton, "The Shakers," *Jubilee* (January 1964): 36–41.

77. Lax to Merton, May 1, 1964, Biddle, 273.

78. Merton to Lax, May 8, 1964, Biddle, 274.

79. *Jubilee* (October 1963): back cover.

80. Robert Hoyt, "Kennedy, Catholicism and the Presidency," *Jubilee* (December 1960): 12–15.

81. *Jubilee* (March 1964): 1.

82. Van Doren to Merton, July 28, 1963, SLMVD, 240.

83. March 17, 1964, SLMVD, 244.

84. "Women in White," *Jubilee* (April 1964): 28–35.

85. Anne Fremantle, "Comment: Latin and the Mass: A Defense of Tradition," *Jubilee* (May 1964): 26.

86. "Marriage, Love, Children II," *Jubilee* (June 1964): 17–32.

87. *The Intimate Merton*, ed. Patrick Hart and Jonathan Montaldo (San Francisco: HarperSanFrancisco, 1995), 221 (journal entries for June 16 and June 20, 1964).

88. Merton, "Flannery O'Connor," *Jubilee* (November 1964): 49–53.

89. Charles E. Curran, "Christian Marriage and Family Planning," *Jubilee* (August 1964): 8–13.

90. "In this issue," *Jubilee* (February 1965): 1.

91. Merton, "Gandhi and the One-Eyed Giant," *Jubilee* (January 1965): 12–17.

92. Karl Rahner, "The Pope and the Bishops," *Jubilee* (February 1965): 16–23.

93. O'Gorman interview, December 17, 1996, New York.

94. Paul Doucet and Denis O'Brien, "Report from Canada: The Revolution in Quebec," *Jubilee* (February 1965): 2–6.

95. Merton to Laughlin, SLML, 263 (February 25, March 19, May 13, 1965). *A Catch of Anti-Letters* was published by Sheed Andrews & McMeel, New York, 1978.

96. Merton to Lax, April 28, 1965, Biddle, 301.

97. Lax to Merton, August 1965, Biddle, 310.

98. Van Doren to Merton, October 8, 1965, SLMVD, 249.

99. Lax, "Sea & Sky," *Lugano Review* (September 1965).

100. Merton to Laughlin, January 4, 1966, SLML, 272.

101. The proceeds from the sales, says Brother Patrick Hart, went toward a college scholarship for a young black girl.

102. January 8, 1966, *LTL,* 5.

103. Merton to Lax, January 28, 1966, Biddle, 320.

104. Merton to Rice, January 27, 1966, RGA.

105. Ibid., February 4, 1966, RGA.

106. Ibid.

7: Romances, Deaths

1. Paul Hendrickson, *Washington Post*, December 27, 1998, F4.

2. April 28, 1966, *LTL,* 48.

3. Rice to Merton, March 1966, RGA.

4. Merton to Laughlin, SLML, 278.

5. Van Doren to Merton, SLMVD, 250–51.

6. Van Doren to Merton, February 16, 1966, SLMVD, 250. Parts of the 1976 journal were eventually published as *Journal F, Kalymnos Journal*, ed. John Beer (Zurich: Pendo-Verlag, 1997). A large segment covering 1964 to 1970 is in *Love Had a Compass: Robert Lax Journals and Poetry*, ed. James J. Uebbing (New York: Grove Press, 1996), 198–252.

7. Van Doren to Berryman, September 20, 1967, SLMVD, 254.

8. Merton to Lax, March 17, 1966, Biddle, 327–28.

9. Merton to Laughlin, March 19, 1966, SLML, 277.

10. Lax, "The Kalymnos Journals," *New Directions Annual* 31 (1975): 74–80.

11. Ibid.

12. Ibid.

13. Merton to Henry Miller, May 12, 1963 (*The Courage for Truth: Thomas Merton Letters to Writers*, selected and edited by Christine M. Bochen [New York: Farrar Straus & Giroux, 1993], 279).

14. Merton to Lax, April 7, 1966, Biddle, 330.

15. Envelope in folder of letters of Sister Thérèse Lentfoehr, September 13, 1966, MCU.

16. May 20, 1966, *LTL*, 66.

17. Merton to Lentfoehr, June 7, 1966, *RTJ*, 256. The O'Gorman book is *Prophetic Voices* (New York: Random House, 1969).

18. Bamberger, in *MBTWKHB*, 120–21.

19. Interview with Bamberger, November 18, 1999, Abbey of the Genesee.

20. Joan Baez, in *MBTWKHB*, 45.

21. Merton to Lentfoehr, July 31, 1966, MCU.

22. *CGB*, 5.

23. *LTL*, 129–30.

24. Merton to Ruether, September 21, 1966 (*Thomas Merton: The Hidden Ground of Love*, selected and edited by William H. Shannon [New York: Farrar Straus & Giroux, 1985], 499).

25. Interview with Bamberger, November 18, 1999.

26. Ibid., March 9, 1967, 502.

27. Ruether to Merton, March 1967 (*At Home in the World: The Letters of Thomas Merton and Rosemary Radford Ruether* [Maryknoll, N.Y.: Orbis Books, 1995], 28–29).

28. Ibid., xvi.

29. Bamberger, in *MBTWKHB*, 121.

30. Merton to Lax, July 21, 1963, Biddle, 247.

31. Jennifer Harford interview with Rice, 1996.

32. *SSM*, 183.

33. Merton to Lentfoehr, June 5, 1967, MCU.

34. Merton to Lax, September 5, 1967, Biddle, 368–69, MCU.

35. Lax to Merton, September 8, 1967, Biddle, 369.

36. Merton, September 14, 1967, *LTL*, 291.

37. Merton to Lentfoehr, September 5, 1967, *RTJ*, 258.

38. Mary Ellen Slate to Merton, October 1967, Merton Bellarmine Archive (MBA).

39. John Slate to Merton, April 29, 1967, MBA.

40. Lax conversation, October 14, 1984, Lausanne, Switzerland.

41. *OSM*, 44–45.

42. Lax to Merton, November 3, 1966, Biddle, 345.

43. Lax, unpublished poem, box 23, LCU.

44. Merton to Rice, January 30, 1967, RGA.

45. Telephone interview with Monaco, September 20, 2001.

46. Interview with Bamberger, November 18, 1999, Abbey of the Genesee.

47. Notes from memo by Father Comber to the staff of *Catholic World*, April 28, 1967, RGA.

48. Jennifer Harford interview with Rice, November 9, 1996, Sagaponack, N.Y.

49. Merton, "The Death of a Holy Terror," *Jubilee* (June 1967): 35–38.

50. Ibid.

51. Lawler to Rice, July 29, 1967, RGA.

52. Rice to Theophil Herder-Dorneich, August 1, 1967, RGA.

53. Sullivan handwritten notes to Harford, February 15, 2004.

54. Sullivan interview, December 3, 1996, New York.

55. "Editors of Jubilee" to subscribers, August 3, 1967.

56. Merton to Lentfoehr, June 5, 1967, MCU.

57. Rice interview, November 3, 1996, Sagaponack, N.Y.

58. "Journal of My Escape from the Nazis" was published as *My Argument with the Gestapo* (New York: Doubleday, 1969).

59. Merton to Lentfoehr, September 26, 1967, MCU.

60. Lax to Harford, August 25, 1967.

61. Interview with Bamberger, November 18, 1999, Abbey of the Genesee, Genesee, N.Y.

62. Merton to Lentfoehr, December 1967, MCU.

63. Merton to Lentfoehr, October 13, 1967, MCU.

64. Ibid., November 16, 1967, *RTJ*, 260.

65. Ibid., September 5, 1967, *RTJ*, 259.

66. *OSM*, 28 (December 22, 1967).

67. Merton to Lentfoehr, January 1968, MCU.

8: Odysseys

1. Merton, *The Ascent to Truth* (New York: Harcourt Brace, 1951), 3.

2. Ibid., 130.

3. Merton to Rice, March 31, 1960, RGA.

4. Merton, "Classic Chinese Thought," *Jubilee* (January 1961): 26–32.

5. *Mystics and Zen Masters* (New York: Farrar, Straus & Giroux, 1967).

6. R. C. Zaehner, "The Idea of God in Hinduism," *Jubilee* (May 1963): 37–40.

7. *MZM*, viii.

8. Heinrich Dumoulin, *A History of Zen Buddhism* (New York: Pantheon Books, 1963).

9. *MZM*, 7.

10. Ibid.; Dumoulin, *History of Zen Buddhism*, 4–5.

11. Paul Tillich, "A Christian-Buddhist Conversation," *Jubilee* (March 1963): 43–46.

12. "In This Issue," *Jubilee* (May 1963): 1.

13. Bede Griffiths, "Report from India," *Jubilee* (May 1963): 2–3.

14. Zaehner, "Idea of God in Hinduism," 37–40. Zaehner would be liberally cited by Merton in his *Mystics and Zen Masters*.

15. Merton to Rice, January 30, 1967, RGA.

16. References are all from "Thomas Merton on Zen," in Merton, *Thoughts on the East* (New York: New Directions, 1995), 30–42.

17. Ibid., 28.

18. Wilfrid Sheed, "The Beat Movement Concluded," *New York Times Book Review*, February 13, 2001, 2.

19. Interview with Bamberger, November 18, 1999, Abbey of the Genesee.

20. Aldous Huxley, *Ends and Means* (New York: Harper & Brothers, 1937), 347.

21. Merton to Huxley, November 27, 1958, *HGL,* 437, 439.

22. Huxley to Merton, January 1, 1959, MCU.

23. Anthony Padovano, *The Human Journey* (New York: Doubleday, 1982), 35.

24. Lax to Merton, October 21, 1965, Biddle, 312.

25. Interview with Forest, November 9, 1999, Red Bank, N.J.

26. Merton to Ruether, March 9, 1967, *HGL,* 502–3.

27. Ibid.; Bamberger interview, November 18, 1999.

28. December 12, 1967, *OSM*, 24.

29. December 15, 1967, *OSM*, 25.

30. December 23, 1967, *OSM*, 29.

31. December 24, 1967, *OSM*, 30.

32. December 2, 1967, *OSM*, 20–21.

33. December 7, 1967, *OSM*, 21.

34. December 9, 1967, *OSM*, 21–22.

35. Merton to Rice, undated, RGA.

36. Dresselhuys letter to various people, undated, RGA.

37. Rice, *Mother India's Children* (New York: Pantheon, 1971).

38. Pagal Baba, *Temple of the Phallic King, The Mind of India: Yogis, Swamis, Sufis and Avataras,* ed. Edward Rice (New York: Simon & Schuster, 1973).

39. Merton to Lax, January 26, 1967, Biddle, 110.

40. Merton to Ruether, February 14, 1967, *HGL,* 501.

41. March 25, 1967, *HGL,* 510.

42. May 27, 1967, *LTL,* 23.

43. January 11, 1968, *OSM*, 39.

44. January 15, 1968, *OSM*, 41.

45. February 12, 1968, *OSM*, 55.

46. *ZBA.* Merton never saw the book before he died.

47. Merton, *Cables to the Ace* (New York: New Directions, 1967).

48. Lax to Merton, March 21, 1968, Biddle, 388.

49. Lax to Rice, July 23, 1984, RGA.

50. Merton, *Monks Pond* (Louisville: University Press of Kentucky, 1968).

51. Merton to Jonathan Williams, December 13, 1967 (*The Courage for Truth: Thomas Merton Letters to Writers,* selected and edited by Christine Bochen (New York: Farrar, Straus & Giroux, 1993), 288.

52. Merton to Lax, December 13, 1967, Biddle, 377.

53. Lax to Merton, December 1967, Biddle, 378.

54. Merton to Lentfoehr, August 20, 1968, MCU.

55. Sister Thérèse Lentfoehr, "You Sing from Islands," *Monks Pond* (Louisville: University Press of Kentucky), 309.

56. Lax to Merton, April 4, 1968, LCU.

57. Laughlin to Merton, July 25, 1968, SLML, 350.

58. Merton, *The Geography of Lograire* (New York: New Directions, 1969), 127.

59. Rice to Phoebe Larmore, probably 1973 or 1974, RGA.

60. Mott, xxiv.

61. Ibid., 640.

62. Ibid.; Merton, *The Geography of Lograire* (New York: New Directions, 1969), 127.

63. Lax to Merton, June 17, 1968, Biddle, 402.

64. Mott to Lax, April 24, 1982, LCU.

65. Lax to Merton, May 9, 1968, Biddle, 397.

66. Lax to Antonucci, May 17, 1968, LCU.

67. Merton to Lax, May 14, 1968, Biddle, 398.

68. Merton to Lax, probably end of May 1968, Biddle, 401.

69. William Claire, *Voyages* (Winter–Spring 1968): 4–5.

70. Levertov, *Voyages* (Spring 1968): 93–94.

71. Lax to Antonucci, probably April 1968, LCU.

72. Lax to William Claire, May 7, 1968, LCU.

73. June 13, 1968, *OSM*, 128–29.

74. June 15, 1968, *OSM*, 130.

75. Merton to Van Doren, April 12, 1968, *RTJ*, 54.

76. Ibid.

77. August 20, 1968, *OSM*, 157.

78. Lax to Merton, August 12, 1968, Biddle, 410.

79. Ibid.

80. Merton and Lax, *A Catch of Anti-Letters* (New York: Sheed, Andrews & McMeel, 1978).

81. Merton to Laughlin, March 10, 1968, SLML, 339.

82. Merton to Lax, August 22, 1968, Biddle, 412.

83. Merton to Lax, September 4, 1968, Biddle, 413–14.

84. Lax to Merton, September 7, 1968, Biddle, 415.

85. Merton to Lax, September 6, 1968, Biddle, 414–15.

86. Merton, September 6, 1968, *OSM*, 165.

87. *MIST*, 120.

88. September 7, 1968, *OSM*, 165.

89. September 18, 1968, *OSM*, 187.

90. September 22, 1968, *OSM*, 189.

91. Cassette of *Thomas Merton in California*, given to author by Lax.

92. October 15, 1968, *OSM*, 4–5.

93. October 19, 1968, *AJ*, 28.

94. Merton to Lax, October 21, 1968, Biddle, 416.

95. Merton to Lax, probably around October 23 or 24, 1968, from Calcutta, Biddle, 416–18.

96. *Bulletin of Temple of Understanding* (February 1969), 1826 R St NW, Washington, DC 20009.

97. *AJ*, 306, 308, from notes prepared for delivery, October 1968, in Calcutta.

98. Lax to Antonucci, November 12, 1968, LSBA.

99. Ibid., December 2, 1968.

100. Lax to Merton, December 5, 1968, Biddle, 419.

101. Lax to Merton, December 8, 1968, Biddle, 420.

102. November 12, 1968, *AJ*, 131.

103. *AJ*, 133.

104. November 13, 1968, *AJ*, 135.

105. November 14, 1968, *AJ*, 138

106. *The Autobiography of the Dalai Lama* (New York: Harper Perennial, 1991), 189–90.

107. *AJ*, 144.

108. December 4, 1968, *AJ*, 236.

109. November 29, 1968, *OSM*, 308.

110. November 22, 1968, *OSM*, 298.

111. November 28, 1968, *AJ*, 199.

112. November 22, 1968, *OSM*, 293.
113. Wire from Van Doren to Lax, December 10, 1968, SLMVD, 259.
114. Patrick Hart, postscript, *AJ*, 259.
115. Rice to Lentfoehr, October 22, 1969, RGA.
116. Van Doren to Lax, December 30, 1968, SLMVD, 260.
117. Van Doren, *America* (January 4, 1969): 22.
118. Lax to Lentfoehr, December 22, 1969, MCU.

9: Laurels

1. *Merton Concelebration*, ed. Deba Patnaik (Notre Dame, Ind.: Ave Maria Press, 1981), 37–40.
2. Lax to Antonucci, January 21, 1969, LSBA.
3. Lax to Antonucci, March 18, 1969. LSBA.
4. Lax to Antonucci, undated 1969 letter, LSBA.
5. Fitzsmimmons to Lax, June 18, 1969, LSBA.
6. Lax to Antonucci, August 3, 1969, LSBA.
7. Guggenheim application, around 1969, LSBA.
8. Comment by Kenedy accompanying Lax Guggenheim application, LSBA.
9. Ibid.; Guggenheim application, LSBA.
10. Lax, *Lugano Review* 1, nos. 3–4 (September 1965). Reprinted in Lax's *33 Poems*, ed. Thomas Kellein (Stuttgart: Edition Hansjorg Mayer, 1987); *Sea & Sky* takes up only sixty-two pages, 74–135.
11. Ibid.
12. Lax to Antonucci, August 31, 1969, LSBA.
13. Lax to Antonucci; Guggenheim application, LSBA.
14. Lax to Antonucci, June 7, 1971, LSBA.
15. Lax to Antonucci, October 10, 1969, LSBA.
16. Ibid.
17. Ibid., January 2, 1970.
18. Ibid., February 20, 1970.
19. Lax, *33 Poems* (New York: New Directions, 1987), 59.
20. Ibid.
21. Lax to Antonucci, June 11, 1970, LSBA. *ZBA*.
22. *ZBA*, 124.
23. Lax to Antonucci, July 16, 1970, LSBA.
24. Lax, *Voyages* (Winter, Spring 1968): 35.
25. Lax, *Fables* (New York: Journeyman Press, 1970).
26. Lax to Antonucci, September 5, 1970, LSBA.
27. Ibid.
28. *AJ*.
29. Lax, From loose pages in his *JRNL SEPT 29–OCT 1 '73 KAL*. There are hundreds of pages in this journal, LCU.
30. Lawrence Cunningham, *Merton Seasonal* (Spring 2003): 28.
31. George Kilcourse, *America* (October 22, 1988).
32. *MIST*. Same title as a book that Merton started in 1940, but never finished. It comes from the Gospel of Luke, chapter 19. Zacchaeus, a rich tax collector, climbed a tree in order to see Jesus walking by. Jesus shocked the crowd by inviting himself

to stay in Zacchaeus's house. Zacchaeus then declared that he would give half of his property to the poor, thereby, said Jesus, assuring his salvation.

33. *MIST,* 139.

34. Rice interview, Sagaponack, N.Y., November 11, 1996.

35. *AJ,* 313.

36. *MIST,* 91.

37. Wing-Tsit Chan, *A Sourcebook in Chinese Philosophy* (Princeton, N.J.: Princeton University Press, 1963).

38. Ibid.

39. *MIST,* 91–92.

40. John Eudes Bamberger, *Cistercian Studies 5,* no. 3 (1970): 160.

41. Ibid., 155.

42. Bamberger interview, November 18, 1999, Abbey of the Genesee.

43. Ibid.

44. Ibid.

45. Bamberger, in preface to Henri Nouwen, *Thomas Merton Contemplative Critic* (New York: Harper & Row, 1981), viii.

46. Letter to Rice from John R. Guinn, University of Detroit, January 4, 1971, RGA.

47. Van Doren to Lax, January 12, 1971, SLMVD, 264.

48. Forest to Harford, e-mail, February 27, 2002.

49. Lax to Rice, May 8, 1971, LSBA.

50. Merton to Lentfoehr, May 27, 1949, MCU.

51. Knight, "The Merton I Knew," www.therealmerton.com.

52. Letter to Rice from Scott Wright, St. Paul, Minnesota, January 16, 1971, RGA.

53. Rice to Lentfoehr, January 16, 1969, RGA.

54. John Howard Griffin, *The Hermitage Journals* (Garden City, N.Y.: Image Books), 162–65.

55. Rice to Lentfoehr, October 22, 1969, RGA

56. Rice to friends, February 14, 1969, RGA.

57. Rice to Phoebe Larmore, June 18, 1972, RGA.

58. Manuscript in archive of Rice's son, Christopher Rice, Princeton, N.J.

59. Laughlin to Lax, July 2, 1969, LCU.

60. Lax, "The Kalymnos Journals," *New Directions in Prose and Poetry 31,* ed. J. Laughlin (1975): 76–77.

61. Van Doren to Lax, 1974, LCU.

62. William Maxwell to Lax, 1974, LCU.

63. R. C. Kenedy, "Robert Lax," in *The ABC's of Robert Lax,* ed. David Miller and Nicholas Zurbrugg (Devon, U.K.: Stride Publications, 1999), 66–79.

64. William Packard, "Interview with Robert Lax," in *The ABC's of Robert Lax,* 15–26.

65. Merton, *The Collected Poems of Thomas Merton* (New York: New Directions, 1978).

66 Richard Kostelanetz, "The Sounds of Silence," *New York Times Book Review* (February 5, 1978): 20

67. Ibid.

68. Robinson to Lax, 1976, LSBA.

69. Lax, *New Poems* (New York: Journeyman Books, 1962).

70. Robinson to Lax, May 8, 1977, LSBA.

71. Robinson to Lax, March 13, 1978, LSBA.
72. Eliot to Lax, September 2, 1977, LSBA.
73. Eliot to Lax, March 20, 1979, LSBA.
74. Dr. Richard Lennon to Rice from Southampton, N.Y., November 21, 1979.
75. Rice to Lax, RGA.
76. Packard to Lax, undated, LCU.
77. Lax to David Kilburn, 1979, LSBA.
78. Antonucci to Lax, undated, LSBA.
79. Williams e-mail to author, November 21, 2004.
80. Williams to Lax, November 14, 1977, LSBA.
81. Lax to Williams, November 7, 1979. The poem that Lax mentions, titled "Floor," is in *C. K. Williams: Selected Poems* (New York: Farrar, Straus & Giroux, 1994).
82. Lax to Williams; Williams e-mail, November 21, 2004.
83. N. Deedy, *Commonweal* (March 3, 1978).
84. Lax, *"One Island"* (Brooklyn, N.Y.: Hanging Loose 29, 1976).
85. Interview with Bannon, November 18, 1999, Rochester, N.Y.
86. Ibid.
87. 1974 Rice résumé, RGA. "Macaronic" means two or more languages jumbled together.

10: Merton Movement

1. Lax, *circus, zirkus, cirque, circo* (Zurich: Pendo-Verlag, 1981).
2. Lax to Rice, July 12, 1977, RGA.
3. Rice to Lax, November 13, 1979, RGA.
4. Lax, "Harpo's Progress," written for, but not read at, Merton/Maritain Symposium, Merton Center, Louisville, September 25–26, 1980, *Merton Annual* 1 (1988): 35–54.
5. Conversation with Lax, Lausanne, October 14, 1984.
6. Interview with Rice, October 31, 1996, Sagaponack, N.Y.
7. Rice to Larmore, October 15, 1981, RGA.
8. Conversation with Lax, September 1982, Zurich.
9. Lax to Rice, February 3, 1983, RGA.
10. Rice to Lax, "Bloom's Day," 1983, RGA.
11. Rice to Lax, July 6, 1983, RGA.
12. Lax to Rice, October 19, 1982, RGA.
13. Lax interview, Lausanne, October 14, 1984, Harford tape.
14. Lax to Rice, July 23, 1984, LCU.
15. Lax to Rice, December 7, 1984, LCU.
16. Lax to Harford, July 19, 1985, Harford archive.
17. Conversation with Lax, Stockholm, October 1985. Harford archive.
18. Ibid.
19. Rice to Lax, November 2, 1983, RGA.
20. Phone interview with Emery, 2003, Harford notes.
21. *Stuttgarter Nachrichten*, April 23, 1985.
22. Lax to Rice, June 3, 1985, RGA.
23. Lax to Rice, June 10, 1985, RGA.

24. Zonov to Harford, January 8, 2001, Harford archive.
25. Lax to Harfords, December 21, 1986, Harford archive.
26. Rice to Lax, July 24, 1987, RGA.
27. Rice to Lax, March 5, 1988, RGA.
28. Lax to Rice, April 19, 1988, RGA.
29. Robert Lax, *33 Poems*, ed. Thomas Kellein (Stuttgart: Edition Hansjörg Mayer, 1987).
30. Eliot to Lax, Good Friday 1988, LCU.
31. Lax, *33 Poems*, 67. Originally published in *R.L.: New Poems* (New York: Journeyman Books, 1962).
32. The remarks, in a review of two books about Merton by M. Basil Pennington in *America* (October 22, 1988) were by George Kilcourse, Bellarmine College. Rice's unanswered letter of protest was sent on December 31, 1988, and Harford's on February 10, 1989.
33. Rice to Lax, February 10, 1989, RGA.
34. Rice to Lax, October 24, 1989, RGA.

11: Ups, Downs, Requiems

1. *AJ*, 143-44. The meeting was at a nunnery near Darjeeling, India.
2. Ibid., 317.
3. Donald W. Mitchell and James Wiseman, O.S.B., ed., *The Gethsemani Encounter* (New York: Continuum, 1999), 5.
4. Walter M. Abbott, S.J., ed., *The Documents of Vatican II* (New York: America Press, 1966), 661-662. *Nostra Aetate* posed such basic questions as "What is a man? What is the meaning and purpose of our life? . . . whither our journey leads us?" and points out that "Buddhism . . . teaches a path by which men . . . can either reach a state of absolute freedom or attain supreme enlightenment by their own efforts or by higher assistance."
5. Coff, ed., *Gethsemani Encounter*, 5.
6. Simon Tonini, "Intermonastic Dialogue: Beginnings and Development," *Pontifical Council for Interreligious Dialogue Bulletin* 23, no. 1 (1988): 12.
7. Coff, ed., *Gethsemani Encounter*, 5.
8. Ibid.
9. Ibid., 9.
10. Dalai Lama, in *Gethsemani Encounter*, 260-61.
11. *AJ*, 308.
12. E-mail from Pascaline Coff, February 28, 2005.
13. *Robert Lax and Concrete Poetry* (press release), Butler Library, August 3-October 23, 1992.
14. Lax to Rice, April 24, 1995, RGA.
15. *Philokalia*, first published in 1782, is, according to Amazon.com, from the Greek "love of the beautiful, the good," and is a "collection of Hesychastic writings written between the fourth and the fifteenth centuries by men devoted to contemplative prayer."
16. Lax to Rice, April 24, 1995, RGA.
17. Ned Chase interview, December 4, 2001, New York.

18. Marvin Rothstein, *New York Times*, September 18, 1990.
19. Lax to Rice, April 24, 1985, RGA.
20. Interview with Victoria Lowe Allen, April 13, 1999, Sag Harbor, N.Y.
21. Lax to Rice, October 29, 1991, RGA.
22. Interview with Lax, May 19, 1997, Patmos.
23. Paul Quenon, *Merton Seasonal* (1991): 26, in "Father Louie: Photographs of Thomas Merton by Ralph Eugene Meatyard" (New York: Timken Publishers, 1991).
24. Rice letter to Quenon, December 29, 1991, RGA.
25. Undated letter, possibly not sent to anyone, RGA.
26. Mary Cummings, *Southampton Press*, July 29, 1999, B8.
27. Lax to Rice, June 30, 1993, RGA.
28. Lax to Rice, January 31, 1995, RGA.
29. *Love Had a Compass: Journals and Poetry of Robert Lax*, ed. James J. Uebbing (New York: Grove Press, 1996).
30. Lax to Rice, March 29, 1996, RGA.
31. Mary Cummings, "Traveling on Unbeaten Paths," *Columbia College Today* (May 2001): 18-29.
32. Telephone comments by Father Callan, November 8, 1996, Sagaponack, N.Y.
33. Rice conversation, November 9, 1996, Sagaponack.
34. Anne Freedgood interview, November 9, 1996, Bridgehampton, N.Y.
35. Uebbing, *Love Had a Compass*, xiv.
36. Michael McGregor, *Poets & Writers* (March/April 1997): 79-87.
37. Conz letter to Zurbrugg, November 14, 1991, in *The ABC's of Robert Lax*, 218.
38. *Peacemaker's Handbook*, the nineteenth book of Lax poetry, published by Moosbrugger's Pendo-Verlag, would come out in 2000, the year Lax died.
39. Interview with Forest, November 9, 1999, Red Bank, N.J.
40. *ABC's of Robert Lax.*
41. C. K. Williams, in *ABC's of Robert Lax*, 183.
42. E-mail from Sarah McCann, April 3, 2001.
43. Ibid.
44. Ibid.
45. Jack Kelly, "Robert Lax—Coming Home," in catalog *ROBERT LAX*, Museum Tinguely, 2004-5. 139-48
46. E-mail from McCann, April 3, 2001.
47. Ibid.
48. Knight phone call to Harford, October 2, 2000.
49. Ibid.; Jack Kelly in Tinguely catalog.
50. Ibid.
51. O'Gorman remarks at Lax memorial service, Corpus Christi Church, New York, November 18, 1999.

12: Legacy

1. Lax conversation, Lausanne, Switzerland, October 14, 1984.
2. *Survival or Prophecy The Letters of Thomas Merton and Jean Leclercq* (New York:Farrar Straus & Giroux, 2002), 175.
3. Ibid. xvi

4. Interview with Shannon, November 18, 1999, Nazareth College, Rochester.

5. Mary Anne Rivera, "Jubilee Magazine and the Development of a Vatican II Ecclesiology" (Ph.D. diss., Duquesne University, Pittsburgh, 2004), 307. Rivera is now assistant professor of sacramental and moral theology, Center of Pastoral Studies, Gannon University, Erie, Pa.

6. "Vatican II: 40 Years Later." *National Catholic Reporter*, October, 2002.

7. Garry Wills, "The Council We Are Still Living," *National Catholic Reporter*, October 4, 2002, 3-6.

8. George Weigel, "Grateful for Vatican II," *National Catholic Reporter*, October 4, 2002, 14.

9. John Allen Jr., "A Musical Challenge to Go Forward," *National Catholic Reporter*, April 16, 2004, 12.

10. Deborah Halter, "Whose Orthodoxy Is It?" *National Catholic Reporter*, March 11, 2005, 8-10.

11. E-mail from Sister Sheryl Frances Chen OCSO, May 8, 2005.

12. Merton, *OSM*, November 11, 1967, 9.

13. Website entry, May 21, 2004, www.compass-points.org.uk.

14. David Gibson, *The Coming Catholic Church* (San Francisco: HarperSanFrancisco, 2003).

15. Tom Beaudoin, in *The Coming Catholic Church*, 81.

16. *Times of Trenton*, February 23, 2004.

17. Rice to Lax, July 6, 1983, RGA.

18. Merton to Lax, July 25, 1966, Biddle, 338.

INDEX